D1119011

INSULÆ BRITANNICÆ

INSULÆ BRITANNICÆ

THE BRITISH ISLES

THEIR GEOGRAPHY, HISTORY, AND ANTIQUITIES DOWN TO THE CLOSE OF THE ROMAN PERIOD

BY

ARTHUR WILLIAM WHATMORE

KENNIKAT PRESS
Port Washington, N. Y./London

INSULAE BRITANNICAE

First published in 1913
Reissued in 1971 by Kennikat Press
Library of Congress Catalog Card No: 72-118508
ISBN 0-8046-1256-0

Manufactured by Taylor Publishing Company   Dallas, Texas

AUTHOR'S PREFACE

IN this work, founded principally upon the classic references
to the British Isles, an attempt is made to review the geography, history, and antiquities of the group from the earliest
times to the withdrawal of the Romans. The task has not
been easy. The mass of matter to be handled, and the innumerable problems involved, have engaged the greater part
of the author's limited leisure for many years. Originating
in an effort to locate the stations noticed in the itineraries of
Richard of Cirencester, so far as they lay in or near the counties
of Leicester and Derby, the plan was extended from time to
time until it embraced the Iter Britanniarum, the Notitia,
Ravennas, Ptolemy, and the whole range of classic literature
to which access was possible, thus springing from a local effort
into a particular survey of all the Britains.

How far the effort has been successful is a point for the
judgment of others. It cannot be hoped that all the views
expressed will be held warranted by the slender materials
which time has spared, or that the deductions drawn from
such sources as Homer, Orpheus, and the early poets will meet
with general approbation. Still, what has been done was
intended to be done well ; and I shall consider myself rewarded
if I have succeeded in unravelling but a few out of the hundreds
of problems which the subject opposed to me.

The difficulties of the work can only be appreciated by
those whose inclinations lead them into the same field. There
was no royal road ; there was sometimes scarcely a beaten
track ; and almost at every step some new light or circumstance made it necessary to review or modify something
which had gone before. Hence many paragraphs had frequently to be revised and rewritten ; and, in particular,

Ravennas was repeatedly laid down as undecipherable, only
to be taken up again as other parts of the work progressed
and threw side-lights upon it.   Ravennas was, in fact, a bait
which offered irresistible temptation.   Its long list of names,
each claiming a place in the map of ancient Britain, excited
curiosity which grew keener as the plan was gradually un-
folded.   The interest aroused by Antonine's Iter Britanniarum was at first less accentuated.   The unfavourable
opinion, long religiously entertained, that the recorded distances in that work were in many cases corrupt, in consequence
of which stations were definitely allocated to sites without the
slightest regard to the numerals, appeared to offer no hope of
a satisfactory solution.   This view was followed until growing
familiarity with Ptolemy's geography led to the identification
of the Devnana of the twentieth legion with Daventry.   If
commentators had been wrong in fixing Devnana at West
Chester, might they not have erred in their general condemna-
tion of Antonine ?   This consideration led to an attempt to
understand Antonine's work as it has been handed down, and
in the result the itinerist seems to emerge with a reputation
for accuracy second to none.   His work should be the more
valuable because it records the distances between the towns ;
but this circumstance is mainly responsible for the unfavourable light in which it is held.   In the commentary contained in
the present volume the English mile is used, and if the reason-
ableness of the sites proposed for the stations is admitted,
the generally received view that the itinerary mile is a different measure must be abandoned.

The Notitia was difficult to handle, but it was not fettered
with the deep-rooted prejudices which had obscured Antonine.
Keys were found in Morbium and Braboniacis, stations of the
Dux Britanniarum, which, when identified with Laughton-en-
le-Morthen and Barbon, formed new starting-points from
which the remaining towns in the list could be sought.   The
stations along the Wall were, perhaps, not less perplexing,
but the area to be studied was narrower, though the nicest
discrimination was still essential.

It is obvious that, in allocating the dry names in the various
lists to their proper localities, etymology must, in the majority

of cases, be the first, and in some cases, the only guide. In the early stages of investigation this guide was sought in the Welsh language, from a preconceived notion that it was the representative of the spoken tongue of the South Britons ; but little progress was made until recourse was had to the Gaelic, through Armstrong's Gaelic Dictionary. The advance from that time was rapid, and the circumstance contributed materially to the views expressed respecting the origin of the primitive Britons. As Gaelic derivations appear copiously throughout, a glossary is added to avoid repetition of meanings in the text.

The tribal history is based generally on Ptolemy, and no towns are noticed in this connection except those named by him ; indeed, care has been taken throughout not to mention any place as connected with a tribe unless etymology or some ancient authority affords sufficient testimony. Equal care has been taken in preparing the map of the islands according to Ptolemy. No colouring or effort to lay down tribal limits is attempted, while the tribe-names are, as far as possible, so written as to cover only the towns which the Greek geographer assigns to each. The same methods are followed in the other maps, and it is conceived that a freer treatment must be deprecated as tending to inaccuracy. Special care was necessary in laying down the coastline after Ptolemy ; the recorded places were first marked, and then the intermediate coast was filled in as closely to modern conditions as circumstances permitted. In the general maps the tribe-names mentioned in Ptolemy are printed in thick type ; those found in other classic authors are distinguished by open type.

In the pages devoted to the Roman walls and roads I have endeavoured to deal concisely with a subject which alone would furnish matter for a volume. Many views are expressed which possess originality, and in every case etymology, coupled with the study of ancient geographical conditions, has been the principal guide. Except in two cases, none of these interesting remains are laid down in the maps ; their delineation would have involved crowding ; added to which the subject is attended with so much uncertainty that it is better to defer their inclusion until further discoveries shall

have added to our knowledge.   Undue importance attached to
the so-called " great roads " accounts in a large measure for
the unfavourable criticisms upon Antonine.

Even greater uncertainty surrounds the native religion ;
yet there are sidelights which point to a connection with the
greatest religions of antiquity.   Many deductions are possible,
and some are ventured ; but the paucity of materials leaves
the problem perhaps unsolvable.   It is clear, however, that
in very primitive ages the cultured nations of the Mediterranean regarded our islands with peculiar reverence and fear.
The entrance to Hades lay in these seas, and here, apparently,
Charon ferried the departed souls across the river of death.
The curious basaltic columns of Ulster and the Western Isles,
and the awe-inspiring portals of Fingal's Cave, probably had
something to do with these extraordinary notions, but, be
that as it may, it is certain that such stories were common
gossip in the time of Homer, and that they were sufficiently
credited after the Christian era to daunt the well-tried soldiers
of Agricola.   The views expressed on this subject are advanced as suggestions, capable of elaboration.   The restricted
leisure and opportunities at my command did not permit
the complicated research which the subject calls for ; hence
no attempt is made in the present work to trace the progress
or influence of religion in Britain beyond the Druidic Age.

The superstitions early current respecting the islands
obviously account for the Kimmerian adventures of Ulysses.
It cannot be expected, however, that the views hazarded
either as to the astronomical aspects of the hero or as to the
signification of the names by which he is known, or of the
names borne by his heroines, will furnish anything like the
last word on the subject ; and the story needs to be compared
with what can be gleaned as to the primitive religion of the
islands.   The accumulation of myth and fable gathered about
the hero makes it seemingly impossible to separate the nucleus
from the matter which has entered into it and obscured it.
Yet there is a strange fascination in the story, and it becomes
of greater interest if the views offered as to the Kymric-
emigration triad are conceded.   Other mythological subjects
are noticed where comment seemed relevant.

The chief circumstance in connection with the " Odyssey " is the identification of Æӕa with Hi. This encouraged a suspicion that the names borne by our island group and its largest members might be connected in some way with the northern adventures of Ulysses, and so with the basaltic formation ; and accordingly the etymologies offered generally conform to this view. It is clear that, whether the names originally had this signification or not, it was expressed very early in transferred or poetical uses, and in these and the classic fables it is possible to detect traces of astronomical mythology. One of the notions involved has reference to the rigid northern winter and the gloomy circumstance of death, suggested possibly at one time by the setting sun, at another by the passage of the sun into the southern signs of the ecliptic, when the region within the arctic circle is enveloped in a six-months' night. It is to astronomy that we are indebted for the first mention of our islands in the poetry of Homer ; and if we except the writings of Cæsar, Tacitus, Dion, and some few others, the astronomical element may be said to have predominated well into the Christian era. References to this aspect are scattered throughout the work in the order in which the authorities or the plan give opportunity ; but, in particular, the reader is referred to the paragraphs dealing with the " Odyssey," the native religion, and the national legends of the Welsh, Irish, and Scots.

It was part of the original plan to incorporate considerable parts of the De Situ and all the Diaphragmata of Richard of Cirencester, notwithstanding the opinion now generally entertained that the work is a forgery of the eighteenth century. If it is a forgery, it reveals very respectable knowledge on an interesting subject ; and in any case it is highly creditable to its author, whether he was Richard or the Copenhagen professor, Charles Bertram. After reflection, Richard's work has been passed over, while no notice has been taken of the coined names Cinnabanta and Venantodunum found in some maps of modern execution.

The present work is numbered off into paragraphs, with an extensive system of cross-reference. This was suggested by experience as a convenient method of obviating repetition, and it had the further advantage of enabling distinctive numbers to be given to those parts of Ravennas and Nennius which bear traces of a regular itinerary or definite plan. In some cases, however, the numbering may be found arbitrary, creating the division or grouping of subjects which it might have been better to treat differently. This is due to alterations made since 1907, when the work was numbered and referenced in its then state for the press. Care, however, has been taken to distinguish authorities from commentarial matter; and it is hoped that the method adopted will be found convenient and free from confusion. An index of ancient and modern geographical names is added; the table of contents will serve, for most practical purposes, as an index of subjects and persons.

The map, according to Ptolemy, was originally prepared on a flat projection. I acknowledge the assistance of my brother-in-law, Mr. George Allen, Quarndon, Derby, in rewriting the same map conically; and of my daughter, Joan Marshwood Whatmore, in writing the final revision of all the maps, and in indexing. In other directions, Doomsday Book, Horsley's " Britannia Romana," and the 1-inch ordnance maps, have afforded material assistance.

A. W. WHATMORE.

ASHBY-DE-LA-ZOUCH,
February 17, 1913.

CONTENTS

NOTE.—*Left-hand numbers refer to paragraphs.*

CONTENTS

CONTENTS

LIST OF MAPS

INSULAE BRITANNICAE
According to Ptolemy

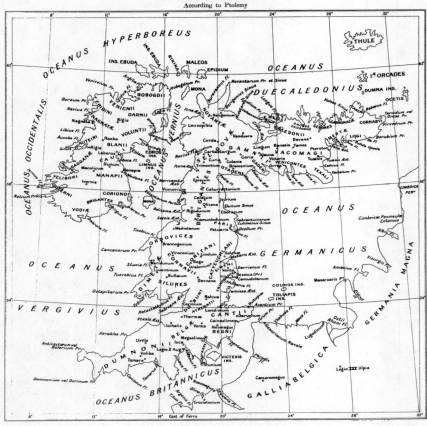

1

INSULÆ BRITANNICÆ

INSULÆ BRITANNICÆ

(Βρεττανικαὶ Νῆσοι)

I

INSULÆ BRITANNICÆ

1. THE term " Insulæ Britannicæ " (*Britannic Islands*) in mediæval times, as now, commonly designated Great Britain and Ireland, with the islands lying immediately off their coasts ; but anciently it had sometimes a wider signification, seeming to embrace all the islands of the northern seas, as well as some parts of the opposite mainland which were believed to be islands. In very remote ages these regions seem to have been known to the Mediterranean traders who preceded the Greeks and Romans, and it is evident from the " Odyssey " of Homer (supposed about the ninth century B.C.) that voyages were then made far into the North Atlantic. The earliest notices are in the poets, and the islands, with the neighbouring coasts and ocean, situated as it were on the edge of the known world, were a subject around which Hellenic mythographers delighted to entangle their themes. Homer divided the earth into two parts, the dark and light sides (west and east), this arrangement originating in the same school whence the Gan-eden Semites derived the division of the day into evening and morning. Calling evening " Ereb," עֶרֶב, the Semites apparently designated the dark or west side of the earth by the same word, thus giving to our Continent the name it still bears—Europe, *evening-land*. Thus the islands lay in that half which Homer called the dark side (πρὸς ζόφον, *towards the west*) ; and this, being the region of the setting sun, furnished the poets with ample materials to work upon. In this direction, but inclining to the north, where the temperate zone approached the Arctic circle, they

3

fitly placed the gloomy Erebus, the dark place beneath the
earth through which the shades of the dead passed into
Hades. Homer, the earliest of poets, locates Hades on the
far bank of ocean-stream, and there Ulysses conversed with
the dead [2a]. As late as the sixth century A.D., Britannia
was the dread island whither departed spirits were conveyed
[25]. Different ideas were associated with the lower region
of the temperate zone towards the Tropic of Cancer, where
Arctic conditions did not prevail ; and there, not far from
the ocean-mouth and on the inner bank of ocean, the great
poet placed the Elysian Fields (*Lusitania*), where the breezes
of Zephyros bestowed perpetual summer, unalternated by
rain, cold, or snow. The brilliancy of sunset was especially
a theme for admiration, and the poets occasionally forgot the
terrors of Hades in their contemplation of the shining rock
Leukas, the sun's passage through which into the underworld
was often signalized by the gorgeous tints of a fiery sky. The
universe of Homer was a globe, the earth, which was flat, being
identical with the plane of its circumference, the upper semi-
sphere being the vault of heaven, the lower that of Tartarus.

2a. Homer's earth was surrounded by ocean, and many
of the adventures of his hero Ulysses are connected with this
ocean, and indisputably with the Britannic group. Sailing
from the Æolian Island in the Mediterranean, Ulysses passed
out upon the ocean to the country of the Læstrygones (the
Elysian Tarraconensis in Spain), and thence voyaged to the
island Ææa (*Hi, Iona, in the Western Isles of Scotland*),
where Kirke, daughter of Helios and Perse, dwelt The
goddess, by means of drugged wines, turned some of his companions into swine. Ulysses, when on his way to liberate
them, was met by Apollo, who counselled him how to proceed,
and gave him the herb moly, which had a black root and milk-
white flower, as an antidote against Kirke's poisons. Thus
provided, he was immune from harm, and having secured the
restoration of his men to human shape, he accepted the
goddess, and became the father of Telegonus. After a year
he obtained permission to return to his own land of Ithaca,
but he must first visit Hades in the north, where the flaming
River Phlegethon (*Plocton*), and also the Cocytus (*Elchaig*),

which rose in the Styx (*Itys*) [134*i*], fell into the Acheron [5] (*Carron*).* Thither he voyaged, arriving after nightfall at the ocean's utmost bounds, in the country of the Kimmerian men—Κιμμέριοι ἄνδρες ("ceum," *step ;* "comar," *a way*, but usually derived from Heb. Kemer, *blackness*—in whose land the mouth of Hades lay, and over whom the sun never shone. Having sacrificed a sheep, he saw and conversed with the shades of the dead, but was unable long to endure the ordeal, and withdrew in terror. Returning to Ææa, he raised a lofty mound over the ashes of his friend Elpenor, who before the departure for Hades had met his death by falling intoxicated from an upper story of Kirke's house, and whose spirit in the underworld had implored this last service from Ulysses. Kirke now instructed the hero concerning his homeward journey, warning him especially of the Sirens (Σειρῆνες), whose island, *Bardsey*, he must pass, and whose sweet voices were irresistibly alluring, so that all who travelled that way were drawn upon their shore, where they were killed, and on which a large heap of human bones and skins lay wasting away. As a protection from this danger, he filled his crew's ears with wax before reaching the island, and, causing himself to be chained to the mast, was thus one of the few mortals who heard the Sirens and survived. Continuing his course, he passed between the rocks Scylla and Charybdis (*Pillars of Hercules*) into the inner sea (" Odyssey," x.-xii.).

2*b*. The story of the Sirens is a play upon the Gaelic word " seirean " [*a leg (cape)*], applicable to the promontory of Lleyn, Carnarvonshire, off which Bardsey lies. Apparently transferring to this word the meaning of Gael. "seirgean" (*a shrivelled person*), Homer equated it with σειραίνω (*to dry up*), and Ptolemy, ten centuries later, substituted καγκανων ἄκροι [135*k*] (καγκαίνω, *to parch*).

Kirke's warning to Ulysses has been rendered thus :

> Next where the Sirens dwell, you plough the seas ;
> Their song is death, and makes destruction please.

* Virgil makes the Acheron a tributary of the Cocytus. In modern geography Loch Duich, joined by the waters of the Ling and Elchaig, expands into Loch Alsh, which meets the waters of Loch Carron at Kyle Akin

Unblest the man, whom music wins to stay
Nigh the curst shore, and listen to the lay ;
Nor more the wretch shall view the joys of life,
His blooming offspring, or his beauteous wife !
In verdant meads they sport, and wide around
Lie human bones, that whiten all the ground ;
The ground polluted floats with human gore,
And human carnage taints the dreadful shore.
Fly swift the dang'rous coast ; let ev'ry ear
Be stop'd against the song ! 'tis death to hear !
Firm to the mast with chains thyself be bound,
Nor trust thy virtue to th' enchanting sound.
If mad with transport, freedom thou demand,
Be ev'ry fetter strain'd and added band to band.

W. H. MELMOTH.

2c. Kirke's story is an echo of the best and noblest of the cosmic views which took root in primitive antiquity, and which clearly embraced accurate knowledge of our islands, whose natural curiosities and position in relation to the heavenly pole could not be neglected in such studies. The foundation of the story is the firmament (Heb. רָקִיעַ, *raqiha*), which Elohim made to divide the celestial waters from the waters upon the earth ; and, calling it "shamaim" *(heaven)*, he placed in it the great lights and the stars, to be for signs and seasons, days and years. This firmament, spreading like a vault above the earth, on the extremities of which it seemed to rest, was first conceived as a half-circle, and the Hebrew word with that signification passed into Latin in the form "arx" (Eng. *arch*) ; but the crowning mystery of the firmament was that point or spot which, shooting outwards into the great background of heaven, appeared as an immense pinnacle or pit, around which the starry signs revolved daily in majestic and unchanging order. This point furnished the noble notion of a celestial and terrestrial pole ; and the celestial prolongation came to be regarded as the summit of the universe, the Greeks, who adopted Eastern science and etymons, terming it "Arktos," while the Latins called it "Aquila" (G. "cuaille," *a post*), both names signifying, in modern acceptation, "the north." Under that part of the raqiha thus immediately associated with the pole lay our own islands, the remotest of lands, whose promontory Orcas stretched towards the Insulæ Orcades and the

Oceanus Arktöus; while directly from our shores and seas, in
North-East Ireland and the Western Isles, rose those wonderful
basaltic columns, which, towering upwards like the pillars of a
gigantic temple, obviously must have done much to establish
the theory of a mundane pole. To these circular pillars we
are indebted for the first mention of our islands in Homer.
Kirke (G. " cearcall," Lat. " circus," Russ. " kryg," *circle*) is
the " circler," or the constellation of Ursa Minor, which, here
overhead, revolves round the celestial pole every day; her
island home of Æxa is the terrestrial counterpart of the
Wain (G. " a," *waggon*), the celestial Wain being the couch of
the goddess, again answered terrestrially by the sacred white-
horsed car of the ancient Germans [364], but in Britain perhaps originally connected with G. " uadh," *cave.* Her father,
Helios, is the sun, whose apparent annual path round the
universe led to the institution of the zodiac. Ulysses (called
Odysseus in Homer) was an unwilling visitor to these seas;
yet his story shows close connection with the northern sky,
and in his visit to Æxa and the underworld he seems to point
to the Bear-Wain in its Eastern acceptation as a bier.

2*d.* It is an important feature of the "Odyssey" that its
hero is driven to Æxa by Neptune, who is incensed at the
blinding of his son Polyphemus, the one-eyed Kyklops.
Polyphemus (πόλος, *the pole*; βῆμα, *step*) may be connected with
the steplike basalts, pointing polewards, which lay in Kirke's
region; and the one eye in the middle of his forehead is the
socket of the celestial pole, viewed as the eye through which
the deity surveyed the world. How the Kyklops was son of
Neptune appears from the name of the father, who as Poseidon
(Russ. " bezdna," *abyss*) is the pit of heaven, whence comes
the deluge of rain, and who as Neptune (G. " neamh ";
Russ. " nebo," *heaven*) is the firmament, above which lies the
celestial sea. This exalted station of Polyphemus accords
with his boast that he cared not for Zeus or the blessed gods,
since the Kyklopes were superior to them ("Odyssey," ix.
275-76); he is, indeed, the common enemy, the inhospitable
and warlike Bel (Heb. " Baal "), who designed the flood in
which Adrahasis (Hassisadra) was preserved by Êa. The same
flood is the tempest which carried Ulysses to Æxa, retold in

the deluge from which Noah was saved by Yhovah, and in
that which carried Deucalion to Thessaly. Êa, like Ææa,
is the Bear-Wain (G. " ær," *a cart*), and the Wain is the
saviour-ship which ploughs the celestial seas uninjured by
storm or tempest. The name of the pilot, Adrahasis, repeats
Tiresias, the blind seer of Thebes (Tape ; Phœn. " dûb," *the
Bear*), while the compound " hasis " appears in Ulysses,
Odysseus, and is possibly related to Russ. " os," *an axle,*
which would seem to furnish the true signification of
" Zeus." Polyphemus was blinded with a sharpened olive-
pole. The olive was sacred; Hercules fetched the plant
from the Hyperboreans [4], and its leaf was connected with
Noah.

2*e*. The firmament was a rich field for poetic themes.
Its abyss, or possibly the bowl-shaped tail of the Bear, found
expression in Kirke's wine-bowls, the contents of which
transformed men into swine, typifying the baneful effects of
intemperance ; while the bowl might also be suggested by
the upper end of the basaltic pillar. This aspect of Kirke
has suggested the crescent moon, which in turn pointed to a
boat ; but it was the special lot of Ulysses to attract to himself the greater number of similes offered by the resemblance
of the firmament and the Bear's tail to an arch or bow.
Thus, Kimmeria was perhaps equated with Gr. $\kappa\alpha\mu\acute{\alpha}\rho\alpha$,
an arch (sometimes *a covered waggon*), and his native Ithaca
was the bow-island. The bow figured prominently in primitive religion*; and Ulysses is pre-eminently the archer. The
god appears in Greece as Eurytus, who instructed Hercules
in the use of the bow. This bow came from Eurytus to his
son Iphitus, who gave it to Ulysses, and the latter prized it so
highly that he would only use it in Ithaca. None but he could
draw it, so that he won an easy victory when the suitors of
Penelope had a shooting contest with it, and he afterwards
used it with deadly effect against the suitors themselves.
Laërtes, father of the hero, was himself the archer (La-
Eurytus). Gr. $\tau\acute{o}\xi o\nu$, *bow*, accounts for Toxeus, son of
Eurytus, and again for $\tau o\xi\acute{o}\tau\eta s$, *the sign Sagittarius*, the latter

* The priests of Iona were called " Culdees," G. "culaidh," *vestment*
(*cf*. Chaldees, *i.e.*, Kasdim, Heb. Kesuth, *vestment*).

connected with Udgudûa, an Akkadian name for the sign. Udgudûa points to Ithaca, and the subdivisions into which the archer-sign is said to have been parcelled out included Kumaru (*cf.* Kimmeria). The latter name may survive in that of the Summer Isles, off Loch Broom.

3a. Ulysses, coming from Æǽa, sailed into the inner sea, landing in Trinacia, and there his crew killed some oxen, part of the sacred herd of Helios. Seven days afterwards Jupiter, angry at this impiety, sent a storm which drove the vessel back towards the rocks Scylla and Charybdis, where it was lost. All were drowned except the hero, who, floating on the broken mast, was impelled out upon the ocean for ten days, when he was washed upon the shore of the island Ogygia. This lay far away in the wide sea, and was the abode of Kalypso, daughter of Atlas ; and she, receiving the visitor kindly, persuaded him to remain with her, offering immortality and eternal youth if he would do so. But when he had lived seven years under her roof Hermes arrived from the gods to demand his liberty, and she sorrowfully bade him go. She helped him in his preparations for the voyage, allowing him to fell poplars, alders, and pines, for building a ship, and finding him a double-edged axe, with a handle of olive-wood, for the work, as well as cloth for the sails. The work was finished in four days, and the vessel having been amply provisioned by the goddess, she lastly sent a favourable wind.

> And now rejoicing in the prosp'rous gales,
> With beating heart Ulysses spreads his sails ;
> Plac'd at the helm he sat, and mark'd the skies,
> Nor closed in sleep his ever-watchful eyes.
> There viewed the Pleiads and the northern team,
> And great Orion's more refulgent beam,
> To which, around the axle of the sky
> The bear revolving, points his golden eye ;
> Who shines exalted on th' ethereal plain,
> Nor bathes his blazing forehead in the main.
> Far on the left those radiant fires to keep
> The nymph directed, as he sail'd the deep.
>   MELMOTH, *Od.* v.

Γηθόσυνος δ' οὔρῳ πέτασ' ἱστία δῖος 'οδυσσεύς·
Αὐτὰρ ὁ πηδαλίῳ ἰθύνετο τεχνηέντως,
Ἥμενος· οὐδέ οἱ ὕπνος ἐπὶ βλεφάροισιν ἔπιπτε,

Πληϊάδας τ' ἐσορῶντι, καὶ ὀψὲ δύοντα Βοώτην,
Αρκτον θ', ἣν καὶ ἅμαξαν ἐπίκλησιν καλέουσιν,
Ἥ τ' αὐτοῦ στρέφεται, και τ' Ὠρίωνα δοκεύει·
Οἵη δ' ἄμμορός ἐστι λοετρῶν Ὠκεανοῖο·
Τὴν γὰρ δή μιν ἄνωγε καλυψὼ, δῖα θεάων,
Ποντοπορευέμεναι επ' ἀριστερὰ χειρὸς ἔχοντα.

Od. v. 269-77.

3b. Kalypso's story is less easily explained than Kirke's. Her father, Atlas, who is generally associated with θάλασσα, (sea) or Phœn. "atel" (darkness), really personifies the aerial vault (Gr. Θόλος) which sustained the firmament, this office being expressed in the fable that he supported the heavens on his head and hands. Possibly his name, still surviving in "Atlantic," may be connected with Heb. תֵּל, "tel," (a mound), since the Bear-Wain was sometimes regarded as a bier, and Atlas's father Iapetus (Heb. "ephathah," darkness) was, as Ptah, the Egyptian death-god. Kalypso herself is the aerial roof, from καλύπτω, to cover, thus reflecting her father, and so she is the same as the Little Bear; and she retains this feature if we view her in her varied acceptations as daughter of Oceanus (Russ. "ocean"; G. "aigean," abyss) and of Tethys (G. "tuath," the north), or as daughter of Nereus (Russ. "nord," north). The seven years Ulysses spends with her are the seven Bear-stars, and his four days of shipbuilding are the four wain-stars. Her island Ogygia (Heb. גג, roof; G. "cuach," a bowl; "cuach-mhullach," a dome) is the island Gigha, off Cantire, in the Cichican Valley of Gildas, now the Passage of Gigha. Ogygia, the celestial dome, was widely worshipped, but all its vestiges betray a common origin. Our Ogygia, which was one of the Ebudæ, and where Ulysses lived seven years, may be compared with that of Bœotia, whose ruler Ogyges, the hero of the Bœotian deluge, laid the foundation for the power of Thebes, the seven-gated city, famous for the War of the Seven and sacred to the constellation of the Bear. Attica also had its flood hero Ogyges, whose son Eleusis, renowned in Attica, repeats Ulysses of Ithaca; and Abram lived near the oak called "Ogyges," belonging to Canaan, and near Hebron, when he received the Egyptian Hagar. The latter (Heb. "hagar,"

girded) is the Albionic Kirke ; and her son Ishmael is
without doubt connected with the Little Bear constellation,
the last compound of his name (Heb. " mal," *circumcised*)
associating him with the pole (G. " mulghart," *the pole*), and
so with Melquarth (Moloch). The archer Hercules, like
Ulysses, is the hero of the northern bow, and so is the
archer Ishmael. The latter, as the progenitor of a great
nation, was the active power in Nature, and clearly the pole
with its celestial socket and the shape of the Bear were
connected with the mysteries of Phallism ; while the Wain was
considered as a bed, cart, chariot, plough, ship, well, bag,
and, indeed, as any object with which the elastic mind of
the priestly astronomer could draw comparison. It occurs
as Jacob's couch, the violation of which by Reuben* ceded
precedence to Benjamin, and again as the vessel containing
the mess of pottage which placed Jacob above Esau ; as a
skin or leathern bag Æolus bound up in it the raging winds as
a present for Ulysses, and it is the stone of Sisyphos and branch
of Tantalos.   Again, as Jacob's couch it was the seat whence
he watched and directed his twelve sons, who are as well the
twelve winds as the twelve signs of the zodiac, and who are,
moreover, only redrawn in the twelve Ishmaeli, Solomon's
twelve officers for provisions, and other twelves.   The Bear,
as the bow, is emphasized in the story of Kallisto. That
goddess, daughter of Lycaon (Russ. " lyk," *bow*), being slain
by her companion Artemis during the chase, was placed by
Jupiter amongst the stars under the name of Arktos.
Another version says that she was metamorphosed into a
she-bear by Hera, and, being hunted by her son Arkas, who
was on the point of killing her, Zeus turned them both
into stars, the mother as the Great Bear, the son as the
Little Bear.

3c. When Ulysses sailed from Ææa he left Telegonus†
behind him ; and the son, being sent by the mother to find the

* The Great Bear, or Wain, appears to be reduplicated in the
Pleiades, which were directly connected with Reuben.

† Telegonus and Telemachus were probably connected in name with
Atlas and Delos ; perhaps Telamon was also.   The latter visited the
Hyperboreans.

father, is cast during a storm upon the island of Ithaca, which he ravages for provisions. Ulysses resists him, but they do not recognize one another, and the father falls. The truth being discovered, the son, accompanied by Telemachus and Penelope, carries the body to his mother in Æaea, where he buries it ; then, marrying Penelope, he becomes the father of Italus. Another account says that Kirke restored Ulysses to life ; and in another he goes to Tyrrhenia, where he is burnt on Mount Perge. Tyrrhenia suggests the Albionic Iona, whose hill, called " Dunbhuirgh " (*hill of mourning ;* G. " buirich," *a lament*), answers Mount Perge ; but be that as it may, it is clear that there was in very ancient times either some connection between the Greek Iona and that of Britain, or that the same astronomical myths or teachings were familiar to both.

4. After Homer there is no direct allusion to our islands for a long period, but the poet Aristeas, who seems to have lived not later than 800 B.C. (" Herod.," iv. 13-15), mentioned the Hyperborei (Ὑπερβορεοι) as inhabiting the north extremity of Europe, extending to the sea, and he related that he personally visited the Issedones (a tribe of the European mainland), who were separated from the Hyperborei by the Arimaspi. He also spoke of the Kimmerii, but as a separate people, and located them by the southern sea (the Euxine), the Scythæ lying between them and the Issedones. As he made his journey under the inspiration of Apollo, to whom his work was probably dedicated as the god of song and music, his geography may have suffered from the licence of poetry, but on the whole it was exact, and Herodotus incorporated the part relating to the most northern nations into his own " Scythia," without altering their relative positions, though also hearing of the people from other sources. Hesiod (735 B.C.), generally followed Homer, speaking of the ocean-stream with its sources in the extreme west, the heavenly vault supported by Atlas, Tartarus beneath the earth, Hades in the extreme west, and the Hyperborei, the latter taking the place of the Kimmerii. The poets in general testify to an intimate knowledge of the north, and describe its inhospitable climate ; with their usual licence, they fabled the darkest and most frigid of these regions as the abode of Boreas, the north wind. The Hyperborei, usually derived from ὑπερ, *above*, and Boreas,* but rather akin to Russ. " phyra " (*waggon*) —*i.e.*, the pole-wain, or Little Bear—were said to dwell beyond the habitation of the wind-god, their land being an ideal paradise, bright with perpetual sunshine. The story was obviously a poetic exaggeration of the circumstance that within the Arctic circle there was continuous day in summer, culminating in a six-months' day at the pole. Herodotus, the first historian (440 B.C.), discredited the accounts which were current concerning the northern regions, and in this respect was unequal to the best intelligence of his age. He ridiculed the notion of an all-encircling sea, believing that the land was unlimited towards the north except by its own extremities, persisting in this view from want of an eye witness to corroborate the older idea. Hence he would not allow that there were islands in the north or west, and denied acquaintance with the Cassiterides [333], from which tin (κασσίτερος) was imported into Greece ; he disputed also that there was a river Eridanus flowing into a northern sea, from which amber came, though he admitted that both tin and amber came from the utmost bounds of Europe (iii. 115). He adds : " I laugh, seeing many persons making charts of the earth without having any knowledge to guide them ; they draw the ocean flowing about the earth, being round as if from a lathe " (iv. 36). He doubts the reality of the Hyperborei, asserting that if there were such there must also be Hypernotii (*dwellers beyond the south*) ; but he treats the Kimmerii as an historical, though extinct, people, who had inhabited the upper coast of the Euxine (iv. 11-13). The truth probably is that Kimmerii was a name strictly belonging to the Britons, as inhabiting the columnar basaltic islands towards the pole—the " ceum," or *step* region (the *dark road*), which probably, in one aspect, suggested the ancient notion of the ladder reaching to heaven (Gen. xxviii. 12). The Hebrew cosmogony is founded upon the same ideas. Japhet (G. " pait," *what protrudes—i.e., a promontory*, celestially *the*

* Diod. Sic., shortly before the Christian era, says : τῶν ὀνομαζομένων Ὑπερβορέων 'απὸ τοῦ πορρωτέρω κεῖσθαι τῆς βορείου πνοῆς (ii. 47).

pole, poetically equated with " ephathah," *darkness**) was an original name for all the northern nations, later subdivided into the western race of Gomer (*Kimmeria*), and the eastern race of Magog ; and Gomer again was split up into the three great divisions of Aschkenaz, the *Iazyges of the Euxine*, Riphath, *North Europe*, and Togarmah, *the British Isles*. The Sea of Togorma† occurs several times in the poems of Ossian [26*d*] under circumstances which point to the west of Scotland.

5. The incredulity of Herodotus is the more remarkable as Orpheus's " Argonautica," supposed *circa* 500 B.C., a little before Herodotus, shows undoubted knowledge of the north and the British Isles. This poem agrees on the whole with Homer, but is richer in details. The Argonauts, voyaging from Kolkis, passed through the Palus Mæotis (*Sea of Azof*), and then along a channel or river on which the Hyperborei and other nations dwelt, to the Oceanus Cronius, called also the " Pontus Hyperboreus " and " Mortuum Mare " (νεκρὰ θάλασσα [351*i*]). The heroes, unable to row the Argo through the thick water of this sea (which was no other than Helice and Tethys, the remotest of waters), took to the shore, and, drawing the vessel along, made their way through the Macrobii, whose name, said to mean the " long-lived," was probably connected with the island of Mageroë, near the Rubeas Promontory, Norway. The adventurers next traversed the Cimmerii, who were hidden from the sun-rising by the mountains of Ripæus (*Yarrow or Morven Hills*), Calpius (*Ben Klibreck in Sutherland*), and Caligo (*Craigellachie*), till they came to a rugged promontory, from which they continued on foot to the Acheron [2], a river of turbid depths, flowing

* The same notion underlay the religion of the Egyptians, with whom Ptah, represented as a mummy, was the god of the nightly sun ; hence the hymn, " I rose up like Horus [the rising sun], I sat down like Ptah."

† Togorma, interpreted by J. Macpherson as " the island of the blue waves " (G. " gorm," *blue*), is by that writer made one of the Hebrides. The sea is the Oceanus Duecaledonius ; and an echo of the Ossianic name may survive in the Grampian Hills stretching east from the district of Etha. Ossian, however, seems to apply it to the sea about S. Skye and Rum. He also mentions the seas of Colgormo.

from the fruitful fields of Ceres (*Cerones*) into a black swamp.
In the vicinity were the gates of Hades. Having passed this
region, Ancæus, distressed at the great difficulties encountered,
threatened to charge his companions with their recent crime
(the murder of Absyrtus) when he should reach the Iernidan
Islands (Νῆσοι Ἰερνίδες* ; " Orph.," 1164), adding that he would
run into the open Atlantic (πέλαγος Ἀτλαντικος), unless they
kept him from the sacred heights by entering the gulf of the
unfruitful land and sea (*west coast of Ross*). The threats caused
great fear, but amity being restored, the heroes set sail, and
were carried past the island Iernis (Νῆσος Ἰερνίς, Orpheus
1179; *Ireland*), being driven by a storm for twelve days to
the limit of the ocean, where they came to an island studded
with pine-trees (Νῆσος πευκήεσσα ; G. " giuthas," *a pine*),
Azores. Here the goddess Ceres (*cf* Azores) had spacious
temples, which were surrounded by an immense cloud, and
lofty rocks girded the island on every side. The Argonauts
feared to disembark, and, altering their course, came in three
days to the land of Lycæus (λυκαῖος χέρσος, *Madeira*), the
abode of Kirke ; but the goddess declined to receive them in
consequence of their guilt, and counselled them to expiate
their crime with Orphic ceremonies at the coast of Maleæ
(παρὰ κροκάλοισι μαλέιης [348]). She, however, provided
them with food and wine to help them on their voyage, and,
crossing the ocean, they came to the Strait of Tartessus and
the Pillars of Hercules. The names in this poem show that
the story was based on geographical knowledge, although
inferentially the oversea passage from Macrobia to Kimmeria
was made on foot, and it is important to notice that the
Insulæ Iernides excluded Britain, being confined to Ireland
and the Western Isles—a distinction recognized by Ptolemy,
who in the second century A.D. grouped the Western Isles
under Ierne.

6. While Carthage was mistress of the West, Himilco, one
of her subjects, navigated the Atlantic to the west of Europe.
His voyage is supposed to have occurred about 500 B.C. ; and
Festus Avienus, a poet of the fourth century A.D., has left

---

* In a various reading the islands give place to the Furies (νήεσσιν
ἐριννύσιν).—*Eschenbach's Edit., Utrecht.*

an account of it.   The navigator passed the Œstrymnides
(*Scilly Islands* [333-34]), which were rich in tin and lead, and
arrived two days afterwards at the Insula Sacra (*Ireland* [294]),
which was the abode of the Hiberni, and near which lay the
Insula Albionum.   The Tartessians traded with these islands,
and the Carthaginians also sent traders and colonists, while
some of the islanders themselves settled on the opposite coast
of the Ligures (on the Liger, *Loire*, in Gaul), which had been
depopulated by the Celts.   Himilco pursued his northward
course until towards the end of the fourth month of his voyage,
when he found himself in waters which were impassable
owing to intense calm and great quantities of seaweed.
Commentators assume that Avienus has misplaced some of the
facts, and that the seaweed was really met with near the
Azores ; but we must accept the account as it stands, remem-
being that the poets generally regarded the extreme northern
ocean as impervious.   Other causes are assigned by different
authors.   Plato attributed it to the muddy matter of a sunken
island called " Atlantis," and Aristotle affirmed that the
ocean was shallow, and that sailing was impossible owing to
dead calms.   The last two notices may have referred to the
low-lying land about the Rhine, considerable tracts of which
are even now only saved from inundation by human industry.
The dangers which ancient navigators of these seas had to
encounter must have been heightened off our own coast by
the Goodwin Sands (" gead faoin "), and in the Netherlands by
the shallows near the mouths of the Scheldt and Rhine.

   7. The text of Avienus, describing Himilco's voyage in
northern latitudes, is as follows :

> Terræ patentis orbis effuse jacet   81
> Orbique rursus unda circumfunditur
> Sed qua profundum semet insinuat salum
> Oceano ab usque, ut gurges hic nostri maris
> Longe explicetur est Atlanticus sinus.   85
> Hic Gaddir urbs est, dicta Tartessus prius
> Hic sunt columnæ pertinacis Herculis,
> Abyla atque Calpe : (hæc læva dicti cespitis
> Libyæ propinqua est Abyla), duro perstrepunt
> Septemtrione, sed loco certæ tenent.   90
> Et prominentis hic jugi surgit caput,
> (Œstrymnin istud dixit ævum antiquius)

Molesque celsa saxei fastigii
Tota in tepentem maxime vergit Notum.
Sub hujus autem prominentis vertice   95
Sinus dehiscit incolis Œstrymnicus,
In quo insulæ sese exserunt Œstrymnides,
Laxe jacentes, et metallo divites
Stanni atque plumbi : multa vis hic gentis est.
Superbus animus, efficax solertia,   100
Negotiandi cura jugis omnibus :
Notisque cymbis surbidum late fretum.
Et belluosi gurgitem oceani secant.
Non hi carinas quippe pinu texere,
Acerve norunt ; non abiete, ut usus est,   105
Curvant faselos ; sed rei ad miraculum,
Navigia junctis semper aptant pellibus,
Corioque vastum sæpe percurrunt salum.
   Ast hinc duobus in sacram, sic insulam
Dixere prisci, solibus cursus rata est.   110
Hæc inter undas multa cespitem jacit
Eamque late genus Hibernorum colit.
Propinqua rursus insula Albionum patet.
Tartessiisque in terminos Œstrymnidum
Negotiandi mos erat : Carthaginis   115
Etiam coloni, et vulgus, inter Herculis
Agitans columnas, hæc adibant æquora
Quæ Himileo Poenus mensibus vix quatuor,
Ut ipse semet re probasse retulit
Enavigantem, posse transmitti adserit :   120
Sic nulla late flabra propellunt ratem ;
Sic segnis humor æquoris pigri stupet.
Adjicit et illud, plurimum inter gurgites
Exstare fucum, et sæpe virgulti vice
Retinere puppim : dicit hic nihilominus,   125
Non in profundum terga demitti maris,
Parvoque aquarum vix supertexi solum :
Obire semper huc et huc ponti feras,
Navigia lenta et languide repentia
Internatare belluas ; si quis dehinc   130
Ab insulis Œstrymnicis lembum audeat
Urgere in undas, axe qua Lycaonis
Rigescit æthra, cespitem Ligurum subit
Cassum incolarum : namque Celtarum manu,
Crebrisque dudum præliis vacuata sunt :   135
Liguresque pulsi, ut sæpe fors aliquos agit,
Plerumque dumos : creber his scrupus locis,
Rigidæque rupes, atque montium minæ
Cœlo inseruntur : et fugax gens hæc quidem
Diu inter arcta cautium duxit diem,   140

Secreta ab undis : nam sali metuens erat
Priscum ob periclum : post quies et otium,
Securitate roborante audaciam,
Persuasit altis devehi cubilibus,
Atque in marinos jam locos descendere.   145
    Post illa rursum, quæ supra fati
Sumus magnus patescit æquoris fusi sinus
Ophiusam ad usque : rursum ab hujus litore
Internum ad æquor qua mare insinuare se
Dixi ante terris, quodque Sardum nuncupant,   150
Septem dierum tenditur pediti via.
Ophiusa porro tanta panditur latus,
Quantam jacere Pelopis audis insulam
Graiorum in agro : hæc dicta prima Œstrymnis est,
Locos et arva Œstrymnicis habitanibus :   155
Post multa serpens effugavit incolas,
Vacuamque glebam nominis fecit sui.
    Procedit inde in gurgites Veneris jugum,
Circumlatratque pontus insulas duas
Tenue ob locorum inhospitas : arvi jugum   160
Rursum tumescit prominens in asperum
Septemtrionem : cursus autem hinc classibus
Usque in columnas efficacis Herculis
Quinque est dierum.

8. The work of Avienus shows accurate knowledge of the coasts opposite Britain. The voyage from the Pillars of Hercules lay by Gaddir or Tartessus [86] to the cape anciently called Œstrymnis [91], where the rocky coast suddenly turned southward [94]. This headland, now Cape Finisterre, was in that angle of the Spanish Peninsula which contained the Astures ; from it the Sinus Œstrymnis [96] (*Bay of Biscay*), stretched out into the Atlantic, giving the name of Insulæ Œstrymnides to some of the Britannic group. The return voyage was by the coast of the Ligures [133], and then through the gulf to Ophiusa [148], which the poet relates was anciently called Œstrymnis, and he adds that it had the same extent as the Peloponnesus [152-155]. This comparison illustrates the exactness of the poet's information, and identifies Ophiusa as the territory of the Pæsici, which consequently once embraced the whole north coast of Spain, leaving traces of itself in the Basque Provinces and Viscaya (*Biscay*). From the recess of the gulf the inland sea called Sardum (*Sardinian Gulf*) could be reached overland in seven days (150). After traversing the Ophiusan Bay (*Bay of Biscay*) the voyagers came to the Promontory Veneris (*Cape Carvœiro*), off which there were two inhospitable islands, *Barlengas Islands*. This cape had a northerly inclination, and lay a five-days' voyage from the Pillars of Hercules [158-164].

9. From the evidence adduced it is certain that the islands opposite Gaul were early known to the Phœnician nations of the Mediterranean and Spain, whose merchants came for native products (lead and tin), to be disposed of in distant marts. These visitors, however, endeavoured to hide the sources of their supplies, and the Greeks, on whose writings we have chiefly to rely, seem themselves to have been only moderately accustomed to maritime enterprise, and to have derived their knowledge in general from outside sources Matters continued thus until about the fourth century, B.C., when the Greeks began to appear as rivals of the Carthaginians, and gradually superseded them. Mention of the Britannic group now occurs, for the first time, under its modern name in the περὶ κόσμου (*De Mundo*), generally attributed to Aristotle, who died 322 B.C. According to this work, the north of Europe above the Palus Mæotis was washed by a vast sea, along which, beyond the Scythæ and Celtæ, the land gradually contracted as far as the Sinus Gallicus and Columnæ Herculis. In this sea, beyond the Celts, were situated two very large islands called " Britannicæ "—Albion and Ierne (Νῆσοι Βρεταννικαὶ, 'Αλβιον καὶ 'Ιέρνη) ; these were greatei than the other islands lying above the Celts, exceeding also Taprobane beyond the Indi (*Ceylon*), and Phebol, by the Arabian Gulf (*Madagascar**). There were also many small islands around the Britannic Isles and Iberia (*Spain*).

10a. Many derivations have been proposed for the terms " Iernides, Britannicæ," the former occurring first in the *Argonautica*, the latter in the *De Mundo*. As to the former the names " Iernus Fluvius " and " Ieron Promontorium " [304g-305c], mentioned by Ptolemy in his description of Ierne, first claim consideration ; but if, as is possible, Ieron

* Britain is smaller than Madagascar in area, owing to its exceedingly irregular coastline ; the greatest length and breadth of both islands are about the same.

signifies " Iernian," the question becomes narrowed down
to Iernus, now represented by Urhin (Ric. " Rhufina ") in
County Cork. If this was really connected with the island
name it might be compared with G. " iarunn " (*iron*), and
Hibernia with Lat. " ferrum " (*iron*), as some antiquaries
have urged ; but Urhin rather points to Lat. " æs " (*copper*),
that metal being still worked at Berehaven, not far from
Urhin, while there is evidence that copper-mining was a
native industry of great antiquity and importance. Eyeries
(*cf*. Lat. " ærarius," *pertaining to copper*), a place near Urhin,
probably indicates old copper-mines ; and so apparently does
Eryr, the old name of Snowdon in Wales (where there are
still copper-mines), though the name is popularly associated
with Wel. " eryr " (*eagle*). The importance of the metal at
Rome was such that copper money only was used there until
the third century B.C., whence " æs " came to signify
" money." The readiest explanation of Britanniæ is G.
" braid " (*mountain*), and of Albion, G. " ailbhe," " ail-
bhinn " (*a rock, mountain-rock—cf*. Breadalbane) ; but it is
possible that the real meaning of these names and Ierne is to
be found in the mythological legends of the Classic Age.

10b. The terms " Iernides " and " Britannicæ," being in
some degree apparently interchangeable, it may be assumed
that Iernides, the earliest name, expressed some feature
common to both Ireland and Britain, and nothing appears
more notable or common to them than the basaltic formation,
which it is clear excited unbounded curiosity before Homer
wrote the *Odyssey*. Guided by this circumstance and the
fables and theories which cluster round it, it is possible to
compare Ierne (Iris [294]) with Heb. אָרָה (orah) (G. " rian,"
" raonadh," " radh," " rais," *a path*), and thus to connect it
with the fabled causeway extending between the two islands,
from the Antrim coast to Staffa. This path, the Giant's
Causeway, once trodden by heroes who must represent the
classic gods, is obviously connected with those views which
caused Ierne to be called the " Insula Sacra " [7] (*Sacred Isle*),
and which perhaps started the story of the wondrous way
(θαυμαστὴ ὁδὸς) to the Hyperborei, which no one could
find (*Pyth*. x. 30). Britannicæ points to G. " bruth " (*cave*),

answered by the caves of the basaltic region. Albion may
be from G. "al" (*rock*), "fainne" (*ring*) ; but Orpheus
mentions mountains called "Alpes" east of Kimmeria,
towards the district called in medieval times " Hilef " (Alp),
now Breadalbane, so that the derivation from G. " ailbhe "
must prevail.

11. In the age of Aristotle parts at least of the northern
seas were tolerably well known. About the time of the De
Mundo, Pytheas of Massilia, having for his object the amber
coasts of the north, sailed to Thule ; then, turning southward,
went through the Gulf of Mentonomon [351*g*], and east along
the coasts of the Guttones and Teutones to Basilia (*Baltia*).
The same navigator related that he travelled all over Britain
on foot (*Strab.*, II., iv. 1). The great political changes
which subsequently swept over the Mediterranean seem to
have caused Britain to be almost forgotten ; but the Greeks
apparently retained its trade. The historian Polybius, in the
third book of the Pragmateia, *circa* 170 B.C., promised to write
an account of the Britannic Isles (Νῆσοι Βρεττανικαί), and the
making of tin, but there is no evidence that he fulfilled his
intention. The Romans themselves, neglecting the commercial
opportunities with the north which their conquests offered,
knew very little of Britain until the time of Julius Cæsar, 55 B.C.
This writer mentions Britannia, Hibernia, and Mona, and was
aware of many contiguous islands. At that time the Veneti
of Gaul were practically masters of these seas, and imposed
tolls upon the merchants who put in at their ports. Diodorus
Siculus (*temp.* Julius and Augustus) mentions many islands
dispersed in that part of the ocean which contracted Gaul,
and lying opposite to the Hercyniæ Saltus in Germany, the
greatest being called " Britannia," which produced tin (v. 21).
A few years later Strabo alludes to the Νῆσοι Βρεττανικαί, and
describes Albion, Ierne, the Cassiterides, and Thule. Roman
knowledge of the group must now have made great strides, yet,
according to Tacitus, they were uncertain until the time of
Claudius (A.D. 43) whether Britain was an island (see Orcades
[327]). The dictators of Europe, however, could not have been
so ignorant, and Tacitus's statement must be discredited.

12. Pomponius Mela, the first Roman geographer whose

works are extant, writing after the Claudian invasion and probably after the conquest of the Orcades, mentions Britannia, Iuverna, the Orcades, Vecta, Æmodæ, and Thule. Pliny (died A.D. 79) mentions the largest as well as many smaller islands ; he states that none of them except Britannia and Hibernia were above 125 miles in circuit ; but his quotations from other sources seem to show that the term " Britannicæ " had become narrowed down, having sometimes embraced all the islands eastward, one of them being the reputed island of Nerigon (*Norwegian peninsula*), which was known to be larger than Britain. Speaking of this larger group, he says : " Britanniæ vocarentur omnes " (*Nat. Hist.* iv., 30). Ptolemy (*circa* A.D. 140), includes the Orcades, Ocetis, and Thule, in the Νῆσοι Βρεταννικαί, grouping them with Albion and the Western Isles with Hibernia. About a century later Solinus wrote a short account of the islands. He remarks that the Gaelic coast would be the end of the world if it were not for Britannia, which from its size almost deserved to be called another world. Many islands, not insignificant, lay around it, of which Hibernia most resembled it in size. The sea which separated the two largest was billowy and restless throughout the year, and navigable only for a few days. The people used osier boats, which with great effort they covered with ox-hide ; when on a voyage they abstained from food. This sea or strait was estimated to be 120 miles broad by those writers who were most exact, and it was distinguished by the island Siluria [332]. The other islands in these seas included Adtanatos, Thule, the Hebudes, and Orchades. Sailors from the promontory of Caledonia [328] to Thule passed the Hebudes, and the second station was the Orchades (*Sol.*). It would appear from the last remark that navigators started for Thule from the Roman frontier near the Clyde, following the west coast to the Orcades, and thence probably by the Faroë Islands.

13. The poet Avienus (fourth century A.D.) describes the Iberians (*Spaniards*) as bordering upon the cold waters of the boreal ocean, having the harsh Britons as near neighbours (*Descriptio orbis Terræ*, 416-18). Another passage mentions two islands (*hæ numero geminæ*), containing high mountains,

at a distance from the Iberian coast, towards the breezes of
the icy north (*aquilo*) and opposite the mouth of the Rhine.
These possessed rich soil and spacious pastures, were inhabited by the horrible Britons, and were washed by immense
tides. Thence a considerable voyage northwards led to
Thule (*ibid.*, 745-60). The poet Priscian (*circa* A.D. 450)
speaks of the proximity of the Britanni to the Hercynian
Forest (*Periegesis*, 273-74). He places the Hesperides
(ἕσπερος, *west*) at the Hyperborean bounds, and mentions
two islands (*geminæ*) near the northern limits of the ocean
towards the Ostia Britannides or Ostia Rheni (*the straits
between Britain and the Rhine*). Here was found the agate
stone which glittered when sprinkled with water, but lost its
brilliancy in oil. Not far distant were the shores of the
Nesides, occupied by the Amnites [328] ; thence voyagers
crossed the open ocean to Thule (*ibid.*, 570-89). In the early
part of the same century (the fifth) Orosius mentions Britannia,
Hibernia, the Orcades, Thule, and Mevania [329], placing the
first two beyond Gaul and opposite Spain. Marcian Hera-
clitus, a Greek geographer, of unknown date, but perhaps
belonging to the same century, speaks of two islands in the
Northern Ocean which were commonly called the Pret-
annicæ (Πρετανvικαὶ Νῆσοι). The largest of these, Albion
('Αλβίων), was the third largest island in the world, and
Hibernia ('Ιουερνία) was the fourth. He also mentions the
Æbudæ. Similar particulars appear in the *Ethnica* of Stephen
of Byzantium. Dionysius Periegetes has the forms Νῆσοι
Βρετανvίδες,* N. Βρετανvοί.

14. Procopius, in the middle of the sixth century, speaks
of war between the Varni and the insular soldiers in the
island Brittia. According to him, the Varni dwelt beyond
the Ister as far as the northern ocean and the Rhine, which
river separated them from the Franks and other nations in

* Possibly the " tres Fortunatæ " Insulæ (" e quibus solum voca-
bulum signandum fuit," *Solinus* xxiii.) had their origin in a pun on
the three Bretannides (Albion, Ierne, and Thule, *Strabo*). Eumenius
seems to associate them with the sea about Thule [116], and there
we now find the Faroë Isles. But Pliny connects them with the
Arrotrebarum Promontory, so that they were probably the Buryos
Isles off Galicia [372].

that quarter. Those formerly on either side of the Rhine had each a peculiar name, of which one tribe was called "Germans"—a name commonly applied to all. In this northern ocean lay Brittia, not far from the continent, at the distance of 200 stadia right opposite to the outlets of the Rhine and between Britannia and Thule. Britannia lay towards the setting sun, at the extreme of the Spaniards, and distant from the continent not less than 4,000 stadia. But Brittia lay at the hindermost extreme of Gaul, where it bordered on the ocean—that is, to the north of Spain and Britannia, whereas Thule, so far as known, lay at the farthest extreme of the ocean towards the north; the latter was ten times larger than Britannia. Three very numerous nations, the Angli [131a], Phrissones, and Britones, possessed Brittia, each having a king. So great was the fecundity of these that every year vast numbers migrated to the Franks, who colonized them in their most desert parts, insomuch that it was said they formed a claim to the island. In Brittia men of old time built a long wall, cutting off a great part of the island; for the soil and men and all other things were not alike on both sides. The east side had wholesome air in conformity with the seasons, being moderately warm in summer and cool in winter, and it contained many men living as other men; the trees bore appropriate fruits in season, the corn-lands were productive as others, and the district was fertilized by streams. On the west side all was different, and it was impossible for a man to live there half an hour. There were vipers and serpents innumerable, and all other kinds of wild beasts, and the natives affirmed that if a man passed to this side of the wall he died immediately, unable to endure the unwholesome atmosphere. In this account Brittia is Britain (cf. Bryttas [176]) and Britannia is Ireland; and the settlement of Britons among the Franks is confirmed by the occurrence of the British language in Little Britany (Bretagne). It has been shown, however, that the latter received British settlers as early as Himilco's age [6].

15. The religion of the British Isles in prehistoric times is a subject upon which little is known, but important side-

lights are occasionally thrown upon it by the classics. The
nucleus around which it developed was the scientific theory
of the pole, conceived in very remote ages, and supported,
if not suggested, by the basalt columns of our coasts, springing
up, as they do, from that sea whence the terrestrial pole
advanced to the highest point of the vault of heaven. This
point or pinnacle (G. " barr," " beur," *pinnacle*) furnished
the classic races with the word " boreus " (βόρειος, *northern*),
the winds blowing from this region being personified as
" Boreas " ; and above the seat of this wind god the ancient
poets placed the blissful race of the Hyperborei [4]. Perhaps through G. " bior " (*water, well*), the notion of the
pole became sometimes lost in that of the abyss or underworld. Some interesting matters concerning the Hyperborei
are preserved by Diodorus Siculus. He relates that the
geographer Hecatæus (*circa* 330 B.C.) and some other writers
reported that there was an island in the ocean opposite Gaul
not smaller than Sicily, and lying under the Septentriones
(Great Bear), which was occupied by the Hyperborei, who
were so called because they were more remote than the
north wind ; the soil was very good and fruitful, the air was
in the highest degree temperate, and there were two harvests
in the year. Leto was fabled to have been born there, and
therefore the cult of Apollo, her son, was pre-eminent ; and
because the chanting of praises to this god was regularly
observed every day and the highest honours were rendered
to him, the priests had the reputation of being priests of
Apollo. He had a magnificent grove there, and a celebrated
temple, round in form and adorned with many votive offerings.
There was also a city (πολις), sacred to the god, in which
there were very many harp-players (τοὺς πλείστους εἶναι
κιθαρίζοντας). These, playing upon their instruments in the
temple, sang hymns extolling the works of the god. The
Hyperborei had a language peculiar to themselves, and were
especially well disposed, from ancient times, towards the
Greeks, particularly the Athenians and Delians. They related that some Greeks had passed over to their island, and
presented noble offerings, inscribed with Greek letters. On
the other hand, Abaris, a Hyperborean, went into Greece and

renewed the old intimacy and friendship with the Delians. They also affirmed that in the island the moon appeared very near the earth, and exhibited some terrestrial hillocks on its surface. Moreover, Apollo visited the island once in nineteen years, in which period the stars, completing their revolutions, returned to their former places. On this account the Greeks called the cycle of nineteen years the " Great Year." In this visitation the god sang to the cithara at night, and conducted ring-dances continually from the vernal æquinox to the rise of the Pleiads, delighting in the praises bestowed upon him for his propitious dispensations. The government of the city and the supreme control of the temple was in the hands of the Boreades (Βορεάδαι), the offspring of Boreas, who held the office in hereditary succession (*Diod. Sic.*, ii., 47). The island intended in this narration is probably Britain, but the statement that it was not smaller than Sicily is more appropriate to Ireland. The term " Boread " (*i.e.*, pole-man, priest of Apollo), in the form " bard," came in later times to signify any poet or minstrel.

16. The Hyperboreans, whom we have seen connected with the Britannic group and Delos, were renowned at Delos about a century before the period of Hecatæus. Herodotus (440 B.C.) says that two Hyperborean virgins, named Arge and Opis, came to Delos attended by the gods, bringing gifts to Ilithya in return for easy labours in child-birth. Dying at Delos, they were buried behind the temple of Diana towards the east. The Delian women collected gifts for them, and invoked them by name in a hymn composed in their praise by Olen the Lycian, who also composed all the other old hymns that were sung at Delos ; and the women of the islands and Iona, borrowing the Delian custom, also invoked them by name and made collections. At Delos when the thighs of the victims had been consumed on the altar, the ashes were thrown and spread on their tomb. The Hyperboreans afterwards sent some sacred things in the care of two virgins called Hyperoche and Laodice, and for the security of the virgins they also sent five of their citizens, who, under the name of the Perphereës, received great honours at Delos. In consequence of the persons thus despatched not coming back, the Hyperboreans for the future wrapped the sacred things in wheat-straw, and took them to the people on their borders (the Scythians), asking them to forward the parcel to some other nation, and by this method it reached Delos. Wheat-straw was also sacred to the Thracian and Pæonian women, who would not slaughter the victims to Royal Diana without it. In honour of the Hyperborean virgins who died at Delos, the young women and men of Delos were wont to cut their hair. The girls, previous to their wedding, cut off a lock of hair, twisted it round a spindle, and placed it on the virgin's sepulchral monument, which stood in Diana's precinct. On the top of the monument grew an olive-tree (*Herod.*, iv., 33-35).

17. Interesting notices of the Hyperboreans are found in other early writers. Pindar (about 500 B.C.) said that no one could find the wondrous way to the Hyperborei, but Perseus had visited them, entering their houses unexpectedly as they were sacrificing their renowned hecatombs of asses to Apollo, and he feasted amongst them under the guidance of Athena (*Pyth*, x.). About 200 B.C. Eratosthenes, recording the slaying of the Kyklopes with Apollo's arrow, says the god hid the fatal missive amongst the Hyperborei, where there was a winged temple (Εκρυψε δέ αὐτο ἐν ὑπερβορείοις οὗ καὶ ὁ ναος ὁ πτερίνος [200 *f*]). Abaris, the Hyperborean priest of Apollo, received the arrow from the god, and went into Greece with it, riding on it through the air, and taking no earthly food. Soline (third century A.D.), speaking expressly of the fabled Hyperborei beyond Pterophoron (πτεροφόρος, *winged*), says that it was usual for virgins of the fairest reputation to send repeatedly the earliest of fruits to the Delian Apollo. But since the virgins sometimes received harm by the treachery of persons with whom they lodged, they at a later period received within their own boundaries a high priest (*pontifex*) of the same religion which they followed when abroad (*Sol.*). Aviene (fourth century A.D.) says that in the two islands of the Britons women danced in the celebration of Bacchic orgies, the sacred rites being continued into the night ; the air rang with shouts, and the worshippers indulged in frenzied processions, carrying their fanaticism to even greater excess than the Thracians or

Indians (*Descriptio Orbis Terræ*, 751-57). Priscian, in the next century, relates that the Amnite women who lived in the Nesides islands [328] performed Bacchic rites and wore crowns of the leaves and berries of ivy (*Periegesis*, 584-86).

18a. Other writers show that divinities either identical with or resembling those of Greece were worshipped in the islands lying off this part of the European coast. Strabo says that in the ocean, not far from the coast of Gaul, there was a small island, opposite to the mouth of the Loire, inhabited by Samnite women who were Bacchantes, and appeased Bacchus by mysteries and sacrifices. No man was permitted on the island, and when the women desired mixed companionship they crossed the sea, and afterwards returned again. They had a custom of unroofing their temple once a year and reroofing it the same day before sunset, each one bringing some of the materials. If anyone let her burden fall, which invariably happened, she was torn to pieces, and her limbs carried round the temple with wild shouts, which the worshippers did not cease till their rage was exhausted (*Strab.*, IV., iv., 6). Artemidorus (*circa* 100 B.C.) mentioned an island near Britain in which sacrifices were performed to Ceres and Proserpine in the same manner as in Samothrace (*ibid.*). Mela says that the island of Sena [335] was famous for an oracle of the Gallic deity. Its priestesses kept perpetual virginity, and were said to be nine in number. They were called Galligenæ, and were supposed to be endowed with singular powers, such as raising the seas and winds by incantations, twining themselves into any animals they choose, curing disorders which others could not cure, and knowing the future and prophesying. They were, however, unfavourable except to mariners and to those who went thither to consult them. Plutarch mentions the genii. He says that many islands, generally uninhabited, lay about Britain, scattered like the Italian Sporades, some being called the Islands of the Heroes [328]. Demetrius, being sent by the Emperor (Caligula or Claudius) to explore, arrived at an island inhabited by a few Britons who were held sacred by their countrymen. Immediately after he arrived the air grew black, apparitions were seen, a tempest arose, and fiery

serpents and whirlwinds flitted towards the earth. The
islanders informed him that when these things occurred some
of the ærial gods or genii, superior to us, ceased to live. " As
a taper while burning affords a pleasing light, and is offensive
when extinguished, so these heroes are beneficent, but at
their death turn all things to confusion, make tempests, and
infect the air with pestilence." There was one island [334]
where Saturn was kept by Briareus in a deep sleep, attended
by many genii as his companions (*Plutarch*). A genius might
be ascribed to almost any object, animate or inanimate ; the
" GENIO TERRÆ BRITANNICÆ " occurred on a stone from
Achindavy [252*a*].

18*b*. Superior to the genii, of course, were the gods. There
is abundant evidence that the principal deities of the Gauls
(Mercury, Apollo, Mars, Jupiter, and Minerva [355]), and
those of the Germans (Mercury, Hercules, and Mars [363])—
Mercury being the favourite with both races, and all familiar
to the Greeks—together with many other deities, were worshipped in Britain. And Ireland undoubtedly shared the
same mysteries and rites, carrying them possibly to a greater
extreme, since Orpheus and Avienus [5, 6] speak of it in
terms implying peculiar reverence. That idolatry was
common in Britain appears from Gildas (*temp*. A.D. 500).
He said he would not enumerate the diabolical idols of
his country, which almost surpassed those of Egypt in number, and of which some were still to be seen in his time
mouldering away about the deserted temples, with stiff and
deformed features, as was customary, and he added that he
would not call out upon the mountains, springs, hills, or
rivers (see Verbeia [282*i*]), which were then subservient to
the use of men, but were once an abomination and destruction,
the people blindly paying them divine honour. In Ireland
the chief idol was Crom, or Crom-cruach (" rig idaill hErin "),
which, after a legendary existence of 2,000 years, was found
by St. Patrick at Mag Slecht (G. " magh," *field ;* " sleuch-
dadh," *a worshipping*) in Cavan, ornamented with gold and
silver, and having about it twelve idols covered with brass.
The priest of this god was called Cruimter (" crom," *circle* ;
" tuir," *lord*), probably identical with Cairnec, or Cairneach,

explained in O'Connor's *Gaelic Grammar* as a *priest of the sun*, and in Armstrong's *Gaelic Dictionary* as *a Druid, in allusion to his dwelling-place* (*i.e., a carn*). G. " Gre," *sun*, may explain the name of Lough Gur, in Limerick, the shores of which are thronged with stone circles, altars, and other rude remains, some of gigantic proportions, but probability points to G. " gearr," *to carve.*

19. The principal religious offices in the islands appear to have been in the hands of the Druids ; but this priesthood is only mentioned in connection with Britain and Mona, and even there direct information of it is found only in three or four passages in Cæsar, Tacitus, and Pliny [47]. Hence our knowledge of these priests is most meagre, and authors are wont to apply to them the classical accounts of the Gallic Druids [352]. Strabo says they had their name from δρῦς (*oak*), which tree was sacred to them ; and Pliny relates that they did not perform any rite without the leaf of the oak, on which account he favours the same etymology (*H. N.*, xvi., 95.) Classic writers only preserve the term in the plural (" Druides," Δρυΐδαι), and give no clue to its singular form, but Strabo's explanation is countenanced by the following words from the native languages :

G. darach, darag,	
Ir. darach	} oak.
Wel. dar, derw, derwen	
G. druidh, *pl.* druidhean,	} *a wise man, diviner, Druid (a*
Ir. drui, drai, *pl.* druite, draite	*priest of the sun,* O'Connor's
Wel. derwydd, *pl.* derwyddon	} *Gael. Gram.,* 52. 189).

It is improbable, nevertheless, that this was the true origin of the term, and the explanation must be guided by the certainty that the insular religion was astronomical, a circumstance already suggested in connection with the Hyperborei. It is clear that Druidism was engrafted upon a profound knowledge of astronomy. The Druids studied astronomy ; they professed to know the size and form of the earth and universe, and the motion of the heaven and stars (*Mela*) ; they reckoned their months and years from the sixth day of the moon [360*a*] ; and the native poetry of prehistoric Scotland mentions the stars Uleirin (Iul Erin, *guide of Erin*),

Cathlinn, and Tonn-theine (*Ossian*). The Boreades closely
observed the moon, remarking upon its undulating surface,
and they were cognizant of the Apollonic cycle [15] ; the latter
represented the Chaldæan period of rather more than eighteen
years, during which the lunar nodes made a complete circuit
of the heavens, occasioning a regular recurrence of eclipses.
According to Plutarch, the inhabitants of an island (which
must have been Albion or another of the Britannic group)
kept every thirtieth year a festival in honour of Saturn, when
his star entered Taurus (*De Facie in Orbe Lunæ*) at the com-
pletion of his revolution round the sun.   The relation of
Taurus to the Saturnian feast is important, and the feast itself,
recurrent every thirtieth year, joins with other astronomical
coincidences in explaining the real significance of the gigantic
remains of Stonehenge.   The outer circle, 360 feet in diameter,
which encloses this temple, represents the celestial sphere,
divided into 360 degrees ; and the outer circle of thirty
upright stones symbolizes the thirty years of Saturn's
revolution.

20*a*. Taurus, thus connected with the Saturnian feast, was
important in Asia from about 4600 to 2500 B.C., when it
was the first sign of the Sumer-Akkadian zodiac, the sun
entering into it at the vernal equinox.   It is, indeed, possible
that the sign was known in Britain at that remote epoch ; and
Taurus itself points to the Gaelic word " turus " (*a course*), a
term not inappropriate to the constellation in which the sun
commenced his yearly journey.   As the first sign it bore in
Euphratean tracts the name of Alpu, which may be compared
with Heb. אַלּוּף (" aluph," *leader ; cf.* Heb. אַדִּיר, " adir ";
G. " triath," *leader*), while in Heb. דּוּר (" dur," *a circuit*)
probably lies the true explanation of the Druids' office as
priests or professors of the Tauric astronomy.   As the leader
of the circuit of the year, Taurus corresponds to the eldest of
Jacob's twelve sons—Reuben, Reubel—who thus has the
first period of office.   About 2500 B.C., however, the preces-
sion of the equinoxes caused this honour to be transferred
from Taurus to Aries, the last sign, the circumstance finding
expression among the Hebrews as the advancement of the
youngest over the eldest son. The preferred son is Benjamin,

who fared five times better than his brethren in Egypt. His
mother Rachel is Hera (Lat. " Juno "), her identity being
placed beyond doubt by the name Ben-oni which she gives
her son ; and his father, as shown by the name which he
bestows, Ben-jamin, is Jupiter Ammon, who as the Egyptian
Baal was known to the Canaani as Abel-mizraim (Gen. l. 11).
There was thus a close connection between Aries, the Ram-
sign, and the Egyptian deity whose sacred animal was a ram.
Aries, again, is Ares, the god of war, a dignity especially
Benjamin's. Jacob, blessing him, says : " Benjamin shall
raven as a wolf ; in the morning he shall devour the prey, and
at night he shall divide the spoil " (Gen. xlix. 27). Aries,
called in the east " Star of Anu, Star of Lulim," explains the
death of Rachel (Juno) in Bethlehem. Her tomb, in the way
to Ephrath, surmounted by a pillar, may be compared with
the circumstance that basaltic Britain was once the spirit-
world of the dead, and when after her burial her husband
journeyed and encamped beyond the Tower of Edar, we
have surely, in the latter name, a definite allusion to the sign
" Taurus," and probably the true key to the interpretation
of the term " Druid." Jacob, blessing Reuben, says, " Thou
art my firstborn, my might, and the beginning of my strength,
the excellency of dignity and of power "; hence no symbol more
appropriate than the tower could be applied to him, and the
importance of the tower, either from this consideration or its
use in the observation of the heavens, may be assumed from
the numerous towers of the Euphratean nations, and again
from the curious round-towers which, scattered thickly over
Ireland (the Insula Sacra), are so ancient that there are no
records to explain their use. Possibly the Tower of Edar is
the Pleiad group, especially as Peleth was son of Reuben
(Num. xvi. 1); and the Pelethi, were important in the time of
David. An ancient conception of the Pleiads as a " mound "
may identify Peleth with the dreaded Pluto ; nay, the seven
maidens of Europa (*darkness*), who gathered flowers upon the
coast of Sidon, are, through Sidon, connected with Satan, lord
of Hell.

20*b*. The suggestion, half-ventured, that astronomy was
Britannic in origin, may seem bold, but if etymology can be

relied on, the evidence is strong, for Gaelic, the prehistoric
native tongue, explains all the celestial objects which are
familiar to an ordinary observer of the heavens. Thus, Lat.
" sol " (*sun*), the great light placed in the firmament by
Elohim to rule the day, is explained by G. " solus " (*light :
cf.* " seol," *to guide*), and Ἥλιος is G. " iul " (*a guide*).
The native word for the luminary, " grian " (*obsolete* gri)
perhaps appears in the name of the Tropic of Cancer, " cinn-
gri " (*the waxing of the sun*), and perhaps also in Capricorn.
The orb which divides with Sol the sovereignty of the daily
period is Metis (*the moon*), from G. " muth " (*to change*),
whence " mios " (*month*) ; her office as measurer of time
furnished the name Σελήνη (G. " seal," *a course*), and the
crescent or vessel-shaped form displayed in her early stage is
expressed by the Latin " luna " (*moon :* G. " lunn," *vessel*).
The crescent-moon is the golden cup, or boat (G. " long,"
ship), given by Helios to Herakles, in which the hero sailed to
Erythia. The Gaelic terms for the stars indicate that the
smaller luminaries likewise served as directors or guides.
Gaelic " astar " (*journey*), " stiuir " (*to steer*) reappear in
ἀστηρ (G. " steorn," *star*) ; G. " rannag," " rionnag," " rean-
nan " (*star*) is related to " rang " (*a row*), and G. " saod "
(*road*), " saodaich " (*to conduct, to guide*) sufficiently describe the zodiac. Lat. " sidus " (*constellation*) has affinity
with G. " saide," (*a swarm*). Such concurrent similarity
cannot be entirely accidental, and if this be admitted, the
question may indeed be asked whether the Biblical story that
the lights were placed in the sky to serve " for signs, for
seasons, for days, and for years," and the Chaldæan story that
they were arranged in months and rows in the forms of animals
to fix the year, did not really emanate from Britain. According to the Triads, Idris (*cf.* Taurus) was the first astronomer
of Britain, the other two being Gwydion, son of Don, and
Gwyn, son of Nudd.

20c. The Chaldæan notion that the stars were from the
beginning arranged in the appearance of animals must be
comparatively modern, springing up when the poets and
fabulists had begun to liken particular clusters to living
objects, or to pervert the names of groups to significations

not theirs. It may have been by a levity of the latter kind that "turus" (*journey*) was changed to "Taurus" (G. "tarbh," *a bull*), and that those myths were started which associate the animal with the sign. It is probable, however, that such associations were never entirely arbitrary, but were founded upon observed characteristics of the sign ; for instance, the blustering winds, which are common about the time of the vernal equinox, might suggest to the poets the freaks of an infuriated bull. The story of Europa is particularly connected with Taurus, and throws much light upon the sign. Zeus, in the form of a white bull, appeared to the goddess when she was gathering spring-buds among her seven maidens on the coast of Sidon, and bore her off on his back through the sea to Crete. The goddess, as already noticed [1], typified the darkness, her companions are the seven Pleiades in Taurus, and when upon the animal's back on the way to Crete she is the black night retreating before the sovereignty of the advancing sun, which brings with it longer days and shorter nights for the northern hemisphere. The truth of this explanation of the myth is confirmed by the mutilated figure of the Zodiacal bull, the hind half being unrepresented, obviously because its burden of darkness (equal night) hid it from view.

21. It has been seen that the revolutions of the heavenly bodies and the spherical form of our earth were familiar to the Druids. Athena's statue by Pheidias represented her holding a globe in her hand, and the same symbol appears in a statue of Helios (*Sol*). The symbol was well known in Britain under the form of a circle or wheel, and it cannot be doubted that its use here was founded upon the same reasons which gave the globe favour in the East. Heb. חוג, Gr. κύκλος, G. "cuach," each expressing the idea of rotundity, point to a common root ; the former is used in Isaiah when speaking of the deity who sits upon the circle of the earth ; the second is compounded with ὤψ (*eye*) in Kyklops (*round-eye*), applied to the one-eyed sons of Uranos, and the Gaelic word may be detected in the name of the hero "Cuchulain" ("cuach; aillean," *causeway*). This hero belonged to the province of Ulster, in which the Giant's Causeway lies, and he is the Irish

representative of κικλην (*the circler*), the Phrygian name
of the Great Bear. He resisted Queen Meave when she
invaded Ulster with the object of seizing the bull Donn
Chualgne, and that he had something to do with the round
towers may be assumed from the reputation enjoyed by the
Kyklopes as the first tower-builders (*Plin, N. H.*, vii. 57).
The curious rocks of the Ulster coast, resembling pillars or
columns (G. " colmhuinn ") recall the Biblical Gilgal (עָגֹל,
round ; גַּלְגַּל, *wheel*) ; and St. Columba, the Christian apostle
of the Western Isles, was apparently a circle-god, whose
church of Iona was a place of circle worship. This church
was dedicated by the voluntary sacrifice of Odran. The wheel
under the name אֹופָן was sacred to the Hebrews of the
captivity, and Ezekiel mentions four, which were full of eyes
round about them ; the word appears in Gael. " fainne "
(*ring*), which gave name to the Irish Fian. How far the
Britons were indebted to the East for some of the mysteries
of their disc worship seems suggested by Crom-Cruach and
his twelve attendant gods [18], who recall the Redeemer and
twelve apostles of Greek scripture, and the Hebrew stories
of the twelve pillars and of Israel and the twelve sons. Nor,
indeed, is it unlikely that Jacob's ladder at Bethel found an
actual echo in the Hebudean Islands. The basalts at Staffa
(G. " stap," *step*), and again at Gometra (" ceum," *a step :*
tir) present in their names an echo of the mysterious creed
which once held such sway, that the causeway of its gods is
still fabled as the giant's path.

22. The round towers of Ireland, like the Ulster columns,
were doubtlessly connected with pillar worship. Job speaks
of the pillars of both heaven and earth, and the Proverbs say
of Wisdom that she has built her house and hewn out her
seven pillars (ix. 1). The number seven and the pillar were
sacred ; hence the Apocalypse mentions seven churches,
seven spirits, seven golden candlesticks, and seven stars
(i. 4, 12, 16), seven lamps of fire which were the seven spirits
(iv. 5), seven seals, seven horns, and seven eyes (v. 1, 6),
with many other instances ; and the same book contains a
promise that he who overcomes temptation shall be made a

pillar in God's temple to remain in it perpetually, and the temple is expressly the New Jerusalem which comes down out of heaven (iii. 12). An Irish poem mentions the seven battalions of the constant Fian, and seven tons of gold offered as compensation for carrying off the wife of the King of Lochlin, and seven score of the Fian were sent to combat with the King (*Poem of Valour*). These passages seem to explain with sufficient clearness the true signification of the round towers, with the seven churches which in various places accompanied them, as at Arranmore, Clonmacnoise, Glendalough, Inch Clorin, Innis Caltra, Rattoo, Scattery Island, and Tory Island. The towers, indeed, echo the Hebrew prophet's figure of a wheel (really four), which worked as a wheel within a wheel, and in which the spirit of the four cherubim lay ; the rings of the wheels were so high that they were dreadful, and they were full of eyes (Ezek. i. ; *cf.* Rev. i.). The four rings were perhaps represented originally by four stages, or compartments, in the towers, the " eyes " being the apertures or windows, each of the lower compartments containing in general one small aperture ; in the highest compartment were four large windows looking north, south, east, and west. If this view be correct there would be seven apertures in all, corresponding to the seven churches, and again to the seven lights of the Bear-sign, which circles round the pole (the pillar) every day. These strange structures are supposed to date back to the introduction of Christianity, usually attributed to St. Patrick. It may be doubted, however, whether the Saint (" Ptah righ ") had a real existence ; he was rather the Irish concept of the Apostle Peter (πέτρα, *a rock*), personifying the astronomical teachings of the Hebrew-Grecian missionary-school of Rome. In early Britain the four wheels full of eyes were represented at Stonehenge by two stone circles and two ellipses, so arranged as to have the appearance of doors upon doors, and evidently intended to symbolize the Tropics of Cancer and Capricorn, and the two outer circles towards the poles. The round tower itself symbolized the pole (G. "mulcheann," " Mulghart " ; Heb. נס, " nes,"*

---

* The poets playing upon the similarity of *nes* to Gr. ὄνος, *ass*, G. " aisiol," *axle*, " asal," *ass*, probably started the belief that the

םוס, "mot," "nesides" [328] ; Gr. πόλος), and it is probable
that the key to the true signification of the greatest religions
of the world will appear from a comparison of these words
with Melquarth, Milcom, Baal, Apollo, the Nazarene, and
Mahomet. The emblem of Assur, a wheel with a winged
upright human figure within (sometimes in front), represented,
like Ixion's wheel, the revolution of the Little Bear round the
pole (Baal), and the name "Assur" (Lat. "circus," ring),
repeated in Israel and in Sarai, throws light upon Hebrew
literature. The study of the universe is very ancient. Gog and
Magog of the north, Kalypso's Island of Ogygia in the north, the
Cuchillan Sea (cf. Wel. "gogledd," north), are all echoes of the
cosmic problems which have agitated man from the earliest ages.

23. The oak has been noticed as sacred to the Druids,
but it is probable that greater importance was attached to
the mistletoe (ἰξός, Lat. "viscum" ; G. "Uileice" ; Arm.
"oil-yiach" ; Wel. "ol-hiach" ; Ir. "uile-iceach "), especially when it was found growing on an oak. Pliny relates that
the Druids called the plant by a word signifying, in their
language, "all-heal" ("omnia sanantem appellantes suo
vocabulo" (xvi. 44), and such appears to be the meaning of
the Gaelic word ("uile," all—ic, a cure) [360a]. The plant
was not only held sacred by the Druids, but seems to have
been well known all over Europe. It was the herb moly
given by Hermes to Ulysses as an unfailing antidote against
the poisonous potions of Kirke, the Homeric name being
still current in North-East Europe (Russ. "omela," mistletoe) ;
and Virgil seems to allude to it when he speaks of the
"golden branch." The Hellenes personified it as Melampous
("omela" ; πούς, foot), who was a great physician, and
introduced the worship of Dionysos or Bakchos ("Ael,"
βισκός, mistletoe) into Greece, being endowed with prophetic
knowledge by the serpents which lived in an oak-tree before
his father's house. The final compound of Melampous is

---

ass was sacred to Apollo. The animal was sacrificed to him both among
the Hyperboreans [17] and at Delphi ; and the esteem in which it was
held among the Israeli is shown by the stories of Samson, Saul, and
Balaam. Solomon on a mule, the Redeemer on an ass, entered
Jerusalem in triumph.

probably a perversion of πόα (*plant*). The sacredness of the
plant is again found emphasized under the name Γλαῦκος
(γλάξ). The dead Glaukos was restored to life by a
herb which a serpent brought into his tomb, and another
Glaukos gained immortality by eating of the divine herb
sown by Kronos. A third Glaukos, son of Sisyphos (βισκος
transposed), fed his mares with human flesh, a story quite
consistent with the well-authenticated Druidic rite of human
sacrifice, the mares being probably horse-shaped effigies in
which the victims were consumed by fire [354, 357]. White
horses were reared in German groves [364], and this custom
points to another Glaukos, whose father, Hippolochos, is apparently the " white horse " (ἵππος λευκός), though his real original is
the all-heal (ποα, *plant;* " uile-ice "). Hippolochos is an interesting figure in connection with British antiquities, for his
apparent status as the " white horse " lends significance to
the celebrated figure in the Vale of the White Horse, Berkshire, and to similar representations which existed at several
places on the Belgic Downs. Eurylochus was the only one
of Ulysses's companions who eluded the arts of Kirke.

24. " Mistletoe " is related to μιστύλη (μιτυλος) (*mutilated*),
from μιστύλλω (*to cut into joints*), and a name more suggestive
of the curious structure of the plant would be difficult to find.
Many deities came to be associated with the plant. Semele,
who died when Zeus visited her in his character as god of
thunder, and whose embryo the god saved and sewed up in
his thigh, is the mother-plant whose berry is engrafted in
the oak ; and the embryo, issuing in due time as Dionysos
(Bacchos), is the infant plant. When Dionysos grew up, he
carried his mother from the underworld to Olympus, where
she was called Thyone. The same story is partly retold in
the myth of Metis. She, in her fruitful state, is swallowed
by Zeus, and her child, Athena, eventually comes forth out
of his head. In like manner the introduction of Bacchic
rites into Greece by Melampous repeats the establishment
of Hyperborean worship at Delos. As Dionysos was connected with the mistletoe, and his namesakes Athena and
Thyone shared the same relation, so the Hyperboreans were
probably in some way or other the mistletoe-bearers (ὕφεαρ,

mistletoe : φέρω, *to carry*), the identity also extending to the
five Pherpherëes, whose wards, the Hyperborean virgins, were
buried in the temple of Artemis (Diana). It seems that
Abaris and Hyperoche, the Hyperboreans, are also connected with ὕφεαρ, and that they must be regarded as priest
and priestess of the northern faith. The sacred flower or
plant is the subject of many names in Hellenic myth. An-
thedon (ἄνθος, *flower*), now Lukisi (*cf.* Glaukos), was the
home of Glaukos the Bœotian ; Potniæ (βοτάνη, *plant*) was
the home of Glaukos, son of Sisyphos ; Melanthius (Omela,
ανθος) was son of Dolios (*cf.* Delos) ; and Antiphates (ἄνθος,
φάτης, *prophet's flower*) displayed in his mad behaviour
towards Ulysses the unbridled violence of Bacchos. In the
legend of Glaukos, son of Minos, omela probably occasioned,
through a free translation, the story of the honey-cask (μέλι,
honey), into which the young hero fell, and was smothered,
being afterwards restored to life by the serpent's herb. As
honey was used in making mead, it is not difficult to see how
the mistletoe became associated with the wine-god. The
story of the mutilated foot was familiar in Palestine. Adoni-
bezek (*cf.* Dionysos, Bacchos) had his thumbs and great toes
cut off—a retaliation of the punishment he had inflicted
on seventy kings (Judg. i.) ; and at Jebusi, where he died,
the lame were an important body until cut off by David
(2 Sam. v.). The mutilated foot is the Great Bear; while
the Little Bear, suspended from the mundane tree (the Druid
oak), is the branch of mistletoe. Hercules, who twice visited
the Hyperborei—the first time in company with Telamon—
undertook the second journey at the time of the institution
of the Olympic games, in order to get the olive-plant for the
ἄλσος, or grove. The olive [2*d*] would not be expected in
these latitudes, and the plant meant is perhaps the mistletoe.

25. Among the religious ideas of the Northern races the
one most deeply implanted was, perhaps, the belief in a
future life, or the immortality of souls. Homer placed Hades,
the abode of departed souls, in the perpetual darkness of
Kimmeria, beyond the ocean [2*a*] ; and Ulysses, having
sacrificed in order that the lifetime memories of the silent
populace might be revived by the blood, conversed there with

the spirits of departed Greeks, including those of his mother
and some distinguished heroes whom he had known at Troy.
But it was a region of cheerlessness and misery. The ghost
of Achilles tells Ulysses he would rather be a poor man's
hireling on earth than a king among the dead ; and Ulysses,
overpowered by the weirdness and dread of the place, withdrew in terror. Hesiod and the Argonauts assign this abode
to the same locality ; the Acheron (a river usually connected
with the lower world) [5], flowing down from the delightful
fields of Ceres, there approached its cities and impenetrable
gates. Claudian places the Homeric Hades at the ocean
beyond the extreme coast of Gaul ; the tearful cries of the
restless shades were heard there, and the natives saw the
pallid and ghostly dead migrating thither :

> Est locus extremum pandit quâ Gallia litus,
> Oceani prætentus aquis, ubi fertur Ulixes
> Sanguine libato populum movisse silentem.
> Hic umbrarum tenui stridore volantum
> Flebilis auditur quæstus. Simulacra coloni
> Pallida defunctasque vident migrare figuras.
>
> *In Ruf.* i.

Procopius (sixth century) definitely places this abode in the
western part of Brittia [14], which was separated from the
eastern or habitable part by a wall. The fishermen on the
opposite mainland were the ferrymen. Aroused in the night
by a shaking of the door and an indistinct voice calling them
to work, they proceeded under an irresistible impulse to the
shore. Vessels not theirs, and seemingly empty, awaited
them, and they embarked ; but, without seeing anything,
they would feel a consciousness that there were passengers
on board, whose weight sometimes sank the boat to within
a finger-breadth of the water. They would reach Brittia in
an hour. Here they heard the names and dignities of their
passengers called over and answered ; the ghosts were landed,
and the ferrymen were wafted back to the habitable world.
Evidence that the doctrine of immortality was held by the
inhabitants of the Britannic group is furnished by the contents of ancient burial mounds. In a tumulus opened at
Gristhorpe, Yorks, in 1834, a skeleton was found in the

hollowed trunk of an oak, along with warlike weapons and
other articles, which were evidently intended for the deceased's use in the future life. Interments with weapons
and domestic utensils are numerous, and show that the
custom was widespread, and probably general. That the
Gauls were equally superstitious is clear from several writers.
Immortality was taught by the Gallic Druids ; and Valerius
Maximus ridicules the Gauls for lending money on the condition that it should be repaid in the next world.

26a. The burial of Elpenor, whose body was burnt upon
the funeral pyre and a lofty mound, surmounted by a
column raised upon the ashes, furnishes a prehistoric instance
of interment in Britain, and it throws so much light upon the
sepulchral burrows and their contents, which still exist
thickly upon our downs, that it must be regarded as the
oldest method of burial in the islands. The importance of
the circumstances connected with the incident is sufficient
apology for giving the whole story.   Ulysses, a sojourner in
Kirke's house, being about to set out for the underworld,
does not lead away his companions unharmed, for Elpenor,
the youngest, not very valorous or intellectual, lay down
heavy with wine, and, being roused by the bustle of his
companions, fell from an upper floor and was killed.   Ulysses,
arriving in the underworld, entreats the nations of the dead
with vows and prayers, and sacrifices a sheep, and the souls
of the dead gather from Erebus.   Then the sheep is skinned
and burnt, and the hero invokes the gods Pluto and Persephone, preventing with his sword the powerless heads of the
dead from approaching until he has inquired of the seer
Tiresias. First the soul of Elpenor comes, for he is not yet
buried, his body being left in Kirke's palace where it fell.
Ulysses, beholding him, weeps, and pityingly addresses him :
" O Elpenor, how came you under the dark west ? You,
being on foot, have come sooner than I with a black ship."
He, groaning, answered : " O Jove-born son of Laertes, re-
sourceful Ulysses, the unlucky decree of the deity and excessive wine hurt me. Lying down in Kirke's palace, I did
not think to descend backwards, having come to the long
ladder, but fell from the roof ; and my neck was broken, and

my soul came down to Hades. Now, I implore you by those who are absent, by your wife and father, who cared for you when little, and Telemachus, whom you have left alone in your palace ; for I know that when you go from Hades you will moor your well-made ship at the island Æaea. There, O King, I entreat you to be mindful of me, that when you go to a distance you do not leave me behind unlamented, unburied, lest I bring to you some wrath of the gods ; but burn me with what arms are mine, and build a monument on the shore of the hoary sea for me, a wretched man, even to be heard of by posterity. Do these things, and fix upon the tomb the oar with which I rowed when alive, being with my companions." Ulysses promises, and continues : " Thus we sat, discoursing with bitter words, I holding my sword over the blood ; but the spectre of my companion on the other side spoke many things. And afterwards the soul of my dead mother came on." Returning to Æaea, Ulysses waited for morning ; " then," he continues, " I sent my companions forward to Kirke's house, to bring the corpse, the dead Elpenor ; and immediately cutting trunks, where the shore projected farthest, we, grieving, and in tears, buried him. But when the corpse was burnt, and the arms of the dead, having raised a tomb and placed a column on it, we fixed the well-formed oar at the top."* (Odyssey x.-xii.).

26b. Various circumstances point to North Scotland as Homer's Hades. Toscaig, above Loch Carron, may not be connected with the dread name ; yet Erbusaig, below the loch, in what was once the kingdom of Moref (magh ereb) and Ross, suggests Erebus (see Ripæus [5]) through which the Shades passed to Hades. In the neighbourhood is Loch Alsh G. "aillse," ghost). Erebus personified was son of Chaos,

---

* Ημος δ' ἠριγένεια φάνη ῥοδοδάκτυλος ἠὼς,

*   *   *   *   *   *

Οἰσέμεναι νεκρὸν Ἐλπήνορα τεθνειῶτα.
Φιτροὺς δ' αἶψα ταμόντες, ὅθ' ἀκροτάτη προεχ' ἀκτὴ,
Θάπτομεν ἀχνύμενοι, θαλερὸν κατὰ δάκρυ χέοντες.
Αὐτὰρ ἐπεὶ νεκρός τ' ἐκάη, καὶ τεύχεα νεκροῦ,
Τυμβον χεύαντες, καὶ ἐπὶ στήλην ἐρύσαντες,
Πήξαμεν ἀκροτάτῳ τυμβῳ εὐῆρες ἐρετμόν.

Odyssey, xii. 8-15.

the latter, perhaps, related to Orcus (*Hades*) : and geographic-
ally the Orcas Promontory here stretched towards the
Insulæ Orcades. The flaming Phlegethon of Homer was in
the neighbourhood of the ἠερα φλέγρη of Orpheus about the
modern district of Applecross. (*Cf.* also Kalypso and the
mountain Calpius [5].) These coincidences may all be accidental ; yet there is sufficient, when compared with the
testimony of later writers, to show that Homer followed the
common view when he made these seas the scene of the dread
home of Pluto and Persephone. The flaming river of these
gods, perhaps, left an echo in the Bealtainn fires which were
lighted in the Highlands on May-day until early in the last
century. The district of Ross points to Tartaros (traith
Ross). The Scythian or Britannic Kimmeria, however, had
an Eastern counterpart, known as Gomorrha, which, with
Sodom, lay in that plain of Jordan (constellationally the
River Eridanos), where wickedness was once supreme, and
where the fire and brimstone reigned down by Yhovah
answered the flaming air of our Erebus. Into this Tartaros,
called the " east country " (Qedem ; *cf.* Gaidel), Abram
(Kronos) sent away his sons—an episode which, with the
Greeks, became the story of Ouranos, who cast his sons into
Tartaros ; and of Kronos, who swallowed his as they were born.

26c. Kimmeria and Sodom had much in common. Lethe,
the personification of oblivion, was a river in Hades, where
the souls drank and forgot the past ; and according to one
fable, Leto (λήθη, *forgetfulness*) gave birth to Apollo (Baal)
among the Hyperboreans. Lot (Heb. לוֹט, *concealed*) lived
at Sodom, and as Abram's brother (Gen. xiv. 16) he represents the Titans, or Ouranids* in Tartaros. The blindness
of the Sodomites is the Kimmerian darkness ; the careless
life of the citizens is the witless condition of the souls in
Hades ; and the apotheosis of Lot's wife into a pillar of
salt is surely the story of the mundane pole so clearly associated with the British basalts. When Abram (who buys
Machpelah) pleads for Sodom (Bera's kingdom), he is Baal

---

* Terah, who migrates to Haran, is Ouranos ; and Lot, called
" son of Haran," but also brother of Abram, and so son of Terah, is
a Haranid (Ouranid).

pleading for his own flock ; and the fire which burns his city
is the fire which on various occasions consumes the priests
of Baal. Thus Pluto's Hades, at first a place of forgetfulness, became the awful place of fire. Lot's unconscious
condition appears in the incestuous crime committed un-
wittingly in a cave, and the cave is but the tomb where the
father and his daughters endure an equal fate. In Albion
this condition is personified as Loda, whose circle and mossy
stone of power are features in Ossian. The poet says : " On
the top [of Uthorno] dwells the misty Loda, the house of the
spirits of men ! In the end of his cloudy hall bends forward
Cruth-loda of swords. His form is dimly seen amid his wavy
mist. His right hand is on his shield. In his left is the half-
viewless shell. The roof of his dreadful hall is marked with
nightly fires ! The race of Cruth-loda advance, a ridge of
formless shades." It is curious that the scene of the event
commemorated in this effusion was in the vicinity of Turthor's
(Tartaros's) stream and plain. In another poem, Loda's
circle is in the Island Inistore, and his spirit, coming on a
blast from the mountain, shakes its dusky spear at the hero
Fingal. The latter, answering defiantly, says : " Fly from
my presence, son of night ! call thy winds and fly." But
Loda threw the command back at Fingal, and boasting that
the blasts are in the hollow of his hands, and that the course
of the storm is his, he adds : " The King of Sora is my son ;
he bends at the stone of my power ; his battle is around
Carric-thura." Then he lifted high his shadowy spear, and
bent forward his dreadful height. Fingal, advancing, drew
his sword, and the gleaming path of the steel winds through
the gloomy ghost. "The form fell shapeless into air, like
a column of smoke, which the staff of the boy disturbs, as
it rises from the half-extinguished furnace. The spirit of
Loda shrieked, as, rolled into himself, he rose on the wind.
Inistore shook at the sound. The waves heard it on the
deep. They stopped in their course with fear." This,
however, is only Loda's aspect to the living. He tells
Fingal that his dwelling is calm above the clouds, and that
the fields of his rest are pleasant. So Lot's chosen plain of
Sodom was " as the garden of the Lord, like the land of Egypt

as you come to Zoar "; and the land of the Hyperborei is called the " ancient garden of Phœbos " (φοίβον παλαιὸς κῆπος, *Strab. è Sophocles*). Phœbos was an epithet of the Hyperborean Apollo, belonging to him as son of Leto, the daughter of Koios and Phœbe.

26*d*. The poems of Ossian [133*c*], emanating from the Highlands, and probably the oldest literary remains of the native Britons, show that the old inhabitants of that region were highly superstitious ; ghosts appear at nearly every step, and with such circumstances as might well suggest the exaggerations of the classic poets. The grave is the narrow-house, the winter-house, or cave ; and the dying heroes impose upon their friends the duty of building it. Oscar says : " Carry me to my hills ! Raise the stone of my renown. Place the horn of a deer, place my sword, by my side." Shilric, about to go to war, says to his love : " If I must fall in the field, raise high my grave, Vinvela. Grey stones and heaped-up earth shall mark me to future times." But false tidings of his death reached the maiden, and when he returned he saw her moving on the plain. " Why on the heath alone ?" he asks. She replies : " Alone I am, O Shilric—alone in the winter-house ! with grief for thee I fell. I am pale in the tomb." Then she flits away as mist before the wind. The fair Lorma awaits at night the return of Aldo, not knowing that he is dead ! she calls upon him to come. " His thin ghost appeared on a rock, like a watery beam of feeble light." Following the empty form over the heath, she found his corpse. In another place " the grey, watery forms of ghosts " are called " the meteors of death." When Colgar, son of Trathal, fell in Erin, and his friends returned to Morven, thrice did the bards at the Cave of Furmono call his soul. " They called him to the hills of his land. He heard them in his mist. Trathal placed his sword in the cave that the spirit of his son might rejoice." The face of Crugal's ghost was like the beam of the setting moon ; his robes were of the clouds of the hills ; his eyes like two decaying flames ; the stars dim-twinkled through his form ; and his voice was like the sound of a distant stream. The ghost of Calmar appears to Cuthullin (Cuchulain) shortly before the latter's death, and seems to invite him to his cave. " Son of the cloudy night," says Cuthullin, " why dost thou bend thy dark eyes on me, ghost of the noble Calmar ? Wouldst thou frighten me from the battles of Cormac ? Thy hand was not feeble in war : neither was thy voice for peace. How art thou changed, chief of Lara, if thou now dost advise to fly ! But, Calmar, I never fled. I never feared the ghosts of night. Small is their knowledge, weak their hands ; their dwelling is in the wind. But my soul grows in danger, and rejoices in the noise of steel. Retire to thy cave. Thou art not Calmar's ghost. He delighted in battle. His arm was like the thunder of heaven." The poet adds : " He retired in his blast with joy, for he had heard the voice of his praise." So the soul of Æacus in Hades " went away, taking mighty steps through the meadow of asphodel, in joyfulness," when he heard from Ulysses of the fame of his son. But Homer and Ossian do not present this mutuality at every step. Nor is Homer always consistent in himself ; for while Æacus was ignorant of his son's renown, Ulysses' mother could tell her son what was happening in Ithaca. Ossian's ghosts sometimes come in crowds, as when " feeble voices are heard on the heath." The soul of one hero " came forth to his fathers to their stormy isle ; there they pursued the boars of mist along the skirts of winds." Again we read : " There silent dwells a feeble race. They mark no years with their deeds as they pass along."

27. The history of the islands down to the end of the Roman period will be found under their respective names, and the plan of this work closes with that period ; but it may not be irrelevant to review some of the interesting notices which have come down to us as to subsequent events in the Farthest North. After the Romans withdrew from Britain, a wave of great religious activity passed over the group, being especially strong in Hibernia and North Britain ; and Christian missionaries and enthusiasts seem to have spread into the remotest inhabitable regions of these seas. According to Adomnan's Life of Columba, some followers of that saint went, about the middle of the sixth century, to seek a wilder-

ness in the ocean, and by the commendation of Brudei, King
of the Picts, were received into the Orcades, where they
possibly became known as the Papæ, who, together with
the Picts, inhabited the same islands in the reign of Harold
Harfager about the year 900 (Ritson's *Annals*, i. 100, 101).
They even appear to have settled in Iceland. Dicuil, an
Irish monk of the ninth century, states that Iceland and the
Faroe Islands were discovered by his countrymen ; and old
Icelandic writings expressly state that Iceland was occupied
by Christians called Papæ previous to its colonization by
the Norwegians. The old Norwegians of that island supposed the Papæ to come from the West, for Irish books and
bells were found, with wooden crosses and other things,
worked after the manner of the Irish and Britons. Such
relics were met with in the Isle of Papey, off the east coast;
and at Papilio in the interior. According to the Icelandic
writings, the Christians left Iceland when the Norwegians
colonized it, but their end was probably like that of the
Picts and Papæ of the Orcades, who were totally extirpated
by the Norwegians. The Papæ were, perhaps, the worshippers of Phœbos Apollo, but the name points to G.
" uamha," *cave.*

28. The destruction of the Papæ of Iceland probably
occurred before A.D. 860. In that year, according to Icelandic
history, the island was discovered by a Norwegian navigator
who landed on the coast, and viewed the surrounding region
from a high hill, without seeing any signs of habitation.
Other navigators quickly followed, and a Norwegian colony
settled in it in 874. Greenland was colonized by the same
people in 986, and by the end of the same century these
adventurers were aware of the existence of extensive lands
to the S.W., forming part of what is now America and
its islands. Leif, sailing from Greenland in that direction,
about 1000, for the purpose of examining the new lands more
accurately, gave the names of Helluland, Markland, and
Vinland, to the successive coasts which he touched ; and
Thorfinn visited the same coasts in 1007, remaining upon
them for four years. An old Icelandic geography contains
the following passage : ' To the south of inhabited Green-

land are wild and desert tracts of ice-covered mountains;
then comes the land of the Skrællings; beyond this Markland, and then Vinland the Good. Next to this, and somewhat behind it, lies Albania—*i.e.*, Hvitramannaland—whither
vessels formerly sailed from Ireland. It was there that
several Irishmen and Icelanders recognized Ari, the son of
Mar, and Katla of Reykjanes, whom there had been no
tidings of for a long time, and whom the natives of the country
had made their chief." The Landnámabók states that this
Ari (Ari Marsson) was driven by a tempest to Hvitramannaland, and detained and baptized there. Icelandic writings
also show that in 1121 Bishop Eirek sailed from Greenland
to search for Vinland, and that in 1347 some sailors arrived
in Iceland from a voyage to Markland.

29. In old Icelandic treatises Newfoundland is called
Litla (*Little*) Helluland, and the name Helluland hit Mikla
(*the Great*) is given to Labrador and the whole coast W. of
Baffin's Bay. Helluland hit Mikla was also called Irland it
Mikla (*Great Ireland*), from Limerick traders, who, it seems,
visited it before it was known to the Northmen, and from
this circumstance possibly arose the Norwegian name
Hvitramannaland (*White Man's Land*). That Irish merchants
were acquainted with these coasts appears from the story
of Ari Marsson, since Irishmen were amongst the men who
recognized him; and the further circumstance that he was
baptized there may be taken to indicate that there was a
Christian community in the country, but whether as the
result of missionary enthusiasm of Irish priests it is impossible to say, though such a result was not improbable.
Some of Thorfinn's followers (1007-1011), being driven from
the coast of Vinland by a westerly wind, were thrown upon
the coast of Ireland, where, according to traders, they were
made slaves; while another party of his followers, having
the misfortune to lose their vessel, escaped to Dublin in a
boat; and it is obvious that Irish and other vessels must
occasionally have found their way to the American coasts by
similar means. The position of Hvitramannaland, somewhat
behind Vinland, points to the neighbourhood of the St. Lawrence as the land of the white men; and Irland it Mikla lay

in the direct course which would be taken by vessels plying between Hibernia and that river.

30a. The names Helluland, Markland, Vinland, are stated to have been bestowed by Leif, A.D. 1000, the first (said to signify "Shistland") from the large flat stones which abounded on the coasts of Newfoundland and Labrador ; the second (from "mörk," *a wood*) signifying Woodland, usually identified with Nova Scotia ; the third implying "land of grapes," that fruit growing wild and abundantly about Massachusetts. But the saga of Eirik the Red which gives the story was, apparently, written in the twelfth century, nearly a hundred years after the voyage, and it may be doubted whether Leif conferred the names at all. Markland (*America-land*) is quite as likely an echo of the dark Kimmerian underworld [200*e*], answering in one aspect to the Euphratæan woman Omoroca, "which in the Chaldæan language is Thalatth, in Greek Thalassa, the sea" (*Polyhist. Alex. è Berossus*), vestiges of this myth being still traceable in the names Morocco and Atlantic. Helluland (*Labrador*) seems to have survived to the time of Cartier (1534), when the natives called the St. Lawrence the Great River of Hochelaga. Vinland seems to be from Albania, which lay behind it inland, and is, perhaps, connected with the Algonquin and Alleghan Indians.

30b. The certainty that America was known to the Northmen is not a circumstance to be wondered at ; indeed, the Western Continent could hardly pass unperceived through the still remoter age when Pytheas of Marseilles and others ploughed the exterior sea. Earlier still, Hanno's voyage from Cerne to the River Chretes must have touched the coast of South America somewhere in the neighbourhood of Brazil. The desecrated pyramids of Mexico irresistibly direct the mind to the prouder but kindred structures of Egyptian Memphis. Yet the remains of classical geography afford no definite knowledge of the distant West ; their earth is but the insular expanse which we divide into the three Continents of Europe, Africa, and Asia, the circumfluent ocean being the Atlantic and Pacific, which meet at the poles. It is obvious such a system must be subsequent to definite know-

ledge that this expanse of continent was circumnavigable ;
and the knowledge must have embraced incidentally that
spur of America which approaches Asia at Bering's Strait.
The truth probably is that America was known in some
commercial circles very early, but the traders in this, as in
other cases, concealed, through jealous motives, the sources
of their merchandise, so that the vague information which
gradually leaked out as to the Western continent never
became matter for strict geography, but, taking the shape
of legend and romance, was moulded by the poets into the
story of the prodigious sea-swallowed island of Atlantis,
with its attendant group of seven islands sacred to Persephone.

30c. The Egyptians, about 600 B.C., confirmed by actual
voyage the fact, already credited, that the ocean flowed all
round Libya except at the Suez Isthmus. Geographers,
however, did not notice all the voyages and settlements
which took place in the eventful period of Phœnician and
Hellenic maritime expansion, and it is not from a classic pen,
but from one of the seventeenth century A.D., that we hear
of the African city of Momotopata, whose supposed site in
the Transvaal has furnished many admittedly Greek archi-
tectural remains. Colonists who were bold enough to venture
thus far would not be daunted by a voyage to America.

II

BRITANNIA, FORMERLY ALBION

English Miles

II

BRITANNIA, FORMERLY ALBION
[10]

31a. The name Albion, usually given by the early Greeks to the island Britain, was a native appellation ; it first occurs *circa* 322 B.C. [9], but was apparently known to Himilco two centuries earlier [6]. It was the old name (Albion ipsi nomen fuit ; *Plin.*, *N.H.*, iv. 30) ; but not, it seems, the oldest, the last honour belonging to Kimmeria. Albion occurs again in Ptolemy's *Geographica*, and was copied from that work by Agathemer in the first half of the third century. The Roman historians never adopted it, but it survived the Roman period as a territorial name among the Northern Britons. It is probably personified in Elpenor, who found a pyre and tomb in the land, and who is celestially connected with the Little Bear.

31b. Britannia (*pl.* Britanniæ) first occurs adjectivally (" Britannicæ ") as a collective name for the British Isles. It underwent slight changes, as might be expected, from its initial, which mutated in Greek with π and μ, and became in Gaelic " mh " (pronounced *v*), the latter corresponding to the Cymric mutation *f*. Thus, it occurs in native records as Clas Merddyn (*Triads*) and Ynys Prydyn (*Brut y Tywysogion*) ; and two Greek writers have Πρεττανικαί [13].

31c. Julius Cæsar describes the island as triangular (*insula natura triquetra*). One side lay towards Gaul, and contained about 500 miles, the angle about Cantium [168] pointing E., the other angle pointing S. Another side inclined towards Hispania and the W., and was 700 miles long, having Hibernia opposite, with Mona in the intervening space ; and many smaller islands were supposed to lie off the same coast. The

53

third side **was** towards the N., in length about 800 miles, no land lying opposite to it, but its angle pointing chiefly towards Germania. Thus, the whole circumference was 2,000 miles (*B.G.*, v. 13).

32. According to Diodorus Siculus, Britain was triangular, resembling Sicily ; but the sides were unequal. One angle was at the mouth of the sea—*i.e.*, the German Ocean—at the province Cantium [168], distant about 100 stadia from the Continent ; another, the Promontory Belerium [135*l*], was four days' sail from the continent* ; the third, called Horcæ [134*l*], stretched out into the ocean. The shortest side lay opposite Europe, and contained 7,500 stadia. The side stretching from the strait (*Cantium*) to the extremity (*Horcæ*) contained 15,000 stadia, and the remaining side 20,000 ; thus the whole circumference was 42,000 stadia (*v.* 21).

33. According to Strabo, Britain was triangular. Its longest side lay parallel to, and of equal length with, Gaul (κελτική), each being 4,300 or 4,400 stadia. The side of Gaul extended from the mouths of the Rhine to the N. spurs of the Pyrenees towards Aquitaine ; that of Britain commencing at Kent, its most eastern part, opposite the Rhine, extended to the W. extremity of the island, opposite Aquitaine and the Pyrenees (IV., v. 1, 4). Towards the E. the two coasts lay within sight of each other, about Kent and at the mouths of the Rhine (I., iv. 3) ; and the distance from Caleti to Britain was under a day's passage (IV., i. 14). But Strabo relates that Pytheas stated the length of Britain to be more than 20,000 stadia, and the circumference above 40,000, and Kent to be some days' sail from Gaul (I., iv. 3 ; II., iv. 1). There were some small islands about Britain (IV., v. 4).

34. Mela, about A.D. 50, placed Britannia between the

* This voyage and the one to Cantium were apparently reckoned from the same port. The average day's sail in the open sea seems to have been about eighty miles. Compare Himilco's five-days' sail between Promontory Veneris and the Pillars of Hercules [7] and the usual six-days' voyage from Britain to Thule [344]. Under peculiar circumstances the distance traversed in a day might be much greater ; Ulysses, driven by a terrific storm, passed from the Pillars to Ogygia in ten days [3*a*], and the Argonauts from N.E. Ierne to Ceres' Isle in twelve days [5].

N. and W., having a great angle stretching towards the
mouths of the Rhenus (*Rhine*). From this angle the coasts
receded obliquely from the continent, one side lying opposite
Gaul, the other opposite Germany, and terminating backwards in other angles, formed a third side ; thus the island
was triangular, greatly resembling Sicily (III., vi.). Pliny,
some years later, placed the island opposite the Batavorum
Insula and the mouth of the Rhenus, and between the N.
and W., in an immense space opposite to Germania, Gallia,
and Hispania, being distant about 50 m.p. from the coast
of Gessoriacum Morinorum (Nieuport, Belgium). The circuit, according to Pytheas and Isidore, was 3,825 m.p. ;
according to Agrippa, the length 800 m.p., the breadth
300 m.p. (*N. H.*, iv. 30).

35. Tacitus says Britannia trended E. towards Germania, and W. towards Hibernia, looking S. towards Gallia,
and N. over a vast, open sea. He relates that Livy and
Fabius Rusticus resembled it to an oblong scutula—*i.e.*,
lozenge-shaped—or a double-edged battle-axe. It had that
appearance S. of Caledonia, and by reputation the similitude
became applied to the whole island ; but an immense extent
of land spread out from the point of this axe (the Clota
Isthmus), into which it narrowed like a wedge. Thule lay
still farther N., cut off by a wintry and inhospitable sea.
He calls Britain the largest island known to the Romans—
" Britannia insularum, quas Romana notitia complectitur,
maxima " (*Agr.*, x.). Solinus states its greatest length to
be upwards of 800 m.p., measuring to the Caledonian angle,
and its circumference 3,600 m.p. According to Orosius,
Britannia, " an island of the ocean," stretched a long distance
into the N., having Gaul towards the S. Persons sailing
from the nearest coast of Gaul arrived at Rhutubi Portus
[168*d*], which looked S. towards the Menapii and Batavi.
The island was 800 miles long and 200 broad, and beyond
it lay the northern ocean ; it had the islands called Orchades
(*Orosius*). According to Marcian, Albion was situated in
the region of Celtogalatia, stretching opposite Gallia Lugdunensis and Belgica as far as Germania Magna. It was not
spherical, like Hibernia, but appeared as if disjointed and

scattered about, having two especially long isthmuses, somewhat resembling feet, extending through a great part of the
northern ocean. The greater of these stretched towards
the N. (?), the lesser towards Aquitania. The island was
bounded N. by the Oceanus Duecaledonius, E. by the Oceanus
Germanicus, W. by the Oceanus Hibernicus (in which direction lay the Insula Hibernia), and partly by the Oceanus Vergivius, and S. by the Oceanus Britannicus and the regions and
provinces of Gaul. Its greatest length from the W. horizon
near the Damnonium Promontory to the Tarvedunum Promontory was 5,225 (?) stadia ; and the greatest breadth from
near the Damnonium Promontory to the Neovantum Peninsula, 3,083 (?) stadia ; its greatest circumference, 28,604 stadia,
its least 20,526.   It contained—

Tribes	..	..	..	..	..	33
Noted towns	..	..	..	..	59
,,	rivers	..	..	..	..	40
,,	promontories	..	..	..	14
,,	peninsulas	..	..	..	1
,,	bays	..	..	..	..	5
,,	ports	..	..	..	..	3

—*Periplus Marciani*, ii.*

Xiphiline gives its length as 7,132 furlongs, its greatest
breadth about 2,310, and its least about 300.

36. The climate, according to Cæsar, was more temperate
than in Gaul, the cold being less intense ; and the same kinds
of trees were found here as there, except the beech and fir
(*B.G.*, v. 12). According to Strabo, the greatest part of
the island was level and woody, although many parts were
hilly.   The atmosphere was more subject to rain than snow ;
and even on clear days the mists continued for a considerable time, insomuch that the sun was only visible for three
or four hours (IV., v. 2). At the distance of not more than
4,000 stadia from the centre of Britain the temperature was
such that it was scarcely possible to exist in it (I., iv. 4).
Diodorus remarks that it was very cold, as might be expected from its situation towards the constellation of the
Bear (*Ursa*) (v. 21). According to Tacitus, the island was

* Marcian generally followed Ptolemy (*cf.* [134-137]).

subject to rains and fogs, but free from excessive cold. The days were longer than in Italy ; the nights were clear, and in the extreme parts of Britain short ; it was said that the sun did not rise or set, but its brightness could be seen by night, if clouds did not interpose (*Quod si nubes non obficiant, adspici per noctem solis fulgorem, nec occidere et exsurgere, sed transire adfirmant*) ; the soil was fertile, and yielded abundant fruits, except olives, grapes, and fruits requiring a warmer climate (*Agr.*, 12). The island was fertile, especially in those things which were useful for the food of cattle and men ; it had forests, lakes, and very great rivers, which were tidal, flowing, now into the ocean, now from it (*Mela*, iii.). Soline also mentions its many large rivers, and adds that there were warm springs, which were fitted at great cost for the use of man.

37. Cæsar relates that the interior of Britain was inhabited by people who had a tradition amongst themselves that they were aboriginals. The maritime parts were occupied by tribes who, for the sake of plunder and conquest, had passed over from Belgium (*ex Belgis*), and, carrying war into the island, began to settle in it. Nearly all these incomers were called by the names of the states from which they came (*omnes fere iis nominibus civitatum appellantur, quibus orti ex civitatibus eo pervenerunt*) (*B.G.*, v. 12). Diodorus Siculus, however, relates that the island had formerly been free from foreign aggression, and, as far as the Romans were aware, neither Bacchus nor Hercules, nor any other hero or king, had afflicted it with war. The inhabitants were said to be aboriginal, and to still preserve their primitive manners (v. 21). Tacitus says that, as was usual with barbarians, it was not clearly ascertained whether the Britons were indigenous or of foreign origin ; their physical characteristics and their customs favoured the latter opinion. The red hair and great limbs of the inhabitants of Caledonia suggested a German descent. The Silures, from their coloured faces and plaited hair, and their position opposite Hispania, were, with some reason, supposed to have sprung from a colony of the ancient Iberii. The people nearest to the Gauls resembled the latter, either by force of origin, which was the

received opinion, or from their enjoying practically the
same climate. They also shared the same superstitions in
religious matters ; spoke nearly the same language ; and
showed the same boldness in courting perils and timidity in
encountering them (*Agr.*, 11). He omits to compare these
characteristics with those of the Northern Britons, but he
states in the *Germania* that the language of the Æstyi, a
German tribe on the Baltic, came nearest to the British speech,
referring clearly in this place to the Caledonian Britons, whom,
as already noticed, he suspected to be of German descent :

> Jam dextro Suevici maris littore Æstyorum
> gentes adluuntur, quibus ritus habitusque Suevorum ;
> lingua Britannicæ propior (*Germ.*, 45).

This observation of Tacitus is supported by many points of
resemblance between the Gaidelic languages of the British
Isles and the languages now spoken by the Baltic peoples.
The common notion of an all-absorbing Celtic immigration is
mistaken.* The only instance of Gaulic or Belgic immigration
recorded in the classics is the expedition of Divitiacus [50],
but this does not prove a Belgic settlement any more than
our early continental conquests prove the establishment of
an English race in France. The expedition of Divitiacus
could scarcely have been earlier than 100 B.C. According
to the Saxon Chronicle the first inhabitants of S. Britain were
the Bryttas, from Armenia (*Armorica*).

---

* Richard's fables as to Gallic or Celtic immigrations may be sum-
marized as follows : (1) All the tract south of the Thames was anciently
occupied by the Sennones. (2) These A.M. 3600 (400 B.C.) passing into
Gaul under their King Brennus, with the design of attacking Rome,
left their land uninhabited and full of spoils. (3) The Belgæ having
crossed the Rhine and settled there in right of conquest, sent out
colonies, " of which Cæsar has spoken more at large," *and occupied
the land of the Sennones ;* arriving about A.M. 3650 (350 B.C.), they
expelled some of the Britons, who passed into Ireland and became the
Scoti. (4) At the last-mentioned period (not many ages before Cæsar's
time) the Celtæ, quitting Gaul, passed over to Britain *and occupied
the region deserted by the Sennones.* (5) Soon after the last immigration
Divitiacus, King of the Ædui, passed over and subdued a great part
of the kingdom (I., i. 12-14 ; II., i. 8, 9). It is to be remarked that the
statements italicized are mutually inconsistent ; and Divitiacus was
not King of the Ædui, nor was his age so early as Richard asserts.

38a. The Æstyan theory is supported by the belief of some of the mediæval Northern Britons, who claimed descent from the Scitiæ (*cf.* Æstyi), and identified them with the Albani. The *Chronica de Origine Antiquorum Pictorum et Scottorum* (*circa* 994) states that the tribes of the Scitiæ were born with white hair, owing to the continual snows, and that this colour gave the race the name of Albani, from whom were descended the Scots and Picts :

> Gentes Scitiæ albo crine nascuntur ab assiduis
> nivibus ; et cujus capilli color genti nomen dedit, et
> inde dicuntur Albani : de quibus originem duxerunt
> Scotti et Picti . . . (*Rit. Ann.*, i. 117).

The Gentes Scitiæ are identical with the Gaidhel. See Picti [199*d*], Scotti [200*a*, 200*d*].

38b. The Welsh had their own traditions. According to the triads, all the primitive inhabitants except two persons were drowned by a flood. After this, Hu Gadarn came with the Kymry from Haf, or Defrobani ; and these and other kindred new-comers, who shared with them the same name and speech, formed three separate tribes—the Kymry, Loegrwys, and Brython. Then three fugitive tribes—the Celyddon, Gwyddel, and Galedin—were allowed to settle among them, the Galedin occupying the Isle of Wight ; and the island also received three hostile tribes, the Coraniaid, Irish Fichti, and Saxons, the latter finally obtaining supremacy over all except the Kymry of Cornwall and Carnoban (see [370]). The hostility of the Fichti (*Picts*) towards the Kymry, appearing from these details, seems to confirm Tacitus' observation that the Northern Britons differed from the Southerners. On the other hand, too great reliance must not be placed upon the triads, which were probably not reduced to writing in their present form before the sixth century A.D., though undoubtedly many emanated as oral traditions from a much earlier age.

38c. Interesting deductions result from the Kymric emigration triad. The land of Haf, called Defrobani, is the territory of the Aii in S. India opposite Taprobane (*Ceylon*), the Môr Tawch being the Indian Ocean, and apparently so named from the neighbouring district of Deccan ;

and the name Kymry still lingers there in that of Cape Comorin, the Comaria Extrema of Ptolemy. Inferentially, " Kymry," either originally or by poetic perversion, had reference to the curious submarine bank, called Adam's Bridge, which runs across Palk Strait from Ceylon to the mainland, and which, leading to the Aii, must have shared with Albionic Æaea the reputation of being in the path to Hades. Clearly the ancients did not err when they wrote of an eastern Æaea as well as a western one, though they sometimes located the former too far away in the direction of the Pacific. Hu, the leader of the Indian Kymry, is a flood-hero, answering generally to Hea [2d]. His relation to Ulysses through the sign Toxetes (*Hindu* Taukshika), may be assumed from the Môr Tawch about the parts of Deccan ; and the flood-hero Ogyges creeps in through the sojourn of Ulysses in Ogygia.

38d. An ancient MS. mentions seven tribes which colonized Britain : the Coraniaid, Draig Prydain, Draig Estrawn (Wel. " estron," *stranger*), Gwyr Lledrithiawg (Wel. " lledrith," *a phantom*), Gwyddyl Ffichti, Cesariaid, Sæson. (Pughe's *Welsh Dictionary*.) The Coraniaid came from Pwyl, usually identified with Poland. It is not impossible, however, to regard them as a branch of the Indian Kymry, and to refer their name to κρεῖον, G. " coire," *a caldron*, whence " coradhan " (*coral*), and so to associate them with the circular atolls (G. " toll," *a pit*), or coral islands, which abound in the ocean contiguous to the promontory of S. India. The atolls may have furnished the bardic story of the Lake of Floods, and it may be that they were once regarded as symbols of the world. Ptolemy groups these curious islands with the neighbouring island of Taprobane, which was probably also associated with the island in the wondrous narratives of early navigators. Moreover, the island was opposite the Cory Promontory, on that part of the mainland still called the Coromandel Coast (*cf.* Symondi, the oldest name of Ceylon). The ancient use of the caldron as a symbol may be inferred from Herodotus, who mentions two—one at Exampæus (Gr. Ἱραὶ ὁδοί, *sacred ways*), in Scythia, the other at the mouth of the Pontus (iv. 52, 81).

39. The population was countless (*infinita*). Their habitations were clustered together, and almost similar to those of the Gauls. They possessed a great number of cattle. Hares, hens, and geese, were kept for fancy and pleasure, but it was considered unlawful to eat them (*gustare fas non putant*) (*B.G.*, v. 12). The most civilized of the inhabitants by far were those in Cantium, who differed little in customs from the Gauls. The people in the interior, for the most part, did not sow corn, but lived on milk and flesh, and were clothed with skins. All the Britons stained themselves with woad (*vitrum*), which imparted a blue colour, and gave them a more terrible appearance in battle. They had long hair, but shaved every part of their body except the head and upper lip. Ten or twelve men had wives between them in common. Brothers especially joined together, as did parents and their children, for this purpose ; but the children of the wife were reckoned to the husband who first married her (*ibid.*, 14). According to Strabo, the men were taller than the Gauls, with hair less yellow, and were slighter in person. He himself saw at Rome some British youths who were taller than any there by as much as half a foot ; but their legs were bowed, and in other respects they were not symmetrical. Their manners were in part like those of the Gauls, though in part more simple and barbarous. Some of them, though having plenty of milk, had not skill enough to make cheese, and were totally unacquainted with horticulture and other matters of husbandry (IV., v. 2). According to Diodorus, they lived in mean cottages, roofed generally with thatch or boughs. In harvesting they cut the ears of corn from the straw, and stored them in roofed barns. They fetched out daily as much of the oldest corn as would suffice for the day, and prepared it into food. Their manners were simple, and far removed from the cunning and depravity of the Romans of that period. They were content with plain living, and were not addicted to the pleasures which attended riches. The island abounded with inhabitants (v. 21). Those dwelling about the Promontory Belerium [135*t*] were especially hospitable, and, owing to their intercourse with merchants, who came for tin, were more civilized than the rest (v. 22). Mela relates that the people of Britain were uncivilized, and the farther they lived from the continent, the more were they indolent. They were merely rich in cattle and territory.

40. Several writers besides Cæsar mention the native custom of staining the body. Mela remarks that it was done with woad for the sake of ornament ; Solinus speaks of it as practised by the barbarians who occupied part of Britain (indicating, probably, the people outside the Roman province). These were accustomed from boyhood to puncture upon their flesh the figures of animals, and to make the marks conspicuous by staining them ; and nothing showed the endurance of the people more than this saturating of fresh wounds with paint. The custom is frequently noticed in the classics—*e.g.* :

> . . . Infectos demens imitare Britannos
> Ludis et externo tincta nitore caput.
> —*Prop.*, III., ix. 23.
> [Foolish to imitate the dyed Britons
> And sport the head with an artificial brightness].

> Non ego Pælignos videor celebrare salubres . . .
> Sed Scythicam, Cilicasque feros viridesque Britannos.
> OVID, *Am.* ii.
> [I seem not to frequent the healthy Pælignian lands,
> But the Scythian land, and fierce Cicilians and green-
>   coloured Britons.]

41. The methods of navigation amongst the Britons were very simple. They used little boats formed of silver willow withes, moistened and covered with bullocks' hide ; and in these they ventured upon the ocean :

> Primum cana salix madefacto vimine parvam
> Texitur in puppim, cæsoque inducta juvenco,
> Vectoris patiens tumidum supernatat amnem.
> Sic . . fuso . . . Britannus
> Navigat oceano.
> LUCAN, *Phars.*, iv. 131.

See also Avienus [7 (104-108)] ; Solinus [12], Pliny [325]. Trunks of oak-trees also appear to have been hollowed out for use as boats. A specimen of this class, nearly 50 feet long by 5 feet wide, is preserved at Brigg, Lincs, where it was found in swampy ground.

42. In battle the natives used chariots called " essedi."

These they drove hither and thither, meanwhile hurling their spears. By the plunging of the horses and the noise of the wheels they generally threw the enemy's infantry into disorder ; and when they succeeded in forcing their way into the squadrons of cavalry, they leapt from the essedi and fought on foot. The charioteers upon this withdrew the essedi gradually from the conflict, and so stationed them as to insure to the warriors a ready retreat to their friends if hard pressed. Thus, this class of warriors exhibited in battle the mobility of horse and the stability of infantry. They became so skilful by daily practice that they were able to rein in their horses on precipitous ground, and to manage and turn them in the shortest space. They were also accustomed to run along the pole, stand upon its extremity, and leap back again into the chariot with exceeding swiftness (*B.G.*, iv. 33). Strabo relates that the Britons used chariots for the most part in war, as did some of the Gauls (IV., v. 2) ; and, according to Diodorus, the Britons affirmed that they used them in the same manner as the Greeks did theirs in the Trojan war (vi. 21). According to Mela, the warriors fought not only on horseback and on foot, but especially in chariots drawn by single horses or pairs (*bigis et curribus*), armed in the Gallic manner. Some chariots had scythed axles, and were called " covinni." Scythed chariots seem to have been at one time well known, since Silius Italicus mentions such vehicles in Thule (*Punic.*, 17, 416). According to Tacitus, however, the foot-soldiers were the chief strength of the army. Some nations (*quædam nationes*) also fought in chariots, and with such as did, the charioteers were most distinguished, their retainers fighting in front (*Agr.*, xii.). The chariot of the Caledonii (A.D. 84) was called " covinus," and the charioteers " covinarii " (*ibid.*, xxxv., xxxvi.).

43. Diodorus states that many kings and princes ruled in Britain, and kept peace between themselves as much as possible (v. 21). Tacitus says the Britons were divided into numerous tribes, which were subject to kings. They were weakened, however, by quarrels with one another, and this and their slowness to unite for the common cause contributed more than anything else to the success of the Romans. It was rare for two or three tribes to act in concert, and fighting singly, all were conquered (*Agric.*, xii.). Mela also states that Britain was inhabited by communities (*populi*) governed by kings, and that there were frequent wars, due chiefly to ambition for power and territorial expansion. They appear to have had fixed camps, which Cæsar calls "oppida." Their oppidum, according to this writer, was a place fortified with a rampart and ditch, situated in the woods, with obstructed approaches, and formed as a common retreat in case of invasion (*B. G.*, v. 21). The native name for such a town is not known, but it is possible we have it in the obsolete Gaelic *poit* (*cf. oppidum*, στρατόπεδον). Strabo says that forests were their cities. Enclosing an ample space with felled trees, they made themselves huts in them, and lodged their cattle, but not for long together (IV., v. 2).

44. The most considerable of the Northern Britons, the Caledonii and Mæatæ, lived, at the end of the second century, in still greater barbarism. They inhabited mountains, very rugged and wanting water, or in desert tracts full of marshes, possessing neither castles nor cities. They lived on milk and the fruits of trees, and by hunting, but never tasted fish, although it was exceedingly plentiful. Those dwelling in woods ate the bark and roots of trees. They prepared for all occasions a certain kind of food, of which as much as the size of a single bean* sufficed to stay hunger or thirst for long together. They were able to bear hunger, cold, and all afflictions, and were even wont to immerse themselves in marshes, and remain there many days, with only their heads above water. They dwelt naked in tents, and without shoes, and had wives in common, bringing up whatever was born to them. The mixed intercourse in the married state was the subject of a taunt addressed by the Empress Julia Augusta (wife of Severus) to the wife of Argentocoxus, a Caledonian ; but the latter lady retorted that, while in Britain they had openly intercourse with the best men, the Romanæ had secretly adultery with the worst men. They were governed, for the most part, in the popular state, were

---

* Compare the Scythian food ἄσχυ, and the lozenges made from it mentioned by Herod. iv. 23.

addicted to rob on the highways, and fought in chariots, their horses being small and fleet. Their infantry was most swift in running and brave in battle. Their arms were a shield and short spear, in the upper part of which was an apple of brass, so that, when shaken, the sound might terrify the enemy. They also used daggers (*Dio.*, L., lxxvi. 12). Another historian, writing of the same period, gives an almost similar account of the Northern Britons. They were accustomed to swim in the marshes and traverse them, immersed as high as their waists ; for, going practically naked, they contemned the mud. They encircled their loins and necks with iron, deeming this an ornament and mark of opulence, in like manner as other savages valued gold. Besides, they punctured their bodies with forms of animals, and on this account wore no clothing, lest they should hide the figures. They were most warlike and sanguinary, carrying only a small shield and spear, and a sword girded to their naked bodies. Breastplates and helmets, as impediments to their progress through the marshes, were not in use. From the vapours and exhalations of the marshes the atmosphere of the region always appeared dense (*Herodian*).

45. The mineral resources of the island seem to have been always considered important. In its prehistoric period its valuable metals were undoubtedly known to foreign merchants, the chief commodity being tin. Cæsar (55 B.C.) mentions both tin (*plumbum album*) and iron, which, he says, were scanty ; but he appears mistaken as to their localities, stating that tin was found in the midlands, and iron about the coasts.* Copper was then used, but was imported (*B. G.*, v. 12). A comment of Cicero upon Cæsar's expedition suggests that the existence of silver here was not then known

---

* Cæsar, perhaps, confused his materials ; but the terms *midland* and *maritime* are more or less vague. The iron district of the Forest of Dean may be designated by both. Favoured by the bold estuary of the Severn, it was almost as accessible to mariners as the tin district of Damnonia. Lead and tin are called " plumbum " in Latin, the former taking the distinguishing suffix " nigrum," *black.* This sameness of name makes it not improbable that " album " may have been substituted for " nigrum " in Cæsar's text ; but the point is unimportant, since the seats of the two industries are scarcely in doubt.

(Illud cognitum est neque argenti scripulum esse ullum in illa insula ; *Ad Att.*, iv. 16). Strabo (A.D. 1-24) states that the island produced gold, silver, and iron, which were exported (IV., v. 2). Diodorus relates that tin was dug up in Britain, being worked by the inhabitants of the Promontory Belerium [135*t*], who obtained it from the ground with great labour. In stony ground it was discovered in veins, whence it was taken, melted, purified, and formed into tales, or blocks. In this form it was carried in large quantities to Ictis [336], an island adjacent to Britain, where, at the time of ebb, a place in the intervening channel was left dry. The islands lying in these parts between Europe and Britain were, in fact, only islands during the tide ; at the ebb, the water, receding from the wide channel, gave them the appearance of peninsulas. The lead being sold by the inhabitants to merchants, was conveyed from Ictis to Gaul, across which it was carried on pack-horses to the mouth of the Rhone, the journey across that country occupying thirty days (v. 22). Mela says the island produced gems and pearls. According to Tacitus, it contained gold, silver, and other metals, which were rendered as tribute (*pretium victoriæ*) ; and the ocean yielded pearls (*margaritæ*), though these were not very clear or numerous. Some considered that the art of collecting pearls was wanting, since in the Red Sea they were torn alive from the rocks, and in Britain were gathered already separated ; but Tacitus believed that the quality was inferior, than that the Romans lacked zeal (*Agric.* xii. ; *Plin., N.H.*, ix. 35). Solinus mentions the lucrative veins which everywhere existed in the island, and furnished metals in great abundance and variety. The stone gagates was most plentiful and best here. It was in appearance a brilliant black, having the property of glittering in water, but losing its brightness in oil ; and, made warm by rubbing, it became adhesive. Amber was also found (*Solinus*). Abundant proofs of extensive Roman industries have been discovered : iron-smelting in the Forests of Dean and Anderida, etc. ; lead-mines in Derbyshire, Cumberland, etc. ; stannaries in Cornwall and Devon ; and potteries in numerous places. Pigs of lead of the time of Claudius and Hadrian have been found in

Derbyshire [283*x*], of Domitian in N. Wales [186*a*], and of
Marcus Aurelius and Verus in Somerset [109]. Quartz ore
appears to have been crushed for gold at Lampeter, Wales;
and this, coupled with the discovery of a square ingot of
silver inscribed in Latin, confirms Tacitus as to the working
of the precious metals. The mines were, perhaps, in general
controlled by the Romans, and worked by forced labour.
Galgacus (A.D. 84), in the speech attributed to him at Mons
Grampius, tells his followers that no mines (*metalla*) are
left to them for their support, and he includes mines among
the pains of slavery involved in submission [99, 100].
For money the Britons in 55 B.C. used copper or bars of
iron (*taleis ferreis*) of fixed weight (*B. G.*, v. 12). Various
coins bearing the names of native princes have been
found; pieces of Tasciovanus bear the words " SEGO,"
" VER " (? Verulamium), and " CYNOBELIN "; and pieces of
Cynobelin are found with " CAMUL " (? Camulodunum),
Verulumum, etc.

46. Among the exports Strabo mentions corn and cattle,
skins, slaves, and dogs sagacious in hunting. The Celts used
the latter as well as their native dogs for the purposes of war
(IV., v. 2). Nemesian mentions dogs from Britain which
were swift and suitable for Roman hunting (Divisa Britannia
mittit veloces, nostrique orbis venatibus aptos; *Cynegeticon*,
124); and Claudian speaks of them as very powerful (mag-
naque taurorum fracturæ colla Britannæ [canes] ; *De Laud.
Stil.*, iii. 301).

Oysters are occasionally mentioned among the delicacies
of Britain [168*d*, Juvenal] :

> Santonico quæ tecta salo ; quæ nota Genonis ; [281*a*]
> Aut Eborum [137*s*] mixtus pelago quæ protegit amnis.
>
>   *   *   *   *   *   *   *
>
> Sunt et Aremorici qui laudent ostrea ponti ;
> Et quæ Pictonici legit accola litoris, et quæ
> Mira Caledonius nonnunquam detegit æstus.
>   —*Ausonii Carm. de Ostreis*, 30-37.

From an altar found at Domburg in Walcheran Island,
and dedicated to the DEÆ NEHALENNIÆ by SILVANUS NEGOT-
TOR CRETARIUS BRITANNICIANUS, it would appear that lime
(*creta*) was a British export (*T. Gale*, 43, *è Reinesius*).

The musical instrument called " crotta " is referred to by
a writer of the sixth century :

> Romanusque lyra plaudat tibi, Barbarus harpa,
> Græcus Achilliaca, Crotta Britannia cantet.
> —*Venantius Fortunatus*, vii. 8.

47. The religion of the Albionic Britons, as already noticed,
was Druidism [19-24]. This was thought to have been
invented in the island, and thence carried into Gaul, and
those Gauls who desired to excel in it resorted to Britain to
be taught (*B.G.*, vi. 13). Tacitus relates that the Britons
and the Gauls had the same superstitions (*Agr.*, 11). The
Druids took part in opposing Suetonius's attack on Mona
[80]. The groves there were consecrated to cruel rites. It
was customary to sacrifice captives at the altars (cruore
captivo adolere aras), and to divine the will of the gods from
the entrails of men (*Tac. Ann.*, xiv. 30). These rites were,
in general, common to the Gallic Druids and to the Germans
[354, 355, 357, 363, 366], and, no doubt, to all Britain. Such
a religion was naturally detested by the Roman Emperors.
Augustus forbade it to Roman citizens (*Suet. Claud.*, 25),
and Tiberius made it and similar practices unlawful in Gaul
(*Plin. H. N.*, xxx. 1). The latter prohibition caused the
Druids to pass over into Britain, where the barbarity of the
inhabitants gave scope for greater ferocity ; and Pliny relates
that the island, frenzied with the rites, celebrated the cult
with such ceremonies that it might almost seem to have
given it to the Persians (ut dedisse Persis videri possit) (*ibid.*).
Claudius finally abolished it in the Empire (*Suet. Claud.*, 25),
and as under this Emperor the Roman power began to be
imposed on Britain, it may be that the Roman advance was
as fatal to Druidism in all parts of the island subdued by
them as it was in Mona. Still, there is no direct evidence
that it was not tolerated in Britain. Pliny justly eulogizes
the act of the Romans in repressing the religion :

> Nec satis æstimari potest quantum Romanis
> debeatur, qui sustulere monstra, in quibus hominem
> occidere religiosissimum erat, mandi vero etiam
> saluberrimum (*H. N.*, xxx. 4).

This is all that is definitely related in the classics regarding British Druidism. The island, however, contains numerous remains undoubtedly Druidic—*e.g.*, the megaliths and trilithons of Stonehenge, the ruder megaliths of Stanton Drew, Somersetshire ; the enfossed area (some time used as a camp) at Avebury, Wilts ; and many cromlechs, rocking-stones, buckstones, and other prehistoric relics of the monumental or altar class. Of literary treasures the Druids have left none, except such as may be wrapped up in the productions of the post-Roman bards. The most remarkable of these productions are the Welsh triads, which are based upon a mystic value attached to the number 3, and are therefore supposed to be so termed from Gr. τριας, *three :* but originally the term may have signified a Druidic aphorism (*cf.* triath [20*a*]), whether involving a profound proposition or dogma, or making a simple statement of fact or record. The subject is full of interest. Whether the mystery had its birth in Britain or not, it appears largely in Scripture, developing into the Trinity of Christianity and the incoherent Creed of Athanasias ; and in mythology finding echoes in the three sons of Kronos and other triad groups, precisely as the next generation of gods, governed by the sign Gemini, faded away in stories of twins. Probably the triadic literature sprang out of the three primary elements of cosmogŏnic speculation referred to in Pythagorean fragments. Taliesin says :

        . . . The circle of Sidin (Zodiac)
        . . . continues revolving
        Between three elements.

48. Inscriptions found in the island show that a host of gods was recognized in the Roman period. The great deities of the Roman Pantheon (Jupiter, Mercury, Apollo, etc.) undoubtedly found their way into Britain before the Romans entered, being common to Gaul and Germany at the commencement of the Christian era ; but many others may have been introduced by the cohorts of different nationalities which were in garrison here. It is probable, however, that there was little material difference in general between the native and introduced worships. Solar and planetary

adoration in some form or other underlay them all ; and if
the ceremonies observed by the Romans themselves were
more humane and refined, there was yet not sufficient advance
to prevent many of the Romans harping back to traditional
rites. This backward inclination, tending to revive the rite
of human immolation, and thus exciting the horror of the
better class of Roman citizens, probably hastened the pro-
hibitive edicts of the Emperors ; but Druidism itself, when
once rid of these enormities, was, perhaps, not more degraded
than the religion of intellectual Greece. Among the deities
or deistic groups mentioned in the inscriptions we find Jupiter
optimus maximus, Mars, Apollo, Hercules, Mithras, Fortuna,
Victoria, Coventia, Deæ Nymphæ, Deæ Matres, and Matres
Campestres. A stone from Housesteads [237h] mentions an
oracle of Apollo—Diis Deabusque secundum interpreta-
tionem oraculi clari Apollonis Coh. I. Tungrorum ; and a
stone from Corbridge [282y] mentions Diodora, ΗΡΑΚΛΕΙ
ΤΥΡΙΩ . . . ΑΡΧΙΕΡΕΙΑ — a description supposed, perhaps without sufficient reason, to refer to the Phœnician
Hercules of Tyre (see HERAKLES PR. [135s]). The occurrence
of so many deities in the grapholithic texts of Roman Britain
show that the religion observed by at least the resident
Romans was highly polytheistic ; yet we may not be far from
the truth if we suppose that the many gods were in the main
regarded merely as diverse attributes of an all-pervading
deity. The supposed Druidic aphorism—

> Nid dim ond Duw, nid Duw ond dim,
> [Not nothing but God, not God but nothing.]

—*i.e.*, everything is God ; what is not God is " nothing "
—is equal to the loftiest sentiment of our own national
creed.

49. According to Cæsar and Tacitus, Mercury was the
favourite god of the Gauls and Germans. In Gaul he had
many images, and was honoured as the inventor of arts, the
guardian of roads and journeyings, and the patron of commerce
[355]. He was probably not less exalted in Britain. A stone
found at Thornborough, near Catterick [191e] was dedicated
to the god of the roads (Deus qui vias et semitas commentus

est), and the stones called Golden Pots in Northumberland [155b] probably owed their origin to the same belief. Thomas Gale (p. 17) makes the following interesting remarks respecting four mercurial stones near Boroughbridge, Yorks [191g] :

Paulo infra Isurium, occidentem versus tria nunc stant præsignia saxa (vulgo, " the devil's arrows ") non dolata, pyramidalis figuræ, in ortum quasi prospicientia. Hæc cum Lelando credas fuisse tropæa a Romanis posita, cum aliis Deos Britannorum ; mihi quidem Hermæ videntur fuisse, qui hic statuebantur ad Quadrifinium. Apud Gromaticos ex editione Gœsii, p. 247, sic ista confirmari existimo. *Petræ si duæ, aut tres, aut quatuor, taxatæ, non perdolatæ a ferro, in quadrifinio inventæ fuerint, ab oriente per convallia limitem ostendunt.* Fuerunt autem ista saxa quatuor numero, jam vero-ponti-culus in viciniâ ex uno eorum subverso constructus cernitur. Habent singula in summitate foramen excavatum, in quod caput olim defixum esse parum dubito. *Quid mirum igitur, inquit Vossius, si et viæ monstratio Mercurii stellæ sit attributa, quando Mercurius fingeretur forma capitis humani impositâ lapidi quadrato, cui inscriptum foret quô via duceret. Ponebantur autem hujusmodi Hermæ in biviis, triviis, quadriviis.* Agnosco jam nullas in illa legi literas, sed edax tempus quod non unum in duris hisce petris sulcum detrivit, istas etiam abrodere possit. Quid nisi deum hunc sub hâc formâ, & nomine ERMINSUL, quod est Mercurii Columna (Ermin, *Mercurius ;* Suyl, *columna*), coluerunt et Saxones ? Quatuor porro illi fines qui quadrifinium conficiebant, quatuor viis publicis limitabantur : nec erit difficile vias illas describere. Primam, perspicuitatis gratiâ, pons illam a Cataractonio ; secundam facio, quæ ab Olecana [191i] ad M. P. xvii. ab occidente descende-bat per Burgum Knaresburgh ; Tertia huc a Legeolio [218m] per vadum Sanctæ Helenæ juxta Wetherby ducebat ; et quarta huc ab Eboraco procedit.

The same writer remarks (p. 14) : " Via quæ ducit a Londinio ad Carleolum Herminstreet [140] dicebatur, nomenque id a Mercurio, sive Hermete, deo qui vias commentus est, iisque præsidet, sortita fuisse videatur."

HISTORY.

50. The island seems to have been anciently well known. Pytheas of Massilia travelled over it before 300 B.C. ; but it appears to have been afterwards neglected, consequent upon the disturbing changes brought about by the wars of Roman expansion. The Marseillaise about 140-130 B.C., when in-interrogated by Scipio, could tell him nothing about Britain (*Strabo* IV., ii. 1) ; and no mention of any military event connected with it is found in any writer earlier than Julius Cæsar. The latter relates that within memory (nostrâ etiam memoriâ) Divitiacus, King of the Suessiones, and the most powerful ruler in Gaul, had obtained the sovereignty of a great part of Britain as well as of Belgium (*B. G.*, ii. 4) ; and in 57 B.C. some chiefs of the Bellovaci who were at war with Cæsar fled into Britain (*ibid.*, 14). At this period the island was visited by the Veneti, a powerful naval people, who lived on the opposite coast of Armorica, and were strong enough to control the trade of these seas. In 56 B.C. they received assistance from Britain in their war against Cæsar, but were vanquished in a naval battle (*ibid.*, iii., 8, 9, 16). Strabo relates that they had prepared to resist Cæsar's passage into Britain, jealous for the commerce which was in their own hands (*Strab.*, IV., iv. 1) ; but, in any case, their over-throw doubtlessly transferred considerable mercantile oppor-tunities to the Romans.

51. According to Cæsar, the Gauls knew very little about the island, its ports, landing-places, or people. None willingly approached it but merchants, and these were only acquainted with the coast and the territories opposite Gaul. When pre-paring for his descent, he summoned many merchants, but they could not tell him the size of the island, the civil or military usages, or how many vessels the ports could accom-modate. His officer, Caius Volusenus, who was sent to recon-noitre the coast, evidently looked upon it with fear, returning on the sixth day without having ventured to leave his ship. It is probable, however, that Cæsar drew too dark a picture. The Gauls, according to his own account, had exercised some sort of mastery in the S.E., and the Veneti also had intercourse ; and it is related that the legates sent to him by British tribes before the first descent were some of the Gallic Morini (*Dion. Cass.*, xxxix. 51). Commius Atrebas, a Briton, was with him in Gaul at the same time ; and Mandubratius, a Trinovantine refugee, accompanied the second expedition. It seems, indeed, that Cæsar magnified his difficulties, but with what object we know not, unless it was for the purpose of excusing the indecisive character of his conquest.

52. The object of Cæsar's invasion was to punish the people for the help they had given his opponents in nearly all the Gallic wars ; but the first descent, made towards the end of summer 55 B.C., was merely exploratory, the lateness of the season making it advisable to defer an organized campaign until spring. He assembled his troops and navy in the territory of the Morini on the Gallic coast, and collected all available information of the island, first from merchants who visited it, and then by means of a warship sent out under Volusenus. His designs becoming known to the Britons, many tribes sent legates to offer hostages and allegiance. These he received kindly, and sent back with them Commius the Briton, whom he had promised to make King of the Attrebates, commanding him to use his influence to persuade the tribes to submit. The Britons, however, answered Commius by putting him in chains (*Bell. Gall.*, iv. 20, 21, 27).

53. Cæsar set sail from Portus Iccius* in Morinia after midnight, August 26, 55 B.C., and arrived off Britain about ten on the following morning. At the spot off which they arrived high hills ran up to the water's edge, with only a narrow beach between, and the place was so unfavourable for disembarkation that the troops immediately on landing would have been within reach of the enemy's spears, the Britons already being in position. Cæsar, spending some time in instructing his officers, was at length carried by a favourable wind and tide about seven miles along the coast, where the hills terminated in an open, level shore, and here he resolved to land. This had to be accomplished in face of

* Portus Iccius (Itius) is now Dunkirk.   Strabo says that Cæsar established a dockyard on the Seine when he sailed to Britain (IV. iii. 3), but used Itium as his naval station (*ibid.* v. 2).

the British horsemen and essedarii, who were drawn up on
the beach ; and the undertaking involved great danger, since
the ships, owing to their size, could only be moored in deep
water, and the troops, besides being unaccustomed to the
native methods of war, had to gain the land by force, through
uncertain depths. Perceiving his troops to hesitate, Cæsar
caused the warships to run farther in shore and harass the
enemy with slings, arrows, and projectiles. This was successful ; the Britons, awed by the ships, to which they were
unused, and by the projectiles from the engines, gave ground.
The depth of the water they were in still deterred the troops ;
but at this juncture the standard-bearer of the tenth legion,
having invoked the gods, and reminding his comrades of their
duty, leaped overboard, and his enthusiasm speedily spread
to the whole fleet. As they leaped down, the British horsemen attacked them, and they were for some time in great
straits, and their unprotected flank was subjected to a shower
of darts. Cæsar ordered the boats of the warships, and the
speculatory vessels filled with soldiers, to their assistance.
These caused the Britons to give ground, and the battle being
transferred to the plain, they were soon put to flight. The
Romans, from want of cavalry, were unable to pursue. The
Britons then sent legates, and Commius with them, to sue
for peace. Cæsar reproached them for their treatment of
Commius, but demanded hostages, part of whom were given
forthwith ; the remainder, having to be brought from distant
parts, were promised in a few days. These things being
arranged, the British leaders commanded their people to
return to their homes, and the princes to assemble to make
submission (*B. G.*, iv. 23-27).

54. Cæsar had now to cope with the elements. On the
fourth day after his arrival, twelve ships which were trans-
porting his cavalry from Gaul were beset by a sudden storm
when within sight of his camp, and were dispersed. The
same night happened to be full moon, when the greatest tides
were experienced. The Romans, who were ignorant of this
phenomenon, were horrified to see immense waves wash over
and fill the warships ; and at the same moment the transports
at anchor dashed one against another. All the vessels were

rendered useless, and means of repairing them were not at hand, creating a position fraught with great danger, since Cæsar, intending to winter in Gaul, had no more supplies with him than were necessary for immediate needs. The British princes who had met to comply with the terms of peace gained new courage from these events, and imagining, from the smallness of his camp, that he had but a meagre following, they resolved to again trust their fortunes to the sword, hoping, by cutting off his supplies and prolonging the campaign into winter, to inflict such a blow that no one would afterwards dare to attack Britain. They secretly proceeded to reassemble the army. Meanwhile, Cæsar, though without knowledge of their designs, adopted prompt measures to ward off the danger in which the disasters to the fleet had placed him, and to meet possible defection, which he half suspected, as the natives had failed to render the remaining hostages. Corn was brought in daily from the fields, and with the materials afforded by the most damaged vessels and other requisites hurried from the Continent, the fleet was, after great labour, put into navigable condition. While this was in progress, and there were still no apparent signs of hostilities, the guards before the camp announced to Cæsar that a greater dust than usual was observed in the direction whither the seventh legion had gone to forage. He hurried out with some cohorts, assigning two others to keep the camp, and ordering the remainder to arm and follow him. The legion, while reaping the only remaining corn in that vicinity, had been suddenly assailed by the Britons, who, expecting the arrival of foragers, had concealed themselves in the woods, so as to surprise them. The Romans had no time to form, and were hard pressed, some being killed, and on Cæsar's arrival they were already surrounded by horsemen and essedarii. The latter, when they saw the reinforcements, desisted ; but Cæsar, considering the time inopportune for a battle, in a short time led his troops back to camp. Some commentators regard his return as a flight, assisted to this opinion by the poet Lucan [64], but it must be admitted that he showed himself at least superior to the Britons in his ability to extricate the legion (*B. G.*, iv. 28-34).

55. This event was followed by many days of stormy weather, unfavourable for operations. The Britons meanwhile collected succours, and soon a great multitude of horsemen and foot-soldiers threatened the camp. Cæsar prepared for battle, including in his dispositions about thirty horse, brought by Commius from Gaul. The conflict was of short duration. The Britons, taking to flight, were pursued, and many of them slain. Peace was solicited the same day, and Cæsar, demanding double the former number of hostages to be delivered to him in Gaul, immediately crossed over to the Continent, the day of the Equinox being near, and his stricken ships being ill-suited for navigating the channel in winter. Two British tribes sent hostages to him there ; the rest neglected (*B. G.*, iv. 34-38).

56. In readiness for the spring of 54 B.C., Cæsar collected a large fleet of over 800 vessels with ample supplies at the Portus Itius, which was the most convenient port for the passage to Britain. He is also said to have established a dockyard on the Sequana (*Seine, Strab.*, IV., iii. 3). He set sail from Itius with five legions and 2,000 horse at sunset. The wind, at first south-west, changed about midnight, and he was carried out of his course by the tide, so that when day dawned he found he had left Britain some distance to the left. He landed about noon at a spot which he had selected in the previous campaign. No Britons were to be seen, for, being terrified at the magnitude of the fleet, they had concealed themselves some distance from the shore. Having formed a camp to protect the ships and placed it under Quintus Atrius with ten cohorts and 300 horse, he set out at night, and, after a march of about twelve miles, sighted the Britons, whose horse and esseda were drawn up behind a river. They offered resistance, but fled before the cavalry into the woods, taking shelter in a camp, strong by nature and art, which he supposed had been made in connection with some domestic war. The seventh legion made a testudo and threw up an agger against this post, from which they expelled the defenders ; and Cæsar, forbidding pursuit, spent the rest of the day in fortifying a camp (*B. G.*, v. 1, 2, 8, 9).

57. The next day the troops were divided into three bodies and sent in pursuit. When they were scarcely out of sight, messengers from Quintus Atrius announced that a tempest in the night had damaged nearly all the ships and thrown them upon the shore, sailors, anchors, and ropes, being powerless against the storm. Cæsar recalled his troops and proceeded to the coast to find the disaster but little exaggerated ; about forty vessels were totally lost. The artificers of the legions were assigned the task of repairing the rest, and workmen were summoned from the Continent to help. A letter was also sent to Labienus in Gaul to have as many ships as possible built by the legions there ; and, to prevent similar disasters, Cæsar had his vessels drawn on shore and enclosed within the fortifications of the camp. These works were hurried forward day and night. Having thus spent ten days, Cæsar returned to the interior with the same troops as before. He found the Britons greatly increased, and commanded, with common consent, by Cassivellaun, whose own territory was separated from the maritime States by the Tamesis (*Thames*), about eighty miles from the sea. This prince had engaged in continual wars with his neighbours until the Roman invasion compelled all to unite for the common good. We know from Cæsar that he killed Imanuentius, King of the Trinovantes, and forced his son Mandubratius to seek safety by flight (*B. G.*, v. 10, 11, 20).

58. Cassivellaun's horse and essedarii resolutely joined battle with the cavalry as it advanced, but were everywhere worsted, and forced back upon the woods and hills, losing many killed ; the Romans, pursuing too carelessly, also suffered loss. Later, while the Romans were engaged in fortifying a camp, the Britons burst from the woods and fell fiercely upon the troops stationed in front. Two cohorts, each the first of a legion, were thereupon sent forward. When these had taken up a position a very short distance from the rest, the Britons, to the no small terror of their enemy, boldly rushed in between them, and succeeded in forcing their way through. By the aid of many cohorts the attack was at length repulsed, but Cæsar's losses on that day included Quintus Laberius Durus, a military tribune, who was killed.

From the lessons afforded by these events Cæsar observed that his troops, owing to their heavy equipment, were at a disadvantage, since they could not pursue, and dared not leave the standards. His cavalry especially fought in great danger of being enticed away from the legions by the enemy, who, pretending retreat, would then leap from their esseda and engage on foot. Equal danger was also threatened by the British horse, which approached, never in close order, but scattered at considerable and defined intervals, so that fresh troops were always at hand ready to relieve those who were wearied (*B. G.*, v. 15, 16).

59. On the following day the Britons were posted on the hills at a distance from the camp, showing themselves in scattered parties, and offering a less spirited opposition to the Roman horse. But at midday, when Cæsar sent out Caius Trebonius, a legate, with three legions and all the cavalry to forage, they suddenly rushed out towards these troops from all points, and came close up with the standards and legions. They were, however, repulsed and pursued by the cavalry, who, seeing themselves supported by the legions, fought with redoubled confidence, and turned the retreat into precipitate flight, denying their enemy opportunity to concentrate, or make a fresh stand, or to get down to fight on foot. Immediately after this flight the reinforcements which had arrived from all parts to aid the Britons went away, and the latter dared not afterwards wage battle with any very considerable body of Romans (*B. G.*, v. 17).

60. Cæsar, having ascertained the intentions of the Britons, advanced to the Tamesis [57], in the neighbourhood of Cassivellaun's territory. This river was only fordable on foot in one place, and there with difficulty, and the enemy was drawn up in great force and in order of battle on the opposite bank, which was fortified by sharp stakes fastened into the ground, while similar stakes were fixed in the river under water. Having acquired this information from captives and fugitives, Cæsar commanded the horse to cross, followed by the legions ; and the passage was effected with such despatch and impetuosity, although the heads only of the foot-soldiers were above water, that the Britons could

not withstand the attack, and fled. Cassivellaun, convinced
of the hopelessness of the struggle, now dismissed the greater
part of his troops, retaining about 4,000 essedarii, with
which he retired into intricate places and woods, some distance from the road (*ex via*). Here he harboured the inhabitants and cattle from the districts through which the
Romans were expected to pass. At the same time he kept
a close watch upon his enemy, and eagerly took advantage
of any indiscretion, so that when the cavalry wandered too
far to plunder or lay waste, the essedarii would issue from
the woods by every possible exit, and sometimes placed them
in great danger. Cæsar, therefore, ordered the cavalry to
keep in touch with the rest of the army, and to desist from
operations involving much risk when the legionary troops
were too fatigued to support them (*B. G.*, v. 18, 19).

61. While in Gaul, Cæsar had received a youthful British
refugee named Mandubratius, whose father, Imanuentis, King
of the Trinovantes [178] had been killed by Cassivellaun,
and the young prince accompanied his protector into Britain.
The Trinovantes, who were nearly the strongest tribe in
those parts, now sent legates to Cæsar, promising submission
and obedience, and praying that he would protect Mandubratius from Cassivellaun, and send him to take up the
government of their State. Cæsar complied, demanding
forty hostages and corn for the army, which were quickly
furnished. This act seems to have calmed the fears of other
tribes, and the Cenimagni [179], Segontiaci [172], Ancalites
[180], Bibroci [169], and Cassii [181], also tendered submission. From the legates of these he learned that Cassi-
vellaum's town (*oppidum Cassivellauni*) [181a] was not far
distant, surrounded by woods and marshes, and that the
Britons were there in great force. Marching thither, he
found the place strongly fortified, but attacked it at two
points, forcing the defenders, after a little time, into flight,
and killing and taking prisoners many of them in the pursuit. A great number of cattle also fell into the hands of
the victors. As a diversion, Cassivellaun ordered four
kings, named Cingetorix, Carvilius, Taximagulus, and
Segovax, who ruled in Cantium, to collect their troops and

attack Cæsar's naval camp ; but they were met and dispersed by a body of Romans, who made captive a chief of
high rank (*nobilis dux*) named Lugotorix. The unsuccessful issue of these events, added to the defection of the
tribes, put an end to the last hopes of the British leader, and
he tendered submission through Commius. Cæsar, resolving
to winter in Gaul, owing to commotions there, and the season
being nearly spent, so that there remained only a short time
in which to make the passage, demanded hostages, fixed the
tribute to be rendered by the island every year, and warned
Cassivellaun not to molest the Trinovantes. The hostages
demanded were given, and he finally sailed away, carrying
with him a large number of captives (*B. G.*, v. 20-23). Strabo
relates that, although he transported only two legions into
Britain, he took away hostages and slaves and much other
booty (IV., v. 3).

62. " So the storm passed away ! No Roman legion
remained to perpetuate possession, no fortress to frown
hostility upon the natives ; no plunder enriched his avaricious
friends, save a few untaught and barbarous slaves, torn from
their rude homes among the woods, to serve as melancholy
and short-lived memorials of his double sword-sweep upon our
land " (*Anthon's Cæs. Comm.* 1872). Thus one commentator
sums up the results of these campaigns. It must be allowed,
however, that Cæsar emerged victoriously from a perilous
enterprise, in which the valour of the Britons seemed allied
to the greatest efforts of the wind and tides; and the plunder,
instead of consisting of only a few slaves torn from forest
homes, is recorded to have been a great number (*magnus
numerus*) taken in a district bright with cornfields, not to
mention the spoil in cattle. As for the short-lived memorials of the sword-sweep, it is fair to Cæsar, and no dis-
credit to the islanders, to admit that he extended his assistance to one tribe at least, and imposed tribute upon
others ; and though we afterwards find Cassivellaun's family
ruling in Trinovantia, it may be assumed that Cæsar's
victories bore permanent fruit from the familiarity which
Cassivellaun's son and other noble Britons acquired at
Rome.

63. It would appear from Cicero, if that writer could be taken seriously, that very little was expected from Cæsar's expedition. He says in one of his letters that the result was awaited. It was certain the approaches of the island were protected by great moles, and there was no hope of prey, except slaves, among whom he exhorts his friend Atticus to expect no one polished in letters or music (*Ad Att.*, iv. 16). In a later epistle he refers to a letter sent by Cæsar from Britain :

> Ab Quinto fratre et a Cæsare accepi a. d. ix. Kalend. Novemb. litteras, confecta Britannia, obsidibus acceptis, nulla præda, imperata tamen pecunia, datas a littoribus Britanniæ, proximo a. d. vi. Kalend. Octob. Exercitum Britannia reportabant (*ibid.*, 17).

64. The unfavourable comments upon Cæsar probably originated with Lucan (died A.D. 65), who makes Pompey say :

> . . . Rheni gelidis quod fugit ab undis,
> Oceanumque vocans incerti stagna profundi,
> Territa quæsitis ostendit terga Britannis ?
> > *Pharsal.*, ii. 570.

> [Is it that he fled from the icy waters of the Rhine,
> And calling ocean the swamps of uncertain depth,
> Showed frightened backs to the Britons he had sought ?]

Other notices occur in Lucan :

> . . . Proh, si remeasset in urbem,
> Gallorum tantum populis, Arctoque subacta,
> Quam seriem rerum longa præmittere pompa,
> Quas potuit belli facies ! ut vincula Rheno,
> Oceanoque daret ! celsos ut Gallia currus
> Nobilis, et flavis sequeretur mista Britannis !
> Perdidit ò qualem vincendo plura triumphum !
> > *Pharsal.*, iii. 73.

> [Alas ! if he had returned to the city,
> When he had conquered the Gallic peoples and the North,
> What a chain of things, what trophies, in long procession,
> He might have sent before !   How he might give fetters
> To the Rhine and ocean ! and how noble Gaul
> Might drive high chariots, mingled with flaxen Britons !
> Oh, what great triumph he lost by conquering more !]

In another passage the poet suggests disordered retreat :

> . . . Vaga cum Tethys, Rutupinaq' littora fervent,
> Unda Caledonios fallit turbata Britannos.
>
> *Pharsal.*, vi. 67.

[When Tethys wanders, and the Rutupine shores become
crowded,
The agitated wave disappoints the Caledonian Britons.]

If, however, the Northern Britons displayed any interest
in Cæsar's departure from Rutupiæ [168*d*], it was more likely
to take the form of a rejoicing than of sincere disappoint-
ment, unless, indeed, it gave them an opportunity of plundering the South Britons, free from the dreaded prospect of
encountering Roman legions. Tacitus is not far from the
truth when he says that Cæsar, the first Roman who led an
army into Britain, although terrifying the natives, and gaining
possession of the coast, merely pointed out the country to posterity without handing it down.   Soon civil wars and internal
troubles diverted public attention, and during these, and for
long afterwards, the island remained unmolested (*Agr.* 13).

65. Eumenius (A.D. 296) says that in Cæsar's age Britain
had no ships of war, while Rome was as strong by sea as land ;
and he adds that the British nation was then rude, and used
only to war with the half-naked Picti and Hibernii, and
therefore yielded easily to the Romans. Sidonius Apollinaris
(*circa* A.D. 470) also mentions the expedition :

> . . . Victricia Cæsar
> Signa Caledonios transvexit ad usque Britannos ;
> Fuderit et quamquam Scotum, et cum Saxone, Pictum.

[Cæsar bore his victorious standards even among
the Caledonian Britons, and routed the Scot, Saxon,
and Pict.]

66. The Roman wish to possess the Britannic islands is
often expressed by the Latin poets of the Augustan age :

> Tibi [Cæsari] serviat ultima Thule.
>
> VIRGIL: *Georg.*, i. 30 (B.C. 30).

[May farthest Thule serve thee.]

> Serves iterum Cæsarem in ultimos Orbis Britannos.
>
> HORACE : *Odes*, i. 35, 29.

[Keep safe Cæsar, about to go among the farthest
Britons of the world.]

Pestemque, a populo, et principe Cæsare, in Persas
atque Britannos
Vestra motus aget prece.—HORACE : *Odes*, i. 21.

[Moved by your prayer, he will turn destruction
from the people and Prince Cæsar to the Persians
and Britons.]

Præsens divos habebitur
Augustus, adjectis Britannis
Imperio.—*Ibid.*, iii. 5.

[Augustus will be held a god, having thrown the
Britons to his Empire.]

Te [Augustum] belluosus qui remotis
Obstrepit oceanus Britannis.—*Ibid.*, iv. 14, 45.

[The monster-haunted ocean, which roars against
the remote Britons (obeys) thee.]

67. Augustus's real relations with the island appear from
Strabo. According to this writer, some of the British Princes
had by embassies and solicitations obtained the friendship
of the Emperor, and dedicated their offerings in the Capitol,
bringing the whole island into intimate union with the
Romans. They paid but moderate duties both on imports
and exports from Gaul, which consisted of ivory bracelets
and necklaces, amber, glass vessels, and small wares ; so that
the island scarcely needed a garrison. He considered it would
require a legion and some cavalry to enforce tribute, and the
military expenditure would be equal to the revenue collected ;
for the levying of tribute would of necessity result in a re-
duction of the imposts, and at the same time the employment
of force would involve some danger. At this period the
island exported corn, cattle, gold, silver, iron, skins, and
slaves, and dogs sagacious in hunting. The Gauls used these
dogs, as well as their native dogs, for the purposes of war.
There were then four passages commonly used from the
Continent into Britain : one from the coast of the Morini,
near the mouths of the Rhine ; and the others from the
mouths of the Seine, Loire, and Garonne (*Strab.*, IV., v. 2, 3).
Moreover, British princes were not unfamiliar at Rome.
Tenuantius, son of Cassivelaun, was in favour with Augustus ;
and Cunobelin, son of Tenuantius, was brought up at Rome,
and accompanied Augustus in several campaigns. More-

over, a coin of Cynobelin, bearing the Latin word " solidu," seems to argue something more than mere familiarity with the Romans. On the whole, it is probable that the Romans possessed important interests in Britain amounting to a virtual paramountcy over the nearest part of the island, and it may well be supposed that these interests represented the fruits of Cæsar's victories, solidarized by half a century of peaceful unaggressive policy at Rome. Propertius a contemporary Roman poet, mentions his *esseda Britanna*, and the painted chariot (*pictus currus*) of Britain.

68. The peaceful policy of Augustus was continued by Tiberius. Caligula, the next Emperor, meditated an invasion, but never embarked upon it, possibly deterred by the failure of the German expeditions. He, however, received the surrender of Adminius, Cunobelin's son, who had fled with a few followers, having been expelled by his father. Upon this, the Emperor sent boastful letters to Rome, as if he had received the cession of the whole island, commanding the messengers to deliver the letters to the Consuls in the temple of Mars in the presence of the Senate (*Suet. Calig.*, xliv.). On another occasion he advanced towards the ocean, as if to carry war into Britain, and, putting his army in order, proceeded a little way out to sea in a galley. Returning suddenly and mounting a throne, he commanded his soldiers as if about to give battle, made the trumpet sound to the charge, and then ordered them to gather shells. With these he sought to adorn his triumph, as if he had gained a conquest, and having liberally rewarded the soldiers, he carried the shells to Rome (*Dion Cass.*). According to Suetonius, he called the shells " spoils of ocean " (*spolia oceani*), and, to declare his victory, erected a very high lighthouse, rewarding the soldiers with a hundred pence each (*Calig.*, xlvi.).

69. The task of real conquest was commenced by Caligula's successor, Claudius, who is said to have been encouraged by Bericus, a British refugee, who had been exiled for sedition (*Dion*). According to Tacitus, Claudius's expedition was the beginning of success, resulting in conquered tribes, captive Kings and great fame for Vespasian (*Agric.*, xiii.). The island, which no Roman had attacked since the time of Julius

(*Eutrop.*, vii.), was then in an uproar, owing to the Romans harbouring refugees (*ob non redditos transfugas*), and Claudius seized the opportunity for war in order to win honour worthy of a triumph which the Senate had decreed him (*Suet. Vita. Claud.*, xvii.). The command was conferred upon Aulus Plautius, an eminent senator, but the war was at first unpopular with the army. The soldiers, unwilling to engage, as it were, out of the world, refused to go, until the Emperor sent Narcissus, who ascended the tribunal of Plautius and attempted to address them. At this they became more angry, and would not hear him ; but immediately chanting the *Io Saturnalia* (for slaves celebrated the feast of Saturn in the guise of masters), they now readily followed Plautius (*Dion*).

70. The army of invasion consisted of several legions and auxiliary troops, Vespasian commanding the second legion (*Tac. Hist.*, iii. 44), and they set out in three divisions A.D. 43. They were hampered in their passage by contrary winds, but were encouraged by a light which ran from east to west in the direction they were sailing ; and they effected a landing without opposition, for the Britons, from the accounts they had received, did not expect them, and were not in great force. Those who were at hand fled into the marshes and woods, hoping that the invaders would be tired with waiting to no purpose, and, like Julius Cæsar, retire without effecting anything. Plautius had difficulty in discovering them, but, coming up with them (they were not a free State, but were subject to several Kings), he first defeated Caractacus, and then Togodumnus, sons of Cunobelin, their father being then dead. The Britons fleeing, part of the Bodunni, who were subject to the Catuellani, surrendered to him, and he, leaving a garrison amongst them, advanced forward to a river, behind which the barbarians lay careless in their camp, thinking the stream impassable for want of a bridge. The Germans, who were accustomed to swim armed through the most rapid streams, were sent over, and surprised them, but did not attack them, only wounding their chariot-horses, which, being thus disordered, endangered the riders. Then Plautius despatched Vespasian and his brother, Sabinus, a legate, who also crossed the river and surprised the barbarians, slaying

many of them, though not obliging them to flee. The battle
was continued next day, and remained doubtful till Sidius
Geta, who narrowly escaped being taken, gave them such a
defeat that triumphal honours were decreed him, although he
had not been Consul. The Britons after this retreated to the
Thames where it empties into the sea. The water, overflowing,
stagnated here, but, being acquainted with the places which
were firm at bottom and fordable, they passed safely, while
the Romans ran great risk in pursuing. The Germans, however, swam over, and others passed at a bridge a little above.
Falling upon the Britons, they made great slaughter, but
rashly going in pursuit, they fell among impassable bogs, and
lost many men. Togodumnus fell in this engagement. The
Britons, not disheartened by his fall, prepared for war with
more vigour, encouraged also by the Roman losses in the bogs.
Plautius therefore advanced no further, and, securing what he
had conquered by a garrison, sent for Claudius, which he had
been ordered to do in case of violent opposition (*Dion*).

71. Claudius, committing affairs at Rome to his colleague
Vitellius, who was joined with him in the Consulate for five
months, went by sea to Massilia, and thence by land and
river to the ocean, which he crossed. Joining his army at
the Thames, he passed the river, and engaged the barbarians,
who had assembled to oppose him, defeating them, and taking
Camulodunum [222*f*], the capital of Cunobelin. After this
many were brought under subjection by force, others by surrender, and were deprived of their arms. Claudius then returned to Rome to celebrate his triumph, leaving Plautius
again *in command*, with orders to subdue the rest of the
country. For these exploits the Emperor was complimented
several times with the title of Imperator, though it was customary to allow it only once for the same war (*Dion*). Suetonius, however, gives a very different account of Claudius's
visit to Britain. He says he passed overland from Massilia
to Gesoriacum, whence he crossed, and without battle or
bloodshed received the submission of part of the island in a
very few days, returning to Rome in the sixth month after
leaving it (*Vit. Claud.*, xvii.). The latter version is probably
correct [see 72]. A magnificent triumph followed the return

to Rome.   Not only the Governors of the provinces, but even
some exiles, were permitted into the city to witness it ; and
among the spoils of war a naval crown was fixed to the pedi-
ment of his palatine house by the side of the civic crown, as
a token that he had passed over the ocean, as if he had conquered it (*Vit. Claud.*, xvii.).   He, moreover, inaugurated on
-the Campus Martius the representation of the storming and
sacking of a town in real fight (*ad imaginem bellicam*), attended
by the surrender of British Kings (*ibid.*, xxi.).

72.   The annals of Tacitus recording the British expedition
having been lost, only a few more fragmentary particulars of
the early stages of the war have come down to us.   Vespasian,
as already noticed, gained great distinction in it.   Under the
commands of Plautius and Claudius, he encountered the
Britons thirty times [*tricies et bis* (*Eutrop.*, vii.)], and reduced
two very strong tribes,* twenty towns, and the Insula Vectis,
Wight [337] (*Suet. Vit. Vespas.*, iv.).   Claudius also added to
the Empire certain islands called Orcades [327], situated in
the ocean beyond Britain, and gave his own son the name of
Britannicus (*Eutrop.*, viii.).   Two inscriptions given by
Horsley (one from the Palace Barbareni at Rome, and the
other possibly from the same place) confirm the latter conquest, as well as Suetonius's statement that Claudius personally witnessed no fighting or bloodshed :

TI . CLAUDIO CÆS.

AUGUSTO

PONTIFICI. MAX. TR. P. IX.

COS. V. IMP. XVI. P.P.

SENATUS. POPUL. Q. R. QUOD.

REGES BRITANNIÆ ABSQ.

ULLA JACTURA . DOMUERIT.

GENTESQUE . BARBARAS.

PRIMUS . INDICIO . SUBEGERIT.

Reges BritANNIÆ . PERDUELLES . SINE.

Ulla JactuRA . CELEBRITÈR . CEPERIT.

Gentesque EXTREMARUM . ORCHADUM.

Primus indicio . FACTO. R. IMPERIO . ADIECERIT.

---

* AM. 4045 (A.D. 45), Vespasian, with the Second Legion, reduced the
Belgæ and Damnonii; A.M. 4047, the Romans occupied Thermæ and
Glebon (*Ric.*, II., i. 14, 15).

The following lines by an unknown author, printed in the *Poetæ Minores*, iv. 539, also possibly contain an allusion to the bloodless character of his personal campaign :

> Semota, et vasto disjuncta Britannia ponto,
> Cunctaque inaccessis horrida litoribus :
> Quam pater invictis Nereus vallaverat undis :
> Quam fallax æstu circuit oceanus :
> Brumalem sortita polem, qua frigida semper
> Præfulget stellis Arctos inocciduis,
> Conspectu devicto tuo, Germanice Cæsar,
> Subdidit insueto colla premenda jugo.
> Adspice, confundat populos ut pervia Tellus.
> Conjunctum est, quod adhuc orbis, et orbis erat.

73. Seneca, about A.D. 45, says of Claudius :

> Ille Britannos ultra noti
> Litora ponti
> Et cœruleos scuta Brigantos
> Dare Romuleis colla catenis
> Jussit.   *Cap.* 12.

[He condemned the Britons beyond the shores of the known sea, and the Brigantes with blue-painted shields, to give their necks to Roman fetters]

Beyond this notice, nothing is known of Plautian warfare in Brigantia [191*a*], or that the Romans penetrated thus early so far to the north. *Eutropius* (vii.), however, says that Britain was conquered (*devicta*) by Cnæus Sentius and Plautius, both illustrious and noble men, and it is certain that considerable progress must have been made by A.D. 47, about which time Plautius, having performed many distinguished acts, returned in triumph to Rome, Claudius even walking on his left in the ascent of the Capitol (*Eutrop.*, vii.). Plautius was succeeded by Ostorius Scapula. According to Tacitus, under these Generals, both eminent in war, the nearest parts of Britain were reduced to the rank of a Roman province, and several tribes were handed over to the government of a native King named Cogibundus [170], who was a steadfast ally of Rome. It was a common custom of the Romans in their conquests to thus make Kings the instruments of slavery (*Agric.*, xiv.).

74. Ostorius found Britain in confusion. The enemy,

encouraged perhaps by the change of the command, poured into the territories of the friendly States, and behaved the more audaciously since they imagined the new Propraetor would be too busy acquainting himself with the army and placing it in winter quarters to attempt an immediate attack. Ostorius, however, aware that fear and obedience must be inspired from the first, quickly collected his cohorts, and fell upon and scattered the Britons, vigorously pursuing them lest they should reassemble ; and, deeming it imprudent to suspend operations until he had secured a sincere peace, he proceeded to disarm suspected tribes, and to enclose the Rivers Antona [161] (*Granta*) and Sabrina [158*f*, 159*a*] (*Severn*) within a line of forts. The demands upon the natives in these matters evoked dissatisfaction. The Iceni, a strong nation, and hitherto not weakened by war, since they had willingly accepted Roman friendship (*valida gens, nec prœliis contusi, quia societatem nostram volentes accesserant*), were the first to refuse to comply, and drawing the neighbouring tribes to their side, awaited attack in a camp formed by a rough mound, and having only a narrow entrance in order to keep out the Roman cavalry. Ostorius went against them at the head of some social troops, no legionaries being at hand, and, using his horse as infantry, surrounded and forced the camp. The Britons, conscious of the consequences of their revolt, and cut off from flight by their own defences, performed many heroic deeds, but in vain. M. Ostorius, son of the legate, won the oaken crown in this battle (*Annal.*, xii. 31).

75. The slaughter of the Iceni quieted those nations who were hesitating between peace and war, and Ostorius led his army against the Cangi [182*f*], laying waste the country, and everywhere taking booty, the enemy not daring to offer battle, and suffering whenever they hazarded a surprise. The invaders had nearly reached the sea opposite Hibernia, when civil war broke out among the Brigantes, and Ostorius hastened thither, determined not to attempt new conquests until he had secured the old ones (*destinationis certum, ne nova moliretur, nisi prioribus formatis*). Some of the rebels being killed, and others pardoned, the Brigantes settled down again ; and Ostorius had now to contend with the Silures, whose per-

sistent hostility neither harshness nor clemency had sufficed
to soften ; and that he might be the more at liberty to erect
forts amongst them for their repression, the colony of Camulodunum [222f] was formed by the veterans in that part of
Britain already conquered as a check to rebels there and for
keeping the allies to their obligations :

> Silurum gens, non atrocitate, non clementia
> mutabatur, quin bellum exerceret, castrisque legi-
> onum premenda foret. Id quo promptius veniret,
> colonia Camulodunum valida veteranorum manu de-
> ducitur in agros captivos, subsidium adversus re-
> belles, et imbuendis sociis ad officia legum.—*Annal.*,
> xii. 32.

76. The Silures relied not only on their own valour, but
upon the energy of Caractacus, whose many deeds and fluc-
tuating fortunes had made him pre-eminent among British
commanders. More cunning than the Romans, and more
artful than they in choosing his camps, though inferior in the
quality of his troops, he transferred the war into the country
of the Ordovices, and, swelling his forces with such of the
people as were fearing to submit to the Romans, he prepared
for battle in a place disadvantageous to the enemy for advance,
retreat, and every purpose, but favourable to himself. Difficult mountains lay behind, and wherever approach was possible, he piled up stones in the manner of a rampart. A river
of uncertain depth flowed in front. The veteran warriors
(*catervaque majorum*) were posted before the fortifications, and
the leaders of the tribes went in and out among their respective followers, exhorting and encouraging. Caractacus himself went hither and thither, haranguing the troops and re-
citing the names of the warriors who had repulsed Cæsar ; and
each soldier vowed, according to the formalities of his own
religion, not to give ground (*ibid.*, 33, 34). Suetonius was
astonished at this activity, but he saw nothing to alarm him
beyond the rude and usual methods of defence, and, putting
his troops in motion, the river was forded without difficulty.
When they came to the mound, and the combatants fought
with missiles, the Romans lost heaviest, but the rude stone
structure, being presently destroyed by a testudo, a hand-to-

hand struggle ensued, and the barbarians retreated to the highest parts of the mountains, pressed on by the light and heavy armed troops in irregular order.   The Britons, having no cuirasses nor helmets, fell thickly.   If they resisted the auxiliaries, they were overwhelmed with the swords and javelins of the legionaries ; and if they opposed the latter, the others brought them down with spears.   The victory was complete.   The wife and daughter of Caractacus were taken, and his brothers made submission (*ibid.*, 35).   He himself sought the protection of Cartismandua, Queen of the Brigantes, but was bound and handed over to the victors in the ninth year of the Britannic War (*ibid.*, 36).

77. The fame of Caractacus was not only known in the neighbouring provinces, but was talked of throughout Italy, and the people thirsted to see the man who for so many years had scorned their power.   His name was not obscure even at Rome, and the Emperor, in extolling the conquest and showing him and his family to the citizens in a triumphal procession, added glory.   The other captives pleaded pitifully for mercy, but not so Caractacus.   He stood unmoved in the tribunal, and in a noble speech contrasted the Emperor's fortune with his own.   Upon this he and his family were pardoned, and were covered with praises and favours.   The capture of Caractacus was by some accounted as glorious as that of Scyphax by Scipio, or of Perseus by Paullus, and triumphal insignia were decreed to Ostorius (*ibid.*, 36, 37).

78. The Propraetor, hitherto successful, now became involved in ambiguous warfare, either because the troops were less intent, as if the removal of Caractacus ended the war, or because the loss of that leader made the enemy more determined for revenge.   The prefect of the camp and the legionaries left to construct forts among the Silures were surrounded, and would have been annihilated if help had not quickly come from neighbouring stations.   As it was, the prefect, with eight centurions and the most venturesome of the companies, were lost, and not long after a party of foragers and the cavalry sent to their assistance were cut up.   Upon this Ostorius used light troops to facilitate retreat when the legions were not at hand.   The conditions of battle were thus equalized, and the

Romans had the advantage in the next conflict, though night enabled the enemy to get off with moderate loss. Frequent engagements followed, generally provoked by predatory bands, who scoured the woods and marshes in search of plunder, often with, but occasionally without, the knowledge of their commanders. The obstinacy of the Silures was still more accentuated by a reported threat to transport them to Gaul, as the German Sugambri had been, so that their name would be all but extinguished. Thus fired, they intercepted two auxiliary cohorts, whom the prefects had sent out to pillage. By liberally bestowing the spoils and captives taken on this occasion, they secured the defection of other tribes ; and at length Ostorius died, weary with cares, to the joy of the Britons, to whom it was an encouragement that so great a General, though unconquered in battle, had yet succumbed during the war (*Annal.*, xii. 38, 39).

79. Claudius, hearing of the death of the legate, gave the province to Aulus Didius, surnamed Gallus, who hurried thither, but found affairs in a disturbed condition. The Silures had meanwhile defeated the legion under Manlius Valens, and magnified their victory with the view of terrifying the approaching Proprætor. Didius himself added to what he heard that he might claim the greater honour if successful, or be the more easily excused if the Britons should sustain the conflict. The Silures followed up their victory with great activity, until restrained by his arrival. He had also to cope with a civil war which had broken out among the Brigantes* under his predecessor. After the capture of Caractacus, their Queen, Cartismandua, had married Venusius, a man celebrated for military skill, and long a faithful supporter of the Romans ; but, quarrelling with him, she treacherously put his brother and relations to death, divorced Venusius, and married his knight, Vellocatum. These things incensed his adherents, who, moreover, considered it a disgrace to be subject to a woman, and a strong and tried body of warriors invaded the State. The Romans, who had foreseen this event, sent, at her request, some cohorts to assist her, and were thus brought into hostility with Venusius. The ensuing war was at first

* The manuscripts here have " Jugantum " for " Brigantum "

doubtful, but ended favourably for the Romans. Similar
fortune fell to the legion commanded by Cesius Nasica.
Didius himself, being old and full of honours, entrusted these
operations to his officers, and was satisfied to keep the enemy
at a distance. The civil war in Brigantia lasted many years
under Ostorius and Didius, but Tacitus related their achievements together, because, if divided, the reputation of neither
would be benefited (*Annal.*, xii. 40 ; *Hist.*, iii. 45). Didius,
however, preserved the Britannic province as he found it, and.
besides, fortified a few advanced positions that he might have
the credit of extending it. The Emperor Claudius died in
Didius's second year. According to Seneca, a temple was
dedicated to the deceased ruler in Britain [222*f*], and the
natives worshipped him as a god (*Lud. de Morte Claud.*).
Nero, who succeeded him in the Empire, would have. with-
drawn from Britain except for unwillingness to detract from
his honour (*Suet. Vit. Neron.*, 18). Didius was succeeded by
Veranius about A.D. 67. The latter wasted the Silures in
moderate excursions, but died in the first year of office before
he could carry the war farther. Accounted severe while he
lived, he manifested his ambition in his will, according to
which he would have put down the war if he had lived two
years longer (*Agric.*, xiv. ; *Annal.*, xiv. 29).

80. The propraetorship was now bestowed by Nero upon
Suetonius Paulinus, an able General, who prepared to attack
Mona [330], an island well fortified and a retreat for fugitives.
He conveyed his troops in flat-bottomed boats across the
strait which separated the island from the mainland. The
cavalry followed, the horses alternately fording and swimming,
as necessitated by the varying depth. The Britons were
drawn up along the opposite shore, presenting a dense but
curious line of battle. Women in funeral attire, with dis-
hevelled hair, and carrying torches, ran in and out, after the
manner of Furies ; and the Druids stood around, uttering fearful imprecations, and raising their hands towards the sky or
throwing them wildly about. The soldiers, at first terrified,
stood as if voluntarily offering themselves to the enemy's
blows ; but called to a sense of their duty by Suetonius, who
exhorted them not to fear a company of women and fanatics,

they advanced to the attack, overthrew those who opposed, and involved the enemy in the fire of their own torches. After this Suetonius placed a garrison in the island, and cut down the sacred groves (*Annal.*, xiv. 29, 30).

81. While the legate was thus engaged, he received intelligence that the Britons had suddenly revolted under the leadership of Boudicea, Queen of the Iceni. Her late husband, King Prasutagus, who had enjoyed great power, left his two daughters and Cæsar his heirs, hoping by this disposition to keep his kingdom and family from injury ; but the Romans acted as conquerors, the kingdom being wasted by the military and the palace by the Ministers. The Queen as beaten, her daughters violated, and the principal Icenians deprived of their estates, the King's relatives being reduced to the level of slaves (*mancipii*). Smarting under these wrongs, and fearing worse would happen when they had passed into the condition of a province, they entered into a secret compact with the Trinobantes, and some others who were actuated by great bitterness towards the veterans. The latter, in the new colony of Camulodunum, were expelling people from their homes, seizing their lands, and calling them captives and slaves, being supported by the military, who hoped for similar license. The Claudian temple was an additional cause for popular hatred, as if it was the seat of perpetual tyranny, and its priests were constantly increasing anxiety by their predictions. The conspirators hoped to make the colony an easy prey, since it had not been enclosed with walls, the Romans having been more taken up with the pleasantness of the place than with their duty of putting it in a condition of defence.

82. Meanwhile, many prodigies inflamed the people. Without apparent cause, the image of the goddess Victoria at Camulodunum fell, and looked backward, as if going over to the Britons ; strange sounds were heard in the public assembly, and shrieks in the theatre ; the estuary of the Thames reflected the colony overturned ; the ocean had a bloody tinge ; and apparitions of dead men were left behind by the receding tide. Frenzied women sang that deliverance was at hand (*adesse exitium*). These things encouraged the Britons, but filled the veterans with fear. Suetonius being absent, aid was demanded from Catus Decianus, the Procurator, who sent not more than 200 men improperly armed. There was, besides, but a small body of troops in the place, and trusting to the protection of the temple, and hampered by dissembling traitors who purposely interposed obstacles, no effort was made to throw up entrenchments. The storm burst with unbridled slaughter and destruction, and the safety of the aged and the women not having been provided for, the military only remained, and these, caught unprepared, as if in the midst of peace, and surrounded by a multitude of barbarians, took refuge in the temple, which was carried by assault after a defence of two days. Petilius Cerialis, legate of the ninth legion, hurrying to the relief, was encountered and routed by the victorious Britons, with the loss of all his foot, saving himself and his cavalry by retiring into camp (*Annal.*, xiv. 32).

83. Suetonius hurriedly left Mona, and, passing boldly through the enemy, reached Londinium ; but his meagre following, and the already evident consequences of the defeat of Cerialis, decided him to abandon the town and wait a more favourable opportunity for battle. Regardless of the tears and entreaties of the citizens, he gave the order to march, and such of the women and infirm as could not keep up with the troops, and those ho for other reasons lingered behind, were overwhelmed. The same slaughter took place at Verulamium [215a]. The enemy, not waiting to reduce the forts in their course, plundered wherever they could, seizing the best of everything which fortune or the cowardice of others placed in their power. About 70,000 citizens and allies perished in the three places mentioned, for no quarter was given (*ibid.*, 33). Eutropius, referring undoubtedly to these events, says that Britain was almost lost, two very noble towns (*oppida*) in it being captured and destroyed (*Eutrop.*, vii.).

Suetonius now had with him the fourteenth legion, the vexillaries of the twentieth, and auxiliaries out of the neighbouring garrisons, in all about 10,000 men, and with these he prepared to give battle, choosing a spot with narrow outlets, and closed behind by a wood. The legionaries were in close order, with the light troops disposed about them, the cavalry protecting the wings. The Britons, in incredible force, paraded about in companies and squadrons ; and, confident of success, they brought their wives to witness the conflict, placing them in waggons at the extreme edge of the camp. Boudicea, in a chariot, with her daughters before her, addressed each tribe as it advanced ; and Suetonius also harangued his troops before giving the order to attack. At first the legion kept the narrow approaches of the camp, but having discharged its darts with good aim upon the Britons as they came nearer, it rushed forward in the form of a wedge. The auxiliaries behaved with equal impetuosity, and the cavalry bore down all who opposed them. The remainder of the enemy turned in flight, impeded, however, by the wreckage of overturned vehicles, and the soldiers, closely pursuing them, did not even scruple to kill the women. The victory was complete, and 80,000 Britons are said to have been slain. The Roman loss was about 400 killed, and not many more wounded. Boudicea poisoned herself. This battle brought great fame to the soldiers of the fourteenth legion, and Petilius Cerialis, in A.D. 70, calls them "Domitores Britanniæ" (*Hist.*, ii. 11 ; v. 16). Pœnius Postumus, prefect of the camp of the second legion, hearing of the achievements of the fourteenth and twentieth legions, killed himself with his sword, because, contrary to military discipline, he had disobeyed the orders of the General, and thereby deprived his own troops of a share of the glory (*Annal.*, xiv. 34-37). The revolt of the Iceni occurred during the consulate of Cæsonius Pætus and Petronius Turpilianus, A.D. 61 (*ibid.*, 29).

Dio relates that Boudicea collected an army of 120,000 men, which increased to 230,000, and that she died a natural death and was honourably buried.

84. The army having been placed in winter quarters, preparations were made for prosecuting the war. Eight cohorts of auxiliaries and 1,000 horse sent by Cæsar from Germany were hibernated in different quarters, and 2,000 legionary troops from the same source were used to fill up the gaps in the ninth legion. Such nations as were inimical or doubtful were wasted with fire and sword. Nothing, however, tried

the enemy so much as famine, for having expected to get
possession of the Roman supplies, they neglected to sow corn,
and, moreover, all ages had been engaged in the war. They
were the less inclined for peace because Julius Classicianus,
the successor of Catus, was unfriendly to Suetonius, and
allowed his personal feelings to interfere with the public
affairs, declaring that Britain wanted a new legate, who would
be neither severe or arrogant towards the conquered, nor
wanting in moderation towards those offering submission.
At the same time he reported at Rome that the end of the
war was not to be expected until Suetonius should be superseded, ascribing every miscarriage to him and every success
to accident (*Ann.*, xiv. 38). Nero therefore sent Polycletus, a
freedman, to inquire into the state of Britain, hoping that his
authority would be sufficient to restore harmony between the
legate and procurator, and peace with the rebellious Britons.
Polycletus set out with an immense retinue, which was a
scourge to the districts through which it passed, and terrible
to the army when it arrived in Britain ; but the natives, who
did not know the power of the freedmen, were merry over it,
being astonished that the illustrious General and his army
obeyed slaves. Matters were effeminately reported to the
Emperor, and the loss of a few vessels and their crews on the
coast (*in littore*) furnishing a pretext, as if it was a disaster of
the war, Suetonius was ordered to hand over the army to
Petronius Turpilianus, who had already vacated his consulship for the purpose (*ibid.*, 39).

85. The British campaigns of Suetonius won him glory
and a name (*Tac. Hist.*, ii. 37). But for his timely energy, the
island would have been lost ; yet he restored the situation by
a single battle, save that some of the enemy, dreading the
consequences of their defection, but above all actuated by
fear of him, remained in arms (*Agric.*, xvi.), as if war was the
least evil. Such stern severity justified to some extent the
anxiety of the procurator for his recall ; yet there can be no
doubt that his victory and policy had far-reaching effects,
and although the full fruits were delayed through the lull of
operations caused by Polycletus's mission, it is more than
probable that he left the province virtually pacified, or, at

any rate, disturbed only by those who would gladly have made peace if the opportunity had been given them. This opportunity was afforded by Petronius, who finally composed the troubles, being more relentful, and at the same time more moderate, towards the enemy because a stranger to their delinquencies (*ibid.*). Petronius dared nothing more, and his reputation hangs upon that of his predecessor, who left him little to do except to persuade.

> Is [Petronius] non inritato hoste, neque lacessitus,
> honestum pacis nomen segni otio imposuit.—*Annal.*,
> xiv. 39.

86. Petronius was succeeded, probably about A.D. 64, by Trebellius Maximus, who held the office during the rest of the reign of Nero (died A.D. 68), and the short reign of Galba (killed January, 69). He was easier than his predecessor, and repeated his unaggressive policy, but directed the affairs of the province with some affectation of impartiality. The natives, giving way to vices, were becoming softened, and the outbreak of civil war in Italy, on the death of Galba, furnished reasonable excuse for inactivity. But the soldiery, wearied by long peace, became troublesome, and Trebellius, who proved himself avaricious and niggardly, was disliked by them. He was especially inimical towards Roscius Cælius, legate of the twentieth legion, and the civil war furnished the opportunity for an open rupture between them. Trebellius accused Cælius of sedition and lack of discipline, and was in turn charged with undermining the efficiency and strength of the legions ; and, the discord spreading to the army, the Proprætor, alarmed at the clamour of the auxiliaries, and being deserted by the cohorts and alæ, which joined Cælius, fled from Britain to Vitellius (A.D. 69). Actual hostilities, however, were avoided, and there was no bloodshed. Vitellius sent Vettius Bolanus to take command. Previous to his arrival the legionary legates, having equal rights, conducted the government, though Cælius arrogated to himself the greater power (*Hist.*, i. 60 ; ii. 65 ; *Agric.*, xvi.).

87. In the struggle for the Empire after Galba's death, the soldiers in Britain favoured Vitellius (*Hist.*, i. 52), the circumstance adding greatly to his prestige, as if duplicating his resources and opportunities for war [*Vitellius duos duces, duo itinera bello destinavit* (*ibid.*, 59-61)]. In his interests British cohorts were stationed in Northern Italy (*ibid.*, 70), but some soldiers of the fourteenth legion who had fought in Britain joined the party of Otho (*ibid.*, ii. 11). Other troops in Britain, upon whom Vitellius could have counted, were either detained by local enemies (the Brigantes) or were unable to join him from want of transports (*ibid.*, 32). A force of 8,000 British recruits, however, evidently part of a larger body, served for Vitellius under Hordeonius Flaccus (*ibid.*, 57). After the Battle of Bedriacum the fourteenth legion submitted to Vitellius with the rest of the Othonian army. Being taunted by the victors, the legion denied that it had been beaten, only the vexillaries having been engaged, while its strength was not tried ; but the incident led to violence, and Vitellius thought it prudent to send these troops back to Britain. The Batavian cohorts attached to the legion were sent by a different route owing to old-standing bitterness and extreme lawlessness, but they committed fearful excesses, and Vitellius was glad to turn them aside into Germany (*ibid.*, 66, 69). On the proclamation of Vespasian, letters were sent on behalf of the latter to this legion, then in Britain (*ibid.*, 86). Troops were also summoned by Vitellius (*ibid.*, 97 ; iii. 15) ; but the latter concealing the reason, and hence conveying no adequate idea of his exigencies, Vettius Bolanus seems to have considered that there was no hurry, and, moreover, excused himself on account of inquietude in Britain (*nunquam satis quieta Britannia*), and his fidelity was doubtful (*ibid.*, ii. 97). Three British legions—the second, ninth, and twentieth (*ibid.*, iii. 22)—were, however, sent, and the vexillaries with other choice troops were among the forces put in motion by Cæcina against the city of Cremona (*ibid.*, ii. 100). The Vitellian leader in Pannonia expected Vitellius with the strength of the British army (*ibid.*, iii. 1), and Vespasian's adherents derived satisfaction from the circumstance that the forces of Britain were separated from them by the sea (*ibid.*, 2). Three cohorts and the Ala Britannica are mentioned as reinforcements sent by Vitellius to Fabius Valens during the operations in Italy (*ibid.*, 41). The capture of Fabius directly afterwards turned the tide in favour of Vespasian, and in Britain, where the latter was held in high estimation from his old connection with it as Prepositor of the second legion, part of the forces espoused his cause (*ibid.*, 44, 70).

88. Before the triumph of Vespasian was complete, letters were sent into Britain by Flaccus Hordeonius for aid against Civilis, the Batavian (*Hist.*, iv. 25). Roman affairs were then in a chaotic state, and many turbulent neighbours were waiting for a favourable opportunity to attack. Rumours even got abroad that the winter quarters in Britain had been besieged (*ibid.*, 54). The troops sent from Britain to assist Flaccus appear to have comprised the fourteenth legion, for Civilis feared a joint attack from it and the Britannic fleet (*ibid.*, 76, 79).

89. The proprætorship of Vettius Bolanus in Britain was characterized by the usual laxity, and the same inertness towards the unsubdued tribes ; but he was harmless in disposition, and ruled rather by affection than authority. He had, however, to cope with a rising of the Britons, who, encouraged by the dissensions in the Empire, took up arms either just before his accession or immediately after, placing themselves under Venusius, the divorced husband of Queen Cartismandua. But a fresh era set in with the triumph of Vespasian, and excellent armies under distinguished Generals reduced the hopes of the islanders. Petilius Cerialis, the successor of Bolanus (A.D. 71), filled them with terror, and attacking the Brigantes, the most numerous tribe of the province, fought many and sometimes bloody battles, conquering or overrunning a great part of their territory. These operations made the Romans better acquainted with the island, and Pliny, writing about A.D. 73, during the proprætorship of Cerialis, and nearly thirty years after the Claudian invasion, shows that the army had extended their knowledge of the country to the vicinity of the Silva Caledoniæ, though not beyond [372]. Cerialis conducted his office with such energy as to threaten to eclipse the possibilities of a successor, but Julius Frontinus, who followed him, proved equally great, and though hampered by the imperial authorities, subdued the Silures. whose valour and difficult country had hitherto been insurmountable (*Agric.*, xvi., xvii.).

90. This was the condition in Britain when Frontinus was succeeded by Agricola (A.D. 78). But when the latter arrived after midsummer, he found the army in a state of retreat, as if abandoning their operations, and the enemy were turning the occasion to their advantage. Shortly before his arrival the Ordovices had nearly annihilated a body of cavalry within their territory. This event put the province in a ferment, and such as wished for war either joined those already in arms or made ready to do so if the character of the new legate should offer any encouragement. But Agricola—although the summer was spent and the troops were scattered throughout the province in quarters for the winter, and some considered the situation called for defence rather than attack—reopened the campaign at once, and collecting only the vexillæ of the legions and a small body of auxiliaries, because the enemy would not dare to meet on equal terms, he placed himself at their head and offered battle. Nearly all the enemy were destroyed. Aware that the impression made upon the people in his first campaign would influence their future conduct, he then led his troops against Mona, from the possession of which Suetonius had been called by the revolt of the Iceni. Not having expected that the short campaign would carry him thus far, no ships were at hand to convey the troops across the strait ; but such of the auxiliaries as knew the fords and were able to swim, and at the same time control their arms and horses, made the passage with great intrepidity, taking the enemy so completely by surprise that they asked for peace and surrendered the island. These successes, won in the first weeks of office, which other legates were accustomed to spend in ostentation and progresses, brought Agricola great renown (*Agric.*, xviii.).

91. Agricola spent the remainder of his first year in conciliating the province. Aware that military success would profit little if followed by injury, he resolved to remove the causes of discontent, first correcting the faults of his own people. He ceased to entrust public matters to freedmen or slaves. The selection of soldiers for the legions was not allowed to be influenced by favouritism, but the most faithful were advanced. All suggestions were listened to, but only the best were followed. Little faults were pardoned ; crimes were punished with moderation, or very often were overlooked on the penitence of the guilty ; and care was taken not to bestow public offices upon those who were unfit for them. The laws relating to corn and tribute were enforced with justice, the abuses, which were more intolerable than the tribute itself, being checked ; and branch roads and administrative districts were formed in order that the people might resort to the nearest quarters for corn, and that the extortion of officials might be restrained (*ibid.*, xix.). These exemplary reforms gave new significance to peace, which until now, either through the indifference or connivance of his predecessors, had been dreaded as much as war (*ibid.*, xx.).

92. Agricola resumed military operations in the summer of A.D. 79, praising moderation in his troops, restraining imprudence, constructing convenient camps, trying the estuaries and woods which lay in his path, and keeping the enemy constantly occupied. But when he had sufficiently terrified an opponent, he offered him the choice of peace. Such mildness induced many tribes who up to then had maintained themselves on equal terms to give hostages and settle down ; and these were now compassed with garrisons and forts, and with such skill and care that a new territory would sometimes pass under the Empire without being attacked—a thing which had not happened before (*ibid.*, xx.). The following winter was devoted to civil reforms. That the inhabitants, who were scattered, and barbarous, and prone to war, might be quieted and softened, he encouraged them privately, and helped them out of the public funds to build temples, courts, and houses, praising the industrious and punishing the idle. He also caused the sons of the Princes to be instructed in the liberal arts, and incited them to surpass the Gauls, with the result that those who had rejected Latin now desired it. The Roman dress and the toga became esteemed, and by degrees the people grew accustomed to banquets, baths, and other accompaniments of luxury and vice which, though called refinement by the ignorant, were really forms of slavery (*ibid.*, xxi.).

93. In the year A.D. 80. new nations were opened up, and the country was wasted as far as the Taum (*Tay*) [137*k*]. Although the weather was severe, the Britons dared not engage, and time was found for constructing forts. Frequent eruptions were made, for by renewing the garrisons with fresh troops every year, he provided against the hindrances of siege, and the enemy were powerless and despairing, because, having counted upon balancing their losses in summer by gains in winter, they now found themselves unsuccessful in both seasons (*ibid.*, xxii.). The next year was taken up in securing the districts already overrun, and if Roman ambition had not been insatiable, the Empire might have found a fit boundary at the Clota [134*e*] and Bodotria [281*c*]. Garrisons were placed in this isthmus, and all the territory in the vicinity of the two bays being in the possession of the Romans, the enemy were forced, as it were, into another island (*ibid.*, xxiii.) [166*a*]. In A.D. 82, Agricola, having been conveyed across the channel by the fleet, fought frequent and successful battles, and conquered tribes hitherto unknown. He also posted troops on the coast opposite Hibernia, not through fear, but in hope [194*a*] (*ibid.*, xxiv.).

94. In the summer of A.D. 83, having secured the nations across the Bodotria, he turned his attention to the more distant tribes. As the tactics of these and the nature of the country necessitated caution, he proceeded along the coast, keeping in touch with the fleet, which he used for exploratory purposes and for supplementing the operations on land. Thus the marines sometimes shared the camp and battle-field with the foot and cavalry. Penetrating at one time the recesses of forests and mountains, at another harrassed by storm and floods, the danger from the enemy on the one hand was counterbalanced by help from the ocean on the other. The Britons, according to the captives, were horrified at the sight of the fleet, as if its presence on the open sea cut them off from their last refuge. At this juncture the people inhabiting Caledonia (*Caledoniam incolentes populi*) appeared in arms, having made great preparations, and persistent rumours of their having assailed the advanced posts increased the anxiety of the soldiery. The timid among the latter, as if counselling prudence, advised Agricola to withdraw behind the Bodotria,

and act on the defensive. Meanwhile, the enemy burst forth
in numerous companies, upon which Agricola, lest his troops
should be overcome as a body and be surrounded, formed them
into three divisions (*ibid.*, xxv.).

95. The Britons, hearing of the division of the army,
suddenly altered their plans, and during the night attacked
the ninth legion [274c], as by far the strongest, and having
slain the guards, who were defenceless from sleep or fear,
forced their way into the camp. Agricola, informed by scouts
of the way the enemy had taken, followed them, and sent the
swiftest of the horse and foot to fall upon their rear. The
others soon joined them. Daybreak revealed the standards
to the enemy, who, having to fight a double battle, lost heart,
while the Romans, relieved from anxiety for their own safety,
fought for glory. Terrible conflicts were waged at the gates,
and the battle would have ended the war if the marshes and
forests had not sheltered the enemy. Hitherto the army had
shown some discontent, being displeased by Agricola's constant activity and by rumour [200f], and they were dis-
quieted with the belief that he intended to penetrate Caledonia and push on his conquests continuously to the extremity
of Britain ; but this feeling now gave way to boasting and
enthusiasm. The Britons, on the other hand, thinking that
their defeat was not due to Roman valour, but to accident
and the skill of the opposing leader, began to prepare for the
next eventualities with their former zeal, arming the youth,
removing their women and children to places of safety, and
ratifying their alliances in assemblies and with sacrifices
(*ibid.*, xxvi., xxvii.).

96. In the same summer a cohort of Usipii, raised in
Germany and sent into Britain, killed its centurion and dis-
ciplinary soldiers, and sailed away in three light galleys, the
pilots of which they killed or dismissed. In their course they
subsisted for a time by plunder and lawlessness, but were at
length reduced to the necessity of eating their companions,
the victim being chosen by lot from amongst the least able-
bodied. Having sailed round Britain, and losing the ships
through ignorance of navigation, they were intercepted, part
by the Suevi, the rest by the Frisii ; and some of them being

carried to Roman territory to be sold as slaves, there revealed the story of their crime (*ibid.*, xxviii.). These troops were probably stationed on the West Coast of Scotland, since their voyage was from west to east (*Dion.*, lxvi. 20).

97. In the spring of A.D. 84 the fleet was again sent out in advance, pillaging many places, and terrorizing the enemy. Agricola, having enrolled some Britons on whose courage and fidelity he could rely, set out with the army, and found the enemy posted on the Mons Grampius [207]. The Britons, expecting nothing but revenge or servitude, but taught by experience, had at length united for the common good. Already they had 30,000 arms, and others were flocking in. They were addressed before the battle by a chief named Galgacus, who was pre-eminent among their many leaders in valour and descent.

98. The speech of Galgacus, interesting as a Roman summary of the wrongs of the Britons, is given by Tacitus as follows :

" Quotiens causas belli et necessitatem nostram intueor, magnus mihi animus est, hodiernum diem consensumque vestrum initium libertatis totius Britanniæ fore. Nam et universi servitutis expertes, et nullæ ultra terræ, ac ne mare quidem securum, inminente nobis classe Romana : ita prœlium atque arma, quæ fortibus honesta, eadem etiam ignavis tutissima sunt. Priores pugnæ, quibus adversus Romanos varia fortuna certatum est, spem ac subsidium in nostris manibus habebant : quia nobilissimi totius Britanniæ, eoque in ipsis penetralibus siti, nec servientium litora adspicientes, oculos quoque a contactu dominationis inviolatos habebamus. Nos, terrarum ac libertatis extremos, recessus ipse ac sinus famæ in hunc diem defendit : nunc terminus Britanniæ patet ; atque omne ignotum pro magnifico est. Sed nulla jam ultra gens, nihil nisi fluctus et saxa : et infestiores Romani ; quorum superbiam frustra per obsequium et modestiam effugeris. Raptores orbis, postquam cuncta vastantibus defuere terræ, et mare scrutantur : si locuples hostis est, avari ; si pauper, ambitiosi : quos non oriens non occidens satiaverit : soli omnium opes atque inopiam pari adfectu concupiscunt. Auferre, trucidare, rapere, falsis nominibus imperium ; atque, ubi solitudinem faciunt, pacem adpellant.

99. Liberos cuique ac propinquos suos natura carissimos esse voluit : hi per delectus, alibi servituri auferuntur. Conjuges sororesque, etsi hostilem libidinem effugant, nomine amicorum atque hospitum polluuntur. Bona fortunasque in tributum egerunt, annos in frumentum : corpora ipsa ac manus, silvis ac paludibus emuniendis, verbera inter ac contumelias, conterunt. Nata servituti mancipia semel veneunt, atque ultro a dominis aluntur : Britannia servitutem suam quotidie emit, quotidie pascit. Ac, sicut in familia recentissimus quisque servorum et conservis ludibrio est ; sic, in hoc orbis terrarum vetere famulatu, novi nos et viles in excidium petimur. Neque enim arva nobis, aut metalla, aut portus sunt, quibus exercendis reservemur. Virtus porro ac ferocia subjectorum ingrata imperantibus : et longinquitas ac secretum ipsum quo tutius, eo suspectius. Ita, sublata spe veniæ, tandem sumite animum, tam quibus salus, quam quibus gloria carissima est. Brigantes* femina duce exurere coloniam expugnare castra, ac nisi felicitas in socordiam vertisset, exuere jugum potuere : nos integri et indomiti, et libertatem non in præsentia laturi, primo statim congressu non ostendamus quos sibi Caledonia viros seposuerit ?

100. An eandem Romanis in bello virtutem, qu m in pace lasciviam, adesse creditis ? Nostris illi discessionibus ac discordiis clari, vitia hostium in gloriam exercitus sui vertunt ; quem contractum ex diversissimis gentibus, ut secundæ res tenent, ita adversæ dissolvent ; nisi si Gallos et Germanos et (pudet dictu) Britannorum plerosque, licet dominationi alienæ sanguinem commodent. diutius tamen hostes quam servos, fide et adfectu teneri putatis : metus et terror est, infirma vincula caritatis ; quæ ubi removeris, qui timere desierint, odisse incipient. Omnia victoriæ incitamenta pro nobis sunt : nullæ Romanos conjuges adcendunt ; nulli parentes fugam exprobraturi sunt ; aut nulla plerisque patria, aut alia est : paucos numero, circum trepidos ignorantia, cœlum ipsum ac mare et silvas, ignota omnia circumspectantes, clausos quodammodo ac vinctos Dii nobis tradiderunt. Ne terreat vanus adspectus et auri fulgor atque argenti, quod neque

* Tacitus probably meant the Iceni. Cartismandua, Queen of the Brigantes, was a constant ally of Rome.

tegit, neque vulnerat. In ipsa hostium acie inveniemus nostras manus : agnoscent Britanni suam causam ; recordabuntur Galli priorem libertatem : deserent illos ceteri Germani, tamquam nuper Usipii reliquerunt. Nec quidquam ultra formidinis ; vacua castella, senum coloniæ, inter male parentes et injuste imperantes, ægra municipia et discordantia. Hic dux, hic exercitus : ibi tributa et metalla et ceteræ servientium pœnæ ; quas in æternum perferre, aut statim ulcisci, in hoc campo est. Proinde, ituri in aciem, et majores vestros et posteros cogitate " (*Agric.*, xxx.-xxxii.).

101. Agricola so disposed his forces that the foot auxiliaries, about 8,000 in number, supported the middle of the line ; 3,000 horse were posted at the wings, the legions being drawn up in front of his entrenchments. The Britons were so posted that the first line occupied level ground, the other troops being arranged closely on the declivity of the mountain. The space between the two armies was thronged with covinarii and cavalry. When his dispositions were complete, Agricola dismounted from his horse, and placed himself before the ensigns (*ibid.*, xxxv.). At first the battle was waged at a distance. The Britons, behaving with firmness and skill, and using great swords and short shields, tried to evade or ward off the Roman missiles, and also threw a great number of darts themselves ; but Agricola changed the battle by ordering three cohorts of Batavians and two of Tungrians to close in a hand-to-hand contest—a mode of fighting to which these troops were accustomed by the military usages of their country, and for which the long pointless sword and small shields of the Britons were ill-suited. The Batavians, striking with their shields as well as with their swords, began to strew the ground with their opponents, to scatter those who were posted on the plain, and at length to ascend the hill. Meanwhile the other cohorts, with similar impetuosity, overturned all who came near them, leaving many of the enemy wounded, and some uninjured, behind them in their haste. While this was going on, the enemy's cavalry fled. The covinarii mingled confusedly with the foot, and though at first a source of dread to the Romans, they now found themselves inextricably mixed in the dense masses, and hampered by the uneven ground. Thus

the infantry, weary of being long on foot, were also surged about by the mounted troops amongst them, and the confusion was heightened by straying chariots and riderless horses, which dashed against whatever came in their way (*ibid.*, xxxvi.).

102. The Britons upon the summit of the hill, who had not yet been engaged, and idly scorned the paucity of their opponents, now began gradually to descend and fall upon their rear. Agricola met the danger by opposing to them four alæ of horse which he had reserved for emergencies, and they were put to flight, but other alæ, which were detailed from the front of the battle for this purpose, intercepted them. Then a grand and horrible spectacle was seen upon the plain. The victors, pursuing and dealing wounds, also took some prisoners, only to slaughter them when others came within reach. Large bodies of warriors fled before a few ; some rushed unarmed amidst their enemies, and voluntarily offered themselves to death. Weapons, corpses, limbs, and blood were scattered everywhere. Here and there the anger and valour of the vanquished were manifested. Parties who had fled to the woods would suddenly fall upon those who were too incautiously pursuing, and the indefatigable alertness of Agricola could not avert some loss ; but no opposition was dared to any considerable body. Night and satiety put an end to the slaughter. The Britons lost in slain about 10,000 ; the Romans 360 (variously stated at 340), among whom was Aulus Atticus, prefect of a cohort, who was carried amongst the enemy by youthful ardour and the unmanageableness of his horse (*ibid.*, xxxvii.). With the victors the night was one of joy ; with the Britons it was a period of wandering and lamentation. To draw away the wounded, to collect the scattered, to desert and burn their houses, to hold disturbed councils and separate again without result—these were but part of the consequences of their overthrow. Some even laid violent hands on their wives and children, as if pitying them. The next day the fruits of victory were widely apparent. Everywhere there was vast silence, a desolate country, and smoking houses, and no enemy were seen by the scouts (*ibid.*, xxxviii.).

103. The summer being already spent, Agricola was unable to prolong the campaign, and led his army into the

country of the Horestii [204].   There he received hostages, and ordered the prefect of the fleet to circumnavigate Britain, furnishing sufficient arms for the purpose, the recent victory having already sent terror before.   He himself conducted the foot and cavalry leisurely through the territories of new tribes, and disposed them in winter quarters.   Meanwhile the fleet, in favourable weather and by continuous voyaging, reached the Trutulensis Portus [281b], on the next side of Britain to that from which it had sailed (ibid., xxxviii.).   Agricola was the first Roman who discovered Britain to be an island (Dion., lxvi. 20) [11].

104.   Agricola's victory, while it won him great renown, raised scruples in the suspicious mind of the Emperor Domitian.   The latter, dissembling his fears, but none the less determined to draw the famous General from Britain, caused the Senate to decree him triumphal ornaments, a statue, and whatever was usual to a triumph ; and it was also rumoured that the Syrian province, which was then vacant, was being reserved for him.   Some believed that the Emperor sent a freedman with letters conferring the province, with instructions to deliver them if he found Agricola in Britain ; but, meeting him on the sea, the freedman returned without delivering the document or making his mission known. Agricola handed to his successor a quiet and safe province (Agric., xxxix., xl.).   His government had been energetic and successful, his achievements eclipsing those of all his predecessors in the same field.   His strategy had been such that not a single fort established by him was taken by the enemy or abandoned either by treaty or flight (ibid., xxii.).

105.   The successor of Agricola is supposed to have been Sallustius Lucullus, " Britanniæ legatus," who was put to death by Domitian for allowing lances of a new pattern to be called " Luculleæ " (Suet. Vit. Dom., x.).   It was probably about this time that the following lines were written by Juvenal (ii. 160).

> . . . Arma quidem ultra
> Litora Juvernæ promovimus et modo captas
> Orcadas, et minima contentos nocte Britannos.

> [We have advanced our arms beyond the shores
> of Hibernia and the lately captured Orkneys, and
> the Britons content with the shortest night.]

During the next forty years we find no mention of Britain,
except in the poets. It is certain, however, that the northern
conquests of Agricola were not destined to be permanent, and
Tacitus, indulging in his usual oratorical language, says that
the province was immediately lost (*statim missa*) (*Hist.*, i. 2).
The truth seems to be, if reliance may be placed on the following extracts from Juvenal, that the Romans found ample
employment in restraining the Brigantes and a British King
named Arviragus, without embarking on more distant enterprises, and that the Briton had as yet lost none of his proverbial savageness :

> Dirue . . . castella Brigantum
> Ut locupletem aquilam tibi sexagesimus annus
> Adferat.　　　　　　　　　　　　　*Juvenal*, xiv. 196.
>
> [Pull down Brigantian forts, that your sixtieth
> year may bring you the senior centurionship].
>
> Omen habes, inquit (Domitiano), magni clarique triumphi :
> Regem aliquem capies, aut de temone Britanno
> Exidet Arviragus, peregrina est belua.
> 　　　　　　　　　　　　　　　　*Ibid.*, iv. 125.
>
> [You have an omen, he says, of a great and
> splendid triumph ; you will capture some king, or
> Arviragus, a foreign monster, will fall from the
> pole of a British chariot].
>
> . . . Nec terribiles Cimbri nec Britones unquam
> Sauromatæve truces.
> 　　　　　　　　　　　　　　　　*Ibid.*, xv. 124.
>
> [Not the terrible Cimbri, nor the ever-savage
> Britons or Sarmatians].

106. Statius, who was born A.D. 61, and therefore probably wrote after the recall of Agricola, makes an old inhabitant
address the son of a former governor in terms which imply
the permanence of Roman conquest in some part of Britain
at least :

> Tibi longævus referet trucis incola terræ ;
> Hic suetus dare jura parens, hoc cespite turmas
> Adfari victor ; speculas castellaque longe
> (Aspicis). Ille dedit, cinxitque hoc mœnia fossa
> Belligeris hæc dona deis, hæc tela dicavit
> (Cernis adhuc titulos) : hunc ipse vocantibus armis
> Induit, hunc regi rapuit thoraca Britanno.
> 　　　　　　　　　　　　　　　　*Silu.* v. 2, 143.

[The old inhabitant of the savage land tells you,
Here was your father wont to give the laws, on
this mound to address as victor his squadrons ; he
established the far-spreading watch-towers and
forts which you see, and surrounded these walls
with a ditch ; these gifts, these weapons, to the war-
bearing gods he dedicated ; see yet the inscriptions !
this corselet at the call to arms he put on ; he tore it
from a British King].

107. About A.D. 120 the Emperor Hadrian passed into
Britain, and, adjusting many things there, was the first to
make a wall (*murum . . . primus duxit*), eighty miles long,
to divide the barbarians from the Romans [Catrail, 164].
(*Spartiani Adrianus Cæs.*, 51). The poet Florus, in some
verses sent by him to this Emperor, and preserved bySpartian,
says :

> Ego nolo Cæsar esse,
> Ambulare per Britannos,
> Scythicas pati pruinas.

> [I wish not to be Cæsar,
> To walk through the Britons,
> To endure Scythian frosts.]

To which Hadrian replies :

> Ego nolo Florus esse,
> Ambulare per tabernas,
> Latitare per popinas
> Culices pati rotundos.

> [I wish not to be Florus,
> To walk taverns,
> To haunt victualling houses,
> To endure biting gnats.]

Inscriptions have furnished various interesting particulars
of this period, serving to show that it was one of considerable
military activity. A stone dedicated to Hadrian has been
found at Netherby, Cumberland. Platorius Nepos was in
command about A.D. 124, and carried out important imperial
works. "Licinius Priscus, Proprætor,"* occurs on a stone to
Hadrian from Bewcastle ; and Marcus Menius Agrippa, according to an altar found at Alneburgh was imperial proconsul,
Admiral of the British fleet, and proconsul of the province of

---

* Priscus LEG. AUG. PR. PR: PROV. BRITTANNIÆ, etc. (*Gruter*, p. 493).

Britain.   In the same reign, about A.D. 131, Julius Severus,
the first of the best Generals of Hadrian, was called from the
command of Britain to go against the Jews (*Dion.*, lxix. 13).

108. Under Antonine Pius, who succeeded Hadrian in July
A.D. 138, the Britons were again in arms, but Lollius Urbicus,
the legate, defeated them, and, driving them back, built
another wall of turf (*alio muro cespetitio*) (*Capitolini Ant.
Pius*, 132).   See " Deil's Dyke," " Graham's Dyke " [165,
166].   Towards the end of the same reign Julius Verus was
legate, being mentioned on stones found at Newcastle and
Brough [282*f*], and also on a stone from Birrens dated A.D. 158.
(*Derbyshire Archæological Journal*, xxvi. 198, 199).   In this
reign (probably about A.D. 140), Ptolemy, the geographer, compiled his *Description of Britain*, which throws considerable
light upon the island at that period.   It was divided amongst
thirty-five tribes, of which twenty-three occupied the part
S. of the Clyde and Forth.   Numerous towns studded the
latter area, and also that part of the northern region which
lay E. of a line drawn from Dumbarton to Inverness, but
only one town [137*d*] is named (if, indeed, the notice is of a
town) to the N. of this line.   It is probable that all the
towns occurring in this author, except, perhaps, the extreme
northern one, were then, or had been, Roman fortresses.   As
towns are wanting beyond this line, the adopted frontier
must have been approximately identical with it, and the
Romans do not appear to have ever pushed their authority
permanently farther into the interior, though their possession
of the Orcades and the existence of Brough as a place-name
in the island of S. Ronaldsha in that group, and at Dunnet
Head and other spots in Caithness and the northern counties,
suggest that the Roman dominion at some time or other
extended even beyond the Moray Firth.   It is certain, however, that the Romans of this period had accurate knowledge
of all Britain.   Yet the Cæsarian notion that Caledonia
trended towards Germany was still entertained, and Ptolemy
held it.   The E. coast from the River Wear upwards appears
in his map at a right angle with the lower coast ; consequently,
what seem to be the N. and S. sides of Scotland are really
the W. and E. sides—a fact which it is important to bear in

mind when construing his geography. Similarly, he tilts the
East Anglian coast towards the N.W. in a manner which
gives some difficulty in identifying the places, and Orford
Ness [137v] is made the most easterly point, that position
belonging to Lowestoft. Even the coast opposite to Gaul
is difficult to follow, and the S. coast W. of the Tamar is
assigned a length almost as great as that given to the coast
E. of that river, the former being esteemed 4' 40", the latter
6' 20". Yet, notwithstanding its faults, Ptolemy's work is of
the greatest value. According to Appian, a contemporary of
Antonine Pius, the Romans possessed more than half the
island, and, moreover, the best of it, and had no need for the
rest, nor was what they had of great use to them. Some time
during the same reign there were troubles with the Brigantes,
who threatened Genonia [281a]. A stone from the Forum of
Trajan, Rome, mentions M. Pontius, who, about the same
period, passed with the Leg. VI. Victrix (in which he was a
military tribune) from Germany into Britain (*Grut.*, 457).
This legion was afterwards stationed at Eboracum amongst
the Brigantes.

109. Antonine died in A.D. 161, and was succeeded by
Marcus Aurelius, who associated Lucius Verus with himself
in the Empire. A stone in Hexham Church, perhaps originally
brought from the neighbouring wall, refers to works executed
in the joint reigns. A pig of lead found at Burton, Somerset,
in digging a hole for a gate-post, mentions both Emperors :
" IMP. DUOR. AUG. ANTONINI ET VERI ARMENIACORUM " (*Reyn.*,
427). Aurelius* sent Calphurnius Agricola against the Britons,
circa 164 (*Capitolini in Commodo*), and the name of this legate
occurs on an altar from Carvoran on the Tyne Wall [282w].
An inscription from Wales affords ground for believing that
in this reign the N.W. extremity of that region was traversed
by regular Roman roads studded with milliare [283u]. The
Britons were formidable in the reign of Commodus (180-192),
the Britannic War of this Emperor being by far the greatest
struggle which he had to wage against barbarian neighbours.
The nations of the island, breaking through the wall (*murus*)

---

* Pio mortuo varias de Brittonibus victorias reportavit Aurelius
Antoninus (*Ric.*, II., ii. 19).

which separated them from the Roman quarters, committed great depredations, killing the Roman General and the troops which were with him, whereupon Commodus, much alarmed, sent Ulpius Marcellus to cope with them. This legate punished them with the utmost severity (*maximis atque gravissimis damnis . . . barbaros affecit*), but his success evoking the Emperor's distrust, he was removed from the command, and narrowly escaped being put to death (*Dion*, l. 72, c. 8). Various inscriptions of this reign have been found along the Tyne Wall. Marcellus is supposed to have been succeeded by Perennis. A mutiny in the army, however, gave great trouble, and the discontents having sent a deputation to the Emperor, charging Perennis with conspiracy against him, the accused was delivered into their hands, and by them scourged and beheaded (*Xiph.*, lxxii. 821). Pertinax was then sent over, and was faced with a fresh sedition among the soldiers, who were disposed to choose another Emperor, and particularly Pertinax himself. The new General was even left among the slain, but having with difficulty suppressed the mutiny, he was, at his own request, recalled (*Capitolini Vit. Pert.*, 301). A writer remarks satirically upon these events that Commodus was styled Felix after the death of Perennis, and also Britannicus when the Britons were ready to choose another Emperor against him (*Lampridius*).

110. The last governor under Commodus was Clodius Albinus, but this legate incurring imperial displeasure, Junius Severus was sent to succeed him (*Script. Hist. Aug.*, 403). On the death of Commodus, December 31, 192, Clodius was, however, still governor in Britain ; and during the turmoil consequent upon the murder of Pertinax in March, 193, and the sale of the Empire to Didius Julianus, he appeared as an aspirant for the purple, being proclaimed Emperor by his troops, who were numerous and þrave (*Xiph. ; Herodian*, ii. 48). Severus, another aspirant, being acknowledged at Rome, secured the neutrality of Clodius by making him Cæsar, with the promise of the succession ; but, having triumphed over a dangerous rival in the East, he accused Clodius of plotting against his life, and advancing in 196 into Gaul, whither Clodius had passed from Britain, he met him

in the following February at Lugdunum. The battle was at
first in favour of Clodius, his Britons pursuing the enemy and
shouting ; but the tide of victory turned against him, and he
was defeated and slain.

> "Sub eo (Severo) etiam Clodius Albinus, qui in
> occidendo Pertinace socius fuerat Juliano, Cæsarem
> se in Gallia fecit: victusque apud Lugdunum est
> interfectus (*Eutrop.*, viii.).

111. Severus ordered the affairs of Britain, and divided
it into two provinces (*Herodian,* iii. 24). His reign was
marked by considerable activity in the island. The Caledonii
[201], about 197, violating their engagements, prepared to
defend the Mæatæ [199], who lived near the great wall, the
Caledonii living beyond them. These tribes were then the
most ample of the Britons, and the names of the rest referred
for the most part to them. The Emperor was at that time
held by a frontier war on the Continent, and Verrius Lupus,
on whom the British war devolved, was forced to purchase
peace from the Mæatæ with a large sum of money, the Romans
receiving a few captives (*Dion,* L., lxxv. 5). Virius Lupus was
legate and proprætor (*Lavatræ,* 214*i*). Not much less than
half the island was then in the possession of the Romans, but
it was kept in continual commotion by restless tribes, which
overran the country and laid everything waste, so that the
prefect sent letters to Rome pressing for more troops or the
presence of the Emperor. Severus, anxious to win a trophy
from the Britons and to reduce the whole island, as well as
to draw his sons from the allurements of his capital to the
discipline of a military life, ordered a vast expedition, and,
though old and arthritic, crossed quickly with his sons into
Britain about 208. His sudden arrival and the vast concentration of troops terrified the Britons, who sent ambas-
sadors to ask for peace and offer reparation ; but these, after
purposed delays, were sent back without having effected anything. Severus, completing his preparations, put the adminis--
tration of the Roman province under his younger son Geta,
with whom he associated the more aged of his friends, and
then, at the head of the army, and accompanied by his son
Caracalla (also called Bassianus and Antonine), passed beyond

the rivers and fortresses which defended the frontier, and entered Caledonia. He advanced with great labour, cutting through forests, levelling obstructions, making causeways across the marshes, and bridging the rivers, and there were frequent attacks and skirmishes. The enemy, however, retired before him, hiding in the thickets and marshes, and refusing a regular battle ; and they resorted to the ruse of driving sheep and cattle towards the Romans, who, when venturing out to seize them, were continually harassed. The troops also suffered from want of water, and, going out in dispersed bands, fell into snares. Some soldiers, when worn out by the fatigues of the march, were killed by their own comrades to prevent them falling into the hands of the enemy. Thus the dead numbered 50,000.* The difficulties encountered protracted the war, but Severus did not desist until he came to the extreme part of the island, when, having almost traversed the whole country, he compelled the Britons to agree to terms, which involved the cession to the Empire of no small part of their region. On one occasion, when Severus rode towards the Caledonii to take arms from them and parley, his son Caracalla, who was with him, tried to kill him (*Dion*, L., lxxvi. 13,´14 ; *Herodian*). About this time mention is made of Argentocoxus, a Caledonian [44].

112. Britain was the greatest ornament of Severus's Empire, and furnished him with the name of Britannicus. He fortified the island with a wall (*murus aut vallum*), which stretched across it, terminating at both extremities at the ocean (*Spart. Sev. Imp.*, 354). Eutropius, calling this work a *vallum*, says it was made to secure the conquered provinces (*receptas provincias*), and extended thirty-two miles from sea to sea (*Eutrop.*, viii.).† It seems to have been the Emperor's last great work, and, when it was complete, and he returned to the next station (*ad proximam mansionem*) as not only victor, but also establisher of a lasting peace, he appears to

* It is sometimes considered that this prodigious number is a mistake for 5,000.

† Þa ȝepophte he (Sevepuꝼ) ꝼeal miꝺ rupꝼum ꝺ bꞃæꝺ ꝼeal þæꝗ on uꝼon ꞃꝼam ꝼæ ro ꝼæ, Bꞃȳrꝼalum ro ȝebeopȝe (*Sax. Chr.*, 189).

A.M., 4207. Destructum à Romanis conditum, murum restituit, transiens in Brittaniam, Severus (*Ric.*, II., i. 27).

have had some consciousness of his approaching end. He was met on the way by a jocular Ethiopian, who was celebrated among the minstrels, and who brought him a crown of cypress, saying by way of joke :

Totum fuisti, totum vicisti, jam deus esto victor.

[You have been all, you have conquered all ; now, victor, be a god.]

Severus regarded the cypress crown, coupled with the complexion of the man, as an evil omen, and angrily ordered it to be taken away (*Spart. Sev. Imp.*, 363). Soon afterwards another revolt broke out among the Caledonii and Mæatæ ; summoning his troops for a fresh expedition, he ordered them to give no quarter, but to kill all whom they met, adding the injunction :

Nemo manus fugiat vestras,
Non fœtus gravida mater gestat in alvo
Horrendum effugiat cædem.

[No one shall flee your hands,
Not the infant unborn
Shall escape the dreadful slaughter.]

He resolved to take the field in person, but died while the preparations were in progress, February 4, 211 (*Dion*, L., lxxvii. 1), at Eboracum (*Eutrop.*, viii.). He obtained a prodigious mass of riches in Britain (*Xiph.*, 76). According to his wish, his two sons were immediately proclaimed joint-Emperors, but Caracalla, though pretending to share the Empire with his brother, really exercised sole authority. Neither remained in the island, and Caracalla, breaking off the war with the rebellious Britons, retired from their territory and abandoned the camps. Geta was assassinated several months afterwards.

113. With the withdrawal of Caracalla, Britain virtually disappears for many years from Roman history, but numerous inscriptions show that the Romans continued in possession of the territory adjacent to and above the Tyne Wall. A stone from Walwick Chesters, dated 3 Kal. Nov., 221, mentions the Emperor Marcus Aurelius Antonine (Elagabalus), who was separated from Caracalla by the brief reign of

Macrine.   Under the next Emperor, Alexander Severus (222-235), a granary was rebuilt at Great Chesters, when Maximus was legate, and a building for equestrian instruction was erected at Netherby, near the Cumberland-Dumfries border, in the legation of Marcus Valerian.   Lampridius relates that the same Emperor gave such lands as were taken from the barbarians to the frontier troops, to be held by them and their heirs on condition of military service, without the right to convert to private use, hoping that the protection of these possessions would impel to greater diligence and courage. The troops thereupon passed the rampart, and settling on the other side, built and manned garrisons, so that the bounds of the Empire were gradually extended to the Forth.   Several Emperors after Alexander are only known in Britain from the monuments.   A stone of the time of Maximin (235-238) occurs at Burdoswald ; others of Gordian (238-244) at Walton Chesters and Papcastle, with two at Lanchester mentioning the Proprætors Cneius Lucilianus and Mæcilius Fuscus,* and one at Old Carlisle, *anno* 242, mentioning the Proprætor Nonnius Philippus.   Stones of Philip the Arabian and his son Philip (244-249) occur at Old Carlisle ; of Decius (249-251) near Aldborough [191g] ; and of Gallus and Volusian (both of whom were slain in Italy in 253 in their year of consulship) at Housesteads and Bowness.

   114. Under Valerian (253-260) and several of his successors the Empire was assailed by numerous border enemies, and great confusion ensued, during which imperial power was assumed in the provinces by military leaders called the Thirty Tyrants.   Postumus, a man of obscure birth, and the second of the Tyrants, assumed the purple in Gaul in 258, and for ten years ruled there and in Spain and Britain, showing skill and moderation, and repairing by his prudence the calamities brought about by late events.   He was slain in 267 by his soldiers, because he refused to give up a rebel city in Gaul to be plundered.   Lollian, who sympathized with the army, was proclaimed successor, but perished a few months later at the same hands, and the purple was bestowed upon Marius, an artisan of the meanest station.   The latter was slain on

* M. Furius, *Ric.*, II., ii. 25.

the second day of his reign, and was succeeded by Victorine, a very able but somewhat sensual man, who had been the colleague of Postumus. Victorine's name is on a milliare dug up at Lincoln [189b]. About this time Porphyry speaks of Britain as a province fertile of tyrants. Victorine himself was assassinated by an officer in the second year of his reign. The army thereupon hailed his mother Victoria as *Mater Castrorum* (Mother of the Camps), and coins were struck bearing her name and effigy; but becoming tired of the burdens of office, she soon conferred the Sovereign dignity upon Tetricus, though retaining the real power. Her end is uncertain, some stating that she was murdered by Tetricus, others that she died a natural death. The new ruler reigned until 274, when he was overcome by Aurelian in Gaul, and the separate sovereignty in the West then came to an end· Probus (276-282) conquered Proculus and Bonosus (said to be Briton by descent) when they aspired to the Empire, and claimed Britain with other provinces (*S. H. Aug.*, 942, 969). The same Emperor in 277 augmented the forces in Britain by some Vandals whom he had conquered on the Rhine, and Zosimus relates that these auxiliaries suppressed some minor disturbances in the island. Zosimus also speaks of a person (but not by name) who was recommended by Victorine Maurus to Probus, and being sent to Britain, caused a revolt, but was slain, and the outbreak suppressed, by Victorine. Carus (282-283) revived the Western sovereignty (consisting of Gaul, Italy, Illyricum, Spain, Britain, and Africa) in favour of Carine, afterwards Emperor (*S. H. Aug.*, 985).

115. At this epoch the Franks and Saxons began to infest the neighbouring seas, and in order to protect the coast of Belgica and Armorica against their piracies, a strong Roman fleet was established at Bononia (*Boulogne*) in Gaul, under an officer styled *Comes Litoris Saxonici* (Count of the Saxon Shore). The office was first bestowed by Maximian, the coadjutor of Diocletian, on Carausius, a German, who was born among the Menapii, and had arisen from the meanest origin to great military distinction (*vir rei militaris peritissimus, Eutrop*, ix.). The Count took many of the marauders (*barbari*), but part only of the booty was made over to the pro-

vincial authorities or sent to the Emperors. Suspicion also
began to be entertained that he wilfully permitted the
marauders to load themselves with Roman spoils before
attacking them, his object being ostensibly to enrich himself.
Maximian therefore ordered his execution, upon which the
Count openly assumed the purple, and seized Britain. The
troops there conferred on him the title of Augustus, and his
fleet, which still held Bononia, became a greater scourge than
the Saxons, carrying its depredations up the Rhine and Seine
and into the Mediterranean. The imperial troops being unsuccessful against him, Diocletian and Maximian acknowledged his imperatorship in 290, and he was now free to
attend to internal affairs, which he conducted with success,
encouraging civilization and repressing the incursions of the
Northern Britons. In 292, however, Diocletian and Maximian,
who had never relinquished the hope of recovering the province,
conferred Gaul, Spain, and Britain on Constantius Chlorus,
and the latter advanced against Bononia, which fell into his
hands with a great part of the fleet. Shortly afterwards, in
293, Carausius, after a reign of seven years, was murdered in
Britain by his Minister, Allectus, who succeeded him, and held
the sovereignty three years, during which time Constantius
was preparing for a descent upon the island. This was made
in 296, when naval squadrons appeared off different parts of
the coast ; but the conquest was facilitated by the energy of
Asclepiodotus (*prefectus pretorio*), who set sail in tempestuous
weather, passed the British fleet in a fog off the Insula Vectis
(*Wight*), and, landing in the West, defeated and slew Allectus
in a single battle. Constantius crossed later into Kent, and
the island was restored to the Empire. In the same year
(296) we find the first mention of the name Picti in an oration
delivered by Eumenius before Constantius in Germany [65].
About this time Dionysius Periegetes writes of these islands :

Τάων τοι μέγεθος περιώσιον · οὐδέ τις ἄλλη
Νήσοις ἐν πάσῃσι Βρετάνισιν ἰσοφαρίζει.
—*Verse* 568.

116. In 305, on Diocletian's abdication, Constantius
became full Emperor in the West, and immediately proceeded
against the North Britons. Setting sail from Bononia with

his son Constantine (afterwards the Great), he defeated the
Picti, but died at Eboracum, July 24, 306. Eumenius says of
this expedition that Constantius did not (as it was commonly
believed) seek British trophies, but came to the secret bounds
of the earth at the bidding of the gods, compassing the woods
and marshes of the Caledones and other Picts (*Caledonum**
aliorumque Pictorum), but scorning to acquire Hibernia, near
at hand, or farthest Thule, or the Insulæ Fortunatorum (if
such there were) [13*n*]. His son Constantine succeeded him
as Imperator, with the unanimous assent of the British army ;
but Galerius, Emperor of the East, merely recognized Constantine as Cæsar, and conferred the superior dignity of
Augustus on Severus. In the following year Severus died,
and Galerius made Licinius Augustus of the West ; while
Maximian conferred the dignity on Constantine, and gave
him his daughter Fausta in marriage. Constantine, after his
father's death, continued the war against the North Britons,
whom he punished with much severity, and then passed over
into Germany. His name appears on a stone found near
Thirlwall on the Tyne Wall. Camden, on the authority of
the Theodosian Code, says that Pacatinus was Vicarius of
Britain about this reign. Constantine eventually secured the
whole Empire, and in 330, on the dedication of Constantinople,
gave Gaul and Britain to his son Constantine II., who became
sole Emperor in those parts on his father's death in 337. The
following inscription, found in 1853 at St. Hillary, Cornwall,
probably belongs to this period (330-337) :

N . . . P . . . LS

FLAV . . . VS . .

CONSTANTINO

PIO AUGUS . .

CAES . . .

DUCI

. . ONSTANTI . .

PIO

AUG.

FILIO.

[Constantino Pio Augusto Cæsari Duci Constantini Pii Augusti
filio] (*Arch. Journ.*, 1855, p. 283).

---

* The text of Eumenius, "non dico Caledonum," is sometimes
thought to be a mistake for "non Deu Caledonum."

117. Constantine II. was killed in Italy in 340, when invading the dominions of his brother Constans, who then succeeded him in the Prefecture of Gaul. On the assassination of the latter in 350, Magnentius was acknowledged in the West ; but, putting an end to his own life in 353, the whole of the Roman Empire was reunited under Constantius II., brother of Constans. At the same time the government of Britain seems to have been held by a Vicarius named Martin, a very just person, who, being offended by the arbitrary conduct of Paul (surnamed Catena), an emissary charged by Constantius with the punishment of some adherents of Magnentius, attempted to kill that officer, but failing, stabbed himself. Paul, however, was afterwards burnt alive. After the death of Magnentius the government was also held by Gratian Funarius, father of Valentinian II. (perhaps as successor of Martin). Two years later this Emperor conferred the title of Cæsar on Julian, and sent him against the barbarians in Gaul. In 360, in the tenth consulate of Constantius, and the third of Julian, the Scoti and Picti (*gentes feræ*), breaking their treaty of peace, wasted the country adjacent to the limes or border, and caused great terror in the provinces, which were still weak from the ravages of former wars. Julian was then among the Parisii in Gaul, but, fearing to leave owing to greater anxieties there, he entrusted the British war to Lupicinius, a warlike General and clever stratopedist, and at that time Master of the Arms (*Mag. Armorum*). This leader, with some light armed auxiliaries consisting of the Æruli and Batavii, and two companies of the Mæsiaci, crossed from Bononia to Rutupiæ in midwinter, and marched to Lundinium, whence he moved forward again with 300 more troops even before his arrival was talked about (*Am. Mar.*, xx.). Nothing more is related of this expedition, and probably attention was diverted from Britain by more momentous events in Gaul, where, in the same year, Julian was proclaimed Augustus by the army. About his time mention is made of Alypius, who had been Vicarius of the Britons (*ibid.*, xxix. 1). Constantius died in 361 when marching to encounter Julian. The latter built a fleet of 600 ships to carry corn from Britain to the seven Roman fortresses on the Rhine, but Zosim says 800 vessels. Julian died 363, and the Empire was now held successively by Jovian (363-364), and Valentinian (364-375). At this period the Picti, Saxones, Scotti and Atacotti [196] harassed the Britons with continual attacks (*ibid.*, xxvi. 5).

118. In 368 Valentinian, being then in Gaul, received tidings indicating that Britain was reduced to the last distress by a barbarian revolt. Nectaridus, the Count of the maritime coast, had been killed, and Fullofaudes, the General, ensnared and surrounded. Severus, one of the domestics, was hastily despatched to attempt to retrieve the situation ; but, being soon recalled, the task was entrusted to Jovinus, who sent Provertuides in advance with all speed to require the concentration of a strong army. Rumours giving rise to increased uneasiness, the command was at last conferred upon Theodosius, a man of well-tried ability, who set out with a picked army of legions and cohorts. At that time the Picts were divided into two races—the Dicaledonæ and Vecturiones —and these, with the Attacotti, a warlike nation (*bellicosa hominum natio*), and also the Scotti, carried devastation through many districts. The difficulties of the Romans were heightened by the Franci and Saxones, who made incursions by land and sea into the parts of Gaul which bordered upon them. Theodosius crossed from Bononia to Rutupiæ, which was outside the theatre of war, and, having awaited there the arrival of the Batavi, Eruli, Jovii, and Victores, advanced to Lundinium, an ancient town which also bore the more modern name of Augusta.* Dividing his troops into many bodies, he fell upon and routed the scattered bands of the enemy, recovering the plunder, captives, and cattle, with which they were hampered, and restoring the same to the Britons, except a small part retained for the army. After a vigorous and decisive campaign, he entered the city (*civitas*, doubtlessly Eboracum) as a conqueror, encouraged by his success to attempt greater things. But he found it necessary to proceed with caution, for it appeared from the statements of prisoners and deserters that the enemy, who consisted of various

---

* Londinium, vetus oppidum, quod Augustam posteritas appellavit (*Am.* xxvii. 8).

Augusta, quæ veteres appallavere Londinium (*ibid.* xxviii. 3).

nations, and were inveterately cruel, could only be overcome
by stratagem and sudden attack. At this juncture a proclamation promising impunity had a good effect, and brought
into the camp many deserters, with others who had dispersed
themselves in the hope of thus eluding their pursuers. The
affairs of the province were now so far restored that he
nominated Civilis, a man of great ability and integrity, to be
Governor of Britain in place of prefects, and Dulcitius a
celebrated strategist, became Dux (*Duke*) (*Am.*, xxvii. 8 ;
xxviii. 3).

119. In the following year, while Theodosius was engaged
in restoring the despoiled cities and fortresses, Valentinus, an
unprincipled man who had been exiled from Pannonia into
Britain, formed a conspiracy, seeking to win over other exiles
and the soldiery by promising rewards, and aiming especially
to get rid of Theodosius, who alone appeared able to thwart
his schemes. The General discovered the plot in time, and
handed over Valentinus and a few of his firmest associates to
Dulcitius to be put to death, prohibiting an inquiry into the
circumstances of the conspiracy, lest the composed factions
in the island should be again disturbed. This trouble being
over, he proceeded with the work of repairing the towns
(*urbes*) and presidiary camps, and protected the boundaries
with watches and advance guards (*vigiliæ et prætenturæ*) ; and,
having recovered the province which had been in the enemy's
power, so restored it to its former state that, according to his
own account, it had a lawful Governor, and was thenceforward
called Valentia [132] by the will of the Prince, as if by way of
triumph. Up to this time a class of men called the Areani
(*rianaiche*), who were of ancient constitution, held the office
of running long distances on both sides of the frontier and
notifying the Generals of any unrest among the neighbouring
tribes. These men were now openly convicted of having
sometimes betrayed the Roman plans to the enemy, enticed
by the promise of plunder, and Theodosius on this account
removed them from their post. These and other reforms
having been effected, he was summoned back to Court, and
left the provinces in a flourishing condition. According to
Marcelline, he returned to the Emperor with a reputation

which vied with that of Furius Camillus or Cursor Papirius (*Am. Mar.*, xxviii. 3). He was accompanied into Britain by his son Theodosius, afterwards the Great. After his departure, Fraomarius was sent to Britain with the authority of a tribune.

120a. Two Latin poets refer to Theodosius's expedition :

> . . . [Theodosium] litus adustæ
> Horrescit Libyæ, ratibusque impervia Thule.
> Ille leves Mauros nec falso nomine Pictos
> Edomuit, Scotumque vago mucrone secutus :
> Fregit Hyperboreas remis audacibus undas.
> <div align="right">CLAUDIAN : <i>Cons. Hon.</i>, iii.</div>

> [The shore of sunburnt Libya,
> And Thule impassable to boats, dread Theodosius.
> He subdued the light Moors and the true-named Picts,
> And following the Scot with a roving point,
> Broke the Hyperborean waves with bold oars.]

120b. Ille Caledoniis posuit qui castra pruinis,
> Qui medio Libyæ sub casside pertulit æstus,
> Terribilis Mauro debellatorque Britanni
> Littoris, ac pariter Boreæ vastator et Austri.
> Quid rigor æternus, cœli quid frigora prosunt,
> Ignotumque fretum ? maduerunt Saxone fuso
> Orcades, incaluit Pictorum sanguine Thule,
> Scotorum cumulos flevit glacialis Ierne.
> <div align="right">CLAUDIAN : <i>Cons. Hon.</i>, iv. 26-33.</div>

> [He who placed camps to the frosty Caledonians,
> Who under the midday sky of Libya bore the heat,
> Terrible to the Moor, and conqueror of British coast,
> And ravager both of the North and South.
> What profits the eternal stiffness, what the cold,
> The unknown strait ?   The Saxon being routed,
> The Orcades reeked, Thule glowed with the blood of Picts,
> And icy Hibernia mourned heaps of Scots.]

> Redactum ad paludes suas Scotum loquar ?
> DREPANIUS, A.D. 391.

> [Shall I mention the Scot driven back to his marshes ?]

120c. Claudius also mentions Britain in his poem on the Dacian War :

> Nonne velut capta rumor miserabilis urbe
> Trans freta, trans Gallos, Pyrenæumque cucurrit ?
> Famaque migrantes succincta pavoribus alas

Secum cuncta trahens a Gadibus usque Britannum
Terruit Oceanum, et nostro procul axe remotam
Insolito belli tremefecit murmure Thulen.
De Bello Get.

[Is it not as if miserable rumour from the eager city
Ran across the straits, across the Gauls and the Pyrenees ?
And report, girded with fears, perturbing all things
From Gades to the British ocean, frightened the migrating alæ,
And made Thule, far from our land removed,
Tremble with unaccustomed murmur of war.]

121. In 370 Severus, Count of the Saxon Shore, defeated
the Saxons. Four years later Valentinian died, and the
Western Empire was divided between his sons, the eldest,
Gratian, receiving Spain, Gaul, and Britain. About this time
Roman Britain contained four provinces [132]. In 378, on
the death of Valens, Gratian also succeeded to the Eastern
Empire, bestowing it almost immediately upon the younger
Theodosius (the Great). Under Gratian the Picti and Scoti
again broke into the Roman province of Britain, but were
driven back by Maximus, who then commanded there. About
the same time (383) the British legions proclaimed Maximus
Emperor, who, crossing over to Gaul, defeated Gratian, put
him to death, and was acknowledged in the Gaulic prefecture
by Theodosius. Claudian thus alludes to this revolution :

Per varium gemini scelus erupere tyranni
Tractibus occiduis, hunc sæva Britannia fudit.
Cons. Hon., iv.

[Through diverse crime two tyrants rose
In western tracts. Savage Britain poured forth the first.]

In 387 Maximus also attacked Italy, and drove out Valentinian II. Theodosius, espousing the cause of the latter,
defeated and slew the aggressor in Italy in 388, and then
proceeded to Gaul against Victor, son of Maximus, who had
been engaged with the British army there against the Franks.
The Britons, on Victor's overthrow, retired to Armorica, for
the purpose of returning home ; but means of transport not
being available, and the Belgæ receiving them kindly, they
settled in that part of the Armorican coast which is now
called Brittany.

122. The victories of Theodosius established Valentinian II. in the whole of the Western Empire. The restored monarch, however, was murdered in 392 by Arbogastes, his General, who conferred the purple on Eugenius, and the latter reigned until 394, when Theodosius slew him and became sole Emperor. The Picts and the Scots still caused trouble in Britain, and Theodosius sent thither Chrysantus,* son of Marcian, who for some time kept them in check, and won great credit in his office. The Emperor died in 395, having parcelled out the Empire between his two sons, Honorius and Arcadius. The former reigned in the West, and had to meet vast inroads of barbarians, among whom were the Picts and Scots in Britain ; but the State was relieved from this last danger in 396 by, or at the instance of, Stilicho, the Emperor's father-in-law, whose success is referred to by Claudian :

> Inde Caledonio velata Britannia monstro,
> Ferro picta genas, cujus vestigia verrit,
> Cærulus, oceanique æstum mentitur amictus,
> Me quoque vicinis pereuntem gentibus, inquit
> Munivit stilicho, totam cum Scotus Iernen
> Movit, et infesto spumavit remige Tethys.
> Illius effectum curis ne bella timerem
> Scotica, ne Pictum tremerem, ne litore toto
> Prospicerem dubiis venturum Saxona ventis.
> > I. *Cons. Stil.*, ii. 250.

[Thence screened from the monster Caledonian,
Her cheeks iron-stamped, her azure vest sweeping her path,
And feigning ocean's tide, Britannia said :
Me also from destruction by neighbouring nations,
Stilicho defended, when the Scot moved all Hibernia,
And the sea foamed with hostile cars.
By his efforts it happened that I feared
Neither Scotch weapons nor the Pict, nor scanned the entire shore
In expectation of the Saxon borne by changeful winds.]

> . . . Domito quod Saxone Tethys
> Mitior, aut fracto secura Britannia Picto.
> > *In Eutrop.*, i.

[That the Saxon being vanquished, Tethys more mild,
Or Britannia safe from broken Pict.]

---

* Chrysantus, styled Vicarius, was afterwards Bishop in the Novatian Church at Constantinople.—*Socrates.*

123a. Claudian refers to the withdrawal of a legion from the island for the war of Stilicho against Alaric (A.D. 403) :

> Venit et extremis legio prætenta Britannis
> Quæ Scoto dat frena truci, ferroque notatas
> Perlegit exsangues Picto moriente figuras.
>
> *De Bell. Get.*

[There came also the legion, advance guard to the Britons
Which gave the bridle to the savage Scot, and saw
The iron-stamped figures fade upon the dying Pict.]

123b. Sparsas imperii vires constringit in unum
> Depositum : quæ Sarmaticis custodia ripis,
> Quæ sævis objecta Getis, quæ Saxona frenat,
> Vel Scotum legio. Quantæ cinxere cohortes
> Oceanum.
>
> CLAUD.: *Epith. Pall. et Celer.*, 87.

[He gathered together the scattered forces of the empire :
The legion which guards Sarmatian frontiers,
Which opposes the Geti, which bridles the Saxon,
Or the Scot. What great cohorts compassed the ocean !]

123c. A few years later Rutilius thus refers to these northern regions :

> Nec tantum duris nituit sapientia rebus :
> Pectore non alio prosperiora tulit.
> Conscius Oceanus virtutum, conscia Thule,
> Et quæcumque ferox arva Britannus arat :
> Qua Præfectorum vicibus frenata potestas
> Perpetuum magni fænus amoris habet.
> Extremum pars illa quidem discessit in orbem,
> Sed tamquam medio rector in orbe fuit.·
>
> CLAUD. RUT., iter. i., 497-504.

124. The withdrawal of troops from Britain at the beginning of the fifth century afforded an opportunity for the Picts and Scots to renew their ravages. The confusion was increased by the revolutionary violence of such imperial troops as still remained, who, fearing that the Vandals might pass over and subdue them with the rest, revolted from Honorius, and proclaimed Marcus Emperor. This man was soon deposed and killed, and Gratian, a Briton, another usurper, who succeeded him, was murdered by the soldiery in 407, after a reign of less than four months. Constantine then assumed the purple, winning favour not so much by his qualities, which were not extraordinary, as by his name, which was considered fortunate, the troops hoping he would do as much as Constantine the Great, who had received the imperial dignity in the same island. Crossing over to the Continent, he seized Gaul and Spain, taking up his residence at Arles, which he called Constantina. A quarrel with his friend Gerontius led to his being besieged in his capital by the troops of Honorius, who captured him in 411, and took him to Ravenna and put him to death. The British troops who were with him in Gaul (described as the flower of the British youth) settled, after his overthrow, with their countrymen in Armorica. The loss of these soldiers to Britain so exhausted the military resources of the island that, according to Sozomen, it was left naked to new invaders. The defeat of Constantine brought Britain once more under the rule of Honorius, who sent thither a new army of occupation under Victorine ; but, in consequence of increasing calamities on the Continent, they were soon recalled, probably about 412, and the Roman dominion in Britain virtually came to an end. The islanders, now harassed more than ever by the northern barbarians, applied to Honorius for help, but he could do no more than advise them to defend themselves ; and in 418 (according to the Saxon chronicle) those Romans who still lived in the island, regarding the situation as hopeless, disposed of their property and retired to Gaul.

125. The Notitia [230-237], an important Roman document referable to about the close of the joint reigns of Honorius and Arcadius (the latter dying A.D. 408), throws valuable light upon the civil and military organizations in Britain in the last years of Roman government. The supreme responsibilities of this part of the Empire were in the hands of four great officers—viz. :

1. *Vicarius Britanniarum*, the principal officer, who was over the five provinces—viz., Maxima Cæsariensis, Valentia, Britannia Prima, Britannia Secunda, and Flavia Cæsariensis : the two former provinces were consular (*i.e.*, engaged in or expecting war) ; the rest were præsidial (*i.e.*, at peace).

2. *Comes Litoris Saxonici per Britanniam* (*Count of the Saxon Shore in Britain*). His office was military, and ex-

tended along the coast from the Wash, Lincolnshire, to nearly
the W. extreme of Sussex, his troops being distributed in
nine garrisons.

3. *Comes Britanniarum* (*Count of the Britains*). His office
was also military, comprising the Provincia Britanniæ, which
seems to have included those parts of the præsidial provinces
which were outside the Saxon Shore. His troops consisted
of three bodies of infantry and six of horse, but their stations
are not recorded.

4. *Dux Britanniarum* (*Duke of the Britains*). His office
was military, and probably extended over the consular
provinces. The Sixth Legion (undoubtedly stationed at
Eboracum) and thirteen other garrisons are enumerated in
his southern command, and twenty-three garrisons in his
northern command, the latter lying along the Linea Valli
[*line of the* (*Tyne*) *wall*].

126. About the period of the Notitia, Roman history
ceases to take notice of Britain, and the only guide to later
events there is the monkish work of Gildas, whose stories were
subsequently copied more or less accurately by Nennius and
Bede. According to this author, the Britons, being driven
to extremities by the Picts and Scots, appealed to Rome, and
were assisted by a legion, which drove back the enemy and
ordered the people to build a wall between the two seas ; but
the structure, being made by the vulgar without a guide, and
chiefly with turf, did no good (*Gild.*, xii.). From the title
of this chapter in the old capitula, the wall here mentioned is
Graham's Dyke :

[Consilium Romani eis (Britonibus) dederunt], ut inter duo maria
murum per millia passuum plurima trans insulam instruerent, a mari
Scotiæ usque ad mare Hiberniæ, à Kair Eden civitate antiquissima,
duorum ferme millium spatio à monasterio Abercurnig (quod nunc
vocatur Abercorn) ad occidentem, tendens contra occidentem, juxta
urbem Alcluth.

Bede assigns the wall to the same isthmus, and defines its
course thus :

Incipit autem duorum ferme millium spatio à monasterio Æber-
curnig ad occidentem, in loco qui sermone Pictorum Pænfahel, lingua
autem Anglorum Peneltun appellatur ; et tendens contra occidentem
terminatur juxta urbem Alcluith (*Ecc. Hist.*, i. 12).

127. Gildas (chap. 13, 14) states that when the legion had returned to Rome in triumph, the barbarians again renewed their incursions, and the islanders a second time appealed for help to their old masters, who sent troops, by which the assailants were driven back with prodigious slaughter. The Romans, with the aid of the Britons, now erected a strong stone wall, at public and private expense, and in a direct line from sea to sea ; they also constructed towers at intervals along the S. coast, where inroads of barbarians were feared, and, having encouraged the Britons with manly advice and given them models for making arms, left the island for the last time. The title of the fourteenth chapter of Gildas identifies the new wall with the Tyne :

Murum [fecerunt Romani] à mari Norwagiæ [351*h*] usque ad Mare Gallwadiæ [351*d*], per octo pedes latum et duodecim altum. Et turres per intervalla construxerunt, eo in loco ubi Severus imperator maximam fossam firmissimumque vallum crebris insuper turribus communiter per cxxxii. passuum longe antefecerat *i.e.* a villa quæ Anglice Wallesende dicitur, Latine vero caput muri interpretatur ; quæ est juxta Tinemuthe.

Bede's account of the second wall follows Gildas', but omits the geographical names, and only fixes the site by the remark that it lay near the trench of Severus (*Ecc. Hist.*, i., 12). The title to Nennius (xxiv) refers to the Tyne wall as made by Severus II. :

De secundo etiam Severo, qui solita structura, murum alterum . . . fieri a Tinmuthe usque Rouvenes (Boulness [214*d*]) præcepit.

128. The Britons solicited help from the Romans a third time, sending into Gaul to Agitius (Ætius), then Consul, to whom letters were addressed styled " Gemitus Britannorum " (*Groans of the Britons*), in which they complained that the barbarians drove them to the sea and the sea drove them back to the barbarians (*Gild.*, 17). Bede relates that this was in the twenty-third year of Theodosius II. (A.D. 446.) The Romans, however, were now too seriously pressed by the continental barbarians to be able to assist the Britons, who soon afterwards called in the Saxons.

129. The stories of Gildas can scarcely be regarded as historical ; and the first and second appeals to Rome, if ever made, most probably belong to the period from Maximus to Victorine (A.D. 388-411). Nennius (chaps. xxx., xxxi.) says, indeed, that both appeals were preceded by revolts against the Empire and massacres of its deputies, thus making them anterior to the voluntary evacuation. Richard (II., i. 36-39), adopting the same view, dates the first appeal A.D. 396, the second (temp. Stilicho) 400, the final evacuation 411, and the appeal to Ætius in 446. He is himself inconsistent, however, for his remark in one place that the appeal to Ætius was in vain (ibid.) is not easily reconcilable with the statement in another place that this General repaired the wall between the Forth and Clyde (I., vi. 42).

130. After the evacuation the old name " Albion," in the form " Albania," appears as the appellation of a native kingdom in N. Britain. The Scottish Chronicle and the De Situ Albaniæ mention the Regnum Albaniæ as extending in A.D. 496, when it was under Feargus mac Earc, from Mons Drumalban or Brunalban [201b] to the Mare Hiberniæ and Inche-Gall (Ritson's Annals, ii., 25). The Albanwyr (Albion ; Wel. " gwyr," men) occur in Welsh annals in 1085, and the Albanyeit in 1091 (Brut y Tyw.) ; and their descendants, the Gael or native Scotch, still call their country Alba and Albuinn (Erse, " Alba," " Alban ") and themselves Alban-naich. Drumalban, mentioned as the farthest limit of Feargus's kingdom, lay S. of Glen More nan Albin (Great Valley of Albin), which stretched from Moray Firth to Loch Linnhe ; but the kingdom also extended over Breadalbane (Perthshire), and in reality comprised most of what is now Scotland. A version of the above legend of Feargus says that he reigned " in Scotia ultra Drumalban usque Sluagh muner et usque ad Inchegal " ; and another that he held part of Britain with the tribe Dalraida (cum gente Dalraida partem Britanniæ). Inchegall ("innis gual ") and Sluagh muner ("moine ") are now the Rhinns of Galloway and Solway Moss.

131a. In S. Britain the semi-Romanized Britons were harassed by Germanic inroads. In the reign of Marcian and Valentinian, who assumed the Roman Empire in A.D. 449, Hengest and Horsa, invited by Vortigern, (" Brytta cyninge "),

came to Brytsn to assist against the Picts, but afterwards
made war on their ally. Then they sent to the Angles, and
desired them to help, describing the worthlessness of the
Brytwalana and the richness of the land. Men accordingly
came from three powers of Germany—the old Saxons, the
Angles, and the Jutes. " From the Jutes are descended the
Kentishmen and Wightwarians (*i.e.*, the inhabitants of
Wight), and the kin in Wessex which men now call the
Jutna-cynn. From the old Saxons came the East, South,
and West Saxons. From Anglia, which has ever since re-
mained waste between the Jutes and Saxons, came the East
Angles, Middle Angles, Mercians, and all those N. of the
Humber." Their leaders, Hengest and Horsa, were descended
from Woden, "from whom arose all our royal kindred, and
that of the South-humbrians " (*Sax. Chr.*).

Oꝼ Iotum comon Cantꝡape . ꞇ ƿihtꝡape . (ꝥ iꞅ ꞃeo mæiᵭ ꝥe
nu eaꝛᵬaᵭ on ƿiht.) ꞇ ꝥ cẏnn on ƿeꞃt-Sexum . ᵭe man nu ᵹẏt
het Iutna-cẏnn : Oꝼ Calᵬ-Seaxum comon Caꞃt-Seaxan ꞇ Suᵭ-
Seaxan. ꞇ ƿeꞃt-Seaxan : Oꝼ Ængle comon ꞃe á ꞃiᵭᵭan ꞃtoᵬ
ꝡeꞃtiᵹ betꝡix Iutum ꞇ Seaxum' . Caꞃt-Cngle . ꞇ ɷiᵬᵬel Ængle.
ꞇ ɷeaꝛce . anᵬ ealle Noꝛᵭẏmbꝛa.

This authority, however, cannot be implicitly relied on.
Procopius (sixth century) [14] speaks of war between the
inhabitants of Britain and the Varni (Varini of Germany) ;
and he states that there were three sovereign nations in the
island. Two of these, the Angli and Phrissones, are regarded
as the Angles and Frisians of Germany ; but it is not improbable that they represented the old Ancalites and Parisi. Still,
the hold which Saxon obtained as the spoken language of
S. Britain is evidence that there was an influx of German-
speaking people considerable enough to overpower the native
tongue.

131b. Bede relates that in his time (*circa* 700) there were
five languages (*quinque gentium linguæ*) used in Britain,
basing his calculation upon the number of tongues into which
the divine law had been translated ; these were the languages of
the Angli, Brittones, Scotti, Picti, and Latini (*Ecc. Hist.*, I., i.),
" Ænglish, Brytwylish, Scyttish, Pyhttish, and Boclæden "
(*Sax. Chr.*). It is probable, however, that the Scottish

and Pictish were only dialects of the Britton or Brytwylish, or at most distinct only so far as they had respectively been varied by contact with other tongues ; while the Anglic also had a partial root-relationship, which probably rendered it not very difficult for the other races to acquire. An interesting comparison of the Pictish, Scotch, British, and Anglic is afforded by the following table from the various descriptions of the Tyne Wall and Graham's Dyke :

WALL-HILL : [126, 166c].

Bede	Pean-fahel.	Pict.	(Beann balla, G.).
	Pen-el-tun.	Ang.	
Nennius	Pen-gaaul.	Pict.	
	Cen-ail.	Scot.	
	Pen-el-tun.	Ang.	

WALL-END : [127, 237d].

Gildas	Walles-ende.	Ang.	
	(Caput-muri).*Lat.		
Notitia.	Vindo-bala.	(Brit.).	(Finid balla, G.).

It will be noticed that in general the Anglic (now called Anglo-Saxon) presents but very slight relationship, its diverse origin being shown by the order of the compounds, which reverses that of the native tongues—e.g., " Walles-ende," " Vindo-bala." Moreover, Peneltun is not a true Anglic name, being a repetition of " Pean-fahel " with " tun " added. " Walles-ende " is thus the only Anglic name in the list which can be called a translation of the British ; yet no proposition can be drawn from " Wall," which was common to the whole of N. Europe, and was in use at Rome under the form " vallum." " Tun " (suffix), though generally admitted to have been introduced by the Angles, probably had even less to do with them ; the nomenclature of their ancestral tract in Germany is sadly destitute of evidence to support the theory, and this is indeed important in view of the fact that the country where they made their new home teems with instances of its use. Probably it is the Anglic form of the Gaelic " tighean " (houses), and sprung into common use to designate the smallest recognized division of the commonwealth as a result of the civil institutions which rose from the

* Caput-muri is an equivalent, not a proper name

contact of the British and Teutonic elements, and which regulated the townships, tithings, and larger divisions in more recent times.

PROVINCES.

132. Until the end of the second century the Roman possessions in Britain constituted a single province, under a legate, or proprætor, and a procurator nominated by the Emperor. Severus then erected it into two provinces: *Britannia Inferior* in the S., *Britannia Superior* in the N. It is said that about the close of the third century Diocletian (or Constantine the Great in the fourth century) formed four provinces. This was the number in the reign of Valens (A.D. 364-378), when Sextus Rufus names them as follows :

> MAXIMA CÆSARIENSIS.
> FLAVIA CÆSARIENSIS.
> BRITANNIA PRIMA.
> BRITANNIA SECUNDA —*Breviarum.*

Theodosius (A.D. 367) added a new province, *Valentia* [119], which was probably formed out of the northern portion of Maxima ; and matters remained thus at the time of the Notitia, when Maxima and Valentia were consular and the other three præsidial [125]. Various boundaries have been proposed for these divisions, but, having regard to the order of conquest, the following seem most probable :

Prima. S. of the Thames.

Secunda. The Midland and Eastern counties between the Thames and Brigantia.

Flavia. Wales.

Maxima. The remainder of Roman Britain before Theodosius' time, afterwards terminating northwards a few miles below the Wall.

Valentia. The district of the Wall.

CALEDONIA. Καληδονια.

133a. A general designation for the extremely rugged, mountainous, and sea-broken region of N. Argyle and W. Perth and the district beyond. The Caledonii Britanni are mentioned in Lucan before A.D. 65 ; Caledonia first occurs in Pliny (A.D. 73) [89]. It is usually identified with the Scotch Highlands, its S. boundary being drawn along the Clyde and Forth ; but as known to Tacitus it could not have extended farther S. than the Tay. Agricola had already conquered the nations above the Forth before the people of Caledonia armed against him [94]. It is mentioned in the speech of Galgacus [99]. The wild and broken coast-line is alluded to by Tacitus. He relates that it was not part of his plan to describe the ocean and tide, that having been done by many writers ; but he ventured one observation, that nowhere did the sea flow erratically, or receive here and there great rivers, so much as in these parts ; nor did it here overflow and ebb as tides upon the coast, but rushed inwards and surrounded it, mingling with the heights and mountains as if they rose from its depths (*Agr.*, x.). Compare the name with G. cala, *harbour*. In Ptolemy the Caledonii are spoken of as a single tribe, but he places above them and the Varar the Caledonius Drumos [201*b*], thus sanctioning the wider Caledonia of Tacitus. Claudian speaks of Caledonian frosts (A.D. 369) [120*b*]. After the Roman period this name became obsolete, the inhabitants using that of Albania, as probably they had always done. Soline relates that Ulysses was driven to the recess of the Caledonian angle, as appeared from an altar there inscribed with Greek letters. In Ossian's poems Caledonia has a powerful hero, Fingal ("fainne gall," *ring-stone*), whose followers are called Feinne (Ir. "Fian"). His kingdom included that part of Caledonia opposite Skye. There lay the palace of Seallma (*Slumba*), not far from Strumon (*Strome*), the latter the name also of Morni's sword ; and at the hill and stream of Lora (*Ben Lair*), N. of Strome, Cathmor encamped when about to engage Fingal. The distinct of Etha lay about Oude Burn, in Lorn. Fingal is said to have lived in the third century. The poem *Comala* mentions a battle which he fought at the Carun against Caracul (the Emperor Caracalla, A.D. 211), and Oscar, his son, fought against Caros, King of Ships, thought to be Carausius (A.D. 287) (*J. Macpherson*).

See [46]; CALEDONII, DICALEDONES [201-202].

BRITANNIA SEPTENTRIONALIS

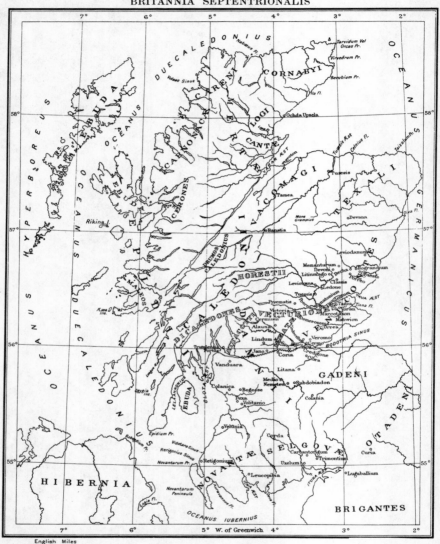

English Miles

COAST-LINE, ACCORDING TO PTOLEMY.

134. Description of the N. and N.W. sides (N., *Ptol.* [193 *note*]), which stretch along the OCEANUS DUECALE-DONIUS [351*e*] :

a. NOVANTARUM PÆNINSULA. Νουαντῶν χερσόνησος. Lon. 21, Lat. 61.40. The Rhinns of Galloway [130]. NOVANTÆ [194].

b. NOVANTARUM PROMONTORIUM. Νουαντῶν ἄκρον. Lon. 21, Lat. 61.40. Mull of Galloway.

c. RERIGONIUS SINUS. Ῥεριγόνιος κόλπος. Lon. 20.30, Lat. 60.50. Loch Ryan, Co. Wigton [194*c*].

d. VIDOTARA SINUS. Ὀυιδόταρα κόλπ. Lon. 21.20, Lat. 60.30. ("Badh eitre"). Ballantrae Bay, Co. Ayr.

e. CLOTA ÆSTUARIUM. Κλώτα εἴσχυσις. Lon. 22.15. Lat. 59.40. Firth of Clyde. Ptolemy's particulars carry this name as far S. as the channel between the Isle of Arran and Ayrshire. This (the Clyde) was apparently the channel crossed by Agricola to the conquest of tribes hitherto unknown [93].

f. LELAANNONIUS SINUS. Λελααννόνιος κόλπ. Lon. 24, Lat. 60.40. ("Lachlan"). Loch Fyne, Argyle; the boundary between the Caledonii and Epidii [201]. Strathlachlan, and not Scandinavia, is the Lochlin [22] of early Irish romance.

g. EPIDIUM PR. Ἐπίδιον ἄκρ. Lon. 23, Lat. 60.40. Mull of Kintyre, the S.W. extremity of the Epidian mainland (199*a*]. CALEDONIÆ PR. [328].

h. LONGUS ÆST. Λόγγου ποταμοῦ ἐκβολαί. Lon. 24, Lat. 60.40. ("Linne Achahoish"). Loch Killisport (with the village of Achahoish).

i. ITYS FLUVIUS [Hades, 2]. Ἴτυος π. ἐ. Lon. 27, Lat. 60. ("Attow"). Loch Duich, near Ben Attow, Ross.

j. VOLSAS SINUS. Ὄυολσας κόλπ. Lon. 29, Lat. 60.30. ("Poll eas"). Badcall Bay, at the mouth of Geisgill, Sutherland. Waterfall ("eas") on Geisgill.

k. NABÆUS FL. Ναυαίου π. ἐ. Lon. 30, Lat. 60.30. ("Cnap"). The Naver, Sutherland.

l. TARVIDUM VEL ORCAS PR. [137]. Ταρουιδοὺμ ἡ καὶ Ὀρκὰς ἄκρα. Lon. 31.20, Lat. 60.15. ("Torr fad"; Arcas [3*b*]). Duncansby (*dun Caithness by*) Head. This headland gave name to the Orcades and Caithness. HORCÆ [32].

135. Description of the W. side, along the oceans IUBERNIUS and UIERGIUIUS, after the Novantarum Chersonesus:

a. AURAVANNUS FLUVIUS. Αὐραονάννου ποταμοῦ ἐκβολαί. Lon. 19.20, Lat. 61. (" Uir beann "). Luce Water, Co. Wigtown ; the old name preserved in Airyhemming, Arriolland, Gleniron Fell.

b. ICNA ÆSTUARIUM. Ἴκνα (ἰηνα) εἴσχυσις. Lon. 19, Lat. 60.30. The Cree. *Cf.* Barbuchany.

c. DEVA FL. Δηούα ποτ. ἐκ. Lon. 18, Lat. 60. The Dee, Co. Kirkc.

d. NOVIUS FL. Νοουίου π. ἐ. Lon. 18.20, Lat. 59.30. The Nith, Co. Dum. [194, 278*r*].

e. ITUNA ÆST. Ἰτούνα εἴσχυσις. Lon. 18.30, Lat. 58.45. The Eden, Cumb.

f. MORICAMBE ÆST. Μορικάμβη εἴσχ. Lon. 17.30, Lat. 58.20. (" Morc mab "). Parton Bay, in Moresby (A.D. 1291, Morisceby), Cumb. Moresby has yielded many antiquities, with an inscr. of the LEG. XX (*temp.* Hadrian), and others, mentioning the COH. II. LING and COH. I. DALMAT.

g. SETANTIORUM PORTUS. Σεταντίων λιμέν. Lon. 17.20, Lat. 57.45. Rampside (" airm seidean "), in Furness. SETANTII [192].

h. BELISAMA ÆST. Βελίσαμα εἴσχ. Lon. 17.30, Lat. 57.20. (" Bla ais-magh "). The Ribble [278*m*], the name connected with Samelsbury.

i. SETEIA ÆST. Σετηΐα εἴσχ. Lon. 17, Lat. 57. The Mersey, which in its higher course is called the Tame. *Cf.* Staleybridge.

j. TISOBIUS FL. Τισόβιος π. ἐ. Lon. 15.40, Lat. 56.20. The Conway [224*c*]. The name perhaps related to Caerdoi, Llyn Syberi, south-east of Caerhun.

k. CANCANORUM PROMONTORIUM [2]. Καγκανῶν ἄκρον. Lon. 15, Lat. 56. The extremity of the Promontory of Lleyn, Carnarvonshire. Cancani [186*c*]. " Lleyn " is perhaps from G. " aillean " (*causeway*), in reference to the rocks called Sarn Badrig, off Merionethshire (" magh "; " rion," *path*). Wel. " sarn "; G. " aisre," *road.*

135*l.* STUCIA FL. Στούκια π. ἐ.   Lon. 15.20, Lat. 55.30.   The Ystwith, Card.

m. TUEROBIUS FL. Τονερόβιος π. ἐ.   Lon. 15, Lat. 55.   The Teifi.

n. OCTAPITARUM PR. Ὀκταπίταρον ἄκρ.   Lon. 14.20, Lat. 54.30.   (" Ceide beithir ").   St. David's Head.   The following equation probably supplies the true signification and origin of the modern name :

Oc tapita ron
St. David's head.

The town of St. David's occurs as Menevia, Menapia in mediæval Latin, and as Mynyw in *Brut y Tyw.* 810, 904.

o. TOBIUS FL. Τοβίου π. ἐ.   Lon. 15.30, Lat. 54.30.   (" Dubh abh ").   The Tawe, Glam., rising in the Black Mountains.

p. RATOSTATHYBIUS FL. Ῥατοσταθυβίου π. ἐ.   Lon. 16.30, Lat. 54.30.   (" Art Stadh Abh ").   The Taff, Glam. This name, referring evidently to the ironstone with which the district abounds, explains Merthyr Tydfil as " Magh-ruathar tathybi," notwithstanding the story of St. Tydfil.

q. SABRIANA ÆST. [278*d*]. Σαβριάνα εἶσχ.   Lon. 17.20, Lat. 54.30.   (" Sopar ").   The Severn.   Wel. " Hafren," (fuaran).

r. VEXALA ÆST. Οὐέξαλα εἶσχ.   Lon. 16, Lat. 53.30.   (" Uig ail ").   The mouth of the Tawe, at Pebble Ridge, near Appledore, Devon.

s. HERAKLES PR. Ἡρακλέους ἄκρ.   Lon. 14, Lat. 53. (" Ear gall ").   Tintagel Head (" dion-aite gall "), with King Arthur's Castle, Corn.   This name is sometimes noticed as indicative of the worship of Hercules in Britain.   [See 293*b*.]

t. ANTIVESTAEUM VEL BOLERIUM PR. Ἀντιουέσταιον ἄκρον τὸ καὶ Βολέριον.   Lon. 11, Lat. 52.30.   Gurnard's Head, 1½ W. of Zennor, Corn.   The first name (" ionad fossaite ") survives in " Boswednach," the second (" bol roinn ") in Ebal Rocks, near Trereen Dinas [32, 39, 45].

u. DAMNONIUM VEL OCRINUM PR. Δαμνόνιον τὸ καὶ Ὄκρινον ἄκρον.   Lon. 12, Lat. 51.30.   Lizzard Head (" lios ard "), Corn.   The first name (" aith mein," *Hill of the Mine*) gave name to the Damnonii [175], the second ("gurna," *cave*) to Cornwall [176]. Goonhilly Down, several miles N.E. of this headland, has a Roman camp and many tumuli.

136. Description of the S. side, which lies above the Oceanus Britannicus [351*b*], after the Pr. Ocrinum :

a. CENIONUS FL. Κενίωνος ποτ. ἐκ. Lon. 14, Lat. 51.45. ("Ceann ain"). The St. Austell River, which falls into the sea at Pentewan ("ceann Ewan") Beach, Corn. Ancient tin-workings occur near Tregonissey, in the vicinity of this stream.

b. TAMARUS FL. [278*e*]. ταμάρου π. ἐ. Lon. 15.40, Lat. 52.10. The Tamar.

c. ISACA FL. Ἰσάκα π. ἐ. Lon. 17, Lat. 52.20. ("Uisge.") The Exe, Devon.

d. ALÆNUS FL. Ἀλαίνου π. ἐ. Lon. 17.40, Lat. 52.40. The Lym, Dorset.

e. MEGASLIMEN. Μέγας λιμὴν. Lon. 19, Lat. 53. ("Magh caois"). See το μεγας λιμην [337]. Bittern ("badh roinn"), on the Itchen, near Southampton. This name in its Greek form signifies "great haven," and is latinized as "Magnus Portus." The place is usually identified with Portsmouth, but wrongly, that position being incompatible with Ptolemy's description, which places Megaslimen only thirty minutes S. from Venta, but forty minutes N. from the middle of Wight ; and the same objection applies to Gosport, which might be suspected to be a Roman rendering of the Greek name. Bittern and the opposite hamlet of St. Mary's were Roman settlements ; the former still possesses vestiges of ramparts of undoubted antiquity, and has yielded Roman coins and inscriptions, and, according to Stukeley, the castrum was surrounded by a ditch into which the sea-water flowed. The local names, Mansbridge and Chissel House, if ancient, may be compared with Megaslimen. See Clausentum [220*c*].

f. TRISANTONUS FL. Τρισάντωνος π. ἐ. Lon. 20.20, Lat. 53. ("Eitre Santon"). Tarring Brook (Broadwater), by Sompting, Sussex. Crescent-shaped Roman entrenchment 1 N. of Sompting, connected probably with Chanctonbury Ring and Camp, 4 N.W.

136g. CAINOSLIMEN. Καινὸς λιμήν. Lon. 21, Lat. 53.30. Acha neas; luimean). D. B. Lamport, Romney Marsh; now lost. Near Dunge Ness (dun; achaneas, *Cainos*).

h. ACANTIUM PR. Κάντιοι ἄκρ. Lon. 22, Lat. 54. (Akin to Kent [168], Wantsum, Thanet [339].) North Foreland [137*y*].

137. Description of the E. and S., lying above the Oceanus Germanicus [351*h*]. After the Tarvidum or Orcas Pr. [134*l*] :

a. VIRVEDRUM PR. Ουιερουέδρουμ ἄκρ. Lon. 31, Lat. 60. ("Fearb druim"). Tang Head, Keiss ("caois"), Caithness.

b. BERUBIUM PR. Βερουβίουμ ἄκρ. Lon. 30.30, Lat. 59.40. ("Ubh Ripæus" [5]). Bruan, under Yarrow Hills, Caithness. Morven Hills ("magh Ripæus"), S.W.

c. ILA FL. Ἴλα π. ἐ. Lon. 30, Lat. 59.40. Dunbeath Water, discharging into the sea near Knockally, Caithness.

d. OCHDA UPSELA. Ὄχθη υψηλη. Lon. 29, Lat. 59.40. ("Achadh fasail"). Dunrobin, near Golspie, Sutherland. The Greek name is apparently a phonetic approximation to the Gaelic, still surviving as the hill-name "Cagar feosaig" ("fasach," *a desert, forest*). Generally latinized as "Alta Ripa."

e. LOXA FL. Λόξα π. ἐ. Lon. 28.30, Lat. 59.40. The Evlix ("Abh Loxa") on which is Loch Laggan. It falls into Dornoch Firth. LOGI [209].

f. VARA ÆST Ουάρα εἴσχ. Lon. 27.30, Lat. 59.40. Mouth of the Farrar (Beauly) in Moray Firth. VARAR [201].

g. TUAESIS ÆST. Τουαίσις εἴσχ. Lon. 27, Lat. 58. ("Dus"). The Spey. TUESIS [207*e*].

h. CELNIUS FL. Κελνίου π. ἐ. Lon. 27, Lat. 58.45. ("Gall"). The Cullen, Banff. The name connected with the rocks called "Three Kings of Cullen."

i. TAIZALUM PR. Ταΐζαλον ἄκρ. Lon. 27.30, Lat. 58.30. ("Tochail"). Quarry Head, W. of Pitsligo, Co. Aberdeen. TEXALI [206].

j. DIVA FL. Διούα π. ἐ. Lon. 26, Lat 58.30. The Dee. Aberdeen.

137k. TAVA ÆST. Ταούα εἰσχ. Lon. 25, Lat. 58.30. The Tay [93].

l. TINNA FL. Τίννα π. ἐ. Lon. 24.30, Lat. 58.45. (" Tain "). The Eden, Fife.

m. BODERIA ÆST. Βοδερία εἰσχ. Lon. 22.30, Lat. 58.45 (" Badh uir "). Budle Bay, at the mouth of the Waren ("uir"), Northumb. Outchester, 1 N.W. of Waren Mills, has the remains of a Roman square camp with foss and double rampart. In the vicinity was Warnmouth, a borough *temp.* Henry III., since washed away by the sea. This estuary must not be confounded with the Bodotria Sinus [281c].

n. ALAUNA FL. 'Αλαύνου π. ἐ. Lon. 21.40, Lat. 58.30. The Alne, Northumb.

o. VEDRA FL. Ὀυεδρα π. ἐ. Lon. 20.10, Lat. 58.30. ("Abh doire "). The Wear; the name connected with Durham [282u]. Ptolemy supposed the coast N. of this place to run eastward ; hence he places the Wear in the same latitude (58.30) as the mouth of the Deva, Co. Aberdeen, and Quarry Head, Banff.

p. DUNUM SINUS. Δοῦνον κόλπ. Lon. 20.15, Lat. 57.30. Scarborough Bay (" scorr ").

q. GABRANTUICORUM EULIMENUS SINUS. Γαβραντουΐκων εὐλίμενος κόλπ. Lon. 21, Lat. 57. (" Gabrantuici " [190b]; "eubh luimean "). Bridlington Bay. Eulimenus survives as Flamborough. Ptolemy's calculations carry the bay S. of Bridlington to the neighbourhood of Auburn, a village now washed away by the sea.

r. OCELLUM PR. 'Ὀκέλλον ἄκρ. Lon. 21.15, Lat. 56.40. (" Iug ail "). Spurn Head, with the village of Kilnsea. The old and modern names are synonymous (" uig," " sprineag," *pebble*).

s. ABUS FL. (Ἄβου π ἐ). Lon. 21, Lat. 56.30. (" Bus," *snout*, probably in allusion to Spurn Head). The Humber. Eborum Amnis [46], whence the modern name (" Amn Ebor"). *Cf.* Foss Way [144].

t. METARIS ÆST. (Μεταρὶς εἰσχ). Lon. 20.30, Lat. 55.40. (" Magh toirrse "). Mouth of the Lymn (Wainfleet Haven), Linc. The name referring to the great sea-bank, supposed Roman, commencing E. of Gedney and passing along this coast.

137*u*. GARRIENUS FL.   Γαρρύενου π. έ.   Lon. 21, Lat. 55.20.
The Yare [235*c*].   *Cf.* Yarmouth ; D.B., " Gerne-
mutha."

v. EXOCA.   Ἐξοχή.   Lon. 21.15, Lat. 55.05.   (" Soc ").
North Weir Point, Orford Beach, Suff., the extremity
of the bank, 10 miles long, which separates the River
Ore from the North Sea.

w. IDUMANIA FL.   Εἰδουμανία π. έ.   Lon. 20.10, Lat. 55.
(" Toman ").   The stream flowing into the Stour, W.
of Dimbols Farm (D.B., " Adem ") and Wrabness,
Essex.

x. IAMISSA ÆST.   Ἰαμισσα εἴσχ.   Lon. 20.30, Lat. 54.30.
JIMENSA ÆST. [178*a*].   (" Gael. I.," *a shallow ;* "mais,"
bank).

y. ACANTIUM PR.   Ἀκάντιον ἄκρ.   Lon. 22, Lat. 54 [136*h*]·

ROADS, WALLS, AND DYKES.

138. Britain was apparently traversed by regular roads at
the time of Cæsar's invasion (*see* " Ex via " [60]) ; but be that
as it may, an elaborate system sprang up under the Romans,
receiving particular attention from Agricola, who, however,
is only associated with the *branch* roads [91], the great roads
being obviously already in existence.   The circumstance
that there were splendid thoroughfares, affording easy inter-
communication between the districts, towns, and ports of
the island, has been evidenced by abundant remains showing
the greatest skill and perfection in the art of road-construc-
tion ; and the enormous expenditure in money and labour
which these works must have entailed appears to have had its
reward in a considerable export trade, apart from the value
of the roads for strategical purposes.   The exportation of
corn to Germany alone employed at one period 600 vessels
[117], so that the carriage of grain and the numerous other
exports to the coasts for shipment must have filled the principal thoroughfares with bustle and activity.   Five great
roads are commonly enumerated—the Watling, Ermine,
Ryknield, and Iknield Streets and the Foss Way—but none

of them, nor, indeed, any other roads, are named in the classics, and the five mentioned come first into notice in Saxon or Early English writings. Their courses have engaged the pens of many mediæval and modern antiquaries, but the lines laid down are in the main conjectural. Ermine Street in particular is carried at one time from London to the North ; at another from South Wales to Berkshire ; and Watling Street, usually carried from London to Wroxeter, is by some continued thence into Scotland. It is obvious that these views cannot be accepted in their entirety, and the great arteries have so many important bifurcations, or are crossed by roads equally substantial, trending to all points of the compass, that outside the early sources indicated, the only materials which can be expected to throw light upon the subject are etymological.

The principal Roman roads appear to have crossed the great rivers by means of fords [218*j*] or ferries [224*b*], but often, and perhaps usually, by bridges, traces of which have been found in many places [267*a*]. In low lying tracts, liable to frequent floods, the roads are sometimes raised upon arches. An instance of this kind occurs in Lolham Bridges [140*b*] ; and it is probable that a similar origin in Roman times should be ascribed to Swarkeston Bridge, across the Trent Valley from Stanton-by-Bridge to Swarkeston, Derbyshire. Tolls were levied at the latter bridge before 1276, and two patents of pontagium of later date are recorded.

The principal Roman roads were constructed with inimitable thoroughness and solidity. Railway engineers, when excavating near Gloucester on the line of the Birdlip-Gloucester road, had to resort to blasting operations to remove the Roman pavement. The parish authorities at Little Chester, Derby, when attempting to break up the disused Roman pavements as materials for their own roads, were obliged to desist owing to the difficulty and expense of the task. Fragments of Roman paved roads still exist open to the eye in rocky places where the character of the ground is unfavourable to the accumulation of rubbish upon them. This is particularly the case in the Forest of Dean, Gloucestershire, where the method of construction called " herring-bone work " was employed ; but in general the pavements lie much below the present

level of the ground.   The road near Gloucester, above mentioned, was met with at the depth of 1½ feet, but in many
places, especially thickly populated towns, the depth is
considerably greater (see London [168b], Lincoln [189b]).   It
is obvious that something more than superficial observation
is necessary to discover the true line of the Roman roads, and
this must be borne in mind in connection with the roads
attempted to be described in the ensuing articles.   An instance
of the consequence of following superficial indications too
closely is seen in the hopeless confusion which Watling Street,
as laid down in official maps, has involved commentators on
Iter. Brit. II.   These commentators, persisting in following
that street, instead of Antonine, have made so many alterations in the work of the Roman itinerist that if only half of
them were justified he must have been a careless author
indeed.   The truth is that Antonine was concerned little
with our Watling Street, and he went along it but a short
distance, using other roads—sometimes running parallel to it,
sometimes touching or crossing it—all apparently equally ser-
viceable, but now generally lost.

Great difficulty also attends the study of the ancient walls
and dykes of the island.   Except in several cases indisputably
determined by history or etymology, it is not certain whether
these monuments of martial art are Roman or British.   That
one of them at least is British may be affirmed from the name
" Attrebatii " [171a], and undoubtedly others are equally
ancient.   Hence the word " Roman " used in the ensuing
paragraphs in connection with these interesting works must
not be construed too strictly.   It was indeed possible for a
British entrenchment to serve the exigencies of the Roman
military, whose strategists were too practical not to seize
advantages which the prior toil of native warriors had left
ready for them.

WATLING STREET (" iadhadh lonaig ").

139. This is said to have run from Richborough to London,
thence obliquely across the island, possibly into Ordovicia,
intersecting in its course Icknield Street, Foss Way, and

Riknield Street. Some authors carry it across Wales to Carnarvon; others describe it as running to Wroxeter, and terminating there; but vestiges of a road in Shropshire bearing the name point to Shrewsbury, leaving Wroxeter S. Beyond Shrewsbury there is no guide, ancient or modern, unless indeed the place-name " Wattlesborough " be admitted as evidence; but it cannot be doubted that substantial roads from the vicinity of Shrewsbury traversed N. Wales, one of such roads evidently running to Carnarvon via Bala, Tomen-y Mur, and the S.W. foot of Snowdon.

The term Watling, signifying " circuitous lane," and probably of post-Roman origin, aptly describes the road so called throughout the bold sweep which it makes between London and Shrewsbury, and this was possibly its original extent. In 1013 King Sweyne, having received the submission of the Five Burghs (Leicester, Lincoln, Nottingham, Stamford, Derby), and all the army · N. of Wæthlinga-stræte, crossed the Street and went to Oxford (*Sax. Chr.*). About 1140 the road was recognized as trending towards Shrewsbury, for Philip de Belmeis, Lord of Tong, Shropshire, then granted in Tong for founding a church, " totam terram que continetur infrà Wethlinge Streete et Merdiche."

Watling Street, so called, cannot be regarded as the work of a single enterprise. Its winding course, not necessitated by apparent difficulties, justifies the inference that it is to some extent an aggregation of roads, some of which were formed to connect particular stations, rather than to provide direct intercoastal communication. Two circumstances favour this view:

1. The direct bearing of the road as it approaches Towcester is through Castle Dikes (near Stowe), Daventry, Dunchurch, Sow, Exhall, Astley, Baxterley, and Fazeley, where it points across Watling towards Lichfield and Stone; at Towcester, however, it leaves this bearing to make a crescent-shaped deviation to Fazeley via Weedon and Witherley (Mancetter).

2. The bearing of Watling between Fazeley and Wall points to Penkridge, and thence by Gnosall Heath, Hinstock, and Whitchurch to the neighbourhood of Erthig, near

Wrexham [187a], at Watt's Dyke. Nevertheless, it deviates at Wall, pointing W. towards Shrewsbury. From Wall it is usually identified with the Shareshill Road as far as Wyrley Common, and thence with the Coldfield Road to Water Eaton ; but the true course to Water Eaton was apparently via Cannock.

These remarks may be compared with *Iter. Br. II.*, between Urioconium and Londinium [214q-215b], which did not proceed uniformly along Watling Street, and, indeed, seldom touched it.

Henry of Huntingdon and Higden state that the street commenced at Dover, the former carrying it to Chester, the latter to Cardigan. This bearing towards Ireland led some to assign the etymology to Gwyddel, *Irish*. Others make it practically coextensive with *Iter. Br. II.* to York, thence with *It. I.* into Northumberland, these being unfortunately followed by the Ordnance Survey authorities, who lay it down for a considerable distance into Scotland, and also southward extend it from Wroxeter towards Kenchester. Those who favour its continuation N.W. beyond Shrewsbury may perhaps find encouragement in the names **Y Wyddfa** (*Snowdon*) and Watt's Dyke, but the derivation proposed at the head of this article is to be preferred.

MALA PLATEA (*Evil Street*).

139b. This occurs (1188) in *Girald Camb.* (ii. 13), who speaks of it as a narrow, rugged road leading from Shrewsbury to Wenlock. The name perhaps signifies no more than that the street led across the Meole at Shrewsbury to Buildwas ("Build"; " eas," *brook*), where the " Devil's Dingle " suggests some superstition of religious origin. Girald quotes a legend which describes the Archdeaconry of Shrewsbury as extending from Mala Platea to Malus Passus (Malpas, Chesh.).

ERMINE STREET ("Aire moine," *Armin ;* D.B. *Ermenie*).

140a. One of the five great roads; mentioned, according to Camden, in a Saxon charter relating to Stilton, Hunts. Its course N. and S. of this place is by no means certain,

but it probably ran from London to Stilton via Royston and
Huntingdon. N. of Stilton, near Norman's Cross, the
road now called Ermine Street turns off N.N.W. at an
obtuse angle, passing between Chesterton and Alwalton,
beyond which it is called " Forty Foot Way," and trends
towards Burghley House; but before reaching the latter
it deviates N.W. across Burghley Park, crossing the
Welland above Stamford, and thence running on to Bridge
Casterton [261d]. Beyond Casterton it is known as Horne
Lane, which points towards West Bridgford, Notts, but
which at Greetham Mill deviates in a circuitous N.N.E.
route, under the name of Ermine Street, to Lincoln, going
thence due N. to the Humber. This tortuous course,
however, cannot be the true line of Ermine Street, and it
seems that, instead of deviating across Burghley Park, it
went on by Burghley House to the Welland below Stamford,
and thence ran by Grantham and Newark, or at some distance
E. of them, to Armin, near Goole.

According to Henry of Huntingdon the street ran from
S. to N. Higden confounds it with the Via Julia. Both
authors write it " Erning," and this has led to the
conjecture that the name is related to Arrington (" Ærninge-
ford," " Earningeford," " Erningefort "—*Lib. Eliensis*, 109,
159, 212 ; " Erningtune," D.B.) in Armingford Hund. (D.B.,
" Erningford "), Camb., by which Ermine Street passes ;
but this view is not applicable to Higden's road nor orthographically to Henry's. Arrington is indeed called " Earm-
ingaford " in a Latin charter of King Edgar (*Lib. El.*, 111),
but this instance cannot be relied on.

KING STREET [182*f*].

140*b*. At the Nen, between Castor and Chesterton, a Roman
road called Long Ditch, or High Street, branches from the
E. side of the so-called Ermine Street, and runs in a direct
line to Lolham Bridges, an ancient structure of many arches,
unquestionably of Roman origin ; thence it continues by
West Deeping, still direct, under the name of King Street, to
Bourn, whence it trends towards Sleaford and Lincoln.

Peddars Way (" feith rais ").

141a. This commenced probably at Colchester, and, crossing Suffolk and Norfolk, terminated at Holme, near Hunstanton, on the Metaris Æst. [137t], where there seems to have been a station or port of some importance. The road entered Norfolk at the Thet, between Brettenham and Bridgeham, and may be traced in its entire course through that county.

EAST ANGLIAN ROADS.

141b. Great roads overran East Anglia in all directions. They included :

1. The road from London to Colchester, which ran parallel to the present road, but from one to two miles E.

2. A road branching from the first near Brentwood, and running through Little Waltham and Braintree to Gosfield, where it seems to have divided, one arm proceeding to Sudbury, the other towards Haverhill.

3. From Great Dunmow towards Abbess Roding, probably proceeding to London.

4. From Dunwich via Peasenhall and Earl Soham to Pettaugh, where it divided, one arm going to the Braintree road at Sudbury, the other to Colchester.

5. From Aldeburgh, via Peasenhall and Waybread, to Semere Green.

Girvian Way.

142. A well-defined road, to which this name may be applied, ran across the Fens from Cambridge to King's Lynn, via Stretham, Eley, and Littleport. S. of Cambridge a road through Grantchester probably connected it with Ermine Street at Royston, and another, crossing Ermine Street at Arrington Bridge, connected it with Iknield Street near Hitchin.

The Girvii were the inhabitants of the Anglian fens. Bede mentions their province, and speaks of Tonbert, Chief of the Southern Girvii (*Ecc. H.*, 143, 204) (Sax. " Suth Gureva ").

Iknield Street.

143*a*. This occurs in several tenth-century charters relating to places in Berkshire between Blewberry and Way-
lands Smithy.   A manuscript, supposed fourteenth century,
speaking of Dunstable, says : " Locus autem ille prope
Houghton ubi Watling et Ickneld duæ stratæ regiæ con-
veniunt." It is again noticed near Dunstable in 1476, and
was known in Oxfordshire (*temp*. Charles II.), as the Icknil,
Acknil, Hackney, or Hackington Way (*Arch. J.*, xiv. 106).
It seems to have started at the Wansdyke, near Morgan's
Hill, and to have gone by Beckhampton and the great temple
at Avebury to Hackpen Hill, near the source of the Kennett
(" ceann aith," *cf*. Hackpen).   Beyond Hackpen it passes by
Barbury Hill Castle and Liddington Castle to Charlbury Hill,
and thence runs under the name of Ridgeway to Wayland
Smith's Forge, near which it seems to have descended the
hills.   At this point it assumes the name of Port Way, proceeding by Wantage and Sinodun Hill, near Dorchester, to
the Thames, crossing which, it apparently went through or
near Lewknor, Chinnor, Tring, Dunstable, Ickleford (near
Hitchin), Baldock, Royston, Newmarket, and Thetford to
Caistor, Norwich.   The road may have been part of Ostory's
scheme for fortifying the Sabrina and Antona.

143*b*. From Wayland Smith's Forge, a road, generally
but erroneously regarded as the true Iknield Street, keeps to
the high ridge, running by Uffington Castle, Hackpin Hill
in Childrey, Letcombe Castle, Scutchamfly Barrow, and
Compton Downs to the Thames near Streatley and Goring,
being in this portion of its course called Ridge Way or
Ickleton Street.   Thence it went by Ipsden to Grim's Dyke
(which ran from it to the Thames at Mongewell), and then
onward, under the names of Ickleton Road and Upper
Iknield Way, by Watlington and Bledloe, beyond which
it is lost.

143*c*. The above description of Iknield Street must be
regarded only as an attempt to unravel a difficult problem.
Some writers carry the street into S. Wilts and Dorset,
where they identify it with Ackling Ditch and Aggleton

Road ; but Ackling, at least, appears to have no etymological connection with Iknield (see Vindocladia [228e]). It can scarcely be doubted, however, that Iknield Street owes its name to the high downs along or under which it passes through Wiltshire and Berkshire. These downs (G. " cinn ") apparently gave their oldest name to the Eoccen, now the River Ock, and to the Kennet, and the first river name in turn, by the addition of a word signifying *hill*, might furnish the name Eoccen-beann, Hackpen (" ceann-beann "). The D.B. " Levecanole " (laib Iknel, *Lewknor*) seems to contain the street-name. " Ickleton " may be compared with Chiltern (" cailc dronn,") but *cf*. Ancalites.

Foss Way (Abus [137s]).

144*a*. From Exeter to the Humber. Ancient charters, some as early as the eighth or ninth century, mention it at Wellow, three miles S. of Bath, and at various places northward ; and a charter of Henry I. gives permission to Alexander, Bishop of Lincoln, to divert the Chiminum Fosse, so as to carry it through the town of Newark, Notts (*Arch. J.*, xiv. 106). This is the most perfect and certain of the great roads, being still open for the greatest part of its course, noticeable interruptions occurring (1) between Honiton and Dinnington, on the borders of Devon and Somerset, for a distance of sixteen miles, where it is much broken ; (2) from Jackments Bottom (where Akeman Street branches out for Cirencester) to Baunton Downs, between the fourteenth and fifteenth milestones from Stow-on-the-Wolds, about eight miles, the true course in this part running by Trewsbury Castle and Stratton, where it crossed the Via Julia ; (3) near Narborough, Leics, about two miles. It exists near Willoughby, Notts, as a broad, green lane, and other portions, though open, are little used. Its course N. of Lincoln is uncertain, but its general bearing through Notts points to the coast about Grimsby. At Leicester the Ordnance Map carries it W. of the town by Danetts Hall and St. Mary de Pratis ; yet it must have entered the town near West Bridge, emerging again by Belgrave Gate.

Higden, following mainly Geoffrey, says the Foss commenced in Cornwall at Totenesse and ended at Caithness. Others carry it through Devon into the present county of Cornwall, perhaps influenced by Ric's 16th iter, which proceeds through Isca to Cenia (see [175*f*]). This street perhaps gave name to Foss Dyke [167], which commences at it near Lincoln, though it is likely that in this part the original road is not exactly identical with the present road.

Buggilde Street (" beic alt ").

144*b*. A Saxon charter of 709 mentions Bugghilde Street on Stanihtan Hyll, and another of 967 mentions Bucgan Streete. This leaves the North Iknield Street at the head of the Cotswolds above Weston-sub-Edge, Glouc., where it is known as Buckle Street, and following the ridge of the hills by Snowshill, Temple Guiting, Benborough, and Wagborough, falls into the Foss near Salmonsbury.

North Iknield Street.

144*c*. Traces of this road are found in Glouc., Warw., and Worc. It occurs near Condicote, Glouc., as Condicote Lane, having in places a crest 3 feet high and 13 feet wide, pointing S. to the Foss, which it must have intersected at Lower Slaughter, near the camp of Salmonsbury. This great camp has uncemented walls, but has furnished many Roman antiquities, and the neighbourhood formerly had traces of a paved aqueduct. Swell (" siubhal ") between the Foss and Condicote Lane, near their junction, has earthworks and barrows. N. of Condicote there are few traces of the lane until it descends the ridge of the Cotswolds at Weston-sub-Edge, whence it proceeds to Alcester [256*c*], being known beyond Church Honeybourne as Icknield Street. From Alcester it runs under the name of Hayden Way to the Arrow near Ipsley, and thence as Icknield Street again to Selly Farm, Selly Oak. Here it is lost, but the pointing is towards Walsall. This street, like the other Iknield, probably owes its name to the hills at the source of the Ock and Kennet, to which Condicote Lane directly points.

Via Devana.

145a. The name (apparently modern) given to a street or line of streets which ran from Colchester to Chester (Deva). It is identical with Ant. V. as far as Huntingdon, and thence proceeded by Barham, Highway Grounds and Oldford in Clapton, Aldwinkle and Medbourn (Roman pavement found), where it crossed the Welland. From the latter place to Leicester it is clearly defined, and called Gartree Road, and has the villages of Great and Little Stretton upon it. Beyond Leicester it ran by Ashby-de-la-Zouch (Roman urns filled with third century coins found, 1818) [259b], Burton-on-Trent (where it crossed Riknield Street), Uttoxeter [259c], Newcastle-under-Lyme [259e], Nantwich, and Bunbury. Though undoubtedly Roman through the entire course indicated, it is now much broken. It is known as Worsted Street in the neighbourhood of Fleam Dyke, Camb.

It may be doubted whether the name Via Devana, if ancient, was derived from Deva. (See next article.)

Devnana Way.

145b. This name may be given to a road which left Worsted Street near Cambridge and ran to Daventry (Devnana [188c]). Leaving Worsted Street at the two tumuli called " The Two Penny Loaves " (which are, perhaps, connected with the name Devana), it went under the name of Worts Causeway [161a] to Grantchester, and thence proceeded W. by N. through Hardwick (where it is called Port Way), Caxton, Eltisley, Eynesbury, Bushmead, Odell, Castle Ashby, Northampton, Harpole, and Classthorpe to Borough Hill, Daventry.

Long Lane.

146. A local name for part of the great road between the Via Devana, at Draycott-in-the-Moors, Staffs, and the Riknield at Derby. From Draycott it passes through Rocester and the village of Longford (Wel. " fordd," *road*), the latter apparently preserving an older appellation of the lane ; thence

proceding by Mackworth and Park Fields to Little Chester,
Derby, from which it went S.E. to Sawley and Six Hills
[219*e*].

SALT WAY (" clawdd")

147. Probably the direct route between London and the
Clawdd Offa [159]. If so, its course near London can only
be conjectured, but it may have gone via Hampstead and
Edgware to Berkhampstead, from which a Roman road
leads through Tring and Aylesbury to Bicester, where it
crossed Akeman Street, thence running by Banbury, Strat-
ford-on-Avon, Alcester, Droitwich, Tenbury, and Ludlow
to Bishop's Castle, in the vicinity of which there are extensive
military vestiges along the Clawdd.

Some antiquaries mention two salt ways from Droitwich,
the Lower being carried by Evesham and Northleach to the
Hampshire coast, the Upper by Birmingham, Saltley, Salt
Hill, near Stretton-en-le-Field, Derb., Six Hills, and Saltby,
Leics, to the Lincolnshire coast.   Salt Hill, however, is wide
of the direct line from Birmingham to Saltby, which would
pass near Castle Bromwich, Mancetter, and the Fenn Lanes,
Leics.

The Upper Salt Way is confounded in part with a considerable road which, entering Staffs from Worcs, passes
three miles N.W. of Birmingham, and on through Perry
(where it crosses Riknield), Sutton Coldfield, Mile Oak
(where it crosses Watling), then leaving Tamworth to the
right, proceeds between Syerscote and Statfold, with a
bearing onward through Clifton Campville and Seal, as if
making for Swarkeston.   It is unlikely that the present road
from Tamworth to Ashby-de-la-Zouch was ever called Salt
Way, or that it was of Roman origin ; the indications rather
suggest a thoroughfare branching from the Worcestershire
road at Statfold, and passing by Chilcote, Stretton-en-le-
Field and Oakthorpe to Ashby-de-la-Zouch, whence its
direct line would point more or less to the angle in the Foss
Way, near Cotgrave, Notts.   This last road, however, rests on
conjecture.

Via Julia.

148. Mentioned by the early poet Necham as passing the Usk at Newport, Mon. Higden, calling it Erning Street, describes it as running from Mavonia (*St. Davids*) to Hamo's Port (*Southampton*). Its course is involved in great obscurity, but from St. Davids it may have gone via Carmarthen (or S. of that town), Pontardulais, Briton Ferry, and Kenfig (**283aa**) ; thence, under the names of Heol las and Heol y Sheel, a road, evidently not the Julia, runs to Bal-las, and on via Ewenny, Cowbridge, and St. Fagans in a winding course to Caerleon (or Newport). The Julia probably went by a straighter route from Punpeius's stone, Kenfig, to Caerleon in the line followed by *It. Brit. XII*. From the Usk it ran via Caerwent to Portskewet, where there was a Roman camp by the Severn, the river being crossed by ferry, said to be one of the three ferries of Britain (*Triads*). The road, if it was ever recognized as extending E. of the Severn, may have started again at Chittening Wharf (" coitean," *boats*), and proceeded as indicated by Higden, but there are no marks to guide inquiry. Camden supposes the street had its name from Julius Frontine, the conqueror of the Silures, but it is possibly from G. "gual," *coal*, that mineral which seems to have been known to the Romans, abounding along the line of this street W. of the Severn. See [293a].

Sarn Helen (" aisre," *sarn ;* " aillean ").

149. A N. continuation of the Via Julia, said to commence at Neath, and thence crossing the rugged counties of Glamorgan, Carmarthen, Cardigan, Montgomery, Merioneth. and Carnarvon, terminates near the Conway. There are many vestiges of this road, its ridge being traceable in places for considerable distances, and its elevated surface, clothed with smooth turf, is in pleasing contrast to the general asperity of the country. It is popularly said to have been made by a British Princess, Helena, mother of Constantine the Great, but this notion rests only on the similarity of names. It was

no doubt the work of the Roman military, whose character-
istic paving is found several feet beneath the turf.

This name seems to be connected with Elennith ("aillean
ait "), used by Gerald Cambrensis of the mountainous region
of Mid-Wales, in which rises the Elan, a tributary of the
Wye. Elennith, by means of the prefix " abh " and the
substitution of " luimean " for " ith," furnished the modern
name Plinlimmon.

AKEMAN STREET (" Ugg moin ").

150. A road branching from the Foss Way at Jackment's
Bottom in Rodmarton, Glouc., and running to Cirencester,
where it points N.E.E. across the island.   From Cirencester
it runs to the Windrush near Burford, being in this portion
designated " the Ikneild Roman Way " on the original
Ordnance Survey.   Thence the same authority carries it
under the name of Akeman to Chesterton, near Bicester,
and then S.E. to Tring, there crossing Iknield Street and
pointing to London.   It is probable, however, that Akeman
Street did not enter Chesterton, but deviated where Avesditch
touched the Cherwell, passing by Stratton Audley, Stony
Stratford, Olney, Harrold, and Kimbolton to Alconbury
(D.B. Acumesberie; A.D. 1199, Gumencestr'), Hunts, where
an old road crosses Ermine Street, pointing to the fenny
tract between Higney, Ugg Mere, and Ramsey.   If this was
the true course of the street (and the old orthography of Alconbury countenances the view), its purpose was apparently to
provide communication between the Antona and Sabrina
lines of Ostory.

The course indicated on the Ordnance maps—Bath to
London, via Bicester—cannot be regarded as a single road,
since the direct route between those places ran through
Silchester, and the road between Bath and Cirencester was
clearly part of the Foss.   The extension of Akeman Street
to Bath was perhaps conjectured from the Roman name
" Aquæ," but the conjecture must have been ancient, as
Bath is called Acemannesceastre by a Saxon antiquary
A.D. 973 :

On þæꝛe ealðan byꝛiᵹ	At the old borough
Acemanneꝛ-ceaſtꝛe	Acemannesceastre,
Ac hie buend	Which those dwelling there
Oðꝛe ꝛoꝛðe beoꝛnaꝛ	(That is, the moderns)
Baðan nemnað.	Have named Bath.

Sax. Chr.

This street, under the name "Iksman," is sometimes carried into S. Wales, and there identified with the Via Julia.

RIKNIELD STREET.

151. A note by Selden to the Polychronicon mentions an ancient deed of land bounded near Birmingham, Warw., by Recneld ; and Pegge, the Derbyshire antiquary, found the name Rignall Street in a map (*circa* 1600) of the country about Tapton Moor, Chesterfield, Derb. (*Arch. J.*, xiv. 101-3). The road commenced in the district of Archenfield (Wel. Ergengl ; Ang. Urchenfield ; *Sax. Chr.*, 918, Ircinga-felda), bordering on the Monnow between Hereford and Monmouth. It ran by Worcester, Droitwich, Sutton Coldfield, Wall, Derby, Tapton, and Temple Brough [2840] to Castleford [218*l*], where it either ended at or intersected the great road of Ant. II. (North Watling Street). If it went further N., it went to Aldborough, and thence to Catterick, the Tyne Wall, and Roxburgh, along the line which is generally regarded as the North Watling.

Beyond Tapton the course of this street is obscure, but it probably proceeded to Castleford via Ridgeway (in Birley) and Masborough. A road leaving this line beyond Masborough passed through Mexborough and Hamphall to Ermine Street. The vestiges called *Roman Ridge*, extending from Sheffield, through Wincobank, towards Mexborough, are too irregular in their course to have been principal roads, and may be either the remains of military dykes or an aggregation of local freight-roads connected with the mines.

According to Higden, Rykeneld Street stretched from Mavonia (*St. Davids*) through Worcester, Wich, Birmingham, Lichfield, Derby, Chesterfield, and York to Tynemouth.

Archenfield, whence this street had its name, was an important district, extending in 1086 from Kenderchurch, in the Golden Valley, to Llanwarne, seven miles E., comprising the bold ridge of Orcop Hill, with which the old name seems synonymous. Offas Dyke, where it touches the N. bank of the Wye at Bridge Sollers, points to this district, and may have traversed it, if the dyke, as sometimes argued, commenced at the mouth of the Wye. There was a strong British fortress in Archenfield, S. of the Monnow [308d].

DOCTORS GATE (" duc toirrse ").

152a. A Roman road running by Alport Moor, Derb, in a N.W. direction to the station now called Melandra Castle ("meallan eitre"), situated on the Etherow (*cf.* Melandra), and connecting that station with the one at Brough in Hope [282f]. A spot upon this road at Hope Woodlands is called Doctors Gate Culvert. Adjoining Melandra is Glossop ("clais abh").

MELANDRA CASTLE.—A stone found here (1771) is inscribed " COHO. I. FRISIANO. Ɔ. VAL. VITALIS." From coins of Carausius and Maximus it is probable that the camp was occupied late in the third century. Part of the site was excavated in 1905 (*Derb. Arch. J.*, xxix.).

STALEY STREET, STALEY LANE (Seteia [135i]).

152b. The continuation of Doctors Gate through Staleybridge to the Manucio-Cambodunum road, near Oldham [214k, l]. Another street connected Staleybridge with the same road at Old Delph.

BATHAM GATE (" Ba tom," *Beelow*).

152c. The road from Brough in Hope to Buxton, Derb., probably connected in name with Beelow, Lower Beelow, and Pedlicote, one mile N., which lie W. of Peak Forest. Batham Edge occurs on this road above Pittle Moor, one and a half miles E. of Peak Forest. Undoubted remains found at Buxton point to that place as having been a Roman station; its name perhaps connected with the Wye, which rises near it.

ARBELOWS ROAD.

152*d*. Vestiges of a Roman road occur S.E. of Buxton, running from that town to Brassington, and passing, at about nine miles from Buxton, the Druidical circle at Arbelows [236*d*], which name may be conveniently applied to it. From Brassington the course is unknown, but it is probable that good roads connected the neighbourhood of that village with Derby through both Kedleston and Turnditch.

MAIDEN WAY (" meidhe ").

153. Commencing at Kirkby Thore, Westm. and running through the rugged districts of Ousby, Melmerby, Gilderdale Forest, Knaresdale, and the S. Tyne valley to Carvoran, on the Tyne Wall. Alio and Bremetenracum [237*t*, *u*] were upon it.

" Maiden " is often found associated with ancient hill-stations [242*c*].

WHEEL CAUSEWAY (" ail ").

154. The name given to the remains of a road lying between the Liddel and Rule Water, Co. Roxburgh, probably of military origin, providing communication between the different posts on the inner side of the " ail " or dyke called Catrail [164], whence evidently its name. It deviates from the Catrail near the head of Liddel Water, and passes Wheel-rig Head, beyond which it is laid down on the Ordnance Map for a distance of two miles. At the latter point it seems to trend to the W. of Wolflee Hill and Rubers Law, possibly rejoining the Catrail by way of Woll Rigg, S. of Selkirk, which may be a part of it. A road from N. Tyne valley joined it near Peel Fell.

DEVIL'S CAUSEWAY.

155*a*. A well-defined road running from Corbridge, on the Tyne Wall, to Berwick-on-Tweed.

OTADINIAN ROAD.

155b. This name may be given to the great road which left the Tyne Wall at the same point as the Devil's Causeway, and crossed Otadinia and the Cheviots into Roxburghshire. Gammels, or Kemmell's Path (anciently Campaspath) was its local name between Chew Green and Cottonshope camp (283b], and the same limits contained the stone pedestals called Golden Pots at distances of rather less than one mile, generally supposed to be Roman milliare.

Salter's Road comes from Scotland into England over Cock Law, and runs to Alnham.

STONE STREET—PORTWAY—RIDGEWAY—HIGH STREET.

156. The names of many roads in Britain, the following being the best known :

Stone Street.—1. From Watling Street at Canterbury to Lymne.

2. Chichester to London, through Bignor.

3. Dunwich to Norwich, thence pointing to Brancaster.

4. Stane Street, from Colchester [218c] to Bishop's Stortford.

Port Way.—1. Near Exeter, pointing to Bridgewater.

2. Salisbury to Silchester.

3. From the Onny, Salop, along the ridge called the Long Mynd, pointing towards Condover, beyond which it seems to cross, or be identical with, King Street.

Ridgeway.—1. West Ridge, a local name for Iknield Street between Speen and the Thames.

2. Roman Ridge [151].

3. Ridge Way, between Milbury Heath and Knole Park, Almondsbury, Glouc, and extending thence to the Avon at Sea Mills under the name of Cribb's Causeway. It joins the Roman road to Gloucester at Lady's Hay Fields, three miles N E. of Berkeley.

High Street.—From Penrith to Windermere, over the mountainous region of Bampton Common and Caudale Moor [264d, 268f].

WALLS AND DYKES.

Sussex Ditches.

157. The Sussex Downs are strewed with tumuli and numerous remains indicative of obstinate warfare, but no traces of a regular vallum system appear E. of the Arun. Two fortified posts there may be mentioned :

Devil's Dyke.—An entrenched camp, three miles N. of Portslade.

Lancing Ditch.—A semicircular Roman work, near Lancing, on the S. slope of Steep Down, with another entrenchment on the N. slope. Cissbury Ring, two miles N.W.

W. of the Arun a series of entrenchments are met with about Chichester [170]. One, commencing at that town, runs parallel to the River Lavant as far as Mid-Lavant. About a mile from Chichester it is joined on the W. by an entrenchment from Oakwood, and at Mid-Lavant it is crossed by another, which was probably the principal vallum. The latter, traceable W. near West Stoke, runs E. in an irregular line through Lavant and Valdoe (N. of which there is a Roman camp) to Warehead (" uir," *mound*), by Halnaker, where the vallum crossed Stone Street [156]. Still in the same direction a ditch is met with in Arundel Park, between Rewell Hill and Houghton. Other ditches exist at Bow Hill, five miles N.W. of Chichester.

Belgic Ditches.

158. Belgia, extending generally from Sussex to Dorset and the Somerset coast, presents the appearance of a vast military amphitheatre, being traversed by stupendous dykes and studded thickly with camps. The chief dykes are—

158*a*. Grim's Ditch.—From Whitsbury [247*e*], across Charlton and Odstock Downs, to Combe Down, where it points to the Sarum - Tarrant Hinton Road, length seven miles. It is sometimes given a continuation W. to Cranborne Chace.

158*b*. Ackling Ditch [228*e*].—The raised road branching from the Sarum Road, on Pentridge Down, thence proceeding across Critchell Moor direct to the great camp of Badbury Rings. The name akin to Critchell.

158c. COMBE BANK.—From Winterborne Clenstone to Crawford Common, whence it seems to have gone towards Shapwick, and perhaps to Badbury Rings.

158d. BOKERLEY DITCH.—Remains of this extend from the Sarum Road, N. of Woodyates Inn, to Stone Hill Wood, N. of Cranborne, distance three miles ; here it points towards Brach Wood. It forms part of the Wilts-Dorset boundary.

158e. OLD DITCH.—An earthwork, eleven miles long, stretching irregularly across Salisbury Plain from Casterley Camp to Knock Castle, and probably to Warminster Down. A ditch from Lake joined it N.E. of Tilshead, and another from Fifield joined it at Ell Barrow [246, c-e].

158f. WANSDYKE [173b] (" uaighean, dig ").—A vast earthwork in Somerset and Wilts, extending to the border of Hampshire. Formed by Ostorius [74]. It commenced at the Severn, on the S. side of the Somersetshire Avon, and, running more or less parallel to the latter, passed over Dundry Hill and by Stantonbury Camp and Bath to Morgan's Hill, whence it proceeded along the hills to Savernake Forest and Chisbury Camp at Little Bedwin. Near the latter it was intersected by the Roman road from Cirencester to Winchester, and apparently passed into Hampshire, pointing to the neighbouring post of Walbury [228b]. The line of this dyke is studded with numerous camps, and ample fragments remain, though in places entirely obliterated. The purpose of this work and Offa's Dyke was undoubtedly to protect Central Britain from the hardy and warlike inhabitants of the great promontories which flanked the Severn estuary. The fortified post of Fosbury, in Pastrow Hundred, Wilts, and the long earthwork or vallum adjoining on Totterdown (" toitear dun") were probably connected with Wansdyke.

OFFA'S DYKE (Wel. " Clawdd Offa," *fos dig*).

159a. The great earthwork crossing part of Wales from S. to N. It commences apparently at the Wye, and, traversing Hereford, Radnor, Salop, Montgomery, Denbigh, and Flint,

ends at Holywell, near the Flint coast, in Ordovicia [187].
Its formation is attributed to Offa of Mercia (*circa* 779), but
it is impossible to regard such a work as Saxon, and it must
be identified with part of the line of forts with which Ostory
enclosed the Severn in A.D. 50 [74]. It served the same
purpose with reference to the Welsh tribes as the S.E. extension of the Sabrina line (the Wansdyke) did with the
Belgæ, or the northern wall with the Picti.

From " Fos " (of which " Offa's " is a corruption, probably
arising from etymological speculation, due to Offa's connection with the dyke when he made it the Mercian boundary)
sprung the name of the post-Roman kingdom of Powys, between the Dee and Severn. In late Saxon times the dyke
gave its name to the district of Salop (*Clawdd Offa*), which
contained part of Powys; and the capital of the district,
Shrewsbury, variantly Salopesburia, D.B. Sciropesberie (Wel.
Pengwern, *Swamp Hill*), is apparently to be read as Scir-
powys-burg; the variant name of the county, Shropshire
(D.B. Sciropescire), signifying Scir-powys-scir.

WATT'S DYKE (" uath ").

159b. Commences E. of Offa's Dyke at Maesbury, near
Oswestry, and after running more or less parallel with it for
a considerable distance, joins it again at Mold. About ten
miles N. of Maesbury Watt's Dyke crosses the Dee, and for
the remainder of its course follows generally the direction of
the river, though at a distance of several miles W. The
ancient native form of this name seems to be contained in
" Clywedog " (" cladh-uath "), a river which is crossed by the
Dyke at the place Erthig [187a]. See Watling Street [139].

GRIME'S DYKE (" griom ") ; AVESDITCH (" fos dig ").

160a. Grime's Dyke extends from the Evenlode at Charlbury, Oxford to the Glyme, near Woodstock. Under the
names of Avesditch, Ashbank (" ais bank "), and Wattlebank
(" uath aill "), the same dyke or another is met with at
the Cherwell, by Kirtlington (" caer wattle "), where it is
crossed by Port Way, and runs for about eight miles, till it

touches the Cherwell again at Aynho. Its course thus far
is generally well defined, and it perhaps had a still more
northerly continuation towards Chipping Warden [258a].
The district has several Roman camps (Chadlington, Ditchley
Park), a villa S.W. of Combe, various military works (Callow
Hill, etc.), and is traversed by Akeman Street. See Bicester
[256b]. Avesditch, connected with the name Attrebates,
and thus older than Cæsar's expedition, cannot be a Roman
work. It probably gave name to the Cherwell (cf. Kirtlington).

GRÆME'S DYKE (" griom ").

160b. A crescent-shaped entrenchment about six miles
long, on Chiltern Hills, E.S.E. of the former, extending from
near Wendover, Bucks, W., to Great Berkhampstead,
Herts, E., the oval camp of Cholesbury being about midway
between the extremities. Ikneild Street passes a little N.W.
of the dyke. At Tring (" dronnag "), N., a Roman helmet
was dug up in excavating the Grand Junction Canal.

GRIM'S DYKE [143b].

ANTONA DITCHES.

161a. These, usually called the Cambridgeshire Dykes,
were erected by Ostory, along the Antona [74], now Granta,
their purpose being evidently to restrain the inhabitants of
the fens and the tribes bordering them W., as also perhaps
to isolate the latter from the Iceni, whose defection may have
been already suspected. The refusal of the Iceni to assist
in this work led to war, and the circular camp at Vandlebury
(" beann tul ") [178a] is probably the earthen mound within
which they awaited the Romans, who, cutting off all exit,
annihilated the defenders. The dykes are four in number,
though five are generally reckoned, and they lie parallel
to Worsted Street [145a], two being S. of that road, the
W. extremities of all either resting upon or pointing to the
Granta. Proceeding from S. to N. they are as follows :

BRAND DITCH (" bre ant ").—Extending from the marsh-
land between Melbourn and Fowlmere to Heydonbury,
three miles.

BRENT DITCH (" bre ant ").—Now visible from Pampisford Hall to Abington Park, one and a half miles.

FLEAM DYKE (" vallum ") or BALSHAM DITCH.—This extends from Balsham to the Granta at Fen Ditton, nine miles ; thence, perhaps, running S.W. by Cambridge [218*f*] to Trumpington (" druim," *ridge*). " Fal" appears in several names on this line : Balsham, Fulbourn, Wilbraham.

DEVIL'S DITCH.—From Reach (Wel. " rhych," *a ridge*), near the Cam, by Prior Swaffham to Wood Ditton, nine miles. At the latter place it points direct to Colchester, and at Reach to Ramsey and Peterborough. The road along it perhaps proceeded from Reach across the Ouse to Ramsey. The crest of the rampart in the highest part is about 30 feet above the bottom of the foss, and it runs parallel to Worsted Street at a uniform distance of eight miles.

WORT'S CAUSEWAY.—Commonly enumerated among the ditches, but apparently only a raised road, the commencement of the Via Devana [145*b*]. Starting from the Twopenny Loaves on Gog Magog Hills, upon which is Vandlebury Camp, it passes to Grantchester (" caer ant castra "). The latter was an important station, and produced the change of the river name from Antona to Granta. Numerous tumuli exist in the neighbourhood of the Cambridgeshire Dykes.

161*b*. ICENIAN DYKES.—Two dykes in Norfolk, called Devil's Dykes, one, three miles long, extending from Beechamwell towards the camp at Narborough ; the other, two miles, lying between Methwold and Weeting. Both run parallel to the Iknield Way and the Ouse (which has now received the Granta). They may be part of the Antona lines of Ostorius.

NOTTS AND YORKSHIRE DITCHES.

162*a*. LONG BANK.—An embankment, three miles long, sometimes called a Roman road, lying E. of, and parallel to, the River Ryton, Notts, from Blyth (" balladh ") towards Bawtry.

162*b*. THE WOLDS' DITCHES.—The York Wolds, embracing the undulating district between Great Driffield, Beverley, Market Weighton, and Pocklington, and extending N to the

Derwent, is thickly studded with entrenchments and tumuli, which indicate that it has been the scene of military operations on a gigantic scale. History, however, is silent respecting their origin, but it would probably be correct to regard them as connected mainly with the desperate civil and defensive struggles in which the Brigantes and, perhaps, the Parisi, were involved in the early period of Roman aggression. Three stations are named in the N.W. of this tract [265*h-j*], and six in the S. [213*g*, 265*k-m*].

162*c*. THE MOORS DITCHES.—The North York Moors, stretching N. from the Derwent, present remains of considerable earthworks—*e.g.*, Casten Dike and Cleave Dike on Hambleton Hill, N.W. of Wass [191*g*]. Lapocarium [265*n*]. Long entrenchments between Slingsby and Coneysthorpe.

TYNE WALL.

163*a*. The great fortification, sixty-eight miles long, which stretched across Britain from Newcastle-on-Tyne (see Vindobala [237*d*]) to Bowness, on Solway Firth, separating the Brigantes on the S. from the Selgovæ and Otadeni, N. Camden calls it the Picts' Wall, and it is also known as the Northumbrian or Roman Wall, and, pre-eminently, the Wall. It is also called Hadrian's and Severus's, but, it seems, erroneously. The district was probably first brought into direct submission by Frontine ; and the presence of hostile nations to the N. would naturally lead to the construction of a chain of forts across this isthmus, which was the narrowest part of the island yet reached by the Romans. Agricola apparently met with no opposition here ; and it may be assumed that, if he did not find the line already fortified, he would be careful to secure it with defensive works before proceeding to new conquests in the wider tract beyond. It is, indeed, possible that the wall was one of the lines of forts and garrisons with which he gradually fettered the Britons. Such a base on the confines of the Selgovæ and Otadeni must have been fatal to the freedom and power of those tribes, while minimizing the danger of revolutionary co-operation between them and the Brigantes.

163b. It seems clear that the line was garrisoned in the reigns of Hadrian and Antonine Pius. From a stone found at Hunnum [237e], it is supposed that some repairs to the wall were carried out in the latter reign (*Hodgson's Northumb.* III., pt. ii., p. 284). It is regarded as the Limes or vallum mentioned in Antonine's *Iter. Brit.*; and this view is no doubt correct. Bremenium, the starting-point of the first Iter a limite, id est, à vallo, is almost as near the Catrail; but Blatum Bulgium, the starting-point of the second Iter à vallo, was twelve miles S. of the Tyne Wall, and the next two stations were situated upon it. It is doubtful if this wall was the one which the barbarians forced (*temp.* Commodus), and which lay between them and the Roman camp. The camp, if not Eboracum, was probably the Tyne Wall itself, and in such case the barrier forced might be either Graham's Dyke, Deil's Dyke, or the Catrail. About the close of the second century, Dion Cassius (as abridged by Xiphiline) refers to a wall very near which the Mæatæ dwelt, and which divided the island into two parts, leaving the Romans with not much less than half the island [111]. These details apply more or less accurately to this wall, but it may be questioned whether Dion did not speak of Graham's Dyke, for his remark as to the extent of the Roman province would apply equally well to the latter if, as is possible, he assumed too great an extent for Caledonia.*

163c. The wall is generally supposed to have been of turf previous to Severus, who is said to have built one of stone on the old rampart; but Severus's wall must be sought farther N. [Graham's Dyke], though it is possible that important works along this line took place under him. A minor work of the latter kind may be referred to in the inscription, " SEPT. SEVERO IMP. QUI MURUM HUNC CONDIDIT," mentioned in *Camden's Britannia*, by Gibson, p. 838. The inscriptions, in fact, furnish practically all we know of this wall; and there is not a single definite reference to it in the Roman historians. The reason is perhaps not difficult to find. The fortification arose, not from a great isolated effort in an anxious time,

* Dion says the least breadth of Britain was 300 stadia (about 34 miles); it is, however, not more than 32 miles.

but gradually, and served less as a frontier work than as a base, from which the changeful limes of the Empire was watched and regulated. The Notitia, about A.D. 400 [234*b*], mentions it unequivocally for the first time. As the result of imperial decay and degeneration, the Roman militia had then fallen back upon it, so that it had become the virtual limes, as well as the only line of defence. No garrison remained beyond the Esk and Liddel, and the farthest station northward was Gabrosentis, in the neighbourhood of Bremenium.

163*d*. A stone in Hexham Church to the memory of Flavinus, an ensign (*signifer*) of the Ala Petriana [237*m*], possibly belongs to the Notitia period. The young eques is represented upon a horse at gallop, with head slightly raised, as if scanning the horizon ; while close by a savage ominously crouches beneath a wall, dagger in hand, as if waiting for a favourable moment to leap up and give the fatal stab. The letters H. S. (*hic sepultus*) upon the stone show that it was raised over the ensign's grave, and it may be inferred that he met his death at no great distance, probably in the defence of the neighbouring portion of the Tyne Wall.

CATRAIL (" uachdar aill ").

164. An earthwork, called also Picts' Work Ditch, said to be twenty-two miles long, traces of which are marked on the ordnance map between the Teviot and Liddel Water, and again between Selkirk and Galashiels. It was, however, of much greater extent, being apparently the wall eighty miles long, drawn across the island by Hadrian, A.D. 121 [107]. It commenced in Cumberland between the Eden and the Esk, where the latter entered the marshes of Solway Firth, and where there are still remains of the bank by the village of Wetherall. It followed the banks of the Esk and Liddell to the W. of Peel Fell, where it deviated in a W.N.W. direction towards Allan Water, thence proceeding to Selkirk and Galashiels, and along the Gala Water to the Forth, where it ended, probably at, or near, Leith. The distance between Wetherall and Leith agrees closely with the eighty m.p. of Spartian. The Wheel Causeway was connected with this line.

CELTIC OR DEIL'S DYKE.

165. An earthwork, Co. Dumfries, remains of which are traceable for five miles, from the Annan by Hightae to the neighbourhood of Tam's Knowe by the Water of Ae, and again three miles W. of Thornhill. Lying in advance of the Catrail, it was perhaps erected in the reign of Hadrian's successor, Antonine Pius, being in all probability the alius murus cespetitius, which Lollius constructed after driving back the barbarians [108]. Alius, indeed, indicates a distinct work rather than the restrengthening of a former one. Its existence when Ptolemy wrote is suggested by the circumstance that three of the four Selgovian towns are clustered in its vicinity.

One of the primary purposes of this earthwork, as also of the Catrail, must have been the permanent protection of this part of the island from the Irish and the Island Picts ; for the possibility of descents by these peoples upon the S.W. coast in the rear of Graham's Dyke could not have been unperceived or neglected. Probably this line was never regarded as a regular boundary of the Empire. Ptolemy notices towns towards the Mull of Galloway, and Ravennas names a number in Ayrshire, in the most accessible part of that coast [271a-e], indicating definite occupation. Corda, the Ptolemaic Selgovian town farthest beyond Deil's Dyke, was nearly thirty miles from Velunia, the nearest of the Ayrshire towns. This wall, perhaps, gave name to Galloway (*cf.* gual), the district confined between it and the western sea ; and the epithet Celtic, as applied to it, if sanctioned by old authority, may be connected with G. gallda, *belonging to the Lowlands* (*cf.* Gall, *Scotch Lowlander ;* Galldachd, *the Lowlands*). "Galloway" and "Galwegians" occur in several forms : 921, Galwalenses ; 1098, Galwedienses, 1102 ; Galewedia ; 1118, Galwethia ; 1138, Galleweienses, Galwenses ; 1142, Galwedienses, Galwaya (*Ritson's Annals*).

GRAHAM'S DYKE OR GRIME'S DYKE ("griom").

166a. A fortification thirty-two miles long, which stretched across the neck of land between the Clyde and Forth, and

originated in the military posts established by Agricola in
the isthmus A.D. 81 :

> Clota et Bodotria, diversi maris æstibus per im-
> mensum revectæ, angusto terrarum spatio dirimuntur :
> quod tum præsidiis firmabatur [Agricola] : atque
> omnis propior sinus tenebatur, submotis velut in
> aliam insulam hostibus.—*Agric.*, xxiii. [93].

These posts served Agricola as a base during his operations against the barbarians, and it can scarcely be questioned
that he was the actual founder of the dyke.   The importance
of the isthmus from a military view seems to have been recognized as fully by subsequent legates ; and it was evidently
retained as the first line of defence of the Roman province,
with some few interruptions, down to a late period of their
rule.   It was not, however, the only vulnerable point of the
northern limes, and the fear of attack by sea in the rear of
this rampart, by Irish and Pictish marauders, must have
suggested the necessity for other and less distant lines, such
as Deil's Dyke and the Catrail.

166*b*. Large works, apparently the reconstruction of the
wall, were carried out at the Clyde Isthmus in the reign of
Antonine Pius, by Lollius Urbicus.   A mutilated stone
found at Bemulie, on the line of the rampart, is said to have
contained the essential parts of the name of that legate ;
and other stones dedicated to Antonine clearly show that
portions of the work were performed by the Leg. II. Aug.,
Vexillations of the Leg. VI. Vict., and Leg. XX. Val. Vict.,
Coh. I. Cugernorum, and Coh. I. Tungrorum (*Roy's Mil.
Ant.*, 151, 165-6).   It is generally assumed upon the authority
of Capitoline, that this new structure was of turf [Deil's
Dyke, 165].   It was clearly the " vast ditch " over which
Severus passed into Caledonia about 208 ; and the wall built
by Severus, 208-210, though now generally identified with
the Tyne Wall, must have been on this line.   Its length
of thirty - two m.p., stated by Eutropius and his contemporary, Aurelius Victor, definitely points to the Clyde
Isthmus ; and it is scarcely conceivable that a wall intended
for the protection of conquests in Caledonia would be built
farther S.   Eutropius, who lived from the time of Constantine

the Great to that of Valens, is entitled to the fullest credence, having held the office of a secretary under the first Emperor, and possessing equal opportunities for obtaining accurate information throughout his career. Moreover, both Herodian and Dion, who were contemporary with Severus, show, by confining the Emperor's active operations to Caledonia, that his most southern conquests were among the Mæatæ [199b].

166c. The uncertainty respecting Severus's Wall originated in the works of Eusebius (264-340), Orosius (*circa*, 417), and Cassiodorus (468-560), who state that it was 132 miles long ; but this length is not answered by any of the Roman ramparts, and is obviously an error for 32. Nennius, placing the line at the Clyde while giving the longer and impossible measure, says that the Emperor ordered a wall and rampart to be made between the Britons, Scots, and Picts, extending across the island from sea to sea ; and that it was called in the British language Gwal ; and was made between the three nations mentioned, because the Scots from the W. and the Picts from the N. unanimously made war against the Britons (*Nenn.* 23). Another manuscript of Nennius adds that Severus constructed it of rude workmanship, in length 132 miles—*i.e.*, from Penguaul, which is called in Scottish Cenail, in English Peneltun (now Kinneil), to the mouth of the River Cluth and Cairpentaloch, where it terminated [126]. Notwithstanding this description, the wall did not commence at Kinneil, but at Carriden eastwards.

There were vast remains of the Clyde Wall about A.D. 700 : " Valli latissimi et altissimi usque hodie certissima vestigia cernere licet " (*Bede, Ecc. Hist.*, i. 12).

Foss Dyke, Car Dyke, etc.

167. These works were not military, but had their origin in enterprises for reclaiming the Lincolnshire Fens. The Foss Dyke connected the Witham at Lincoln with the Trent at Torksey, a distance of ten miles ; and is supposed to have been formed to intercept the water from the heaths, which otherwise would have often inundated the adjacent level. Henry I. is said to have made the dyke in 1121, both for the purposes of navigation and drainage. The Car Dyke commenced near Peterborough, and ran through Bourn and Kyme to within a few miles of Lincoln. An extensive bank of Roman construction, intended to keep back the sea, ran from Gedney Marsh, near the Norfolk border, to the Welland, and then to Swineshead ; and others were carried along the coast from the mouth of the Witham northward as far as Mablethorpe, being known as the Old Sea Dyke, Sand Hills, and by other names. Roads are almost invariably formed upon them. (Mablethorpe, *magh-bulg*.)

TRIBES.

CANTII. Κάντιοι.* (" ceann at," *fore land*.)

168a. The inhabitants of Cantium (*Kent* [31, 32, 291g]), and part of Essex, extending W. to the Attrebatii, S.W. to the Regni, and N. to the Trinobantes. ACANTIUM PR. [136h].

In the time of Julius Cæsar nearly all vessels which came from Gaul touched at this coast (*B. G.*, v. 13), and Cæsar landed upon it in both invasions. All the operations prior to the passage of the Thames also occurred within its limits. The Cantii, however, are not named among the tribes which opposed or submitted to him ; but he mentions four Cantic kings (*reges*), who were overcome in the attack on the Roman naval camp, near the close of the second war [61]. These kings were probably subordinate chiefs, or district governors, owing obedience to Cassivellaun as the supreme commander in the war. Q. Laberius Durus was killed in this territory [58], and the mound called Jul Labor, at Chilham, near Canterbury, has been thought to be his grave. Very many tumuli, early called Dane's Banks, existed at Chartham in the same neighbourhood. On the Claudian invasion Cantium was again doubtlessly the landing-place of the Romans ; and its Essex territory, at the mouth of the Thames, was the boggy retreat of the Britons prior to the death of Togodumn [70]. Cantium maintained its importance as the great *entrepôt* of Britain as long as Roman

* The Greek quotations in the tribal section, unless otherwise stated, as well as the latitudes and longitudes, are from Ptolemy.

influence lasted. Ptolemy mentions three towns : one, Londinium, being in the territory N. of the Thames, the others
S. of that river.

168b. LONDINIUM [117, 118, 214a, 216-222], Londinium
Augusta [260a] ; Cair Londein [290c]. Λονδίνιον, Lon. 20,
Lat. 54 (Lon, *Holborn Brook*, " dun "), London. The modern
Gaelic name Lunnuinn, seems composed of Lon-beann. This
place rose to great importance under the Romans, but its
earlier history is unknown. First noticed A.D. 61, when,
although not a colony, it was a great emporium :

> Londinium cognomento quidem coloniæ non in-
> signe, sed copia negotiatorum et commeatuum
> maxime celebre.—*Tac. Ann.*, xiv. 33.

In that year the strategy of Suetonius led to its temporary
abandonment to destruction at the hands of the Iceni and
allies [83] ; but it soon recovered from this blow, and in less
than a century afterwards it was the best-known city of
Britain, judging from the *It. Brit.*, for eight of the fifteen
Iters mention it.   If reliance may be placed upon the panegyric
of Eumeny on Constantius Chlorus, the Franks appeared
in Britain in the time of that Emperor, and engaging with
the Romans, sacked London ; but some imperial troops·
missing their way on a foggy sea, arrived at the town, and
destroyed promiscuously the whole remains of the mercenary
multitude of barbarians, which attempted flight. The Roman
antiquities of London are numerous, but in general, the site
of the city lies many feet below the present surface. Sir C.
Wren, when excavating for the foundations of St. Paul's,
found British graves intermixed with Roman urns at a depth
of 18 feet ; and he laid the foundations of the steeple of
St. Mary-le-Bow, Cheapside, on the causeway of a Roman
road, which the excavations had brought to light. This
causeway was " 4 feet thick, of rough stone, close and well
rammed with Roman bricks and rubbish at the bottom."

Fable states that the city was anciently called Trino-
vantum, that the walls were rebuilt by King Lud, who was
buried by the gate called Parthlud (Sax. " Ludesgata "), and
in whose honour the city was called Kaer-lud, whence

London (*Geoff*. iii. 20).   Ludgate, however, seems to be simply G. " allt-geata," Sax. " Leothes-gata," *hill-gate*.

168c. DARUENUM.   Δαρούενον. Lon. 21, Lat. 53.40. (" Doire uaighean ").   Wye, Kent (D.B., Darenden in Wi Hundred).   Crundell (" cron tul," *dark mound—i.e.*, *burial-place*), N.E.   Dar (" doire ") appears in Grandore, Rich-dore, Hand-dore, all near Crundell, and in many Kentish place-names.   Roman antiquities at Eastwell Park, W. of Wye.

168d RUTUPIÆ [35, 64, 117, 118, 215*h*, 229*b*, 255*d*]. ʿΡουτούπιαι. Lon. 21.45, Lat. 54. (" ard fè ").   Worth, Sand-wich.   Usually, but wrongly, placed at Richborough [339], which was probably once an island, or liable to be occasionally insulated by the tides.   The valley, or plain, of the Stour, between this place and the Thames Estuary at Reculver, was anciently a considerable water-channel ; before A.D. 735 it was called the River Wantsum, and was about three furlongs (*stadia*) across, fordable only in two places, and both ends of it ran into the sea (*Bede, Ecc. Hist.*, i. 25).   These fording places, according to a charter of King Egbert, were at Sarra (" Sarr ") and Lundewic (" Sandwich ").   It was still navig-able (*temp*. Canute), who in 1023 granted to Christ Church, Canterbury, the haven of Sandwich, and all the dues from both sides of the river from Pipernaesse (*i.e.*, Ritupæ point), to Maercesfleote, as far as a taper-axe could be cast upon the land from a ship at high tide.   Another charter of the same King serves to identify Maercesfleote with Northmouth by Reculver, where the Wantsum falls into the Thames Estuary (*Thorp's Dip. Ang.*, 315-335).   Peperness, on Sandwich Haven, two miles N.E. of Richborough, was at the mouth of the Portus Ritupæ of Ant. II. [215*h*], and contains part of the old name.

Under the Romans Rutupiæ was the chief port for trade with the continent.   It was also their great military port ; hence we find it the starting-point of Watling Street.   Shortly before they left Britain it was a station of the Litus Saxoni-cum [232].   At Richborough there are remains of a Roman citadel.   These are described, with other interesting particulars, in the *Antiquities of Richborough, Reculver,* and *Lymne,* by C. R. Smith, 1850.

The place is mentioned by several Roman poets :

> . . . Circeis nata forent, an
> Lucrinum ad Saxum, Rutupinove edita fundo,
> Ostrea, callebat primo deprendere morsu.
> JUVENAL, *Sat.,* iv. 139.

> Et patruos elegeia meos reminiscere cantu ;
> Contentum, tellus quam Rutupina tegit ;
> Magna cui et variæ quæsita pecunia sortis,
> Hæredis nullo nomine tuta perit.
> AUSONIUS, *Parent,* vii.

> Militiam nullo qui turbine sedulus egit ;
> Præside lætatus quo Rutupinus ager.
> *Ibid.,* xviii.

Ausonius died about A.D. 390. The first quotation from him states that his Uncle Contentus was buried at this place ; the second, which refers to his brother-in-law, Flavius Sanctus, speaks of the latter as præses, or governor, of the district.

Rutupiæ long retained its importance under the Saxons. While the first part of the name became perpetuated in Worth, the latter part came to designate the port, which, as Ypwinesfleot, now Ebsfleet, was the landing-place of Hengist and Horsa A.D. 447.

BIBROCI (" beabh bruach ").

169. Between the Thames and North Downs, occupying the hilly district of Bracknell and Bagshot Heath, Berkshire— D.B., Berrochescire (the latter a corruption of the name)—and parts of Hants and Surrey. Cæsar enumerates them among the tribes which submitted after Cassivellaun's defeat [61], but nothing more is heard of them, and they must have been incorporated with the Attrebates, whose town of Calleva was in Hants. Bagshot Heath has many vestiges of the Romans, including the great post called Cæsar's Camp.

REGNI. 'Ρῆγνοι. (" Regnum " [220*b*]).

170*a*. Below the Attrebatii and Cantii (*Ptol.*) occupying in A.D. 150 all Sussex and parts of Surrey and Hants, extending W. probably to Southampton Water, where they adjoined the Belgæ. Not named by Cæsar, in whose time this territory seems to have been held by the Segontiaci and Bibroci. Vespasian penetrated the district, but the tribe probably had its origin in the several states (*civitates*), given to Cogidubn [73]. His province as legatus Augusti included Chichester (ancient name unknown), where, among other antiquities, an inscription was found which has been read as follows :

NEPTUNO ET MINERVÆ TEMPLUM PRO SALUTE
DOMUS DIVINÆ ET AUCTORITATE TIBERII CLAUDII
COGIDUBNI REGIS LEGATI AUGUSTI IN BRITANNIA COL-
LEGIUM FABRORUM ET QUI EO SODALES DE SUO DEDI-
CAVERUNT, DONATE AREAM PUDENTE PUDENTINIS
FILIO.

The only actual mention of the tribe occurs in *Ptolemy*. The people are commonly but wrongly identified with the Bibroci. A part only of the latter tribe was merged in them. Ptolemy mentions one town.

170*b*. NEOMAGUS. Νοιόμαγος. Lon. 19.45, Lat. 53.25. (" Nith magh.") Meon (" magh neo ") on the Meon, Hants. This station was the large camp on Old Winchester Hill.

ATTREBATES (*Caes.*). 'Ατρεβάτιοι. (" Eitre fos," *Avesditch*[160]).

171*a*. Between the Dobuni and Cantii (*Ptol.*) stretching to the Cornavii N.W., the Catyeuchlani N.E., the Belgæ S.W., and the Regni S.E. They lay along both banks of the Thames, in parts of Surrey, Berks, Hants, Hertford, Bucks, and all Oxford, except a narrow strip adjoining Warw. and Gloucs. Their name connected with the large earthworks about the River Dorne (" dronn," *a ridge*), known E. of that river as Avesditch and W. as Grime's Dyke. The tribe name is interesting as evidence that the construction of gigantic entrenchments was a feature of native warfare before the arrival of the Romans.

171b. The Attrebates are the first British people noticed by Cæsar. Commius Attrebas was with him in Gaul, and on intimate terms, before the first invasion, and rendered his patron valuable services both before and during the expedition. The Britons twice solicited peace through him [53, 61]. He occurs in *Cæs.* also as Attrebas Commius, and it is likely, belonged to the tribe   His services to Cæsar may explain why, in Ptolemy's time, the Cassii were merged in this tribe. Ptolemy names one town.

171c. NALCUA. Ναλκούα. Lon. 19, Lat. 54.15. (" Innill acha "). Knoll Hill, three N.W. of Quainton, Bucks. The so-called Akeman Street at Chesterton, Bicester, points hither.

SEGONTIACI (" Sægon " [283v]).

172. The inhabitants of the marshes about Titchfield Hundred, W. of Portsmouth Harbour, Hants, and probably extending E. into Sussex. They submitted to Cæsar after his victory at the Thames, and their legates shared with others the reputation of having supplied him with the information which led to the capture of Cassivellaun's stronghold [61]. As they occupied the coast opposite Wight, which island Vespasian reduced, they were probably one of the two tribes which that general subdued. They are not mentioned by Ptolemy, having perhaps been absorbed first in Cogidubn's kingdom.

BELGÆ. Βέλγαι. (" Bolg," *cf*. Wiley).

173a. Bordering on the Dobuni N., and on the Durotriges S.W. (*Ptolemy*), the Attrebates being N.E., and the Regni E. ; they extended W. to the Damnonii and the Sabrina, embracing the Parret Marshes, but probably having their capital upon the Wiley, which seems to contain the old name (*cf*. Wilton, Wiltshire). Near Wiley (D.B., Wilgi), there are several camps (Belbury, etc.), and all the surrounding district is covered with tumuli and earthworks. The temple at Stonehenge was within their territory, being distant five miles from the Wiley River at its nearest point. The existence of this gigantic and sacred structure within their boundaries must

have shed great lustre on the tribe ; and possibly it was the
desire of their neighbours to possess a spot so celebrated which
led to some of the vast military operations, evidence of which
lies thickly around and within the Belgic country. In no
part of England, except, perhaps, near the Tyne Wall, are
there so many or such extensive remains.

173b. Nothing is expressly related respecting the part
played by the Belgæ in resisting the Romans. They were
outside the area of Cæsar's operations, and are not named
by him. It is uncertain whether they were involved in
Vespasian's campaign (A.D. 43) ; but it is curious that a
fortification between Stonehenge and Amesbury is called
Vespasian's Camp. Richard says the two tribes then conquered were the Belgæ and Damnonii, but though Vespasian
may have been opposed by the Belgæ, he certainly did not
subdue them, and several years later Ostory found them
formidable. and still in possession of extensive territories,
since it was obviously against them, if also against the
Damnonii, that some of his operations were directed, and
tnat he designed the lower line of forts at the Sabrina. This
fortified barrier, the Wansdyke [158f] shows how far the
Romans had asserted their authority towards the S.W. To
this period may belong some of the other great earthworks
called the Belgic Ditches, and perhaps also the desecration
of the Stonehenge temple, though it is not clearly ascertained whether the Roman advance was generally fatal to
Druidism.

173c. Stonehenge, unless it is the round temple of the
Hyperborei [15], is first mentioned by Henry of Huntingdon
before A.D. 1150, and within a few years other writers referred
to it :

> Apud Stanhenges lapides miræ magnitudinis in
> modum portarum elevati sunt, ut portæ portis
> superpositæ videantur, nec potest excogitare qua
> arte elevati sunt, vel qualiter constructi.—*Hen.*
> *of H.*

> þe stude wes Ælenge,
> Nu hatte hit Stan-henge.
> > > *Layamon.*

> [The place was Ælenge ;
> It is now called Stan-henge.]

Breton les solent en Bretan
Apeler Karole-as-gaians ;
Stanhengues ont non en Englois,
Pieres pandues en François.

Wace.

[The Bretons are wont in Bretagne
To call them the Giants' Dance ;
They have the name Stanhengues in England,
Hanging stones in France.]

Ælenge ("ail aonach," *stone-hill*), passed into Stonehenge ("stone aonach") partly by translation, and partly by phonic approximation. Wace's explanation is poetical.

173d. Geoff. of Monmouth, pretending to narrate the origin of the circle, says that the stones were carried by the giants of old from the farthest parts of Africa, and put up on Mount Killaraus in Ireland [309]. Thence Aurelius and Merlin, after a victory over the Irish, removed them to the mountain of Ambrius, near Caer-caradoc (which Geoff. identified with Salisbury), where he used them to enclose the sepulchre of the nobles slain by Hengist. Merlin is made to call it the Chorea Gigantum (*Giants' Dance*) ; aud Wace's Karole-es-gaians has the same meaning. Layamon calls it the eotende ring (*Giants' ring*). Merlin ascribes to the stones a medicinal value. The method was to wash them, and put the sick in the water, which infallibly cured. Hence Ælenge has been interpreted *healing.*

Ptolemy mentions four towns.

173e. ISCHALIS. Ἴσχαλις. Lon. 16.40, Lat. 53.30. ("Easgaidh lios"). Glastonbury, on Sedgemoor, Som.

173f. THERMÆ. AQUÆ CALLIDÆ. Ὕδατα Θερμά. Lon. 17.20, Lat. 53.40. Bath, the chief watering-place of Roman Britain, situated on the Abona and Foss Way. Its antiquities include remains of baths, a temple of Minerva, an altar of Sulis (a British goddess, supposed by some to have given the epithet Solis to this place, but incorrectly, as it was not anciently so called), and inscriptions mentioning the Legions II. and XX. The Saxons called it Bathan-ceaster, or poetically Acemannes-ceastre (*Sax. Chr.* 577, 973).

173g. VENTA. VENTA BELGARUM [220, 228a, 249a]. Οὐέντα. Lon. 18.40, Lat. 53.30. ("Beannte"). Winchester, on the Itchin. It was approached by important Roman roads, and in the Saxon period attained eminence as a bishopric and the capital of England.

DUROTRIGES. Δουρότριγες. (" Dorr traigh ").

174. Situated S.W. of the Belgæ, and extending W. to the Damnonii (*Ptolemy*), their name referring to the pebbly spur called Chesil Bank. Asser, King Alfred's biographer, mentions the district called in British Durngueis, in Saxon Thornsæta, Dorset. The former ("dronn," *ridge;* "cas," *leg, foot*) alludes to the leg-like shape of Chesil Bank and Portland Isle. The Durotriges are not noticed by the classic historians, but Ravennas mentions various towns which must have been within, or near, this territory, indicating the presence of a strong military force. Ptolemy mentions one town.

DUNIUM. Δούνιον. Lon. 18.50, Lat. 52.05. (" Dun "). Downshay, two miles S.E. of Corfe Castle, Dorset.

DUMNONII. Δουμνόνιοι. [135u].

175a. Next to the Durotriges, and in the most W. part of the island (*Ptolemy*), being bounded on all sides except the E. by the sea. They inhabited Cornwall, W. Somerset, and Devon. Their territory was rich in tin, which attracted Phœnician merchants hither some centuries before the Christian era [6]. Their name is sometimes regarded as the source of "Defenas" (*Sax. Chr.*, 897), the inhabitants of Defena-scire (*ibid.*, 851), now Devon ; but the latter must be attributed to Deventia [243b].

b. History is almost silent as to this people. If unsubdued in the time of Ostory, they would at least be curbed by his Sabrina defences ; but in any case, we must suppose them to have succumbed not later than the proprætorship of Frontine, whose conquest of the Silures seems to have removed the seat of war from the S.W. There is evidence, however, that the district was strongly garrisoned. Ptolemy mentions two stations near the Tamar, Ravennas others much farther W. [241], and vestiges of Roman occupation

are met with in many places. After the withdrawal, the
territory seems to have formed a kingdom. Gildas (iii. 28;
circa 520-550), upbraids the wickedness of Constantine " the
tyrannical whelp of the unclean lioness of Damnonia." This
Prince, supposed to be the Cystennyn of the bards, is said
to have abdicated the throne of Cornwall, and become a
Christian missionary among the Picts and Scots. Antiquities
on Dartmoor make it evident that it was once addicted to
druidical rites. Ptolemy names five towns :

175c. VOLIBA. Ὀυολίβα. Lon. 14.45, Lat. 52.20. (" Bol
ubh "). The camp at Polyphant, between the Inny and
Penpont Water, Cornwall.

d. UXELA. Ὀύχελα. Lon. 15, Lat. 52.45. (" Aigeal ").
Clawton, on River Claw, Devon, three miles S. of Holsworthy.

e. TAMARE [241*e*]. Ταμαρή. Lon. 15, Lat. 52.15. Cartha-
martha, Cornwall, within a curvature of the Tamar, half a
mile S. of Dunterton, Devon (circular camp).

f. ISCA. Ἴσκα. Lon. 17.30, Lat. 52.45. Axminster on
Axe [278*h*], Devon.

Isca is commonly identified with Exeter, *Sax.* " Exan-
ceastre (*Sax. Chr.*, 876) ; Wel. " Caer Wysg yn Dyfneint "
(*Caer Wysg in Devon*). Antiquities found at Exeter show
that the latter was a station of the LEG. II. AUG. ; but
in Ptolemy's time the legion was posted near Axminster.

g. LEGIO SECUNDA AUGUSTA. Λεγίων δευτέρα σεβαστή.
Lon. 17.30, Lat. 52.35. The situation of this station, ten
minutes S. of Isca, points to the camp on Hawkesdown Hill,
Axmouth, five S.W. of Axminster. Nearly midway is the
camp of Musbury Castle.

BRYTTꞆS, BRYTƿYLISL, ƿꞆLꞆS, ƿEꞆLꞆS.

176a. The Brytwylisc occur in the *Sax. Chr.* as the indigenous inhabitants of Brytene, excepting the Picts and
Scots. Their name signifies the Wealas of Brittia [14] ;
hence they were only a portion of the Wealas, the latter
apparently referring particularly to the Irish, and owing their
name to the basaltic columns (G. " fail," *a ring ; cf.* " Ynysfail "

[301]). The Irish inroad, however, must have been very early, as the Wealas are traceable in the Roman province-name Flavia [131]. Wealas (*Sax. Chr.*, 465, 473, 477, 485, 597, etc.). The Bryttas evidently called themselves Kimmerii, since their descendants, the modern Welsh, call themselves Cymry, the name surviving territorially in Cymru, *Wales*, Lat. *Cambria*, and perhaps in Cumberland. The Welsh possibly owed their " Cymru," to the Sarn Badrig, and not to the northern Causeway.

LORNWEALAS (*Sax. Chr.*, 891, 997) ; CORNUBII (*Anno* 994, *Dip. Ang. Ævi Sax.*, 286; " Ocrinum [135u], ubh ").

176b. The inhabitants of Cornwall (D.B., Cornvalge). This name does not occur until well into the Saxon period, and seems to have sprung up among the Saxons to designate those independent Welsh who maintained themselves in the rugged country about the Pr. Ocrinum.

SUMURSAETAS (*Sax. Chr.*, 845) ; SUMERSÆTAS (*ibid.* 1015).

(" sumair " ; A.S. sætas).

177. A Saxon name for the inhabitants of the sea-washed fens about the Parrett, comprised in modern Somerset.

TRINOVANTES (*Cæs.*) ; TRINOBANTES (*Tac.*).   Τρινοάντες.

(" eitre beannte ").

178a. Situated more easterly than the Catyeuchlani, and beside the Jimensa Æst. [137x] (*Ptolemy*), lying S. of the Iceni, and occupying parts of Suffolk and Essex, and extending into Cambridgeshire. Their name probably connected with Vandelbury, a circular hill-post lying near the Cambridgeshire Dykes [161], and perhaps the ancient capital of the tribe. This post lies upon Gog Magog Hills (" magh cuach," Gog being probably a facetious adjunct), near Mag's, or Meg's, Hill (" magh caois "), and the neighbourhood appears to have abounded with tumuli. The erection of Camalodunum [222*f*], ten miles S.S.E., into a colony, indicates the existence somewhere hereabouts of a native metropolis of considerable strength.

178b. The earliest events recorded of this tribe are the killing of their King Imanuentis by Cassivellaun, and the flight of his son Mandubrati to Cæsar, who restored him to the kingdom [61]. At that time the tribe was powerful. At a later period Cunobelin, Cassivellaun's grandson, was King, and friendly to the Romans, but his sons Caractac and Togodumn, opposed the armies of Claudius, and the capital, Camalodunum, fell, perhaps as the result of the battle which was fatal to Togodumn [70]. This town was afterwards made a colony by Ostory (A.D. 50) to check the lawless elements and rebels. In 61 the Trinobantes joined Boudicea, and their territory became the theatre of stirring events ; but the ultimate triumph of the Romans brought terrible consequences, and the Trinobantes do not appear any more in history [81-83]. Shortly before the withdrawal of the Romans, the coast was part of the Litus Saxonicum [232]. Ptolemy names one town.

178c. CAMUDOLANUM. Καμουδόλανον. Lon. 21, Lat. 55. (" Cam tul "). Candlet (D.B., Candelenta), near Walton, Felixstowe (D.B., Burg). This name is usually confused with Camalodunum.

CENIMAGNI (*Cæs.*) ; ICENI (*Tac.*) ; SIMENI. Σιμενοί.
(gaineamhach, guin, *sand*).

179a. The Cenimagni, or Iceni, were an ancient tribe, extending N. to the Wash, and W. towards the marshes of the Ouse, occupying Norfolk and part of Suffolk. Some suppose the name to be connected with the Ouse (*T. Gale*, 109), but it is more probable that it refers to the Iken Marshes, which stretch inland along the River Alde from the curious promontory of Orford bank.

These people opposed Cæsar, but submitted after his compact with the Trinobantes [61]. On Claudius's invasion, they appear to have been friendly towards the Romans, though it is probable that the Ouse bogs adjoining their

territory are the marshes into which the Romans pursued
the Britons after the fall of Togodumn [70], and they continued well-disposed until Ostory, in A.D. 50, called upon them
to assist in constructing forts along the Antona [161a] and
the Sabrina ; receiving the assistance of neighbouring nations,
they then took up arms, but were totally overthrown [74].
A few years later their King, Præsutag, bequeathed the kingdom
to his two daughters and Cæsar ; but his widow, Boudicea,
ill-brooking the violent and oppressive conduct of the Romans,
who were thus introduced to a share of the immediate government of the State, broke out in revolt (A.D. 61), and with her
allies, gained various successes, which, however, Suetonius
soon retrieved and revenged with stern severity [81-83].   They
do not occur again under their old appellation, except in the
town-name Venta Icenorum.   Ptolemy calls them the Simeni
(a form of Cenimagni), and he places them next to (i.e., E. of)
the Catyeuchlani and above the Trinovantes.   About 400
their entire coast was within the Litus Saxonicum [232].
Ptolemy names one town.

179b. VENTA.   VENTA ICENORUM [222, 260h].   ("Cair
guent " [390]) ; 'Ονεντα.   Neat's Ling, Ringstead, on Peddars
Way, two N.E. of Heacham.   This station is generally placed
at Caister [283z], but in utter disregard of the numerals of
Ant. IX.

ANCALITES ("aonach allt," Waulud's Bank).

180. These stretched N. from Hertfordshire over parts of
Beds, Bucks, and Cambridge, their name connected with
Leagrave (Lightgrave) and Luton on Chiltern Hills.   Their
boundaries seem to have been the Iceni and Trinovantes E.,
the Cassii S., and the Attrebates W.

These people submitted to Cæsar 54 B.C. [61].   They are
not afterwards mentioned, but as they lay at no great distance
from the Thames, they must have been involved in the
Claudian wars.   At this period, however, they had probably
ceased to exist as a separate State, being apparently absorbed
by the Catuellani (see Boduni [182e]).   This tribe, rather than
the Germanic Angles, is perhaps to be looked to for the origin
of the names England and East Anglia (see 131a).

CASSII *(Cæs.)*.   ("Chess").

181a. Separated southward from the maritime provinces by
the River Thamesis *(Cæs.)*, being bounded by the Trinobantes
E., the Ancalites N., and the Attrebates W. ; and dwelling
about the Chess (a tributary of the Colne), upon which lay
their stronghold, the Oppidum Cassivelauni [61], the Cassi-
bellaum of Bede *(Hist. Ang.,* i. 2), now Cashiobury. This
place, the Caissou of Domesday Book, was considerable *(temp.*
Edward the Confessor), when it was the most valuable of
the Hertfordshire manors belonging to St. Albans Abbey.
Cæsar's statement that the Cassii were about eighty m.p. from
the sea answers approximately to the distance of Cashiobury
from the coast between Sandwich and Deal.

181b. Previous to 55 B.C. the Cassii were very powerful.
Their Prince, Cassivelaun (Cassi-belin, said to mean Prince of
the Cassii), was engaged in continual wars with his neighbours,
and appears to have imposed his power upon the Trinobantes
[61]. He was appointed to the supreme command of the
Britons against Cæsar, whom he opposed with great vigour,
keeping the field after some of the tribes had submitted. It
is possible that his want of success did not impair his influence
in Britain, for his grandson Cunobelin resided in the Trinobantine capital, Camulodunum ; and Caractac and Togodumn,
Cunobelin's sons, are the only Britons mentioned by name
as resisting the Romans in the Claudian period [70]. In the
latter period, however, the Cassii themselves are not expressly
named, being evidently comprised in the Attrebates.

CATUELLANI. Κατουελλανοί. *(Dio.)*. CATYEUCHLANI. Κατυευχ-
λανοί. *(Ptol.)* ("achadh" ; balla, Lat. vallum, *cf. Welland)*.

182a. The inhabitants of the Welland fens at the Claudian
invasion, and possessing a dominion which extended S. over
the Boduni. In the next century they lay next to (*i.e.,* E. of)
the Coritani *(Ptolemy)*, bordering also upon or towards the
Cornavii, Trinobantes, and Iceni.

The Cantuellani were attacked by Plautius in A.D. 43, and
some of the Dobuni, their tributaries, submitted to him

after the defeat of Caractac and Togodumn [70]. It is probable that these Princes (the great-grandsons of Cassivelaun) belonged to the Catuellani ; and, further, that the latter people were paramount over a considerable part of E. Britain, since Cunobelin, father of the Princes, resided in Trinobantia. The extended power of the Princes, however, may have arisen by Roman favour, as in the case of Cogidubn. Caractac, retreating W. before Plautius, became famous as the leader of the Silures [76-77]. The territory of the Catuellani, comprising the fen corn-district, was in all likelihood one of the sources whence the Romans supplied their armies on the Rhine [117]. The etymology adopted above presupposes that even at the Claudian invasion the Welland fens were drained by means of banks and dykes in much the same way as now. Ptolemy names two towns.

182b. SALENAE. Σαλῆναι. Lon. 20.10, Lat. 55.40. (" Salann "). Wainfleet (" uaighean balladh "), on the River Lymn, or Steeping, Lincs; moat and tumulus. Vestiges of Roman salt-works at Wainfleet Tofts, one mile S.

182c. UROLANION. Οὐρολάνιον. Lon. 19.20, Lat. 55.30. (" Uir lon," ? Welland). Little London (" lon dun "), with Winsover (" uaighean uir "),˙ S.W. of Spalding.

Spalding ("siubhal aith ; leanag." Sax. " Spaldelyng ") has furnished relics of undoubted antiquity, including cisterns of Roman construction ; and Stukeley mentions a square Roman camp there on the Boston Road. A great bank, fifteen miles long, supposed Roman, confining the E. bank of the Welland, runs from this place to Crowland (Croyland, Curach-land) and Peakirk, and once formed the regular road thither, but is now partly unserviceable.

BODUNI. Βοδουνοι. (*Dio.*) (" Badan ").

182e. In Bedfordshire (Bedanford, *Sax. Chr.*, 919 ; Bedanfordscire, *ibid.*, 1011) and the fenny district extending thence along the Ouse towards the Wash. Their name probably survives in Potton, Beds ; Galley Hill, Chesterfield, in Sandy, three miles W. of Potton, in the line of a Roman road from Baldock, has the remains of a Roman camp, and has afforded many antiquities. Another Roman road, running along Hasell Hedge, connected Sandy with Lanslinsbury, Hunts.

The early submission of some of the Boduni to Plantius does not seem to have freed them from the yoke of the Catuellani ; they do not come into notice again, and it is evident from Ptolemy's geography that in the second century their territory was within the sovereignty of the superior tribe.

CANGI (*Tac.*).   (" ceann acha ").

182f. The inhabitants of the N.E. extremity of Northants, and the neighbouring parts of the counties of Lincoln, Cambridge, and Huntingdon, where they have left their name in that of King Street [140b].   Proceeding from Icenia against them, Ostory advanced, plundering and destroying, pushing his way across the island almost as far as the sea, which looked towards Hibernia [75].   Their principal town seems to have been Castor, near Peterborough.   *King* Street starts near Castor ; Lady *Cony*burrows (or Kyneburga's) way leads from the S. of the Nen to the village, and one mile W. is *Gun*wade Ferry ; these circumstances and names suggest that Cangum was the ancient name of Castor.   The Castrum occupied the summit of the hill, the church standing within it, and extensive Roman remains have been brought to light. Chesterton, S.W. [218h].   On St. Edmund's Balk in Castor Field, near Gunwade Ferry, were two long stones, niched like arrows at the top, and called St. Edmund's stones (probably mercurial).

DOBUNI.   Δοβοῦνοι.   (*Ptolemy*.)   (" Taip ").

183a. Situated between the Silures W., the Attrebates E., and the Belgæ S. (*Ptolemy*), the Cornavii N. ; inhabiting parts of Glos. E. of the Severn, the Cotswold's being within their territory.   The name, probably connected with Tuffley, on the W. slope of the remarkable Robin's Wood Hill, survived territorially to later times as Duffin.   This territory seems to have furnished the Romans with an important base for their operations against the Silures and Belgæ ; and towards their W. and S. confines Ostory constructed Offa's Dyke and Wansdyke.

The Foss Way and Via Julia traversed them, and Akeman Street started within their limits. Ptolemy mentions one town.

183b. CORINIUM. CORINIUM DOBUNORUM [253c]. Κορίνιον. Lon. 18, Lat. 54.10. (" Churn "). Cirencester, on the Churn, Glos., near the intersection of the Foss and Via Julia. The town was walled, and has yielded beautiful tesselated pavements and innumerable proofs of former magnificence.

SILURES (*Tac.*). Σίλυρες. (" Sal oir ").

184a. Between the Dimetæ W., and the Dobuni E. (*Ptolemy*), the Ordovices being N., and the Severn Estuary S. Their precise limits are quite uncertain, but they occupied the Forest of Dean, Glos., and thence extended over Hereford, Radnor, Brecknock, Monmouth, and part of Glamorgan, and Pliny places them on the St. George's Channel. Their seat was apparently the promontory of Awre, opposite Saul, on the Severn, the name pointing to the marshy ground along that river, which here formed their boundary.

Tacitus considered that the Silures were of Iberian origin [37]. They come into notice during the propraetorship of Ostory, their military being then under Caractac, who retired among them when driven by Plautius from the E. provinces. Emboldened by his presence, they carried on the war with great tenacity. Ostory having overcome the Iceni and Brigantes proceeded against them in person ; whereupon Caractac passed into Ordovicia, and prepared to receive him, but was overthrown [76]. The Silures, however, were not subdued, and Ostory's successes were followed by events less favourable to their enemies ; and matters continued in this state through the propraetorship of Didius and Veranius [79]. But under Suetonius, who succeeded Veranius in A.D. 57, the Roman arms appear to have triumphed in Siluria, and thence to have been carried through N. Wales and into Mona, extending the Empire over all the island S. of Brigantia, excepting, perhaps, Damnonii and part of Belgæa. Hence, if they seconded the attempt of Boadicea in A.D. 61, their assistance must have been of an indirect kind, cut off as they were by.

strong garrisons, and curbed by the presence of the Leg. II.,
which at this period was probably already established within
their territory at Caerleon [225*f*]. They were finally vanquished by Frontine. In A.D. 823 the Denas (those Silures
who inhabited the Forest of Dean = " dinn," *hill*) fought a
battle with the Wealas at Gaful-ford (Yeovil, Somerset ;
cf. Givelceaster ; *Sax. Chr*.). In the twelfth century Gerald
Cambrensis called the forest Sylva Danubiæ, and added " quæ
ferinam ferrique copiam Gloverniæ ministrat." Ptolemy
names one town.

184*b*. BULLÆUM. Βούλλαιον. Lon. 16.20, Lat. 55. (" Bol
aoi "). Hay, co. Brecknock. Roman camp.

DIMETÆ. Δημῆται. (" Aith Mowddwy ").

185*a*. In the most western part, below the Ordovices, having
the Silures E. (*Ptolemy*), on which side they extended to the
neighbourhood of the Neath ; they thus occupied the S.W. angle
of Wales, extending N. over Cardigan and parts of Montgomery
and Merioneth to Dinas Mowddwy. They are not noticed
by the historians, but the Via Julia traverses the territory.
There are many vestiges of Roman occupation. Pliny locates
the gens Silurum about St. Davids [372]. In 918 the Lid-
wiccii, leaving their camp on the island Bradanrelic at the
mouth of the Severn, went to Deomod, and thence to Yrland
(*Sax. Chr*.). Dimetia is said to have passed into Saxon times
as Dyfed, a small British principality, which is frequently
mentioned, but it is probable that the two names were diverse
both in origin and import. The following notices from the
Brut y Tyw. afford no proof of their identity :

893. Keredigyawn and Ystrat Tywi invaded.

981, 1020. Dyfet and Mynyw devastated.

986, 1091. Keredigyawn and Dyfet.

1045. Ystrat Tywi and Dyfet devastated.

1071. Keredigyawn, Dyfet, and Mynyw ravaged·

1092. All the castles of Dyfet and Keredigyawn demol-
ished, except those of Penuro (*Pembroke*) and Rhyd y
Gors.

1100. Powys, Keredigyawn, and half Dyfet given to Iorwerth ; the other half, with Ystrat Tywi, Gwhyr, and Kedweli had been given to Mab Baldwin.

Ptolemy mentions two towns.

185b. LUVENTINUM. Λουέντινον. Lon. 15.45, Lat. 55.10. ("Lia beannte"). Castle Hill, between Blaen Glowen-fach and Esgair Einon, at the source of Clettwr Fawr, five miles S. of New Quay, co. Cardigan. This station usually placed at Caer Castell, Llanio, on Sarn Helen, three miles S.W. of Tregaron, where Roman remains are found.

185c. MARIDUNUM. Μαρίδουνον. Lon. 15.30, Lat. 55.40. ("Mur dun"). Cefn-caer, by Morben in Pennal, Merioneth ; two and a half miles W.S.W. of Machynlleth. Roman fort.

CEANGI ("gaineach," sand).

186a. An early tribe in N. Wales, on the Dee, near Connah's Quay and the old Welsh district of Tegeingl (Tegengel, *Gir. Camb.*, ii. 10 ; Tegigyl, 1164, 1166, 1244, *Brut y Tyw.*), now comprised in Flintshire. The mining importance of this district is seen in the name Tegeingl ("tog," *to lift, raise;* hence "tochail," *to dig, delve;* "tochail," *a mine;* "gual," *coal*). *Cf.* Coleshill (D.B. Coleselt) — *Hill of coals*—a village and hundred near Holywell. Deva Victrix [214n] was in this territory.

The name does not occur in the classic writers, but appears on pigs of lead found in Flintshire and the vicinity, inscribed "IMP. DOMIT. AUG. GER. DE CEANGIS," from which it is evident they existed as a community in the reign of Domitian, though under tribute. When Ptolemy wrote, their territory was part of Ordovicia. The name, perhaps, appears in King or Kind Street, which points from Kinderton, Middlewich, Cheshire towards Northwich, Senna Green (Condate [214m]), and Warrington.

CANCANI ("ceann cian ").

186b. Occurs only in the name Cancanorum Pr. [135k], but perhaps authentic. (For a similar instance in Ptolemy see Setantii [192], which is vouched by independent testimony.)   The name points to the village of Llangian in Lleyn.

Horace (iii. 4) speaks of the Concanus delighted with horses' blood ("laetum equino sanguine Concanum "), but this is usually understood of a tribe in Hispania.

ORDOVICES (*Tac.*).   Ορδοΰϊκες.   (" Ard uaigh ").

187a. Situated, about A.D. 150, below the Parisi and Brigantes, but in the extreme W., having the Cornavii E. (*Ptolemy*). Under them lay the Dimetæ and Silures.   They held N. Wales and a great part of Cheshire ; but (*temp.* Domitian) the N.W. portion of this territory belonged to the Ceangi.   Watts and Offas Dykes [159] traversed their territory ; and upon the former, one mile S.W. of Wrexham, is Erthig, which contains their name, and was probably their early capital ; it has an artificial mound called The Mount.

The Ordovices were involved in the early Silurian wars. Caractac carried the operations into this district against Ostory [76], and received near the S. border the defeat which resulted in his captivity [288e].   The tribe comes into notice again at the close of Frontine's propraetorship, when advantage was taken of the interval before the arrival of Agricola to wipe out a body of Roman cavalry.   The new legate arrived to find the army in winter quarters, but with such troops as were at hand he immediately attacked, and nearly annihilated, the Ordovices [90].   A revival of their power may be inferred from their subsequent absorption of the Ceangi.   The kingdom of Powys was conquered by the Saxons in 823 (*Brut y Tyw.*). Ptolemy names two towns.

187b. MEDIOLANUM [214a, 223i, 257b].   Μεδιολάνιον.   Lon. 16.45, Lat. 56.40.   (" Miad lon ").   Maiden Castle, Bickerton Hill, four miles N.N.E. of Malpas, Cheshire.   Mad Allen's Hole adjacent.

187c. BRANNOGENIUM.   Βραννογένιον.   Lon. 16, Lat. 56.15. (" Broin Ogwen ").   On the Ogwen, near St. Ann's Chapel, co. Carn.   The name preserved in that of Nant Francon, borne by the valley of the Ogwen above St. Ann's Chapel.

CORNAVII. Κορναύϊοι. CORNONINI [256d]. (" Cuirn abh ").

188a. More E. than the Ordovices, and next to them (N.E.),
were the Coritani (*Ptol.*). They extended E. to a line drawn
approximately from Northampton to Chipping Norton, and
occupied Worcester, Warwick, and parts of Salop, Staffs,
Northants, and Oxford, being bounded S. and E. by the Dobuni
and Catyeuchlani. Their seat was probably at Cornwell
(" Carn balla "), one mile S.E. of Chastleton Hill Camp, and
their name seems to refer to the neighbouring antiquities,
called Rollerich Stones, on Bright Hill (" Bruach aith," *Edge
Hill*), Rollwright (D.B. " Rollandri," *Rollan aitreabh*), three
miles N.W. of Chipping Norton. These stones, formerly sixty
in number (one called the King, others the King's Men and the
Five Knights), were supposed by Stukeley to be Druidical ;
but the readiest explanation of Rollerich is " Oir ail araich "
(*Edge Hill Field*) ; and the name can scarcely be so ancient as
Ptolemy's time, since it obviously relates to the boundary
between the counties of Oxford and Warwick, which here runs
along the ridge of Edge Hill for some miles.

188b. Nothing is definitely related of the history of this
tribe. It is likely they were checked early in the Claudian
invasion, when the Romans pushed their conquests, at first
with great celerity, towards the N. and W., eventually securing
their acquisitions by great military roads, three of which
(Watling, Foss, and Ryknield) traversed this territory. The
Claudian war began in 43 ; about 49 the Romans certainly
carried their arms into Cornavia, since Ostory would traverse
it in his progress from the Cangi towards the Irish Sea. On
the side towards Avesditch [160] there are extensive military
remains at Wroxton, Madmarston, Tadmarton, Ilbury, Chadlington, and other places. About 150 the Legio XX. was
stationed within their N.E. boundary. Ptolemy names two
towns.

188c. DEVNANA. Δηούνανα καὶ λεγίων κ̄ νικηφόριος. (*Devnana
and the Leg. Vicesima Victrix*). Lon. 18.30, Lat. 55. (" Taip
Nen "). Daventry (" Devnana aitreabh "), on the Nen,
Norhts. Great camp on Burrow Hill, three miles in circumference, lying between the modern town and Watling Street,

was the military city.   The Leg. XX. Victrix, sometimes styled
Valeria, and also Britannica (*Grut.*, 548, 4), came into Britain
in the consulship of Galba and Titus Vinius (*Camd.*), and was
in the island in 69, when it favoured Vitellius, afterwards acknowledging Vespasian, whose adherent, Agricola, was appointed prefect of the legion in 70. See [86-87]. From
numerous inscriptions, found in various parts of the island,
the legion saw extensive service. Coins of Septimius Geta
(joint-Emperor 211-212), bearing on the reverse " COL.
DIVANA. LEG. XX. VICTRIX.," show that this place was a colony ;
but the honour is usually claimed for Chester [282c]. Numerous military vestiges occur in the neighbourhood of Daventry.

188*d*. VIROCONIUM. Ὀυιροκόνιον. Lon. 16.45, Lat. 55.45.
(" Uir ceann "). Wroxeter, E. of the Wrekin, Salop. This
place was surrounded by a rampart and foss, and contained
a forum and thermæ ; its site has been extensively explored,
yielding many antiquities [290*d*].

CORITANI. Κοριτανοί. (" Carr," *cf.* Soar ; " Ritheadhean ").

189*a*. Next to (E. of) the Cornavii, and adjoining (E.) the
Catyeuchlani (*Ptol.*), being bounded N. by the Brigantes and
the Abus [137*s*], which separated them from the Parisi.
Their name, still existing partially paraphrased as Charn-
wood, points to the rocky forest tracts about the Soar,
Leicestershire.

The tribe is not noticed by the historians, but from its position below the Brigantes, and what is known of Brigantian
history, it is probable that Roman supremacy was imposed
upon it in the time of Plautius. Two great roads, Foss and
Ermine, traversed Coritania ; Watling skirted it S.W., and
Ryknield W. Ptolemy mentions two towns.

b. LINDUM [218*a*, 219*a*, 221]. LINDUM COLONIA [261*a*].
Λίνδον. Lon. 18.40, Lat. 55.45. (" Linnte "). Lincoln,
situate on a steep hill above the marshes of the Witham.
This appears from Ravennas to have been a colony.
Adelphius Episcopus de Civitate Colonia Londi, found amongst
the signatories at the Council of Arles, A.D. 314, is thought to
refer to Lincoln ; and Linde*collinum* and Linde*collina*, occur-

ring in Bede, are often quoted as if forms of the name in Ravennas. Bede, however, would scarcely write Collina if he meant Colonia. Under the Romans, Lindum was an important place, surrounded by a wall, and fossed on all sides except the S. The N. gate, called Newport, is still in existence, forming the N. entrance to the city ; and there is another fragment of Roman work, called the Mint Wall. Ermine Street, so called, in its passage through the town, lies 8 or 9 feet beneath the present thoroughfare. In 1879 a milliare was dug up from it at the point where it is intersected by the old street between the E. and N. gates, and has the following inscription :

IMP. CAES.
MARCO
PIAVONO
VICTORI
NO. P. F. INV.
AUG. PONT.
MAX.
TR. P. PP.
A. L. S. M.
P. XIIII.

Victorine was one of the thirty Tyrants, and ruled in Gaul and Britain A.D. 267-268 ; but the milliare is particularly valuable as confirming Antonine's distance between this town and Segelocum (a *Lindo Segelocum*, m.p. xiiii.). See Foss Dyke [167].

189*c.* RAGE. Ῥάγε. (Εραται*). Lon. 18, Lat. 55.30. (" Araich "). Rice Rocks (D.B. Ricoltorp), one and a half miles N.W. of Markfield, near Bardon Hill, Leic. Billa Barrow Hill and Battle Flat, S.W., separated from this place by the Roman road from Leicester to Burton-on-Trent. This name (" araich," *battlefield*), coupled with " Battle Flat," is evidence that the spot had been, prior to A.D. 140, the scene of some important military event.

PARISI. Παρίσοι. (" bior ouse ").

190*a.* Beside the Brigantes, about the Eulimenus Sinus [137*q*] (*Ptol.*), occupying Holderness, in the S.E. angle of Yorks ;

* Ἐράται, a various reading, is probably a conjectural amendment by some transcriber.

being bounded S. by the Abus [137s], their name referring to
the long, narrow promontory of Spurn. History is silent as
to this people, but the wolds to the N.W., constituting apparently the border between them and the Brigantes, are
covered with military remains [162b] (see [131a]). Ptolemy
names one town.

PETUARIA. Πετυαρία. Lon. 20.40, Lat. 56.40. (" Feith
uir"). Patrington, near Spurn Head.

GABRANTUICI.

190b. This name occurs in Ptolemy in the plural—Γαβραν-
τουίκων [137q], but is nowhere else met with. He uses it in
relation to the coast near Flamborough Head, Yorks, and it
clearly refers to the remarkable echoes produced by the caves
at that headland (" gabair-ionad uagh," *tattler-place cave*).
The caves are also referred to in Bridlington (" bruth," *cave*).

BRIGANTES. Βρίγαντες. (" Bre gant," *Pen y Ghent*).

191a. S. of the Selgovæ and Otadeni, and reaching from sea
to sea ; the Parisi lay beside them, and below were the Ordovices and Coritani (*Ptol.*). They were the most populous of
the British tribes ("numerosissima provinciæ totius," *Agric.*
xvii.), and the greatest territorially, occupying the whole region
between the Mersey and Humber S., and the Solway and Tyne
N., except the small district of Parisia.

Seneca, A.D. 45, mentions the Brigantes as having been
subdued by Claudius [73]. They appear to have acknowledged some sort of dependence upon Rome previous to 49,
for about that time Ostory relinquished the war in Cangia in
order to quell disturbances amongst them [75]. Cartismandua, their queen, surrendered Caractac A.D. 52 [76] ; she
married Venusius, who had long been friendly towards the
Romans, but afterwards, separating herself from him and
marrying his knight Vellocat, some of her subjects took um-
brage, and had recourse to arms. In this extremity she demanded assistance from Didius, who with difficulty released
her from danger, though the party of Venusius was not put
down. After Vespasian's accession in 69, the war was pursued

with more vigour, and the troops led into Brigantia by Cerialis reduced a great part of the province, while Frontine seems to have broken the spirit of the tribe (79, 89]. Agricola, in 78, found them submissive, for there is no mention of any opposition from them, and his northern campaigns were apparently conducted against more distant tribes. Before 100, however, the valour of the tribe was talked of at Rome as if formidable [105]. The most southern of the N. frontier walls ran along the entire upper boundary of this kingdom [Tyne Wall, [163]]) Immense bodies of troops were permanently stationed at different points along this line ; and the territory lying immediately N. and S. of it was in 369 formed into a separate military district called Valentia [132]. Owing to the influx of traders and others consequent upon the presence of such a numerous military, the rugged hills of Northumberland must in those days have presented a scene of animation not less striking than that of the busiest manufacturing and mining districts of our own times. Ptolemy mentions nine towns.

191b. After nearly two centuries of violence and destruction, following the Roman evacuation, Brigantia, in the seventh century, became a Saxon kingdom, under the corrupt name of Bernicia (the people, Bernicas). The Sovereignty of Deira (*cf.* Cartor [282u]) was formed out of it, the separation of Deur from Berneich being effected, according to Nennius, by Soemil, a descendant of Woden. Another portion became known as Westmoringa-land (West Berneich, Westmorland) (*Sax. Chr.*, 966).

c. EPIACUM. Ἐπείκον. Lon. 18.30, Lat. 58.30. (" Fe ach"). Bewaldeth, N.E. of Bassenthwaite Water, Cumb. ; placed by Ptolemy between the Æst. Ituna and the Æst. Moricambe [135e, 135f]. Roman camp between Over Water and Nevin Tarn.

d. VINNOVIUM. Οὐιννούιον. Lon. 17.30, Lat. 58. (" Beann ubh "). Ravenglass by Muncaster, Cumb. ; placed by Ptolemy between the Æst. Moricambe and Setantiorum Portus [135f, 135g]. Remains called the Old Walls. Roman inscriptions said to have been found.

e. CATURRACTONIUM [265f]. CATARACTON [213a, 214a, 218a]. Κατυρρακτόνιον) Lon. 20, Lat. 58. (" Cathair uchdan "). Catterick, Yorks. Camden notices an altar to the " DEUS VIARUM ET SEMITARUM," found at Thornborough in this vicinity. This place is usually identified with Cattraeth, where Ida defeated the Britons in 547 [357 note].

191f. CALATUM. Κάλατον. Lon. 19, Lat. 57.45. ("cladh "). Caldbergh in Coverdale, Yorks. Camp at Middleham, two miles N.E. Druidic circle at Knowle six and a half miles S.E.

g. ISURIUM [49, 213f, 214a]. ISUBRIGANTUM [218a]. Ἰσούριον. Lon. 20, Lat. 57.40. (" Eas ur "). Wass, under Wass Moor, one and a half miles W.N.W. of Ampleforth, Yorks. Numerous tumuli on the adjacent moors. Double Dikes and the camp of Studford Ring one and a half miles E. Extensive earthworks N.W. [162c].

Isurium has hitherto, by general consent, been placed at Aldborough, by Boroughbridge. Portions of the Roman Wall of Aldborough have been excavated, and numerous pavements and antiquities discovered there. Three miles N. of Aldborough a milliare was found towards the end of the eighteenth century, said to be inscribed :

IMP. C.
ÆS C ME
SSIUS
Q DECI
TRA PIO
FELICI
AUG.
XX. C
S.

—i.e., " XX. Catarracton S. (the initial S. representing the place three miles distant, where the stone was found). Decius reigned 249-251."

h. RIGODUNUM. Ῥιγόδουνον. Lon. 18, Lat. 57.30. (" Araiche dun "). Arco, one mile S. of Horton in Ribblesdale. Supposed Roman camp one and a half miles S. near Staniforth, and several barrows.

i. OLICANA. Ὀλίκανα. Lon. 19, Lat. 57.30. (" All ceann "). Helks, above the Nidd, one-half mile N.E. of Ramsgill, in Kirkby Malzeard, Yorks. Camp and tumuli.

This station is generally placed at Ilkley [282j], an error followed by T. Gale [49].

191j. EBORACUM.   EBORACUM LEGIO VI. VICTRIX [213*a*].
EBURACUM [214*a*, 218*a*, 221, 236*a*, 265*g*].   CAIR EBRAUC
[287*a*].   'Εβόρακον, Λεγίων ἕκτος νικηφόριος.   Lon. 20, Lat.
57.20.   (" Bruach ").   York, the station of the Leg. VI. Vict.,
both when Ptolemy wrote (*c*. A.D. 150) and at the date of the
Notitia *c*. A.D. 400 ; and probably the most important, as it is
the most celebrated, of the Roman cities in Upper Britain, if
not in the whole island.   Here the Emperors Severus and Constantius Chlorus* died [112, 116], and it is the reputed birth-
place of the latter's son, Constantine the Great.   The greater
part of the enclosing wall has been traced, and many antiquities
have been brought to light, including votive tablets to Serapis
and Mithras.   Goltzius notices a coin of Severus, bearing the
legend, " COL. EBORACUM LEG. VI. VICTRIX "; and some copies
of Antonine read, " EBORACUM M.P.M. VI. VICTR." (*T. Gale*):
whence it is sometimes spoken of as a colony and municipium ;
but the words " VIR. COL. EBOR.," found upon a sarcophagus,
afford the argument that Severus's coin refers to a college
here :
      M. VEREC. DIOGENES. IIIIII VIR. COL. EBOR.
      IDEMQ. MORT. CIVEIS BITURIX HÆC SIBI VIVUS
      FECIT.—*Grut.*, 485.

Eborius Episcopus subscribed to the acts of the Council of
Arles, 314.

About 866 this city was called Kair Efrawc by the Britons
(*Brut y Tyw.*), and Eoforwic ceastre by the Saxons (*Sax. Chr.*).
In Domesday Book it is called Eboracum civitas, and the
county Eurvicscire.   The transition to York was gradual.

k. CAMUNLODUNUM [262*a*].   Καμουνλόδουνον.   Lon. 18.15,
Lat. 57.   (" Cam ol dun ").   Leeds, at the confluence of
Holbeck with the Aire.   Numerous Roman vestiges exist
between this place and Tadcaster, and traces of roads are met
with traversing the district in all directions.   Addle, five miles
N.N.W. of Leeds, has the remains of a Roman camp, and near
it the outlines of a Roman town were discovered in 1702
(*Reynolds*).   Aberford, eight miles N.E. on the Roman Ridge,
has an earthwork called Becca Banks or the Ridge ; Ardsley

* According to Nenn. Constantius was buried at Cair Segont, also
called **Minmanton** (xxv.).

four and a half miles S., has also yielded Roman remains. Leeds was of considerable importance under the Saxons. The city of Judeu, to which Penda was accompanied by some of the Kings of the Britons previous to the battle of Gai Campi [236*j*], should probably be read Luden, for it was unquestionably Leeds.

SETANTII (" Seidean ").

192. The sole classic authority for this tribe is the Portus Setantiorum of Ptolemy [135*g*]. This port is placed between the Æst. Moricambe N. and the Æst. Belisama S. ; hence the tribe occupied parts of Cumberland and Lancashire contiguous to the sands of the Duddon, Leven, and Kent, the name still appearing in Seathwaite Fells about the Duddon, and in Satterthwaite between Coniston Water and Winder Mere. Ravennas calls them the Sistuntii, and says they divided Britain in the third portion [266], meaning, apparently, that they lay in the region where the tertia pars commenced.

SELGOVÆ. Σελγοῦαι ('Ελγοούαι). (" Slug fè ").

193*a*. Bounded by the Novantæ W., the Damnii N., and the Otadeni E. (*Ptol. corrected**). The Brigantes bordered them S.E., and the Æst. Ituna S., the latter afterwards receiving from them the name of Solway Firth. Their name alludes to the quicksands of the Ituna.

Selgovia was apparently of great importance to the Romans as a frontier dependency. Deil's Dyke lay within it towards the W., and it contained very many fortresses, among which were the strongly entrenched post of Birrenswark, near the Annan, and the station of Birrens, near Middlebie ; the latter has furnished numerous inscriptions referring to the " LEG. II. AUG.," the " COH. II. TUNG.," etc. In later times Selgovia formed the S. confines of the Pictish kingdom of Albania [130]. Ptolemy mentions four towns :

* Ptolemy considered Britain above the Solway to stretch towards the east ; hence his points of compass in respect of all the northern tribes are wrong. Literally, he describes the Selgovæ as under the Novantæ, the Damnii being east in a more northerly situation than the Gadeni. See map and [108].

193b. CARBANTORIGUM. Καρβαντόριγον. Lon. 19, Lat. 59.20. ("Carr beann torrach"). Gairloch, Castleyards, above Roucan in Torthorwald. Forts on neighbouring hills.

c. UXELUM. Ὄυξελον. Lon. 18.30, Lat. 59.20. ("Aigeal"). Kelton, Dum., between the Nith and Craigs Moss. Vestiges of Roman camp on the high ground two and a half miles S.E. of Dumfries.

d. CORDA [267k]. Κόρδα. Lon. 20, Lat. 59.40. ("Corr aith"). Castle Hill, Corrodow, on Dalwhat Water, Dumfries. Vestiges of fort.

e. TRIMONTIUM. Τριμόντιον. Lon. 19, Lat. 59. ("Eitre monadh"). Dormont, between Dalton and the Annan, Dum. Fort E. of Dalton Church.

NOVANTÆ. Νουάνται.

194a. Placed by Ptolemy on the N. side of the island, in the projection which contained the Novantarum Peninsula [134b], having the Selgovæ S. Strictly, they were bounded by the Oc. Hibernicus W. and S., the Damnii N., and the Selgovæ E., being separated from the latter by the Kenn Water.

In A.D. 82 Agricola placed troops in this territory (" eam partem Britanniæ, quæ Hiberniam aspicit, copias instruxit "), to protect his conquests and be at hand for an invasion of Ireland [93]. It was possibly relinquished before Ptolemy's time. Ptolemy mentions two towns :

b. LEUCOPIBIA. Λευκοπιβία. Lon. 19, Lat. 60.20. ("Leac beabh"). Pibble, by Money Pool, under Pibble Hill, co. Kirkcudbright, two and a half miles N.E. of Creetown.

c. RETIGONIUM. Ῥετιγόνιον. Lon. 20.10, Lat. 60.40. ("Ard ceann "). Finnarts Hill ("beann ard "), at the entrance of Loch Ryan, near the mouth of the Water of App. Traces of fort [135c].

OTADINI. Ὠταδινοί. (" Tweed ").

195a. Situated along the Oc. Germanicus, having the Gadeni N. and the Brigantes S. (*Ptol.*), being separated from the latter by the Brigantian Wall or the Tyne, and extending to the

Tweed. They appear in the post-Roman period as the Gododin, or Gododiniaid, who were among the Britons opposed to Ida at Cattraeth, 547 (*Triads*). The Britons, under Cunedda, are said to have abandoned Manau Guotodin, and settled in Guenedota, N. Wales (*Nenn.*, 62). Otadinia, comprehending a considerable part of the advance lines of the wall, was thronged with strong Roman posts ; many are noticed by Ravennas [266]. Ptolemy names two towns :

195b. CURIA. Κουρία. Lon. 20.10, Lat. 59. Crew Castle, under Crew Crag, two miles N. of St. Cuthbert's Church, Cumb. A Roman road from St. Cuthbert's passes this place, and thence over Skelton Pike into Scotland.

c. BREMENIUM [213*a*, 270*a*]. Βρεμένιον. Lon. 21, Lat. 58.45. (" Bri muin "). Old Man's Shield (" Alt muin "), Mantle Hill, two miles W. of Bellingham, Northumb., and nine miles S.S.W. of High Rochester. It occupied an eminence, on which are traces of military works, its identity being established by Ant. I., which places it twenty m.p. from Corstopitum. The Explorates garrisoned here, and were styled " of Bremenium," as appears from two stones found at High Rochester [266*k*] : " DUPL. N. EXPLOR. BREMEN," " *Duplares Numeri Exploratorum Bremeniensium.*"

GADINI. Γαδινοί. (" Gead ").

196. Situated more E. than the Otadeni (*Ptol.*), their boundaries being the Selgovæ and Otadeni S., the Damnii W., the Boderia Æst. N., and the Oc. Germanicus E. Ptolemy mentions no town. They probably had their name from the rocks about Arthur's Seat, Edinburgh ; and the latter town was undoubtedly their capital, which, under the name Eiddyn (a form of Gadeni) is noticed in the triads of the sixth century. Cynon mab Clydno Eiddyn (*Clydno of Edinburgh*) was slain at Cattraeth, his grave being honoured by the bards ; and Ida the Saxon, the victor at this battle, joined Dynguayth (" dinas Gad ") to Bernicia, forming the kingdom of Dynguaythguarth Berneich (" guarth," A.S. *burh*) (*Nenn.*, 61). In 685 Brudei, King of the Picts, expelled the Saxons, and called the territory Gueithlin Garan (" Guidi-ail guarth ") (*ibid.*, 57).

Bede, about 700, called the city Giudi, and described it as in
the midst of the eastern inlet of the ocean which separated the
Britons from the Picts (*i.e.*, the Firth of Forth) (*Ecc. H.*, i. 12).
Geoffrey of Monmouth called it the town of Mount Agned
(ii. 7) ; in Modern Gaelic it is Dun-eudainn (*Armstrong's Gael.
Dict.*).

DAMNII. Δάμνιοι. ("Toman").

197a. Bounded by the Selgovæ and Novantes S., the Gadeni E., and the Epidii N.W. (*Ptol. corrected*) ; the Caledonii
being N., the Venicontes N.E., and the Æst. Clotta W. They
thus occupied the isthmus between the Forth and Clyde, and
a considerable territory to the N. and S. of it.

Agricola overran Damnia in A.D. 80, when he advanced to
the Tay. In 81 he fortified the Clyde Isthmus (Graham's
Dyke [166]), thus constituting the territory a base for future
operations. In 83 he set out from the Bodotria against the
more northern nations, and when apprehending attack from
the Caledonii was counselled by some of his officers to retire
upon this barrier [94]. Lollius, about 139, fortified the isthmus afresh [166b]. The Damnii are not named after Ptolemy's
time ; those N. of the Dyke were absorbed by their neighbours
and kinsmen, the Meatæ, and those S. formed, several centuries
later, the British kingdom of Strathclyde. Ptolemy mentions
six towns ; from this circumstance the military importance of
the district may be inferred, yielding precedence only to the
larger state of Brigantia, with nine towns (Dumnonia, five ;
Selgovia and Vacomagia, four each).

b. COLANIA. Κολανία. Lon. 20.30, Lat. 59.10. ("Aigealan"). Drochil Hill, above the Lyne, one mile S. of
Calland's House, co. Peebles. Forts.

c. VANDUARA. 'Ουανδούαρα. Lon. 21.40, Lat. 60. ("Beannte
uir"). Ranfurley, at the Bridge of Weir, Renfrew. Military
works on the hills N.E. and N.W.

d. CORIA. Κορία. Lon. 21.30, Lat. 59.20. Castle Cary,
on Graham's Dyke, six miles W. of Falkirk. The fort here has
yielded Roman inscriptions and other antiquities.

e. ALAUNA. 'Αλαῦνα. Lon. 22.45, Lat. 59.20. Dunblane,
on Allan Water.

197*f*. LINDUM. Λίνδον. Lon. 23, Lat. 59.30. ("Linnte"). Flanders Moss, Perth ; the Roman camp two miles S.E. of Menteith Lake.

g. VICTORIA [276*b*]. 'Ουικτορία. Lon. 23.30, Lat. 59. ("Uachdar"). Auchterarder, Perth. The notion that this name is the Latin Victoria is erroneous (VECTURIONES [203]).

AITEACHTUATH ("Aiteach tuath," *inhabitants of the north*).

198*a*. These people appear in the Irish annals of the first century, as enemies of the native Irish. It has been suggested that they are identical with the Attacotti [196], but the name is probably a general one for all the Northern Britons.

ATTACOTTI.

b. These first occur *temp*. Julian, 361-3, when they were warlike. In conjunction with the Picts and Scots, they made inroads into the Roman province, but were defeated in 368 by Theodosius [117-118]. The Auxilia Palatina vi. Atecotti juniores Gallicani occur among the continental garrisons about 400 (*Not.*). The Attacotti Honoriani (seniores et juniores) also occur, the Seniores in Gaul, the Juniores in Gaul and Italy. Attacori [200*c*].

The classic historians furnish no clue to the precise location of this people, but the circumstance that there were troops in Gaul bearing their name as late as Honorius affords the inference that they were then, or lately had been, dependent upon or friendly to the Romans, and therefore lay at no great distance from the frontier. The name seems to remain in that of Goodie Water in Menteith above Graham's Dyke, within twenty miles N.E. of Duntocher.

EPIDII. 'Επίδιοι. ("Uadha," *cave*).

199*a*. The Epidii lay W.N.W. of the Damnii, inclining N. from Epidium Pr. [134*g*] ; next to them (on the mainland N.) were the Cerones (*Ptol. corr.*). Their mainland territory included the headland of Kintyre ("ceann tir"), whence some derive their name, but they also occupied at one time or other all the islands off the W. coast of Scotland, called the Western Isles or Inner Hebrides [348]. The name Epidii is found only in Ptolemy.

MÆATÆ. Μαιάται. (*Dion*). (" Magh aith ").

199b. " Mæatæ " is first found in Dion, who was contemporary with Severus (193-211). These people then dwelt near the great wall in what had been part of Damnia, and they and the Caledonii, who lay behind them, were the most ample of the Britons. They were in arms in the early years of Severus's reign, perhaps encouraged by the departure of Clodius Albinus for Gaul, and were supported by the Caledonii. Apparently they acted with great vigour, since Virius Lupus, the legate, was obliged to purchase peace. The war being renewed, Severus went against them in person about 207 or 208, and some of their territory must have been involved in his conquests. Another rising of the Mæatæ and the same allies broke out in 210 ; but Severus died when preparing to coerce them, and Caracalla, his successor, broke off the war [111-112]. They do not occur again, but in the second half of the third century the Attacotti, who probably incorporated some, if not all of them, became formidable to the Romans. They have left their name in Dun Myatt between Stirling and Clackmannan.

PICTI (" uaghaidh," *cave*).

c. " Picti " is first found in Eumenius, A.D. 296, but he speaks of the people as enemies of the Britanni in the time of Julius Cæsar, and Sidonius Apollinaris assigns them as high an antiquity [65]. Eumenius mentions them again about 309 as including the Caledones, dwelling among woods and marshes, and as having been attacked by Constantius [116]. An unknown Latin writer states that this Emperor died post victoriam Pictorum (*Ritson's Annals*, i. 138). Marcellinus calls them savage. About 359 they and the Scotti assailed the Roman territory, and, together with the Attacotti, occur as enemies of the Empire several years later. They were driven back by Theodosius, 368-369 ; the Picti were at that time divided into two tribes, called Dicaledonæ and Vecturiiones [118]. In 383 they were defeated by Maximus, and in 396 by Stilicho [121-122]. After the withdrawal of the Romans they committed fearful ravages upon the Romano-Britons, and had great power in Scotland, but between 838 and 843 they were subdued by the Scots under Kenneth II., who took Camelon, their capital, and put its inhabitants to the sword. They are last mentioned as a separate people at the Battle of Brunanbyrig, or Weondune (Brun, Brynnev, Brunandune, Dumbrunde, Etbrunnanwerch), 937, when they and the Scots were vanquished by the Angles [223g]. The Latin writers down to the eighth or ninth century generally call them Picti, but later writers, perhaps following local pronunciation, somewhat varied the orthography :*

> Peohtas, *Alfred from Orosius ; Ethelwerd.*
> Peohtas, Pyhtas, Pihtum, *Sax. Chr.*
> Pehiti, *Witichind.*
> Peihtes, *Rob. of Brunne.*
> Petæ, *Thos. Bp. of Orkney.*
> Peychtis, *Wyntown.*

199*d.* In the time of Marcelline the Picti occupied the territory between the Forth and Tay, extending E. to W. from sea to sea. They always looked upon Albion as their home, but also had settlements in North Hibernia. They claimed descent, in common with the Scots, from the Albani or Gentes Scitiæ [38] ; and honoured, as their founder, Cruidne or Cruithne (son of Cinge or Kinne), who is called Pater Pictorum, and after whom all the Pictish people of Britain and Hibernia were called Cruithne by the Irish, and Cruithnich by the Gaels. See *Ritson's Annals,* i. 113, 254, *è Cronica Pictorum.* Cruithne, however, is probably only a personification of the Coraniaid, and in any case it is only possible to regard him as a mythical figure, who must have occupied the same position with respect to the Picts and their kinsmen, the Scots, as Woden† did with the Teutons, and Targitaus with the Scythians. The Picti themselves are Gaidhel (Gael)—a name possibly possessing a root relationship with Pict—their

---

* See Ritson's *Annals,* i. 97.

† It is not accidental that " di-ciadain," *day of Gaden,* became the Gaelic name for Wednesday (Wodnesdæg, Dies Mercurii).

principal mainland territory being Arregaithel (" Ary gaidhel ")
Argyle, the Ary being a small river flowing into Loch Fyne ;
and those who inhabited the Ebudæ Insulæ and Caledonia
(called Epidii and Caledonii), became the leading tribes in the
N. ; they or some of them were known to Dion, as the Mæatæ
and Caledonii, and he says that the names of the remaining
nations referred in general to them [III]. Still later the
Picts possessed the sovereignty of the whole country beyond
the Clyde and Forth, except the portion held by the Scots ;
giving name to Pentland Firth (Mare Petlandicum, Pightland
Firth), which separates Caithness from the Orcades. At a
later period the Picts also imposed their authority upon a
considerable district S. of the Forth, and are said to have given
name to Pentland (Pehtland) Hills. It must have been this
southern expansion which gave the Tyne Wall the name of
Picts' Wall. Interesting antiquities, referred to the Picts,
are scattered over the N.—*e.g.*, the Pictish brough or tower
at Mousa in the Shetlands, about 100 feet high, shaped like
a dice-box, and containing compartments approached by
circular stairs which ran to the top ; the somewhat similar
broughs at Burra and Hoxay in the Orkneys, the former
40 feet in diameter, the wall 12 feet thick at the foundations ;
the underground, cone-shaped Picts' houses of Quanterness
and Wideford, near Kirkwall, Orkneys, rising as green mounds
above the surface of the ground ; and among very many
Pictish broughs on the mainland of Britain, those at Caisteal
Coille, Carril, Carn-liath, and Cinn-Trôlla, near Brora, Sutherland, the former built of uncemented stone. That the religion
of the wheel was common to this remote district with the rest
of Britain may be gathered from the " Standing Stones " of
Stennis, near Kirkwall, consisting of the remains of two large
circles ; while a vestige of Scandinavian worship is furnished
by the curious stone barrow of Maeshow, near Stennis, containing runic inscriptions, one of which relates that the
building was erected as a sorcery-hall for Lodbrok. The
Picts' underground houses point to the winter dwellings of
their distant cousins of Scythian Siberia.

199*e.* The views of the monkish historians are sometimes
divergent. According to Nennius, the Picts came not later

than 800 (or 900) years after Eli the High-Priest judged Israel,
and established themselves in the Orcades. From the neighbouring islands they ravaged many regions, seizing the tracts
on the left side of Britain, where in his time (the end of the
eighth century, A.D.) they still possessed territories amounting
to a third of Britain. Gildas calls them a transmarine nation
from the north. Bede says they were called " transmarine "
because they dwelt beyond the estuaries of the Forth and
Clyde ; they came from Scythia, and desired to settle in
Hibernia among the Scots, but by the advice of the latter
occupied the N. part of Britannia, dispossessing the Britons,
and making a second nation in the island. Of the territory
thus acquired, that lying along the N. bank of the Clyde was
afterwards seized by the Scots themselves, who came in under
Reuda, and still held settlements among the Picts in the time
of Bede (*Ecc. Hist. I.* i. ; *Sax. Chr.*). Richard's first mention
of the Picts locates them no farther away than the Western
Isles, and he makes Reuda to be King of the Picts, instead of
the Scots, and says it was supposed he brought his people
from the islands into Britain about A.D. 170, the Scots
entering under Fergusius in 320 (*Ric. II.*, i. 26, 34).

199f. Two old authors speak of the Picts as neighbours of
the Scots :

> [Pictorum plebem et Scottos Britanniæ] utrosque
> Dorsi montes Britannici disterminant.—*Adomnan II.*,
> 47, *anno* 664.

> *After* A.D. 450. [Ochta et Ebisa] cum [petirent Scotos
> et] navigarent circa Pictos, vastaverunt Orchades insulas,
> veneruntque et occupaverunt plurimas regiones trans
> mare Fresicum—*i.e.*, quod inter nos Scotosque est, usque
> ad confinia Pictorum.—*Nenn., circa* A.D. 760.

It is thought that Ochta sailed up the W. coast of Britain,
and after wasting the Orcades attacked the Scotch territory
on the E. coast. The Fresic Sea beyond which these conquests
lay was perhaps that part of the German Ocean which was
supposed to form a huge gulf between the Parisi and the
conjectured E. prolongation of N. Britain.

It has been seen that, according to Bede, the Scots from

Ireland dispossessed the Picts of the N. bank of the Clyde. The De Situ Albaniæ, however, distinguishes Argyle from Scotia :

Montes qui dividunt Scotiam ac Arregaithel.

199g. On the whole, it seems that whatever changes came over Argyle and the Western Isles, the predominating element of the population was maintained unaltered. This population, extending to, and probably of the same race as the Homeric Kimmerii, first came upon the historic stage as the Epidii, then as the Picti (Ang.-Sax. Peohtas), these names, which only differed from each other dialectically, conforming respectively with the Gaelic words " uadh " " uaghaidh " (meaning *cave*). to which the etymology is referred. Thus the Picti were *cave-men*, dwelling amongst the cavernous rocks of the Ebudæ ; and the circumstance that the winter-house or tomb was often a cave, or from its peculiar construction was regarded as such, points to the source of the poetic notion that here, under the celestial pole, the souls of the departed had their abode. So Ptah was in origin, as in worship, the god of the cave or tomb, and also inevitably of darkness, and all the phenomena which the grave suggests. So also it is incontrovertible that the Epidii who lay between the Caledonii and Oc. Duecaledonius in A.D. 140, are the same people as the Pictish Dicaledonæ who occupied the same territory in 368. This circumstance is important in connection with the immigration triads.

h. The Welsh legends, though obscured by their adaptation to triadic composition, do not subvert the views just expressed as to the origin and nation of the Picts. The triads, it is true, anticipate the classics, since they bring the Kymry from Defrobani [38], while Homer finds them already in Britain ; but coming down to more recent triads, the Coraniaid, the first hostile tribe, who came from Pwyl (*cf.* Ynys Fail), and then the Gwyddyl Fichti, who came across the Sea of Llychlyn [134*f*], apparently present in their sequence a version of the legend of Cruithne, father of the Picts. The subsequent absorption of the Coraniaid by the Saxons, which left only two Kymric tribes in Britain—those of Cornwall and Carnoban —is interesting, for Carnoban is answered by Cairnbaan, a small place near Crinan, Argyle ; and the only Kymric peoples whose independence outlived Saxon power were the Welsh and Scots.

Scotti (*Am. Mar.*) ; Scoti (*Claudian*).

200a. A savage Caledonian people whose first historical settlements in Britain were N. of the Clyde and Forth, and who, with the Picts, were reputed descendants of the Albani or Gentes Scitiæ* [38]. The view early took root that they were a Scythian race, a theory favoured by Tacitus's opinion that the characteristics of the Caledonii suggested a Germanic origin, and by his opinion that the language of the Æstyi, an East Baltic people, was nearest to the British speech [37]. Æstyi, indeed, appears to be but a form of Scythæ, and Tacitus's remark gives it superficial significance in connection with the etymology of Scoti.

b. Sidonius Apollinaris, a fifth - century poet, says that Julius Cæsar routed the Scoti among other British nations [65]. The poet Florus states that Hadrian endured Scythian frosts in Britain [107], and the latter, it may be argued, is a definite allusion to the Scoti, since they dwelt in that part of the island where the winters were most severe. The Ancients, however, designated the entire N. of the globe by the term Scythia, and hence Ovid seems to make the latter extend from Cilicia (in Eastern Germany) to Britain [40]. The certain conclusion to be drawn from these notices is that Britain was almost as much Scythian as the rest of N. Europe ; that it was generally included in the indefinite use of that term, and

* It is unsafe to found an ethnological assertion upon a mere coincidence of names, yet the Scythic emigration theory, indirectly sanctioned by Tacitus, and supported by a comparison of languages, may be thought to receive confirmation from many northern names. Thus, the Æstyi may be regarded as either the source or a ramification of the Sitones of Scandinavia ; and the Sitones were predecessors if not ancestors of the Scandinavian Goths (Gutones, Codani), many traces of whom are met with in Sweden, and "Sweden" is related to Sitones. The Sitones, again, were neighbours, if not collateral kinsmen, of the Scandinavian Hilleviones, whose name orthographically is scarcely distinguishable from our Albani (Albion), and may still survive in Lapland. Lapland, again, may be‑compared with Labrador, and Scandinavia (Scandia) with Canada. *Cf.* Kimmeria, America.

that Scythæ was poetically applied to all those northern nations, whether Britons or not, whose manners, customs, and languages were savage and barbarous, and presented more or less such similarities as to suggest a common origin. That the Gaelic of Britain is of Scythian or Gothic origin is supported by the Gothic substructure which may be traced in it. The many word-roots common to the Moeso-Gothic of the time of Ulphilas and to the Gaelic, point to a single source, though the divergencies are such that the separation must have taken place very early. Tacitus's remark that the British speech did not differ much from the Gaulic, applied particularly to the parts of the island towards Gaul ; and his remarks respecting the Æstyan language must be understood as of the remainder of the island, or at least of the parts about Caledonia. Yet there must have been close affinity between the native tongues of Germania and Gaul, but whatever modifications crept into the spoken tongue of S. Britain through intercourse with Gaul, the speech of the whole of Britain at the arrival of the Romans was decidedly Gaelic.

200c. Porphyry, about A.D. 267. says that neither the province of Britain. nor the Scotticæ Gentes, nor the barbarous nations thereabouts, as far as the ocean, had known Moses and the prophets. This notice of the Scottish races after the province of Britain points obviously to the nations dwelling beyond the Roman limits in the island, and consequently the presence of the Scoti there at this period may be definitely assumed, especially as Porphyry appears to have had intimate knowledge of the then state of Britain [114]. St. Jerome (Hieronym 340-420) copies Porphyry's statement in his epistle to Ctesiphon against Pelagius, but has Scythicæ Gentes ; and in another epistle (the eighty-third) he mentions the Scotti, a British race (Gens Britannica), but it may be questioned whether he drew any distinction between the two terms. With the Scotti he also mentions the Atticori (Attacotti [196]), and remarks of both that they had wives mixedly, the children being regarded common. These customs repeat what earlier writers had written respecting the Mæatæ and Caledonii [44], and what Julius Cæsar had, with some difference, affirmed of the Britons [39]. St. Jerome also speaks with detestation of the Scotti, alleging that when in Gaul in his youth he had seen them eat human flesh. About 360 (Jerome being then twenty years of age) they occur in the contemporary history of Ammian Marcelline, who enumerates them among the nations which then broke into the Roman province ; and thenceforward they are intimately associated with Roman history until the evacuation, being driven back successively by Theodosius, 367-368, Maxim, 384, and Stilicho, 398 [118, 121-122]. Claudian, who was contemporary with these events, twice mentions the Scots as if closely connected with Ireland [120-122]. After the withdrawal of the Romans, they made constant plundering inroads into S. Britain until restrained by the Angles and Saxons, and in the first half of the ninth century they became paramount in Scotland by the overthrow of the Picts.

200d. Post-Roman writers held the view that the Scoti were closely connected with N. Ireland. Bede states they were living there before the Picti arrived from Scythia, and that they afterwards migrated to N. Britain under Reuda, and obtained settlements among the Picts in the W., above the Clyde, where they became known as the Dalreudini (*Ecc. H. I.*, i. 12). These newcomers are said to have given name to Dalriada, or Dalrieta, which, according to Bede, signified dal-Reuda, the *part or territory of Reuda ;* but this hero was apparently as mythical as his Pictish counterpart Cruithne [199d]. Dalriada is probably to be explained as dal-Riddon, implying the glen above Loch Riddon in Cowal, though the old historian evidently connected it with Reuta (N. Antrim). According to the De Situ Albaniæ, Scocia lay E. of Arregaichel, the boundary between them being apparently the mountain range extending from Ben Lomond to Ben Nevis.

e. It would seem that the Gentes Scitiæ embraced in common acceptation all the tribes of N. Britain. The interchangeability of " Scoti " and " Albani," the gradual displacement of " Caledonii " by " Albani," and the circumstance that the Gentes Scitiæ included the Picts, and that the whole country beyond the Picts Wall became finally known as Scotland, countenance, directly or indirectly, the same view. So the circumstances that the people were regarded as emigrants from the Scythæ of the European mainland, and that their language approached nearest to that of a tribe of Russian Scythia, are points which cannot be ignored in determining the etymology of the name. While the subject is surrounded with difficulty, it is possible at least to point to the ancient observation that the W. and N. were the dark quarters of the earth, and so associate the name with Gr. σκοτος, *darkness ;* G. "sgath," Corn. "sgeth," *a shadow, shade,* in allusion to the long dark nights which prevailed there when the sun traversed the region of Hea (*cf.* Europe, *darkness*). This explanation makes intelligible the scheme of those ancient geographers who, dwelling between the Mediterranean and Persian Seas, appropriately regarded the N. and W. as the land of night. To these people Scythia was more or less definitely the region about the nearest pole, characterized by short summers and long winters, and stretching from the extreme N.E. of Asia along the northern coasts of that continent and Europe to America (Russ. "mrak," Dan.-Nor. "merke," *darkness ; cf.* Merkland [30]), where it approached Asia again. Perhaps the Tuatha de Dannan of Irish legend were the Scythæ, connected with Russ. "tyan," *shadow ;* their country, Murias, being the land of frosts (Russ. "moroz" *frost*) ; *cf.* the Scythian and Caledonian frosts of Florus and Claudian. Their antagonists, the Fomorians, were the Pictish cave-men (" uamha," *cave ;* " fir," *men*).

200f. There were circumstances which pre-eminently associated the Albionic home of the Scythæ with the powers of darkness. Here lay the causeway to Hades (G. " ifrinn " often equated with Ierne) ; here, too, was the sepulchral mound of Elpenor whose obsequies form the only instance of the kind in the Odyssey, and hither the dead Ulysses was borne for burial. Even in historic times, Iona, the scene of the classic funerals, was the favourite sepulchre of Scotland's illustrious dead. So the curious rocks of the neighbouring sea, long and shaft-like as arrows, evidently combined with G. " saighead," *arrow,* to give to the dark or smiting sign the name of Sagittarius (*archer*). Again G. " sgud," *ship,* containing the elements of saighead, may have suggested the boat of Charon in which the departed spirits were ferried

across the river of Hades. It cannot be a matter for surprise
that Agricola's army, " famâ ferox," refused to be led into a
region associated with such stories [95]. Here, too, almost
overhead, in the vicinity of the basalts, the two bears, ever
visible, winged their flight around the celestial pole. In some
way or other the wing became associated with the Scythian
legends, perhaps through G. " sgiath," *wing*. The same word is
associated with the Isle of Skye, G. " an t'eilean Sgiathanach,"*
interpreted " winged island." However that may be, the
winged temple of the Hyperboreans [17] was in these seas,
and though classical literature contains no indication of its
precise site, it is not improbable that its original, or at least
a temple of the same kind, survives in the monolithic structure
of Turusachan, at Callernish, Isle of Lewis. This temple,
which consisted of forty-eight upright stones, and had a sunk
altar-chamber, calling to mind the deep compartments in the
pyramids, is in the form of a cross, the point of intersection
being enclosed within a circle ; the shaft, which points N.. is
392 feet long, the cross-shaft or wings 141 feet long, and the
diameter of the circle 42 feet. It is impossible not to see in
this temple the emblem of Assur, in which the god, encircled
at the waist by a ring, or sometimes standing before a circle
tilted upright, is the shaft or pole, the wings being the arms
or cross-shaft. Evidently the early Christian church-builders
adopted the forms and symbols of their predecessors, omitting
the circle, this style being exemplified in the remains of the
Cathedral of Iona and very many churches of historic date.
The winged temple is connected with the four-faced cherubim
which, according to Ezek. i., accompanied a whirlwind from the
north, while its astronomical purpose may be assumed from the
name of the Callernish temple, Turusachan (*cf.* Taurus [20*a*]).

CALEDONII ; CALEDONES. Καληδόνιοι, *Ptol.* (" coille,"
forest).

201*a*. First mentioned before A.D. 65 as the Caledonii
Britanni, designating the Britons of Caledonia [133]. Ptolemy
about A.D. 150 mentions the Caledonii as a tribe extending

* *Cf.* Gr. σκια, *shade:* Dan.-Nor., ("sky," *cloud;* "skygge," *shade.*

from the Lelannonius Sinus [134*f*] as far as the Varar Æst. [137*f*] ; al·ove them was the Caledonius Drumos, and more to the N.E. the Cantæ (*Ptol. corr.*). The term was at first used by the Romans to designate all the nations beyond the Tay, but Ptolemy restricts it, as above, to those occupying the most mountainous part of that region (*i.e.*, the district extending in a N.E. direction through Breadalbane and Badenoch). Agricola came in contact with these people in 83, and defeated them in the following year at Mons Grampius, traversing their territory on his way back to the Clyde [97, 103]. They had treaty obligations with the Romans early in the reign of Severus, but nevertheless espoused the cause of the Mæatæ. Severus, attacking them in person, forced concessions, which seem to have been soon relinquished [111-112]. In 296 they are mentioned under the name Caledones by Eumenius, who says they were Picts [116]. Thenceforward the place of the Caledonii in history is taken by the Picti and Scoti, though in poetry Claudian speaks of the monster Caledonian as late as 396 [122]. See [46].

201*b*. Caledonius Drumos. 'Ο καληδόνιος δρυμός ("druim"). The mountainous ridge lying above the Caledonii, the situation and name both pointing to Coil More Forest, about Loch Laggan, S. of Glen More nan Albin. This region perhaps supplied the best known of the ancient names of the Highlands :

Caledonia ; *cf.* Gulban (? coille ; "beann," *hill*), a stream which rises about Luban Loup, and skirts Coil More Forest.

Albion [10*b*] ; *cf.* Levin Water.

Drumalban ; *cf.* Drumouchter ("druim," "uachdar "), S.E. of Coil More Forest.

Dicaledonæ (Etha [133*a*] ; Caledonæ).

202. Mentioned by Marcelline about 361 as one of the two nations into which the Picts were divided [118]. They occupied Cowal and the neighbouring parts of Epidia, lying S. of the Caledonii of Ptol., and extending eastward to their Pictish kinsmen, the Vecturiones. The name, though only occurring ethnically as above, is much more ancient, the Duecaledonian Ocean being mentioned by Ptol., *c.* 140 [134]. Etha is possibly from the same root as " Pict."

VECTURIONES (" uachdar ").

203. Mentioned by Marcelline as one of the two Pictish nations, 361. They occupied at least the E. portion of Damnia N. of the Wall, and apparently had their name from the Damnian town Victoria [197g].

HORESTII, *Tac.* (" Ericht ").

204. These dwelt in Athole and Stormont, between Loch Ericht and Ericht Water, the latter a tributary of the Isla, which falls into the Tay. After the Battle of Mons Grampius, 84, Agricola led his army (exercitum deducit) through this territory, where he received hostages [103].

VENICONTES. Οὐενίκοντες. (*Benchinnin*, " Mount Keen.")

205. Situated S.E. of the Vacomagi, and S. of the Texali (*Ptol. corr.*), in the eastern projection of the Highlands, and probably separated from the latter by the Benchinnin Range, their western neighbours, A.D. 140, being the Caledonii and Damnii, and their S. boundary the Forth. Agricola was probably in their territory in A.D. 80, when he halted at the Tay in order to secure his rear, but Ptol. alone mentions them. This district must have been the most permanent of the Roman possessions beyond the Forth. It contained the town Orrea (*Ptol.*). The Promontory of Fife (Faobh) was in their territory.

ORREA. Ὀρρέα. Lon. 24.0, Lat. 58.45. Lochore, on Orr Water, under Benarty Hill, Co. Fife, possessing vestiges of a Roman fort.

TEXALI. Τεξάλοι. [137i].

206. Situated E. of the Vacomagi (*Ptol.*), having the Venicontes S.S.W., and extending along the Oc. Germanicus from the neighbourhood of the Diva, *Dee*, to the Doveran. Agricola must have been near their S. confines in 83, when the

Caledonii assailed the camp of the Ninth Legion in his rear [274c]. Ptol. names one town.

DEVANA. Δηούανα. Lon. 26.15, Lat. 59.45 [274a]. Glendavan, at Loch Davan, Aberdeen. Camp at Fernyhowe, one and a half miles N.E. Ptol.'s calculations, perhaps by an error of transcription, place this town too far W.

VACOMAGI. 'Ονακόμαγοι. (" uaigh magh ").

207a. E. of the Caledonii, and W. of the Texali (Ptol. corr.) ; having the Venicontes S.E. and the Æst. Vara N.W. Their name survives in Fochabers, near Speymouth. Agricola, supported by the fleet, approached this tribe in 84, but his troops, having shown disinclination to advance into Caledonia, he struck inland, towards his base, coming to Mons Grampius, Cairn Gorm, in the vicinity of which he defeated Galgacus [95, 97]. This hill was near their S. confines, and the victors probably advanced to it up the Spey. This territory was the farthest possessed by the Romans. Ptol. mentions four towns, whence it may be inferred that it was strongly garrisoned.

b. BANATIA. Βανατία. Lon. 24, Lat. 59.30. (" beann ait "). Etteridge, in Glen Truim, Inverness ; the name paraphrased in the neighbouring hill-name, Meall Odharaich.

c. TAMEA. Τάμεια. Lon. 25, Lat. 59.20. (" tom "). Tomatin, with Inverbrough and Corybrough on the Findhorn, Inverness.

d. PTEROTON. Πτερωτὸν στρατόπεδον, Pteroton camp. Lon. 27.15, Lat. 59.20. (" fad ord "). Tom Fade, under Ord Loch, Nairn. Tumuli. The camp, as indicated by Ptol.'s notice, was at some distance, being apparently the entrenched hill of Raitknock (" ord cnoc "), near Raitcastle, on the E. bank of the Nairn, two miles S. of Nairn. Pteroton is obviously the Gaelic appellation accommodated to Greek sounds, but Ric., misled by the Greek, Latinizes the word as Alatra Castra.

e. TUESIS [273a]. Τούεσις. Lon. 26.45, Lat. 59.10. (Tuæsis [137g]). Rothes, on the Spey. This post was probably important, since it anciently gave its name to the river.

CANTÆ.   Κάνται.   (" ceann ait ").

208. More to the N. than the Caledonii, and between the latter and the Logi (*Ptol. corr.*).   They inhabited the peninsula of Tain (Tarbet Ness), in Cromarty.

LOGI.   Λόγοι.   (" Evlix ").

209. Between the Cantæ and Cornabii, and E. of the Mertæ (*Ptol. corr.*); dwelling in S.E. Sutherland, about the small river Evlix [137*e*].   Near their confines, towards Cornavia, was the River Lotha of Ossian's poems, now Loth.

MERTÆ.   Μέρται.   (" magh ord ").

210. W. of the Logi (*Ptol. corr.*); separating the latter from the Carnonacæ and Cerones, and extending over the Caledonios Drumos to the Muir of Ord and the town of Cromarty (" crom ord "), thus comprising part of Cromarty-shire [200*d*].

CERONES.   Κέρωνες.
CARNONACÆ.   Καρνονάκαι.
CARENI.   Καρενοί.
CORNABYI.   Κορναβύοι, Κορναύιοι.

211. Next to the Epidii were the Cerones, then the Carno-nacæ, then the Careni, and last and most northerly the Cornabyi (*Ptol. corr.*).

CERONES.   On the mainland, opposite Skye, dwelling about the Croe (a tributary of Loch Duich ; *cf.* Ceres [5]), near the scene of some of Ossian's poems [133*a*] ; perhaps connected with Ardgour and the medieval kingdom of Gouerin.

CARNONACÆ.   (Gruin ; " ard," *cnag*, *cnoc*).   In Gruinard and parts of Ross and Cromarty.

CARENI.   (" Acharn.")   About Acharn, in the vicinity of Cape Wrath.

CORNABYI.   In Caithness, bounded S.E. by the Logi, and perhaps connected with the name Duncansby.

ANTONINI ITINERARIUM BRITANNIARUM.

212. This work is usually attributed to Antonine Pius, A.D. 138-161. If such was its date it must have been compiled before the wars of Lollius, for the boundary indicated by it is inconsistent with Lollius's murus, if that murus was Deils Dyke [165]. It is more probable that the work belongs to the reign of Antonine, otherwise Caracalla (211-217), who, abandoning the advanced possessions of the empire, seems to have fallen back upon the Tyne Wall, which ever afterwards marked the limit towards the N.W. The purpose of the Iters was obviously military ; many of the stations are hill-posts, some over 1,000 feet above sea-level, as Brocavum Iter V., and in those cases, as in others, the situations are generally unfavourable for large industrial or agricultural populations. Many cities which must have been pre-eminent in commercial importance are not noticed at all.

ITER I.

213a. A limite, *i.e.* a Vallo Pretorium usque M.P. CLVI.

	M.P.	
A Bremenio		[195c]
Corstopitum	XX.	
Vindomora	IX.	
Vinovia	XIX.	
Cataractoni	XXII.	[191e]
Isurium	XXIIII.	[191g]
Eboracum Leg. VI. Vict...	XVII.	[191j]
Derventione	VII.	
Delgovitia	XIII.	
Pretorio	XXV.	
	CLVI.	

b. LIMES, *i.e.* VALLUM [214a, 218a]. The Tyne Wall.

c. CORSTOPITUM (cor stob aite). Ouston, Stob Hill,
 . 1 S.E. of Stamfordham, Northumb.

d. VINDOMORA (" beannte iomaire "). Gibside, Marley
 Hill, E. of the Derwent, 3 S. of Blaydon, Durh.

e. VINOVIA (" beann Eu "). Redford Grove, near
 Pennington, on Euden Beck, 4 S. of Wolsingham,
 Durh.

213*f*. DERVENTIO [236*k*] ("dur vent"). Thorganby (Derwent-by), on the Derwent, Yorks. In 866 (867, *Sax. Chr.*) the Danes, having routed the Northumbrians at this place, then called Dubkynt, entered and plundered York (*Brut y Tyw.*). The Roman station probably stood in the neighbourhood of Thicket Priory, where the Derwent formerly made a considerable curvature.

g. DELGOVITIA ("Tulach fad"). Goodmanham, by Market Weighton, Yorks. Some earthworks here, supposed to have been a heathen temple, probably mark the site of the Roman station. The neighbouring hills have many tumuli and entrenchments. "Del" in this name survives in Towthorpe (D.B. Toletorp), an adjoining hamlet, and "govitia" in Goodmanham.

h. PRETORIUM ("bior eitre"). Halsham, by Ottringham, 4½ N.W. of Patrington. Intrenchment, within which is Halsham Church.

ITER II.

214*a*. A Vallo ad Portum Ritupis M.P. $\frac{\text{CCCCLXXXI}}{\text{CCCCCXXXI.}}$

	M.P.	CORRECTED NUMBERS.	
A Blato Bulgio			
Castra Exploratorum	XII.		
Luguvallio	XII.		
Voreda	XIV.		
Brovonacis	XIII.		
Verteris	XIII.		
Lavatris	XIIII.		
Cataractoni	XIII.	XIX.	⎫
Isurium	XXIIII.	XXIII.	⎬ Iter 1.
Eburacum	XVII.	XVII.	⎭
Calcaria	IX.		
Camboduno	XX.	XXX.	
Manucio	XVIII.	XXIII.	
Condate	XVIII.		
Deva Leg. XX. Victrix	XX.		
Bomio	X.		
Mediolano	XX.		[187*b*]
Rutunio	XII.		
Urioconio	XI.		
Usocona	XI.		

		M.P.	CORRECTED NUMBERS.	
Pennocrucio ..	..	XII.		
Etoceto	.. ..	XII.		
Manduessedo ..	..	XVI.		
Venonis	.. ..	XII.		
Benavenna	.. ..	XVII.		
Lactodoro	.. ..	XII.		
Magiovinto	.. ..	XVII.		Iter VI.
Durocobrivis ..	..	XII.		
Verolamio	.. ..	XII.		
Sulloniacis	.. ..	IX.		
Londinio	.. ..	XII.		[168b]
Noviomago	.. ..	X.		
Vagniacis	.. ..	XVIII.		
Durobrivis	.. ..	IX.		
Durolevo	.. ..	XVI.		
Duroverno	.. ..	XII.		
Ad Portum Ritupis ..		X.		
		CCCCLXXXXIX.	CCCCCXIX.	

214b. VALLUM [213b].

    c. BLATO BULGIUM (" balladh bolg "). Pelutho, in Holme Cultram, Cumb.

    d. CASTRA EXPLORATORUM (" ach poll ard "). Herd Hill, Bowness [127], at the W. extreme of the Wall. Roman remains : camp at Campfield, Bowness Common. Inscription found 1739 : " I.O.M. PRO SALUTE D.D. N.N. GALLI ET VOLU- SIANI AUGG." &C. A°. 251.

    e. LUGUVALLIUM [264f]. CARLEOL, *Sax. Chr.*, 1092 (" Loich balladh "). Carlisle. Roman remains. The wall approached the Eden at Stanwicks, where it crossed to this place.

    f. VOREDA [264e] (" bor aite "). Near Park House, Greystoke Park, 1 N. of Berrier Hill, Cumb. Roman camp on Gillcambon Beck, 1 N.W., and on Berrier Hill. Usually placed at Old Penrith.

    g. BROVONACIS (" bru whin ach "). Julian Bower, Whinfell Park, near the confluence of the Lyvennet and Eden.

    h. VERTERIS [234a] (" bru toirrse "). Fox Tower, near High Burtergill, 1 N.W. of Brough, under Stainsmoor.

214i. LAVATRIS [234a] (" lab toirrse "). Lathbury, by Cotherstone, 3 N.W. of Barnard Castle. Butter Stone, S.W. Camden and later writers place Lavatris at Bowes. Numerous inscriptions at Bowes :

IMP. CÆSARI DIVI TRAIANI PARTHICI *FIL*
DIVI NERVÆ NEPOTI TRAIANO *HADRIA*
NO AUG. PONT. MAXM. . . .
COS. I. . . . P.P. COH. IIII. F. . . .
        IO SEV   —*Reyn.* 187.

DAE . . . FORTVNÆ
VIRIVS LVPVS
LEG. AVG. PR. PR.
BALINEVM VI
IGNIS EXVST
VM COH. I. THR
ACVM REST
ITVIT CVRANTE
VAL. FRON
TONE PRÆF.
EQ. ALÆ VETTO.

                —*T. Gale,* 41.

j. CALCARIA (" calc ar "). Tadcaster, in an extensive limestone district. Cealca-ceaster (*Bed. Ecc. Hist.*), iv. 23. In the seventeenth century the old name was still retained near the town in a hill called Kelchar (*Reyn. è Camd.*, 191 ; Kelc-barr, *T. Gale,* 45). Gale says (p. 44) : " (Tad-caster) in Monastico Anglicano audit Helecester nomen sanè mutuatum a calce pedis, ita enim vocatur pars ista Saxonicè, quemadmodum et alia appellatione in eadem lingua Tah." Hele-cester, however, is directly from " aol," G. *lime :* and " Tad " is perhaps a corruption of " hýðe " this place probably being the " cealc-hýðe " where a tumultuous synod was held in A.D. 785 (*Sax. Chr.*).

k. CAMBODUNUM (" cam bow dun "). Gomershall, near Birstall, 3 N.W. of Dewsbury ; Carlingbow S.E. Edwin of Northumbria built a church in Campodunum, but after a few years it was burnt, with all the town, by the pagans, 633 (*Bed. Ecc Hist.*, ii. 14). The Saxon paraphrast of Bede understood *camp* in this word as *campus* (Lat.), *field*, and adding the latter to the remainder of the word, formed Donafelda. Cambodunum is sometimes placed at Huddersfield (D.B. Oderesfelt), where were found in 1743 the foundations of a temple dedicated to Fortuna by Antony Modestus, or Modestine, of the Leg. VI. Vict.

The shortest distance from Gomershall to Manchester (the vicinity of the next station) is 29 miles, but the Iter has only 18, so that apparently an intermediate post has dropped out. This lost post, if it did not deviate from a direct line to Manchester, would be in the neighbourhood of Bolster Moor, S.W. of Golcar.

214*l.* MANUCIUM ("magh cnag"). At or near Manchester, in the vicinity of Nico Ditch (which preserves the name), perhaps at the point where the Roman road to Stockport intersects the Ditch near Levenshulme (Burnage, S.W.). This station is by general consent placed at Manchester, and considered to be the Mancunium of Iter X. ; the distance to Condate (Iters II. and X.) suits both Manchester and the site near Levenshulme. The flaw in Iter II., between Cambodunum and Manucium, precludes a satisfactory solution of the question. See Mancunium [*223h*].

m. CONDATE [*223a 258e*] ("ceann tot"). Senna Green, 1 N.W. of Comberbach, near Northwich, Chesh. Condate is usually placed at Kinderton, 23 miles from Manchester, but erroneously, the recorded distance of 18 miles being confirmed by Iter X.

n. DEVA LEG. XX. VICTRIX [*224a, 257d*]. At the mouth of the Dee, near Queen's Ferry, by Aston, [*186a*]. Usually placed at Chester, but inadmissibly. See Brig [*282c*]. D.B. notices, in Atiscros Hundred, Hamo's manors of Estone and

Castretone ; and perhaps Deva may be identified with the latter.

214*o.* BOMIUM ("uaimh"). Bryn Bowlio, W. of the Alyn, 2 S.E. of Moel Fammau, Denbigh ; in the line of Iter XI.

p. RUTUNIUM ("Roden"). Blackhurst Ford, on the Roden, Salop, 2 S.E. of Welch Hampton.

q. URIOCONIUM [225*a*] ("uir-aoi ceann"). Ebury Hill Camp, Haughmond Hill, 4 N.E. of Shrewsbury.

r. USOCONA ("ais ceann"). Waxhill, 1½ N.E. of St. George's Church, near Wombridge, Salop.

s. PENNOCRUCIUM ("beann cruach"). Penkridge, on Penk, Staffs. Beyond this place the Iter falls into Watling Street, along which it proceeds to Wall

t. ETOCETUM ("tacaid"). Wall, Staffs, 2 S.W. of Lichfield. The modern village stands within the camp, and derives its name from the Roman wall, a fragment of which exists on the E. side. Chesterfield, S. Roman antiquities. The adjoining city of Lichfield (Licedfeld, Licitfeld) probably had its name from G. "lag" *hollow ;* "aith," *hill.*

u. MANDUESSEDUM ("monadh siat"). Hartshill, by Mancetter, S.E. of Atherstone, Warw. Tumuli. Roman station at Oldbury, W. By general consent, Manduessedum is placed 1 N.W. of Hartshill, at the Roman walled town on Watling Street, 15 miles from Wall ; but the distance negatives this allocation ; this last post is divided by Watling Street into almost equal parts, and the rampart mound is still traceable nearly throughout its whole circuit.

v. VENONIS [219*a*, 221] ("beannan"). Ullesthorp ("aill"), by Claybrook (formerly Claychester), 3 N.W. of Lutterworth, near the intersection of Watling Street and the Foss. The road which connected the station with Ratæ [219*d*] is probably partly identical with the Foss.

3½ S. of Ullesthorp is Cestre Over, on the

Warwickshire side of Watling Street, with entrenchments and tumuli in the townships of
Brownsover and Churchover.

214w. BENAVENNA. BANNAVANNUM [221] (" beann abhainn "). Vengeance Hill, Charwelton, at the
source of the Cherwell, Northants.

x. LACTODORUM [219a] (" loic," " toitear," whence
Tove). *Cair draithou* [290f]. Towcester, Northants. The Tove here forms an islet, perhaps
artificial, within which is Bury Mount, probably
the site of the Roman fortress. Tofeceastre was
fortified by King Edward in 921, and successfully
resisted a Danish attack the same year (*Sax. Chr.*).

y. MAGIOVINTUM [221]. MAGIOVINIUM [219a] (" magh
Wavendon "). On Wavendon Heath, Bow
Brickhill (" bruach "), 2 N.E. of Fenny Stratford,
Bucks. Entrenchment towards Woburn Sands.
Watling, 1½ S.W.

z. DUROCOBRIVIS [219a, 221] (" doireach fearb ").
Warden Hill, near Bramingham, 3 N. of Luton,
Beds. Drays Ditches (preserving part of the
old name), intersected by Icknield Street, trend
between Warden Hill and Galley Hill. The
camp of Waulud's Bank, 2 S.W. " Brivis," occurring in this and two other words in Ant.,
is variously interpreted *bridge* and *town*, but the
modern name of Durocobrivis (Drays Ditches)
shows that it was applied to artificial mounds or
earthworks.

215a. VEROLAMIUM [221] (" uir lom "). Verulam, St.
Albans, on the Ver ; an important city, possessing
a theatre and mint, and defended by a wall and
foss. Cæsar does not mention it, but it was
afterwards under a Prince named Tasciovanus,
some of whose coins have been found [45] ; the
Romans occupied it *temp.* Claudius, and it was
pillaged by the Iceni and allies A.D. 61 [83]. The
abbey church of St. Albans is built of Roman
materials.

215*b*. SULLONIACIS ("slinn acha"). Near Weald Park, 1 W. of Great Stanmore, Middl. Earthworks 1 mile long between Hatch End and Harts Burn. The road hence to Londinium apparently went by Kingsbury Green and Hampstead.

c. NOVIOMAGUS ("cnap magh"). Croydon, on the Wandle, Surrey.

d. VAGNIACIS ("uaighean acha"). Falkham (D.B. Fachesham), E. of the Darent, Kent. This station generally placed at Southfleet, 3 N.E., near Watling Street.

e. DUROBRIVIS [216-217]. DUROBRABIS [255*e*] ("dur fearb" [214*z*]). Rochester. Bede calls this place Rhofescestir, and, adopting the easy but reckless etymology usual with early monkish writers, says that it had its name from Rhof, who was the chief man in it (*Ecc. Hist.*, ii. 3). A charter of Ethelwulf of Wessex, A° 844, calls it Durobrevum, "id est civitas Hrofi" (*Dip. Ang.*, 98), and it appears occasionally as Hrobum. In the Medway marshes between the town and the Thames the Romans had extensive potteries, as is evident from vast accumulations of potters' rubbish.

f. DUROLEVUM [229*b*] ("dur lab"). Holbourn, near Throwley, 1 N. of Stalisfield, Kent.

g. DUROVERNUM [216-217, 255*c*] ("dur feoran"). Canterbury. From the sixth century onwards this city was called Durovernia, or Durobernia (Sax. Cantwareberig, Sax.-Lat. Cantuaria). No doubt behind the Stour, either at or near this place, the Britons awaited the first conflict with Cæsar [56].

AD PORTUM RITUPÆ [168*d*]. The Iter numeral locates the station at Woodnesborough, 1½ from Worth ; hence the formula AD PORTUM—*near the port.*

ITER III.

216. A Londinio ad Portum Dubris M.P. LXVI.

			M.P.	
Durobrivis ..	..	..	XXVII.	Iter. II.
Duroverno ..	..	..	XXV.	
Ad Portum Dubris		..	XIV.	
			LXVI.	

DUROVERNUM. XXVI. m.p. from Durobrivæ, according to Iter II. ; the extra mile being due to the deviation to Durolevum.

PORTUS DUBRIS [229*b*, 232, 255*b*] (" dobhar "). Dover, at the mouth of the small stream formerly called the Dubris [279*c*]. The site of the old port is uncertain ; anchors and remnants of ships excavated at the modern town suggest that the sea has receded, but the discovery of coins and antiquities on the beach has led to the counter-argument that the sea has encroached. Tiles found here inscribed CL. BR. (Classiarii Britannici) show that it was a naval station. It was attached to the Litus Sax. Roman roads, still clearly traceable, connected it with Rutupiæ and Durovernum. But little remains of the castrum except entrenchments, the principal of which, occupying the summit of the hill, contains what is regarded as the Roman pharos, or lighthouse. The Iter station, situated " ad portum," was probably towards Charlton. Various reading of numerals, XV. m.p.

ITER IV.

217. A Londinio ad Portum Lemanis M.P. LXVIII.

			M.P.	
Durobrivis ..	..	..	XXVII.	Iters. II., III.
Duroverno ..	..	..	XXV.	
Ad Portum Lemanis		..	XVI.	
			LXVIII	

PORTUS LEMANIS [229*b*, 232, 255*a*] (" luimean "). Lymne, Kent ; connected with Canterbury by Stone Street. Antiquities : Tiles of the CL. BR.;

also an altar discovered built up in the great gateway of the castrum, inscribed :

. . . IV . . .

ARAM.

. . . AVFIDIV

PANTERA

PRÆFECT

CLAS. BRIT.

This station was attached to the Litus Sax. The River Lemanus [279*d*] formerly flowed by the town, but has disappeared, probably in consequence of the receding of the sea, which has transformed the place into a rural village. In a charter of Ethelbert of Kent, A.D. 732, relating to the fourth of a ploughland near Limenee, convenient for preparing salt, the bounds are " ab austro fluvius qui dicitur Liminæe ; ab occidente et in septentrione Hudan fleot " (Hythe) (*Dip. Ang.*, 20, 21). The military station was *near* the port (" ad portum ").

ITER V.

218*a*. A Londinio Luguvallium ad Vallum M.P. CCCCXLIII.

	M.P.	CORRECTED NUMBERS.	
Cæsaromagus ..	XXVIII.		
Colonia	XXIII.		
Villa Faustini ..	XXXV.		
Icianos	XVII.		
Camborico ..	XXXV.		
Duroliponte `..`	XXV.		
Durobrivis ..	XXXV.		
Causennis ..	XXX.		
Lindo	XXVI.		[189*b*].
Segeloci ..	XIIII.		
Dano	XXI.		
Legeolio ..	XVI.		
Eburaco ..	XXI.		It. I., II.
Isubrigantum ..	XVII.		,, (Isurium).
Cataractoni ..	XXIIII.		,,
Lavatris ..	XVIII.	XVIIII.	It. II.
Verteris ..	XIII.	XIIII.	,,
Brocavo ..	XX.		
Luguvallio ..	XXII.		It. II.
	CCCCXLI.	CCCCXLIII.	

218b. CÆSAROMAGUS [222, 229b, 260b] ("casair magh"). High Easter (D.B., Estram), 5 S. of Great Dunmow, Essex. Keeres Green, E.

c. COLONIA [260d]. Cair collon [290b] ("Coln"). Colchester, on Colne, Essex. Numerous antiquities. The ancient name of this town is usually identified with Lat. *colonia*, encouraging the assumption that the town is the colony Camulodunum [178b]; but there is no evidence that Colchester was a colony.

d. VILLA FAUSTINI ("bol ous-tighean"). Euston, on the Little Ouse, Suff., 2 S.E. of Thetford.

e. ICIANI ("uaighean"). Shingham, 4 S.W. of Swaffham. The old name is also probably contained in Beachamwell, between Shingham and the Devil's Dyke ([161b].

f. CAMBORICUM ("cam bruach"). Cambridge. Vestiges of an entrenched town, yielding Roman antiquities. Camden supposed Grantchester, 2 S., to be the site of this station, but the notion is untenable. See Fleam Dyke [161a].

Cam and Rhee, variant names of the Granta, seem to be modern appellations of that river.

g. DUROLIPONTE ("dur ol beannte"). Pond's Bridge, on Holme Brook, 6 S.E. of Peterborough. Arlmynde's Hills, 2½ W., probably connected with the name. Oakley Dyke points from this place towards Peterborough, passing, about midway, the ancient entrenchment at Horsey Hill.

h. DUROBRIVIS ("dur fearb"). Thorp Arnold, 1 N.E. of Melton Mowbray, Leics.

This station is generally placed at Chesterton on Nen, W.S.W. of Peterborough. There, vestiges exist of a large Roman camp, intersected by Ermine Street; and N. of the Nen, within 1 mile, is Castor [182f]. Normanton Fields, near Castor, said to be properly Dormanton Fields, may have furnished Richard with his Durno Magus.

218i. CAUSENNIS ("casan"). Bicker, 1½ S.W. of Swineshead ("causennis head"), Lincs. This name
probably refers to one or some of the several
banks or walls, conveniently used as roads, which
converged upon Swineshead—viz., the Roman
Bank [167], Bridgend Causeway, and Gosberton
Bank.

Roman remains have been found at Swineshead. Near the abbey is Manwar (? Maincester,
temp. Henry II.), a double-fossed circular camp,
about 60 yards in diameter.

j. SEGELOCUM [277g]. AGELOCUM [221] (" aiseag
loich "). Littleborough, Notts. The Roman
road here crossed the Trent by a paved ford (see
milliare [189b]). Roman coins and pottery are
found in the neighbourhood in abundance. This
is the place (described as near Tiovulfingacestir—
i.e., Tilchester—now Stowe), where Bishop Paulinus baptized a great number of people in the Trent
in the presence of Edwin of Northumbria (*Bede,
Ecc. Hist.*, ii. 16).

k. DANUM [234a]. Doncaster, Yorks. The castrum
is supposed to have stood towards the curvature
of the Don by St. George's Church. Remains of
the dykes and foundations of walls were visible
in Leland's time ; and a votive altar to the Deæ
Matres was dug up in St. Sepulchre's Gate in 1781.

l. LEGEOLIUM. LAGECIUM [221]. Castleford, Yorks.
The Ermine Street, so called, crossed the Calder
here, and Roman antiquities have been found at
the town and on Hoile Hill, 1 S. ; the latter probably a corruption of the Iter name. The road
hence to York proceeded through Aberford and
Tadcaster.

m. BROCAVUM (" bruach abh "). The castle, on High
Street, above Ulleswater, 3½ N.W. of Bampton,
Westm. Brock Crag, 1½ S.W. Eamont (the
water connecting Ulleswater with the Eden)
seems to paraphrase this name.

ITER VI.

219a. A Londinio Lindum M.P. CLVI.

	M.P.	CORRECTED NUMBERS.	
Verolamio ..	XXI.		Iter. II.
Durocobrio ..	XII.		„ Durocobrivæ.
Magiovinio ..	XII.		„ Magiovintum.
Lactodoro ..	XVI.		„
Isannavatia ..	XII.		
Tripontio ..	XII.		
Venonis ..	IX.		Iter. II.
Ratis	XII.		
Verometo ..	XIII.	XII.	Iter. VIII.
Margiduno ..	XIII.	XII.	„
Ad Pontem ..	VII.		
Crococolana ..	VII.		
Lindo	XII.		Iter. V.
	CLVIII.	CLVI.	

b. ISANNAVATIA (" sunn Wed "). Staverton, 2 S.W. of Daventry, at the source of Weedon Beck (commonly confounded with the Nen). Arbury Hill camp, 1½ S.

c. TRIPONTIUM (" eitre avonta "). The Roman camp (D.B., Derbingerie), S. of the Avon, near Wolston, Warw. At this place the original Watling Street probably intersected Foss Way.

d. RATÆ [221]. RATECORION [259a]. CAIR LERION [290e] (" ritheadh "). Leicester, on the skirt of Charnwood Forest, and the ancient woodland of Kirby Frith or Leicester Forest (cf. Rutland, grove-land). Ratæ Corion is clearly an ancient form of Charnwood (stone-wood: G. " carn," plur. " cuirn," stone) ; and the River Soar, which flows past the rocky heights of this interesting district, signifies carn-water (cf. Sharnbrook). The old name Ratæ survives in Raw Dykes, about 1½ S. from the centre of the town. A massive piece of masonry, evidently Roman, called the Jewry Wall, set with arches, stands near St. Nicholas' Church ; and in 1793 a Roman sewer was dis-

covered between this wall and the Soar. Other
antiquities include fragments of tesselated pavements ; a piece of a Samian patera, perforated for
suspension, bearing in gold characters the names
VERECVNDA LVDIA, LVCIVS GLADIATOR ; and a
milliare found in 1771, on the Foss Way, 2 N.,
inscribed :

IMP CAES.

DIV. TRAIAN. PARTH. F. DIV.

TRAIAN. HADRIAN. A. P. M. TR.

POT. IV. COS. III. A RATIS

II.

In the unsettled times following the Saxon im-
migration Ratæ probably became one of the most
important towns, if not the capital, of the Middle
Angles (afterwards Mercia), under the name
LYGERA (LEGRA) CEASTRE ("leac," *slate, flat
stone ;* " Ra," *Raw, Ratæ—i.e., slate-wood chester.
Sax. Chr.,* 917, 920). Its importance under the
Middle Angles is attested by the fact that the
Cymry called England Lloegr, and the English
Lloegrwys. Leicester was a bishopric in the
seventh, eighth, and ninth centuries. In 1086 it
was styled Civitas de Ledecestre (D.B.). The
Saxon name is a variant of Coritani, referring,
however, to the roofing slates of Charnwood, in-
stead of the generally rocky character of that tract.

219e. VEROMETUM. VERNOMETUM [221] (" bru mat ").
Six Hills, on the Leics and Notts boundary, where
Great Lane crosses Fairham Brook and Foss Way.
The station gave name to Framland Wapentake,
Leics., and to Fairham Brook, which rises in the
vicinity, and flows N.W., falling into the Trent at
Wilford. Tumulus W. of the Foss at Broughton
Lane End. The Roman road from Derby ran
direct to this station, being identical with Great
Lane ; and its continuation S.E. led to the camp
at Burrow [289a].

f. MARGIDUNUM [221] (" murach dun "). Castle Hill,
East Bridgeford, Notts. The station is inter-

sected by Foss Way, and an ancient road, called Bridgeford Street, leads from it to the Trent..

219g. AD PONTEM (" aite vont " *Devon*). Farndon, Notts, on the Foss between the Trent and Devon, near their confluence.

h. CROCOCOLANA [221] (" cruach cluain "). Brough, Notts, 1 S.E. of Collingham, which contains the name. Many antiquities : iron-ore, iron-cinders, pots, urns, bricks, etc. (*Stukeley*).

ITER VII.

220a. A Regno Londinium M.P. XCVI.

	M.P.	
Clausento	XX.	
Venta Belgarum	X.	[173g].
Calleva Attrebatum	XXII.	
Pontibus	XXII.	
Londinio	XXII.	[168b].
	XCVI.	

b. REGNUM (" rucan "). Racton, Sussex, 2 N.E. of West Bourn, at the W. extremity of the Lavant Ditches [157] (see [170a]).

c. CLAUSENTUM (" clais ionad "). On Netley Common, near the point where the great ditch there is intersected by the road from Bittern [136e] to Bursledon, Hants. This ditch (G. " clais "), starting from Bittern, is traceable thence past the tumuli on Bursledon Heath, where it points to the Hamble, near Ridge ; its purpose was, perhaps, to curb the Segontiaci.

d. CALLEVA ATTREBATUM. CALLEVA [253d] (" colbh ") Silchester, Hants, in Attrebatia [171] ; a walled town which has yielded many Roman antiquities [283v] ; remains of amphitheatre outside the E. gate. The name perhaps related to the Nymph or Imp Stone, 1 W. Coins of Eppillus rex found here bear the word CALLEV (CALLE). Ogham inscription found in 1893.

220e. Pontes (" beann dus "). Wentworth, Virginia Water, near Egham, Surrey. The Roman road approaches this place over Bagshot Heath, on which there are extensive military remains, and proceeds to London via Staines.

Iter VIII.

221. Ab Eburaco Londinium M.P. ccxxvii.

	M.P.	CORRECTED NUMBERS.	
Lagecio	xxi.		Iter. V., Legiolium.
Dano	xvi.		,,
Ageloco ..	xxi.		,, Segelocum.
Lindo	xiv.		Iter. VI.
Crococolana ..	xiv.	xii.	,,
Margidunum ..	xiv.		,,
Vernometo ..	xii.		,,
Ratis	xii.		,,
Venonis ..	xii.		,,
Bannavanno ..	xviii.		*Iter. II. Benavenna.
Magiovinto ..	xxviii.		* ,,
Durocobrivis ..	xii.		,,
Verolamio ..	xii.		,,
Londinio ..	xxi.		,,
	ccxxvii.	ccxxv.	

Iter IX.

222a. A Venta Icenorum Londinium M.P. cxxviii.

				M.P.	
Sitomago ..	..	..	..	xxxi.	
Combretonio	..	..	..	xxii.	
Ad Ansam ..	..	..	..	xv.	
Camaloduno	..	..	..	vi.	
Canonio ..	..	..	..	ix.	
Cæsaromago	..	..	..	xii.	[218b].
Durolito ..	..	..	..	xvi.	
Londinio ..	..	..	..	xv.	[168b].
				cxxvi.	

b. Venta Icenorum [179b].

c. Sitomagus (" siat magh "). Stow Bedon, by Thompson, 5 W. of Attleborough, Norf.

* These distances differ one mile from those stated in Iter. II., apparently owing to the inclusion in Iter. II. of the intermediate posts of Tripontium and Lactodorum

222 *d.* COMBRETONIUM [*229b*] ("cam breath"). Denham Castle, in Barrow, 6 W. of Bury St. Edmunds. Usually placed at Brettenham on Brett.

e. AD ANSA [*229b*] ("aite neas"). Shudy Camps, Nosterfield, 6 N.E. of Saffron Walden. Numerous military remains.

f. CAMALODUNUM (*Tac.*). Camulodunum [*229b, 260c*] ("cam oll dun"). Saffron Walden, near the Granta, Essex ; *temp.* Tiberius, the residence of Cunobelin [45], and *temp.* Claudius, the Trinobantine capital ; as Camelot, honoured as King Arthur's capital. Its capture by the Romans was one of the early incidents of the Claudian invasion [71], and under their rule it became an important city and a colony [75], possessing (A.D. 61) a curia, a theatre, and a temple dedicated to Claudius [79] ; its destruction in that year [82] was only a temporary misfortune, and it probably continued one of the chief cities of Britain throughout the whole period of Roman rule. Camp on Ring Hill, E.

CN. MVNATIVS. M.F. PAL.

AVRELIVS. BASSVS.

PROC. AVG.

PRAEF. FABR. PRÆF. COH. III.

SAGITTARIOR. PRÆF. COH. II.

ASTYRVM. CENSITOR. CIVIVM.

ROMANORVM . COLONIÆ . VICTRICENSIS.

QVÆ . EST . IN . BRITANNIA . CAMALODVNI.

CVRATOR . VIÆ . NOMENTANÆ.

PATR . EIVSDEM . MVNICIPI.

FLAMEN . PERPETVVS . DVVMVIRALI.

POTESTATE . ÆDILIS . DEDICATOR . IIII.

—*Grut.* 439.

g. CANONIUM [*229b*] ("ceann aon"). Hawkins Hill, between Finchingfield and the Pant, Essex.

h. DUROLITUM ("dur allt"). Haroldwood, on Weald Brook, 2 N.E. of Romford, Essex. Vestiges of Roman road pointing towards Chelmsford. Camp at Weald.

Iter X.

223a. A Glanoventa Mediolanum M.P. CL.

					M.P.	
Galava	..	..	..	..	XVIII.	
Alone..	..	..	..	..	XII.	
Galacum	..	..	..	..	XIX.	
Bremetonacis		..	..	..	XXVII.	
Coccio	..	..	..	..	XX.	
Mancunio	..	..	..	..	XVII.	
Condate	..	..	..	..	XVIII.	Iter. II.
Mediolano	..	..	..	..	XVIII.	,,
					CXLIX.	

b. GLANOVENTA (" gil Ann beannta "). Benty, in Cockfield, at the confluence of the Anngill and Gaunless, Durham.

c. GALAVA (" gil Au "). Augill, on Augill Burn, near Dummah Crag, 1½ E. of Brough on Stainsmoor ; on the Roman road from Bowes.

d. ALON (" ail aon "). Hell Gill, under Lunds Fell, 7 N.W. of Hawes.

e. GALACUM (" gil ach "). On Doe Beck, near Ingleton, under Scales Moor and Ingleborough Hill.

f. BREMETONACIS ("bru mata,"—" bru fad,"—*Long-ridge :* " acha "). Burys, near the source of Tun Brook (which contains the name), 1 S.E. of Long-ridge, Lancs. This place gave name to a troop of the EQ. SARMAT. [263*b*].

g COCCIUM (" cuachan "). Wigan. 3 S. from Wigan lies the camp of old Bryn, about ½ E. of the Roman road to Warrington ; this place is the site of the battle of Brunanburgh, or Weondune, *Hindley*, where Athelstan overthrew the Scots [199*c*].

h. MANCUNIUM (" Manuc " [214*l*] ; " aon "). Manchester (with Ancoats), 2½ N.W. of Nico Ditch. Its antiquities include a milliare of the COHORS I. FRISONVM [282*g*], and an altar to Fortuna Conservatrix, dedicated by an officer of the LEG. VI. VICT. (*Gale*, 48).

223*i*. MEDIOLANUM. The iter passed to this station via Little Leigh, Little Budworth Common (near which are the Seven Lows and other tumuli), Tiverton, and Peckforton.

ITER XI.

224*a*. A Segontio Devam M.P. LXXXIII.

					M.P.	
Conovio	..	..	..	..	XXIIII.	
Varis	..	..	..	..	XIX.	
Deva	..	..	..	..	XXXII.	[214*n*].
					LXXV.	

b. SEGONTIUM [256*g*, 287*g*] (" aiseag ionad "). Llanbeblig, Carnarvon, situated on a knoll within a curvature of the Seiont. Llanbeblig Church is on the site. This place was probably the ferry-station for Mona, and perhaps the contiguous sands (G. " gain," *sand*) gave the name Guineth to N. Wales [282*b*]. Lavan Sands (G. lab) N.E.

From Segontium the road seems to have gone 2 N.E. towards Llanrug, thence along the Dinas-Ty Coch road [283*u*], and on through Llandegai, Penmaenmawr, and Conway.

c. CONOVIUM ("gaineamh," *sand*). Deganwy (aith Conwy), near Llandudno. This name appears in Conway, River Conwy [135*j*]. Several local names are interesting. Cyngreawdr (" ceann "; " gearradh " *a quarry, Creuddyn*), said to be a medieval name of Great Orme's Head ("ruamhair " *a delving*), afterwards gave place to Gogarth (Wel. " ogo garth," *cave-place*). *Cf.* Cerrig Uffem [" uaimh "] and Hyfnant [" nant," Wel. *dingle*], which are place-names on the headland. Creuddyn ("gearraidhean," *quarries*) gave name to the Hundred.

Several miles S. of Conway is the Roman station called Caerhun, at the mouth of Afon-Ro, probably the capital of the British kingdom of Rhuvoniog (" Ro-afon ach "), taken by the Saxons when they ravaged the mountains of Eryri in 817 (*Brut y Tyw.*).

224*d*. VARIS (" foraos "). Pentre Voelas, co. Denbigh. Bryn Brys and Garn Brys, S.E. The road thence to Deva probably proceeded via Cerrig y Druidion, Ruthin, Bryn Bowlio [2140], and Mold.

ITER XII.

225*a*. A Mariduno Urioconium M.P. CLXXXVI.

				M.P.	
Leucaro	..	..	..	XV.	
Nido ..	..	..	..	XV.	
Bovio..	..	..	..	XV.	
Isca Leg. II. Aug.	..	..	..	XXVII.	
Burrio	..	..	..	VIIII.	
Gobannio	..	..	..	XII.	
Magnis	..	..	..	XXII.	
Bravinio	..	..	..	XXIIII.	
Urioconio	..	..	..	XXVII.	[214*q*].
				CLXVI.	

b. MARIDUNUM (" iomaire dun "). *Cair Merdin* [288*a*]. Caermarthen ; Kaer Vyrdin, *Brut y Tyw.*, 1136. Many antiquities.

c. LEUCARUM. Llanelly, Caermarthenshire, on the estuary of the Llwchwr (Burry River). The distance from Maridunum requires this station to be sought in the neighbourhood of Mach-ynys ; Loughwr, where it is usually located, is 3 E.

d. NIDUM. Neath, on the River Neath, Glam.

e. BOVIUM (" beabh "). Byeston, ½ N.E. of Coity Castell, Glam. Roman camp and tumuli at Pen yr heol, 1 N.W.

f. ISCA LEG. II. AUG. [226-227]. ISCA AUGUSTA [251*a*]. CAIR LION [288*c*, 293*a*]. Caerleon on Usk, Mon. (" Caerllion ar Wysc," Wel.). From the Legio Secunda Augusta, which was stationed here, the town derived its name (Wel. " Lleng," *legion, leon*). An amphitheatre, inscriptions of the legion, and altars to Fortuna and Mithras, are among its numerous antiquities.

225g. BURRIUM [226a)] (" bru ") Cwrt-y-gaer, by Wern
   Biree, in Wolves Newton, Mon.   The large camp
   of Gaer Fawr, 1 S.W.

   h. GOBANNIUM [250b] (" ach amhain," Wel. " gwaun ").
   Near Craig y Bodau, on the Afon, 3 N. of Ponty-
   pool, Mon.   Usually identified with Aberga-
   venny, where bricks inscribed LEG. II. AUG.
   and a balneum are said to have been found
   (*Horsley*).

   i. MAGNIS [251f] (" magh gann ").   Aconbury, 4 S. of
   Hereford.   Large Roman camp on Aconbury
   Hill.   This station is generally, but incompatibly
   with the numerals, identified with Kenchester
   [251g].

   j. BRAVINIUM (" bar beann ").   Pervin, between Led-
   wyche Brook and Caynham, Salop.   Caynham
   camp N.

ITER XIII.

226a. Ab Isca Callevam M.P. CIX.

				M.P.	
Burrio	..	..	..	.. VIIII.	[225g].
Blestio	..	..	..	.. XI.	
Ariconio	..	..	..	.. XI.	
Glevo	..	..	..	.. XV.	
Durocornovio	..	..	.. XIV.	
Spinæ	..	..	..	.. XV.	
Calleva	..	..	..	.. XV.	
				XC.	

   ISCA [225f].

   b. BLESTIUM (" poll sead ").   Aust Pill, on the Severn,
   1 S.W. of Aust, Gloucs.   The Iter probably proceeded from Cwrt y Gaer to this place via Chep-
   stow, and thence across the Wye, and along the
   Roman road to Cliff Wood ; old entrenchments at
   the last place indicate the site of a fortified post
   whence the passage of the Severn was apparently
   made to Aust Pill.

   c. ARICONIUM (" ar ceann ").   Bainham (" beann "),
   with Ryeham and Battle, near Berkeley, Gloucs.,
   on the Ridgeway [156].   This station has, by

almost general consent, been hitherto placed at Ross, Hereford.

226*d.* GLEVUM. CAIR GLOUI [288*g*] (" glaib "). Gloucs. This station has furnished many Roman anti- quities. The neighbouring Forest of Dean had extensive iron furnaces under the Romans, and, indeed, has had ever since ; its importance to Gloucester at the Norman Conquest is shown by the circumstance that the crown received from the city yearly, amongst other dues, 36 dicræ of iron, also 100 iron rods, capable of being hammered thin for rudders for the navy. Accord- ing to a stone from Bath, inscribed DEC. COLONIÆ. GLEV., this place was a colony. It must not be confounded with GLEBON COLONIA [252*d*], to which the Roman road which issues from the Southgate, Gloucester, probably led without deviation.

e. DUROCORNOVIUM (" dur-cor cnap "). Tarlton Down, by Churnhill (Carnhill), 1 N. of Rodmarton, Gloucs. Roman villa towards Rodmarton.

f. SPINÆ [227*a*] (" spin "). Stratton St. Margaret, 2 N.E. of Swindon, Wilts.

g. CALLEVA [227-228] (" colbh "). Knap Castle, Golden Ball Hill, 1 N.E. of Alton Priors, Wilts. The name probably connected with the large stones by Wansdyke, 1 N.N.E. Many military remains in vicinity.

ITER XIV.

227*a.* Alio itinere, ab Isca Callevam M.P. CIII.

				M.P.	
Venta Silurum	..	..	..	IX.	
Abone	..	..	..	IX.	
Trajectus ..	..	..	..	IX.	
Aquis Solis	..	..	..	VI.	
Verlucione	..	..	..	XV.	
Cunetione	..	..	..	XX.	
Spinis	..	..	..	XV.	Iter. XIII.
Calleva	..	..	..	XV.	,,
				XCVIII.	

Isca [225*f*].

227*b*. Venta Silurum [250*a*]. Caerwent, Mon. ; E. of
the Nedden, with which the name is probably
connected. Numerous antiquities. Hence the
iter proceeded N.E. across the Wye to the Severn.

c. Abone (" beann "). Painstard, Hewelsfield, Gloucs.
Remains of long entrenchments S.

d. Trajectus (" eitre ceide "). Near Broadmead, between Acton and Cats Castle, 1 S.E. of Tites
Point and Purton Passage, Gloucs.

e. Aquis Solis (" uisge all "). Uley Bury, 1½
E.N.E. of Dursley, Gloucs. Roman camp with
antiquities. This name survives almost literally
in Wisloe (near Slimbridge, D.B. Heslinbruge
[253*b*]), probably the ancient name of Cam
Brook, which has one of its sources at Uley
Bury. Ric. confounds this place with Thermæ
[173*f*], and is universally followed.

f. Verlucio (" uir leac "). Leckhampton Hill Camp,
2½ S. of Cheltenham. Roman remains.

g. Cunetio (" ceann aite ") Sturt, near Signett,
2 S.S.E. of Burford, Oxon.

Iter XV.

228*a*. A Calleva Iscam Damnuniorum M.P. cxxxvi.

				M.P.	
Vindomi ..	..	..	..	xv.	
Venta Belgarum ..	..	..	..	xxi.	Iter. VII.
Brige ..	..	..	..	xi.	
Sorbioduni	..	..	..	viii.	
Vindocladia	..	..	..	xii.	
Durnovaria	..	..	..	viiii.	
Moriduno	..	..	..	xxxvi.	
Isca Dumnuniorum	..	..	..	xv.	
				cxxvii.	

Calleva. Iter VII.

b. Vindome (" finid Em "). Walbury, near West
Woodhay (D.B. Windenaie), at the source of the
Emborne, Hants.

228c. BRIGE ("bruach"). Cold Harbour, Broughton, Hants. On the Roman road from Winchester to Old Sarum, locally called the Causeway.

d. SORBIODUNUM ("sgarbh dun"). Old Sarum, between the Avon and Winterbourn. Extensive mounds and ditches. This once-important cathedral fortress declined on the erection of a new cathedral in the Avon Valley, and the consequent rise of New Sarum (Salisbury). From this station the iter ran via Bemerton and Toney Stratford.

e. VINDOCLADIA [248b] ("finid cladh"). At Woodyates Inn, between Vernditch Chace and Pentridge (the latter partly repeating, partly paraphrasing, the name), near the head of Ackling and Bokerley Ditches [158b, d). Hence the iter proceeded via Farnham.

f. DURNOVARIA ("Dur No," *Tarrant :* "uir"). Long Barrow, Tarrant Hinton, 3 N.E. of Blandford, Dorset. Roman villa at Tarrant Hinton, and numerous barrows in neighbourhood.

g. MORIDUNUM [229b, 245b] ("mur dun"). Meare, 3 N.W. of Glastonbury, Som. Various sites have been proposed for this station, but they are generally based on the untenable view that Durnovaria is Dorchester.

h. ISCA DUMNUNIORUM. SCADUM NAMORUM, CIVITAS SCADONIORUM [229b, 243h, 245a] ("ciadan uir"). Cheddon Fitz-paine, 2 N.E. of Taunton. The Antonine form of this name probably originated in a transcriber's error in confusing the station with the Isca of Ptolemy, and again with Exeter. The forms in Ravennas must be preferred.

PEUTINGER'S TABLE.

229a. This ancient map-roll takes its name from its first recorded owner, Conrad Peutinger. It is drawn upon strips of parchment sewn together, the whole measuring 22 feet by 1 foot, and forming a sort

of road chart of the provinces of the Roman
Empire. The countries, owing to the narrow-
ness of the roll, are drawn without any fixed
regard to their latitudes and longitudes, appearing as narrow elongations which stretch generally
towards the west. Along these elongated tracks
the towns are laid down in lines or iters, following
generally the same direction, but not in strict
accordance with their actual distances or situations. The island of Britain is laid down at the
end or outer extremity of the roll, with the east
coast of Kent placed opposite to Batavia and
Lugdunensis ; between, in mid-channel, is an
island (evidently Thanet), with the words " hic
nascitur," probably indicating that the Britannic
Itinerary commenced within it. The roll, however, is damaged in that part which contained
Britain, and nothing remains but the outline
of the S.E. coast, with the names of the towns.
The entire table was published by Moret in 1598,
and Horsley later enumerated the British towns
in his " Britannia Romana " in the order in the
first column below :

229b. 1. AD TAUM, XXII.   ("Aite Taum "). Near Worthing
("uir Taum "), 4 N. of East Dere-
ham, Norf.   Roman station.

2. SINOMAGI, XV.   ("sunn magh "). Santon Downham,
by Brandon, 5 N.W. of Thetford,
Norf.

3. CONVETONI, XV.   Combretonium
4. AD ANSAM.

5. Baromaci, XII.   Cæsaromagus
6. Caunonio, VIII.   Canonium   [222].
7. Camuloduno, V.
Ad Ansam

8. MADUS, XVII.   ("magh Ight "). Oldbury Hill, Ight-
ham, 3 E.N.E. of Sevenoaks,
Kent.   Large Roman camp.

9. RARIBUS, VII.   Hornmill Green, Harrietsham, D.B.
Hariardesham, 6 S.E. of Maid-
stone, Kent.

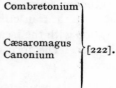

10. BUROLEVO, VII.	Durolevum [215*f*].
11. DUROAVERUS.	("dur uir"). Fairbrook, between Goodnestone and Herne Hill, Kent.

12. RATUPIS.	[168*d*].
13. DUBRIS.	[216].
14. LEMAVIO.	Lemanis [217].

15. Isca Dumno-morum, xv.	[228*h*].
16. Ridumo	Moridunum [228*g*].

229*c*. Eleven of the sixteen Peutinger towns appear in the Iter Brit. ; but the latter, if used in its compilation, was largely supplemented from other sources. The distances between the Antonine towns confirm the Iter Brit., differing only one mile in each of the items 6 and 7. It has been conjectured that the work was executed about the time of the Emperor Theodosius, on which account it has sometimes been called the Tabula Theodosiana.

NOTITIA [125].

230. Notitia utraque Dignitatum cum orientis tum occidentis ultra Arcadii Honoriique Tempora.

SECTIO XL.

Cum viro spectabili Comite Britanniarum :
  Victores juniores Britanniciani.
  Primani juniores.
  Secundani juniores.

Intra Britannias cum viro spectabili Comite Britanniarum.
  Equites Cataphractarii juniores [284*k*].
  Equites Scutarii Aureliaci.
  Equites Honoriani Seniores.
  Equites Stablesiani.
  Equites Syri.
  Equites Taifali.

SECTIO XLIX.

231. Sub Dispositione viri spectabilis Vicarii Britanniarum.

Consulares :
  Maximæ Cæsariensis.
  Valentiæ.

Præsides :   }[132].
  Britanniæ primæ.
  Britanniæ secundæ.
  Flaviæ Cæsariensis.

Officium autem habet idem vir spectabilis Vicarius hoc modo:
  Principem de schola agentum in rebus ex ducenariis.
  Cornicularium.
  Numerarios duos.
  Commentariensem.
  Ab actis.
  Curam epistolarum.
  Adjutorem.
  Subadjuvas.
  Exceptores.
  Singulares, et reliquos officiales.

SECTIO LII.

232. SUB DISPOSITIONE viri spectabilis Comitis Litoris Saxonici per Britanniam :

  Præpositus Numeri Fortensium. Othonæ.
  Præpositus Militum Tungricanorum. Dubris.
  Præpositus Numeri Turnacensium. Lemannis.
  Præpositus Equitum Dalmatarum Branodu-
                        nensis. Branodunum.
  Præpositus Equitum Stablesianorum Garrio-   [235].
                        nensis. Garrianono. [284].
  Tribunus Cohortis primæ Vetasiorum. Regulbio.
  Præpositus Leg. II. Aug. Rutupis.
  Præpositus Numeri Abulcorum. Anderidæ.
  Præpositus Numeri Exploratorum. Portu
                                    Adurni.

Officium autem habet idem vir spectabilis Comes hoc modo :
  Principem ex officio magistri præsentalium a parte
    peditum.
  Numerarios duos, ut supra, ex officio supradicto.
  Commentariensem ex officio supradicto.
  Cornicularium.
  Adjutorem.
  Subadjuvam.
  Regerendarium.
  Exceptores.
  Singulares, et reliquos officiales.

Sectio LIII.

233. Sub Dispositione viri spectabilis Comitis Britanniarum :

Provincia Britanniæ :

Officium autem habet idem vir spectabilis Comes hoc modo :
Principem ex officio magistri militum præsentalium alternis annis.
Commentariensem ut supra.
Numerarios duos singulos ex utroque officio supradicto.
Adjutorem.
Subadjuvam.
Exceptores.
Singulares et reliquos officiales.

Sectio LXIII.

234a. Sub Dispositione viri spectabilis Ducis Britanniarum :

Præfectus Legionis Sextæ.
Præfectus Equitum Dalmatarum. Præsidio.
Præfectus Equitum Crispianorum   Dano.
Præfectus Equitum Cataphractariorum. Morbio.
Præfectus Numeri Bracariorum Tigrisiensium.
                                                                 Arbeia.
Præfectus Numeri Nerviorum Dictiensium. Dicti.
Præfectus Numeri Vigilium. Concangio.
Præfectus Numeri Exploratorum. Lavatris.
Præfectus Numeri Directorum. Verteris.
Præfectus Numeri Defensorum. Braboniaco.
Præfectus Numeri Solensium. Maglove.
Præfectus Numeri Pacensium. Magis.
Præfectus Numeri Longovicariorum. Longovico.
Præfectus Numeri Derventionensis. Derventione.

[236].
[284]

b. Item per Lineam Valli :

Tribunus Cohortis quartæ Lergorum. Segeduno.
Tribunus Cohortis Cornaviorum. Ponte Ælii.
Præfectus Alæ primæ Astorum. Conderco.
Tribunus Cohortis primæ Frixagorum. Vindobala.
Præfectus Alæ Sabinianæ. Hunno.
Præfectus Alæ secundæ Astorum. Cilurno.
Tribunus Cohortis primæ Batavorum. Procolitia.
Tribunus Cohortis primæ Tungrorum. Borcovico.
Tribunus Cohortis quartæ Gallorum. Vindolana.
Tribunus Cohortis primæ Astorum. Æsica.

[237].
[285].

Tribunus Cohortis secundæ Dalmatarum.   Magnis.
Tribunus Cohortis primæ Æliæ Dacorum.   Ambo-
                               glanna.
Præfectus Alæ Petrianæ.   Petrianis.
Præfectus Numeri Maurorum Aurelianorum.   Aba-
                               llaba.
Tribunus Cohortis secundæ Lergorum.   Congavata.
Tribunus Cohortis primæ Hispanorum.   Axeloduno.   [237].
Tribunus Cohortis secundæ Thracum.   Gabrosenti.   [285].
Tribunus Cohortis Aliæ Classicæ.   Tunnocelo.
Tribunus Cohortis primæ Morinorum.   Glannibanta.
Tribunus Cohortis tertiæ Nerviorum.   Alione.
Cuneus Armaturarum.   Bremetenraco.
Præfectus Alæ primæ Herculeæ.   Olenaco.
Tribunus Cohortis sextæ Nerviorum.   Virosido.

234c. OFFICIUM autem habet idem vir spectabilis dux hoc modo :

> Principem ex officiis magistrorum militum præsentalium alternis annis.
> Commentariensem utrumque.
> Numerarios ex utriusque officiis omni anno.
> Adjutorem.
> Subadjuvam.
> Regerendarium.
> Exceptores.
> Singulares, et reliquos officiales.

LITUS SAXONICUM [232].

235a. OTHONA ("athan"). Down near Bradwell, in Dengie Hundred, Essex. Ithanceaster on the Pante (*Bed. Ecc. H.*, iii. 22). D.B. Effecestre. Effecestre and Daneseia were held in 1086 by the Prior of St. Waleric, who also held in 1291, when these places occur as " Bradewell cum capella de la Walle " and " Danesey " (*P. N. Taxatio*, 21b.).

DUBRIS [216].

LEMANNIS [217].

b. BRANODUNUM (" broin dun "). Brancaster, Norf. Roman remains.

c. GARRIANONUM (" Yare " [137u]). Burgh Castle, Suff., at the confluence of the Yare and Waveney

There were considerable remains of the camp in Camden's time.

235*d*. REGULBIUM ("araiche lab"). Reculver, Kent, situated opposite Thanet, in the angle formed by the Thames Estuary and the Wantsum. The latter river, now a brook, was navigable for large ships, thus affording a waterway between this place and Portus Rutupiæ. Vestiges of the station are discernible, and it has yielded almost all kinds of antiquities of the Roman period. Raculf occurs in charters of the eighth and ninth centuries (*Dip. Ang.* 30. 73).

RUTUPIS. [168*d*].

e. ANDERIDA ("ionad ritheadh"). Netherfield, at the source of the Brede ("abh ritheadh"), Suss. An important station in a wooded district, in which are the vestiges of extensive iron-ore smelting ; it gave name to the Anderidan Forest, which in Saxon times was said to be 120 miles long and 30 broad, extending E. to Lymne Mouth, Kent (*Sax. Chr.*, 893). Ella, landing at Cymenes-ora, drove the Britons into this wood, A.D. 477 ; and he and Cissa in 490 besieged Andredes-ceaster and slew all its inhabitants (*Sax. Chr.*). Some time after 755, Sebright, being driven by Cynewulf to Andred (on Andred), remained in it until stabbed by a swain at Pryfetes-flodan (*ibid.*)

f. PORTUS ADURNUS ("adur" [278*s*]). Aldrington (Atherington), near Portslade, mouth of the Adur, Suss. ; the harbour now choked up with sand. Camden, supposing the station to have been higher up the Adur, states that the river was formerly navigable for ships as far as Bramber ; but this seems to rest only on tradition.

This port has been sometimes identified with Cymenes-ora, where Ella, with his sons Cymer, Wlenking, and Cissa, landed in 477 (*Sax. Chr.*) ; but Ella's landing-place was rather west of the

Adur, where the sons seem honoured in the place-
names Sompting, Lancing, and Cissabury. The
story is probably mythical, for *Cissa*bury referred to the Roman period [284*g*].

SUB DUCE BRITANNIARUM [234*a*].

236*a.* LEGIO SEXTA. Their station was Eboracum [191*j*].
    b. PRÆSIDIUM (" Bru siat " [268*a*]). Appersett, under
      Widdale Fell, 1 N.W. of Hawes, Yorks. Roman
      camp at Gayle, 2 S.E. This name is usually
      identified with Lat. " presidium " (Gael. " freicea-
      dan," *a watch, guard*), but the similarity is acci-
      dental.
      DANUM [218*k*].
    c. MORBIUM (" iomare fè "). Laughton-en-le-Morthen,
      6 S.E. of Rotherham. Vestiges of the station.
    d. ARBEIA (" ur ubh "). Arbelows, Middleton Com-
      mon, 2½ N.E. of Hartington, Derb. The circular
      enclosure here, with remains of a stone circle, is
      generally regarded as a Druidical temple ; a semi-
      circular earthwork or bank runs from it towards
      the Roman road from Buxton to Derby. Parsley
      Hey, 1 N.W., probably marks the camp of the
      N. Bracarii [284*j*].
    e. DICTE (" dig aite "). Castle Hill, Hickleton (D.B.
      Dictenebi), 6 W. by N. of Doncaster. Ancient
      road to Mexborough on Marr Moor (" iomare "),
      1 E. Roman camp at Ringston Hill, 4 N.W.
    f. CONCANGIUM (" ceann cnag "). Conisbrough (D.B.
      Coningesburg), 5 S.W. of Doncaster. Earthworks
      in Edlington Wood, 2 S.E.
      LAVATRIS [214*i*].
      VERTERIS [214*h*].
    g. BRABONIACUM (" Barbon acha "). Casterton,
      Westm., at foot of Barbon Low Fell, 1 N.E. of
      Kirkby Lonsdale, and 2 S. of Barbon Brook.
    h. MAGLOVE (" magh cladh "). Castle Hill, Townley,
      in Cliviger, 1½ S.E. of Burnley, Lanc. Stump,

Maiden, Dukes and Stiperden Crosses on the Long
Causeway, at distances of about a mile apart, are
evidently milliare stones.

236i. MAGIS (" magh cais "). Chesham by Bury, Lanc.,
on the Chess Rivulet. Camp and antiquities.

j. LONGOVICUM (" lonach fos "). Cowick, between
Langham and Snaith, Yorks, on the Aire marshes.
At Egbrough, 5 W., occurred the Battle of Gai
Campi, or Winwidfeld, near the River Vinwed
(" went feith "), in which Penda of Mercia was
defeated and slain by Oswy of Northumbria.
The river was then in flood owing to heavy rains,
and more were drowned in the flight than were
slain by the sword (*Sax. Chr.,* 655 ; *Bed. Eccl.,*
xxiv. ; *Nenn.,* 64).

k. DERVENTIO [213*f*].

PER LINEAM VALLI.

237a. SEGEDUNUM [266*a*] (" aiseag dun "). Seghill, on
Seaton Burn, Northumb., several miles N.E. of
the extremity of the Wall.

b. PONT AELII. (" Pont aill "). Ponteland, on the
Pont.

c. CONDERCUM [266*b*] (" ceann dur Ous "). Kenton,
by Ouse Burn, 5 S.E. of Ponteland. This station
and the two preceding were advance-posts,
covering the E. extremity of the Wall.

d. VINDOBALA [266*c*] (" finid balladh "). Benwell, at
the E. end of the Wall, adjoining Newcastle, the
latter town springing from its ruins. Inscriptions to the Ala I. Astorum ; and an altar dedicated to Jupiter by Marcus Liburnius Fronto for
the health of Ant. Pius and the Leg. II. From
Vindobala the Notitia proceeds along the Wall
to Amboglanna.

e. HUNNUM [266*d*] (" aon "). Halton Chesters., 3
S.W. of Matfen. Inscriptions of the Dupl. Ala
Sabiniana and the Legions II., VI., and XX. ;

Remains of baths found here in 1827. See [163b]. The words LEG. XX. V. V. HORTENS. PROCUL. on an inscription from this place seem to indicate that the Leg. XX. had special duties along the Wall for 8 miles on each side of this station, from Rutchester to Carrawbrough [237g, 283n].

237f. CILURNUM [266e] (" cala rion "). Walwick Chesters, near Chollerford, where the Wall crosses the N. Tyne. Inscriptions of the ALA II. ASTURUM, LEG. VI. V., and COH. I. VANGION [283h]. It appears from a stone dedicated to Marc Aurelius that the Ala II. Asturum was here in 221 ; the same body was still here at the time of the Notitia. The Roman road crossed the river here by a bridge.

g. PROCOLITIA [266f]. PROCUL. [237e] (" bruach alt "). Carrawbrough, Teppermoor (" tiobair "), at the most northerly angle of the Wall. Inscription of the COH. I. BATAVOR. An ancient well here, in existence in Horsley's time, was subsequently lost, but brought to light again by lead miners some years ago. On being cleaned out it yielded about 16,000 Roman coins, from Marc Antony to Gratian, with inscribed altars and numerous antiquities. It was dedicated to Coventina.

h. BORCOVICUM (" bruach fos "). Barcombe (Borcum) Hill, by House Steads and Broomlee Lough. At Sewingshields, N.E., the Wall and Vallum separate, the former running along high basaltic crags to this place, the latter keeping to the valley. The earthwork called Black Dike here descends the crags into the valley, and is probably the foss referred to in the name of the station. Here the Notitia leaves the Wall and passes to the most northerly of the ridges which traverse the district hence towards Haltwhistle Burn (see Tungrum [285e]).

237*i*. VINDOLANA (" finid linne "). Bonnyrigg by Green-
lee Lough. Inscriptions of the COH. IV.GALLORUM
at Chesterholme, 1 S. of the Wall ; one of these,
on an altar found in 1831, mentioning this cohort
as from Italy, and dedicated by a member of a
family at Brixia in Gallia Cisalpina, apparently
proves the foreign origin of those troops (*Hist.
Picts' Wall*, 31`). Gallashawrigg, W. of Bonny-
rigg, and Pont Gallan Burn, farther W., appear
to contain their name.

> *j*. AESICA [266*h*] (" uisge," *Caw Burn*). Sook Hill,
between Caw Burn and Melkridge Common. This
station is generally placed at Great Chesters.
Astum [285*f*].

> *k*. MAGNIS [264*g*] (" magh gnuis "). Blenkinshop
(" baillean gnis "), W. of Tipalt Burn. Roman
camp. Usually identified with Carvoran, from
the similarity of the latter to Wel. " caer vawr,"
Lat. " castra magna," but this derivation is untenable.

> *l*. AMBOGLANNA (" mob glinn "). Willowford (which
contains part of the name), within a curvature
of the Irthing, where the Wall crosses that river
to Burdoswald (" bru dac-balladh "). Numerous
Roman antiquities here and at Burdoswald, with
inscriptions of the COH. I. AELIA DACORUM, and
LEG. VI. VIC. A dated stone shows that the
Daci were here in Perpetuus's consulship, 3
Maximin, A° 237 (see 285*g*). The Notitia left
the Wall at this place to notice the advanced
posts not already catalogued, proceeding generally
in the reverse direction (W. to E.).

> *m*. PETRIANIS (" feith Irthing "). Moss Peteral, 1½ N.
by E. of Thirlwall. The Petrianian cavalry
(AL. PETR.) occurs on an altar from old Penrith,
and in the following inscription from Hexham
Church : DIIS MANIBUS FLAVINUS EQ. ALAE PETR.
SIGNIFER TUR. CANDIDI AN. XXV. STIP. VII. H.S.
The Turma Candidi (? " ceann Dodd ") was prob-

ably a troop of the Ala stationed I W., at Inner Dodd. Stone from Carvoran: DEO VITIRINE . . . LIMIO. ROV. P.L.M. (*Grut.* 89).

237*n.* ABALLABA ("poll ubh"). Blackpool, with Bellevue in Bewcastle, on the Black Line, near the confluence of Bailey Water. Roman camp.

   o. CONGAVATA ("cnoc fad"). St. Cuthbert's, Shopford, under Pikefoot. Roman station. Inscription of the LEG. II. AUG. ET. XX. V. and COH. I. DAC. Pikefoot ("pike fad") partly paraphrases the old name, and is probably represented in Bothrigg Burn ("fad rigg"), which falls into the White Line at Ellery Clough (*cf.* COH. II. LERG).

   p. AXELODUNUM [238*d,* 266*j*] ("gil dun"). Gilsland, on the Irthing, Cumb., I N. of the Tyne Wall.

   q. GABROSENTIS ("cabrach-ionad"). Rushend, 4 N.W. of Bellingham. Roman camp above the confluence of the N. Tyne and Tarset Burn.

   r. TUNNOCELUM ("tuin aigeal"). Tone, above Blackbog Burn, Shieldgreen, 3 N.E. of Wark. Tunnocelum, being garrisoned by the Coh. Alia *Classica,* has been sought upon the coast, and generally located at Bowness, Cumb. ; but its identity with Tone cannot be questioned.

   s. GLANNIBANTA ("glinn Pont"). Gilchesters, Stamfordham, on the Pont. This is the last Notitian station N. of the Wall ; the enumeration hence passes S. of the Wall, proceeding in the reverse direction generally E. to W., ending at Old Carlisle.

   t. ALIO ("Ayle"). Whitley Castle, Knaresdale, Northumb., at the confluence of Ayle Burn with the S. Tyne. The following local inscription (corrupt and imperfect) is remarkable as illustrating the descent of the empire from Nerva down to the Antonines, but differing in some respects from the histories :

IMP. CÆS. L.
BICI. ADIABENICI. PARTHICI.
MAX. FIL. DIVI. ANTONINI. P.
SARMA. NEP. DIVI ANTONI. P. PRON.
DIVI. HADRIANI. ABNEP. DIVI. TRAJANI.
PARTH. ET DIVI NERVÆ ADNEPOTI
M. AURELIO. ANTONINO. PIO.
FEL. AUG. GERMANICO. PONT. MAX.
TR. POT. X. IMP. COS. IIII. P.P.
PRO. PIETATE. ÆDE. VOTO.
COMMUNI CURANTE
            LEGATO AUG.
PR. COH. III. NERVIO.
RUM.   GR. POS.

—*T. Gale*, 118.

The following descent appears from this grapholith :

> Nerva.
> Trajan.
> Hadrian.
> Antonine Pius.
> Antonine Pius Sarmaticus.
> Lucius Verus Adiabenicus Parthicus Maximus.
> M. Aurelius Ant. Pius.

The Nervii still garrisoned this place at the Notitia, when they also occur at Dicte and Virosidum. Vestiges of another Roman camp at Alston (" alio ton ") 1 S. of Whitley.

237*u*. BREMETENRACUM (" bru meidhe araich"). Kirkland, 9 E. of Penrith, Cumb. The Hanging Walls of Marc Antony (the latter a corruption of the old name) locate the Roman camp (see Maiden Way [153]).

Six miles N.W., near Little Salkeld, are the stones called Long Meg and her Daughters, the remains of a circle, which about A.D. 1700 consisted of seventy-seven stones, many 10 feet high, one 15 feet (*T. Gale's It. Brit.*, 39).

v. OLENACUM (" oll cnoc "). Roman camp on Gillcambon Beck, Cumb., between Nook W. and Lamonby and Ellonby E.

237w. VIROSIDUM ("uir Wiza-aite"). Old Carlisle, on
Wiza Beck, 1½ S. of Wigton, Cumb. Numerous
Roman antiquities. The Ala Augusta (Equites
Al. Aug.) occurs here in 185, 188, and subsequent
years and at the Notitia. Many inscriptions:

ALA. AUGUSTA OB VIRTUTEM APELLATA.—*Grut.* 1007.
I.O.M. PRO SALUTE IMPERATORIS M. ANTONI. GORDIANI
P.F. INVICTI AUG. ET SABINIÆ FURIE TRANQUILLE
CONGUGI EJUS TOTAQUE DOMU DIVIN. EARUM ALA
AUG. GORDIA. OB VIRTUTEM APPELLATA POSUIT CUI
PRÆEST ÆMILIUS CRISPINUS PRÆF. EQQ. NATUS IN
PRO. AFRICÆ DE TUSDRO SUB CUR. NONII PHILLIPPI
LEG. AUG. PROPRÆTO . . . ATTICO ET PRETEXTATO
COSS.—*Ibid.* 1006, *anno* 242.

RUDGE CUP.

238a. This cup (brass) was found in 1725 in Rudge Coppice,
Froxfield, 6 E. of Marlborough, Wilts, during
excavations by the Earl of Hertford. Round the
rim is the following inscription: A.MAIS ABALLAVA
UXELODUM CAMBOGLANS BANNA (*Arch. Journ.*
1857, p. 283). The names are those of stations
in the Linea Valli, and the cup probably belonged to a cohort or some body of troops
quartered there.

b. AMAIS ("magh foss"). Mavis, by Foxton Burn,
2½ N.E. of Holystone, Northumb., on the Roman
road from Rochester to the Devil's Causeway at
Callaley.

c. ABALLAVA ("balladh fè"). Hepple, on the Coquet,
2 S.E. of Holystone, Hetchester, 1 N.

d. UXELODUM [237p].

e. CAMBOGLANS ("cam bol wans"). Cambo, above
Wansbeck, 2 N.E. of Kirkwhelpington. Several
camps in vicinity of this place and Wallington.

f. BANNA [266i, 283g] ("beann"). Benridge, 2½
N.W. of Ponteland.

RAVENNAS.

239. This author is commonly called the " anonymous Ravennas." His Chorographia of Britain mentions the Saxon race as having " formerly " (*olim*) arrived in the island under Anschis (Hengist) ; hence his earliest possible date is the beginning of the sixth century. His work contains a list of 245 towns and 35 rivers, the former being arranged in six groups—viz. :

1. Prima pars Britanniæ, comprising the district S. of the Thames, with S. Wales and the counties of Gloucester, Worcester, and Hereford.
2. Secunda pars, the remainder of the island up to the Brigantian Wall, including several stations upon and beyond it.
3. The line of the Wall, including some towns where the " Sistuntiaci divide Britain in the third portion " —*i.e.*, in Cumberland, Westmorland, and West York, overlapping No. 2.
4. The narrowest part of the island, between the third district and the Forth isthmus.
5. In and beyond the Isthmus.
6. Eight towns between the Humber and the Wash.

The names thus collected include many found in Ptolemy, Antonine, and others, so that Ravennas must be allowed to have had authentic sources open to him—a circumstance claiming equal respect for the numerous names for which he is now the sole authority. The forms commonly present the appearance of genuine Romano-British names ; some are in the nominative, others in the dative or ablative, from which it may be surmised that amongst other authorities the compiler used documents (now lost) constructed like the Iter Brit. or the Notitia, in which those inflections are regularly employed. In general, the work supports this theory, and the present writer, in numbering the text of Ravennas, has endeavoured to show that there are in places distinct traces of an itinerary (see [256 *et seq.*]). Notwithstanding its difficulties, the work of Ravennas possesses great interest and value ; and the circumstance that it doubles the number of Romano-British town-names found in all other authors put together, and that the sites of many of the towns may be fixed without reasonable doubt, entitles its author to something better than· the scant recognition usually accorded him.

Anonymi Ravennatis Britanniæ Chorographia.

240. In oceano vero occidentali, est Insula quæ dicitur Britannia ubi ·olim gens Saxonum, veniens ab antiquâ Saxoniâ cum principe suo, nomine Anschis, in eâ habitare videtur. Quamvis insulam, ut diximus, quidam Gothorum Philosophi quasi Micosmi appellaverunt.˙ Nam nos tam magnam insulam, neque in supra scripto mari magno, neque in præfato oceano dilatissimo, neque in quo prædiximus sinu oceani, legendam nullo modo reperimus. In qua Britanniâ plurimas fuisse legimus civitates, et castra, ex quibus aliquantus designare volumus, id est ;

Prima pars Britanniæ ;

241a. Giano* (" gann "). Chun Castle, a circular camp 1 S. of Morvah, Corn.

b. Eltabo (" aill taip "). Tubboo Hill, ½ N.E. of St. Stithian's, Corn.

c. Elconio (" aill ceann "). The Roman camp on the Camel near Penaligon Downs, 2 W. of Bodmin.

d. Nemetotacio (" neimhead duc "). Berry Down, ½ N.E. of Tremaddock, St. Neots, Corn. Remains of camp. Roman camp on Goonzion Downs, 1 W. of St. Neots.

e. Tamaris. Tamare [175e].

f. Durocoronavis. Purocoronavis *Vat.* (" dur-cor-cnap") Coryhill, Coryton, Devon, separated from Cury Park by a small tributary of Lew Water ; 2 N.E. of Mary Stow.

242a. Pilais (" fail ais "). Pilsdon, Dors. (D.B. Pilesdone). Roman camp on Pilsdon Pen.

b. Vernalis, Vernilis *Vat.* (" broin lios "). Eggardon Hill, with Nallers, between Poorstock and West Compton,

---

* The names from Ravennas' list are printed in small capitals, *e.g.*, Giano, Eltabo. *Vat.* indicates various readings from the Vatican MS.

Dors., connected with Dorchester by a Roman road. Extensive Roman camp.

242c. ARDUA (" ard "). Maiden Castle, between Winterborne St. Martin and Winterborne Came. Camp 115 acres enclosed by treble ditch. D.B. Ertacomestoche, *Came*.

d. REVENTIONE. RAVENNATONE. (" uir beanntan "). The station of Poundsbury, a Roman camp of about 20 acres on the N.W. side of Dorchester. Dorchester has furnished many antiquities. Parts of its walls were standing *temp*. Stukeley, and outside, on the road to Weymouth, are the remains of an amphitheatre.

e. DEVIONISSO (" taip neas "). Dewlish, D.B. Devenis, Dors. Tesselated pavement and other Roman remains discovered in 1740. Weatherbury Castle, 2½ S.E.

243a. STATIO (" stuadh "). Stadbury (Stodbury, D.B. Stoteberie), 1 S.W. of Aveton Giffard, Dev. The identification of this station and the iter of which it forms the starting-point is important as illustrating a part of the map of Roman Britain which has hitherto been destitute of names.

b. DEVENTIA (" taip ionad "). Denbury, D.B. Deveneberie, 3 S.W. of Newton Abbot, Devon. Camp on Denbury Down [175a].

c. STENE (" ais Teign "). Wooston Castle, 2½ N.E. of Moreton Hampstead, Devon. Ancient camp. Camps at Preston Berry Castle, 1 N.W. towards Drewsteignton, and at Cranbrook Castle, 1½ S.W.

- [STATIO DEVENTIASTENO *Vat.*]

d. DURIARNO (" dur Arno "). Darniford, 3 S.W. of Exeter. Camp near Higher Cotley.

e. UXELIS (" clais "). Clist Heath, on Clist River, Dev.

f. VERTEVIA (" uir taip "). Tiverton, Dev.

g. MELARNONI. MELAMONI *Vat.* (" magh ; luimean, Loman "). Uploman, Dev.

h. SCADUM NAMORUM [228h].

244a. TERMONIN (" Ter," *River Ottery ;* " moine "). Cairo, D.B. Caer, by Otterham, Corn.

244b. MOSTEVIA (" magh stob "). Castle Hill, by Penstowe and Stibb, Kilkhampton, Corn. Several camps in vicinity.

c. MILIDUNUM (" meall dun "). Berry Castle, Emlett, D.B. Mildedone, in Wolfardisworthy, Dev.

d. APAUNARIS (" abh Venners "). Castle Neroche, on Venners Water, 1 N. of Buckland St. Mary, Som. Roman camp.

e. MASONA. Sinners Hill, 3 S. of Castle Neroche. Roman villa at White Staunton, 1 S.E.

f. ALONGIUM. ALOVERGIUM *Vat.* (" lon acha "). Caroling, by Holditch, 2 S.W. of Thorncombe, Dors.

245a. Item juxta suprascriptam civitatem Scadoniorum [228h] est civitas que dicitur.

b. MORIDUNO [228g].

c. ALAUNA (" lon "). Chesterblade (" caster balladh "), near the Aln, 3 S.E. of Shepton Mallet, Som. Camp on Small Down.

d. SYLVA (" slob "). Jack Straw's Castle, by Blackslough, Kingsettle Hill, Som. In the vicinity, at Peonna, near Penselwood, Cenwal defeated the Welsh in 658 (*Sax Chr.*).

e. OMIRE (" iomaire "). Mere, Wilts. Extensive earthworks on Mere Down.

246a. TEDERTIS (" toitear dus "). Tedbury Camp, Elm, Som. Melbury and Newbury camps, N.W.

[OMIRE TEDERTIS *Vat.*]

b. LONDINIS. LINDINIS *Vat.* (" lon dun "). Little London, Edington, on the N.W. ridge of Salisbury Plain. Here the Roman road from Old Sarum descends into the Valley of the Gloucestershire Avon, pointing in the direction of Sodbury and Purton Passage [227d]. Bratton Castle, 2 S.W.

c. CANCA (" cnoc "). Knook Castle, D.B. Cunuche, on Salisbury Plain. Military remains [158e].

d. DOLOCINDO (" tul ceann "). Tilshead, on Salisbury Plain, 5 N.E. of Knook Castle. Military works and barrows [158e].

e. CLAVINIO. CLAVIMO *Vat.* (" cladh beann "). Casterley Camp, by Cleave Hill, 1½ S.W. of Upavon, Wilts [158e].

246*f*. MORIONIO ("magh raon"). Rainscombe, Martensell Hill, near Wootton Rivers, Wilts, 1½ S. of Wansdyke. Large camp and many earthworks.

g. BOLUELANIO (" bolg lon "). Polton with Folly Farm, E. of Marlborough. Roman station and antiquities.

247*a*. ALAUNA ("lon "). Lyneham, 5 N.E. of Calne, Wilts. Avebury, 8 S.E.

b. COLONEAS ("coïlle neas "). Calne. Supposed site of Roman station. Oldborough Castle, 3 S.E.

c. ARANUS. ARAMIS *Vat*. ("raon "). Arn Hill, Warminster. Military remains. Roman pavements at Pitmead 2 E. of Warminster.

d. ANICETIS ("cnoc dus "). Castle Ditches, Ansty, by Tisbury, Wilts. Extensive camp.

e. MOIEZO. MELEZO *Vat*. ("magh ais "). Mizaze Hill, 1 N.E. of Breamore, Hants. Castle Ditches, Whitsbury, Wilts, 1 S.W. at head of Grims Ditch [158*a*].

248*a*. IBERNIO ("Ewerne "). Iwerne Courtney, on the Ewerne, Dors., 4 N.W. of Blandford. Two large encampments, Hamilton Hill and Hod Hill.

b. BINDOGLADIA. Vindocladia [228*e*].

c. NOVIOMAGUS ("cnap magh"). Knap Hill, Anfield, Hants, 4 N.E. of Romsey ; 3 S. of the Roman road from Winchester to Old Sarum, and 3 N.E. of that from Winchester to Nutshalling.

d. ONNA ("ainn "). Abbots Ann, Hants. Circular camp called Bury Hill ; Balksbury Camp between the last and Andover.

249*a*. VENTA BELGARUM. VENTAVELGARUM *Vat*. [173*g*].

b. ARMIS ("ar mais "). Ramsden, in East Meon, 2 S.W. of Petersfield, Hants. Barrow Hill ; tumuli and vestiges of entrenchments on Butser Hill.

c. ARDAONEON ("ardanan "). Castle Farm, West Harting Down, Suss., 3 S. of Petersfield. A Roman road running from Winchester via Bramdean seems to have connected Armis and Ardaoneon with Chichester.

d. RAVIMAGO ("ramh magh "). Rowlands Castle, 3 N.E. of Havant, Hants, on the Roman road from Chichester to Winchester via Bere Forest. Roman remains on Rowlands Hill.

249e. REGENTIUM ("araich ionad"). Camp on Roches Hill, D.B. Rochintone, 4 N.N.E. of Chichester. Roman camp on Lavant Down.

[RAVIMAGO REGENTIUM *Vat.*]

f. LEUCOMAGO. LEUCU-MAGNA *Vat.* ("leac magh"). Uckfield in Loxfield Hundred, Suss.

g. CIMETZONE. CUNETZONE *Vat.* ("ceum dus"). Kemsing, 3 N.E. of Sevenoaks, Kent. In A.D. 822 Ondrede (Forest of Anderida) bordered upon this place (*Thorpe Dip. Ævi Sax.* 65).

h. PUNCTUOBICE ("beann coit beic"). Boxley, D.B. Bichelei, 2 N.E. of Maidstone. Deptling S.E. In the vicinity is Kit's Cotty House, a cromlech, consisting of three stones, weighing respectively about 8, 8½, and 2 tons, and supporting at a height of from 7 to 8 feet a fourth or covering stone, which slopes slightly from south to north, and weighs about 10 tons. Some writers ascribe its erection to the post-Roman period, but the etymology here proposed infers a greater antiquity.

250a. VENTA SILURUM. VENTAS LUXUM *Vat.* [227b].

b. JUPANIA. Gobannium [225h].

c. METAMBALA ("magh-tom balladh"). Caerphilly, 2 S.E. of Mynydd Mayo, Glam. The last compound of the old name appears in Caerphilly. The castle there, enclosing about 30 acres, probably occupies the site of the Roman fortress. The road, Heol Adam, trending from Bryn Adam along Cefn Gelligaer perhaps led to the town, but its present pointing at Gelligaer is more eastward. Caer Filii (*Brut y Tyw.*, 1270).

d. ALBINUNNO. ALBINUMNO *Vat.* ("aill binnein"). Castle Ditches, N.E. of Pennon, in Llancarvan, Glam.

251a. ISCA AUGUSTA. Isca (Silurum) [225f].

b. BANNIO* ("beann"). Banton, in Penterry, Mon.

c. BRENNA.* BREMIA *Vat.* ("bri magh"). Bream, Gloucs. Roman coins found in the Scowles, 1854.

251d. ALABUM ("all abh"). Howl Hill, 1 N.W. of Hope Mansel, Gloucs. Square camp called the Tump.

* These names suggest Penhow with the neighbouring post of Castle Prin, the former 3 W. of Caerwent, on the Via Julia ; but the two next stations favour the allocation in the text.

e. CICUTIO ("acha gead"). Camp Field, Pengethly, 1 S.E. of Michaelchurch, Hereford. Large station. Tumulus S. at Treaddow.

f. MAGNIS [225*i*].

g. BRANOGENIUM ("broin gann"). Kenchester, by Brinsop ("broin abh") and Brienton, 4 W.N.W. of Hereford. Many Roman antiquities. Large camp on Credenhill, N. The S. Watling Street, or a branch of it, ran to this place.

252a. EPOCESSA ("beic eas"). Box at Minchinhampton Camp ("moinsean" Hampton) 3 S. of Stroud, Gloucs. This camp, formed by a mound and ditch, contains about 600 acres, and has Minchinhampton Village within it. Across the Frome is Bisley ("Epocessa leac"), where there are Roman remains. In 1845 a villa was discovered at Lillyhorn in Bisley, consisting of twenty-nine rooms, and among the antiquities within the ruins was a round earthern pot filled with a globular mass of metal, which was found to consist of 1,223 coins from Valerian to Diocletian, A.D. 254-305.

b. UPOCESSA. YPROCESSA ("fireach eas"). Castle-rag, Boxwell Wood, 3 S.E. of Ozleworth, Gloucs. Tumuli near.

c. MACATONION ("magh ceide"). Mangotsfield, Gloucs., near source of Siston Brook, both names containing the old appellation. Bury Hill Camp, 2 N.W.; Little Sodbury Camp, 7 N.E.

d. GLEBON COLONIA. GLEBON, COLONIA *Vat.* ("gall Avon"). Clifton, Bristol. A strong camp, treble-ditched, said to have been known to the Britons as Caer Oder, formerly existed on the summit of St. Vincent's Rocks, Clifton Down. On the opposite side of the river, in Stokeleigh Woods, there are two other fortified posts, called Stokeleigh Camp and Bower (or Borough) Walls. From the extent of these works this station must have been important.

e. ARGISTILLUM ("ar caisdeal"). Regilbury (D.B. Ragiole), 1½ N.W. of Chew Stoke, Som. Wansdyke on Dundry Hill, 2½ N.

253a. VERTIS ("uir dus"). Portishead, Som. Cadbury Camp, 2 S.

253b. SALINIS. SALMIS *Vat.* (" Wisloe "). Slimbridge [227e], Gloucs., 3½ N.W. of Dursley.

c. CORINIUM DOBUNORUM. CIRONIUM *Vat.* [183b].

d. CALEBA ATREBATUM. CALEBA, ARBATI *Vat.* [220d].

254a. ANDERESIO ("ionad rais "). Windrush, on the Windrush, Gloucs. Circular camp, 1 S.W. The great camp of Salmonsbury at Bourton on the Water, containing 60 acres, is 5 N., opposite Rissington ; near it Foss Way crosses the Windrush. Roman villa at Bourton.

b. MIBA (" mob "). Norbury Camp, 80 acres, in Farmington, between Empshill Farm and Hampnet, Gloucs., adjacent to Foss Way ; 4 S.W. of Bourton on the Water. Roman villa.

[ANDERELIOMIBA *Vat.*]

c. MUTUANTONIS ("magh Tuantonis "). Whittington, by Dowdeswell, 5 E.S.E. of Cheltenham. Vestiges of station at Wycombe by Andoverford, and villa and many antiquities. Two camps at Dowdeswell.

255a. LEMANIS [217].

b. DUBRIS [216].

c. DUROVERNO CANTIACORUM. DUROVERNO, CANTIACORUM *Vat.* [215g].

d. RUTUPIS [168d].

e. DUROBRABIS. Durobrivis [215e].

f. LONDINI (" lon dun "). Holwood Hill, Keston, 1 N.W. of Down, Kent. Camp, containing about 100 acres, and nearly 2 miles in circumference. Roman antiquities.

Secunda pars Britanniæ :

256a. TAMESE (" tom ouse "). Tempsford, D.B. Tamiseforde, Beds, at confluence of the Ouse and Ivel. The surrounding district contains numerous vestiges of the Romans. Sandy, 3 S., has remains called Cæsar's Camp.

b. BRINAVIS (" broin fos "). Bicester, Oxf. (*Saxon* Burenceaster, Beranceaster). Avesditch, 4 N.W. [160]. The Roman station of Alchester, 2 S. (see Akeman Street). Traces of Roman road pointing from Alchester towards Dorchester, Oxf.

c. ALAUNA (" lon "). Alcester, Warw., on Riknield Street, at the confluence of the Alne and Arrow. Roman antiquities.

The old town is fabled to have been swallowed up by the earth because its inhabitants, who were all smiths, contemptuously beat their hammers on the anvils to drown the exhortations of St. Egwin, when he attempted to convert them.

256d. UTRICONION CORNONINORUM. U. CORNOVIORUM *Vat.* (" eitre ceann "). Dodder Hill, Droitwich, Worc., in Cornavia [188].

e. LAVOBRINTA (" lab broin "). Brandon Camp, 1 S. of Leintwardine, Hereford. Tumulus at Walford, W.

f. MEDIOMANUM (" magh toman "). Caer Flôs by Rhyd Whimman, E. of the Severn, 2 N.W. of Montgomery. Roman camp.

g. SEGONTIO [224b].

257a. CANUBIO (" ceann Hope "). Queens Hope, with Caergwrle and Cair Estyn, by Hope Mountain, S.E. of Mold, Flint. Camps and antiquities.

b. MEDIOLANO. MEDIOLANA *Vat.* [187b].

c. SANDONIO. SAUDONIO *Vat.* (" sunn dun "). Saighton, D.B. Santune, Chesh., $3\frac{1}{2}$ S.E. of Chester ; connected with the latter by Sandy Lane, probably a Roman road.

d. DEVA VICTRIX. DEVAVICTRIS *Vat.* [214n].

258a. VERATINO ("uir din"). Chipping Warden, Northants, N.E. of Banbury. Roman remains at Arbury Banks and Wallow Banks (coins). Aston le Wall, N.

b. LUTUDARUM. LUTUDARON *Vat.* (" aill toitear "). Lighthorne, anciently Listecorne, Lettethorne, Lythtehirne, 3 N. of Kineton, and 1 E. of Foss Way, Warw. Chesterton, with Roman station intersected by the Foss, 2 N.

c. DERBENTIONE (" dur beannte "). Castle Hill, Beaudesert Park, near sources of Handsacre and Bentley Brooks, $2\frac{1}{2}$ S.W. of Longdon, Staffs. Wandon, 1 N.

d. SALINIS. SALMIS *Vat.* Slindon, on Meese, 2 N. of Eccleshall, Staffs.

e. CONDATE [214m].

259a. RATECORION. Ratæ [219d].

b. ELTANORI. ELTAVORI *Vat.* (" alt near "). Alton, D.B. Heletone, above Normanton Brook, 2 S.E. of Ashby de la Zouch [145a], Leic., on the line of the Via Devana. This place is in the Ashby coalfield, and coal was once worked here (*cf.* Colley Lane). " The outcrop of the coal in the parishes adjoining Ashby has been worked at early periods. In Measham, where the bed was not more than 40 or 50 feet from the surface, indications of ancient workings were found in stone hammer-heads, and large wedges of flint with hazel withes round them ; also wheels of solid wood about 18 inches in diameter. In the N.W. corner of Ashby parish, in South Wood, and at Heath End, very extensive remains of iron furnaces appear ; the surface is exceedingly broken, and scoriæ fill a valley of considerable size. There is no date for this, or tradition. The vicinity was probably occupied by the Romans, as various pots of Roman coins have been discovered in it. . . . A singular pathway, or causeway, called ' Leicester Headland,' runs across the [Ashby] woulds, in a direction nearly E. and W., about 10 feet wide, and raised throughout with a red clear gravel which must have been brought from some distance, as no such gravel is found in the neighbourhood. Tradition states that this is part of a road which originally stretched from Leicester to Stapenhill " (Mammatt's *Ashby Coalfield*, p. 9). At Cadley Hill, Gresley, adjoining the woulds, and in the line of this road, there is an ancient tumulus, erroneously said to be the remains of the keep of a castle of the Gresley family. This tumulus obviously gave name to the Doomsday Manor of Bolun (G. " bolg "), 30 E.I. Bulmeley ; and local nomenclature points to a battle here in remote antiquity (G. " cad," " greis," *battle*).

259c. LECTOCETO. LECTO CETO *Vat.* (" loic tacaid "). Loxley, in Dagdale, 2 S.W. of Uttoxeter, Staffs. Uttoxeter [145*a*], D.B. Wotocheshede, *dag's head*, has yielded Roman remains, but lies N. of the line traversed by this iter.

d. JACIO (" caois "). Hanchurch, D.B. Hancese, N.W. of Trentham, Staffs.

e. DULMA (" tul magh "). Chesterton, by Dimsdale, D.B Dulmesdene, N.W. of Newcastle under Lyme, Staffs.

2 N.E. is Burslem, D.B. Barcardeslim, above the Slum, now Fowlea Brook, which rises near Slum Wood, N. of Talk.

[JACIODULMA *Vat.*]

259f. VIROLANIUM (" uir lann "). Harecastle, Linley Wood, ½ S.E. of Talk on the Hill (" tulach "), Staffs, on the Roman road called Street Lane, which, after passing Linley Wood, and Hollins, received near Talk the Roman road called Booth Lane from Middlewich.

260a. LONDINIUM AUGUSTA [168b].

b. CÆSAROMAGUM. CÆSAROMAGO *Vat.* [218b].

c. CAMULODULO. MANULODUNO *Vat.* [222f].

d. COLONIA [218c].

e. DURCINATE (" dur ceann tigh "). Dorking Tye, 2 N.E. of Bures St. Mary, Suff.

f. DUROVIGUTO (" uaigh ait "). Wixhoe, 3 S.E. of Haverhill, Suff., D.B. auo Keduna, Hauokeduna. *Testa de Nevill*, Wykedeho, Wydekesho.

g. DUROBRISIN. Bressingham, near Diss, Norf.; Fersfield, D.B. Frisa, N.W., near the source of a tributary of the Waveney.

h. VENTA CENOMUM [179b].

261a. LINDUM COLONIA [189b].

b. BANOVALLUM. BANOVALUM *Vat.* (" beann balladh"). Willoughby (" balla ") with Bonthorpe, 5 N.N.W. of Burgh le Marsh, Linc. Roman camp called Dam Close at Willoughby ; Roman camp at Claxby, 1 E.S.E.

c. NAVIONE (" cnap "). Navenby, on Ermine Street, 9 S. of Lincoln. Roman camp at Welbourn, 2½ S.W. Stone from Foligno, Italy : CENSITOR BRITTONUM ANAVION.

d. AQUIS (" uisge," *Gwash*). Bridge Casterton, Rutl., within a curvature on N. side of the Gwash. Slight vestiges of the Castrum, two sides being protected by ditches called the Dikes, the other two sides by the river.

e. ARNEMEZA ("raon mais"). Ramsey, with Bury, Hunts.

f. ZERDOTALIA (" sraid tul "). Eley, with Cratendon (formerly Cradindone), Camb. The Roman road from Grantchester, crossing the Ouse at Stretham Ferry Bridge, passes through Eley in its course towards Littleport and Kings Lynn. Thetford and Shore, 3 S., seem connected with the ancient name.

g. MANTIO. MAUTIO *Vat.* (" iumaidh "). Methwold (" iumaidh balladh "), Norf. [161b], D.B. Metalwald.

261*h*. ALUNNA ("lon"). Kings Lynn, D.B. Lun.

262*a*. CAMULODUNO [191*k*].

b. CALUNIO. CALUVIO *Vat*. ("gallan"). Cullingworth, 3 S. of Keighley, Yorks. Encampments called Catstones Ring N. and Castle Stead Ring, W.

c. GALLUNIO. GALLUVIO *Vat*. ("glinn"). Colne, on the Laneshaw, Lancs. Caster Cliff, 1 S., where Roman remains.

d. MODIBOGDO. MEDIOBOGDO *Vat*. ("magh-taip gead"). Middop, under Weets, Yorks, 4 N.W. of Colne. Roman camps at Hesketh towards Gisburn, near the Roman road from Skipton to Ribchester.

e. CANTIUMETI ("ceann Hodder miad"). Jumbles at the confluence of the Hodder and Ribble, Lancs. Mounds here, and across the Ribble at Mitton Wood.

f. JULIOCENON ("gual ceann"). Gaulk Thorn ("julioc torran"), by Icconhurst, 1½ S.W. of Accrington, Lancs. Earthworks.

g. GABROCENTIO ("cabrach - ionad"). Cowpe, by Rossendale, S.E. of Haslingden, Lancs. Cowpe Low.

263*a*. ALAUNA ("lon"). Lancaster on Lune.

b. BRIBRA ("fearb uir"). Ribchester, Lancs. Local inscriptions:

> DEO SAN.
> POL'N¹ MPON
> O SALVE D.N.
> ET. EQQ. SAR.
> BREMETENN.
> ORDIANI
> OR. ANTONI.
> NVS LEG. VI.
> VIC. DOM. VO.
> MERITEN. L.S.
> —*Arch. Journ.*, xii. 226.

On one side of the above altar is a figure of Apollo resting on a lyre.

> DEO MARTI ET.
> VICTORIÆ DEC.
> ASIATIC. AL. SARMAT.
> —*T. Gale*, 119.

See [282*o*].

c. MAIO OLERICA ("magh larach"). Mellor, on Mellor Brook, Lancs. Roman station.

263*d*. DERVENTIONE ("dur beannte"). Lower Darwen, on the Darwen, Lancs. This station was probably at the cross roads by Darwen Church.

e. RAVONIA ("ar beann"). Harrobin, by Turton, Lancs. Tumulus E. and Druidical circle on Turton Heights, N.

264*a*. BRESNETENATI VETERANORUM. BRESNETENACI *Vati* ("bru ; snetenati," *Saint Sunday*). Natland, between Saint Sunday Beck and the Kent, Westm., 2 S. of Kendall. Castle Steads 1½ S.E. Between Natland and Kendall, within a curvature of the Kent, is Watercrook, a Roman camp which has yielded coins, altars, and inscriptions. At Levens Hall, 3 S.W., remains of Roman temple.

b. PAMPOCALIA ("fè mab cala"). Clappersgate, Ambleside ; vestiges of Roman camp at head of Windermere.

c. LAGENTIUM. LAGUENTIUM *Vat*. Dunmail Raise, under Dollywaggon ("tul lagent") Pike, 2 S. of Thirlmere. Tumulus.

d. VALTERIS ("faill toirrse"). Whelter, under Bellty Howe, where Blea Water falls into Hawes Water. Traces of fort. High Street, 1½ W.

e. BEREDA. Voreda [214*f*].

f. LUGUBALUM. LAGUBABAMI *Vat*. Luguballium [214*e*].

g. MAGNIS [237*k*].

265*a*. BABAGLANDA. GABAGLANDA *Vat*. ("beabh gleanntaidh"). Ebchester, Durham. Roman remains.

b. VINDOLANDE (beann toll-ionad). Handwell Hill, Iveston, 2 N.W. of Lanchester.

c. LINEOJUGLA ("linne gual"). Lanchester, Durh. Traces of Roman reservoir. Inscription of the Cohors II. Lingon.

d. VINONIA. VINOVIA *Vat*. ("beannan"). Binchester, near the confluence of the Wear and Gaunless, Durh. [282*u*].

e. LAVARIS ("lab rais"). Piercebridge, Durh. Roman camp between the Tees and Dyance Brook.

f. CATARACTONION. CATABACTONION *Vat*. [191*e*].

g. EBURACUM [191*j*].

h. DECUARIA ("dig uir"). Duggleby, in Wharram le Street, Yorks. Traces of entrenchment pointing towards Grindalythe, probably a continuation of the Double Dykes by Weaverthorpe [162*b*].

265*i*. Devovicia. Devovitia *Vat.* ("taip fich"). Bessing-dale, Towthorpe, 4 S.E. of Wharram le Street. Traces of an entrenchment extend from this place to Weaverthorpe Ling (8 miles), and another, starting from the last at Bessingdale End, points to Thixendale [162*b*].

j. Dixio ("dig"). Thixendale (D.B. Xistendale), in Wharram Percy, Yorks. Entrenchments and tumuli [162*b*].

k. Lugunduno ("leog dun"). Leckonfield (D.B. Lugu-fled, Lucufled), W. of Hull River, Yorks. This station occurs only in the *Vat. MS.*, in which it is joined to Dixio ("Dixio-lugunduno") [162*b*].

l. Coganges. Ceganges *Vat.* ("cuach cnoc"). Gan-stead, D.B. Gagensted, Yorks. Circular camp, Castle Hill, 1 W. Roman camp 2 N.W. between Swine and Waghen [162*b*]. The neighbouring carrs about Waghen were prob-ably the scene of the Battle of Cocboy ("cuach bog") or Maserfield (Meaux), where Oswald of Northumbria was defeated and slain by Penda of Mercia, A.D. 642 (*Bede, Ecc. H.*, iii. 9 ; *Nenn.* 65). Perhaps the numerous miracles which happened upon the spot where Oswald fell were the cause of the foundation of the neighbouring monastery and minster of Beverley (*cf.* Pighill Moat and Figham, in Beverley).

m. Corie ("corr"). Gardham, in Cherry Burton, 4 E. of Market Weighton, Yorks. Entrenchments and tumuli [162*b*].

n. Lapocarium ("lab carr"). Pickering, Yorks. At Cawthorne, on Pickering Moor, 2 from Lewisham, are vestiges of four Roman camps [162*c*].

266. Iterum sunt civitates ipsâ in Britanniâ, quæ recto tramite de unâ parte in aliâ, id est de oceano in oceano, & Sistuntiaci [192] dividunt in tertia portione ipsam Britan-niam, id est,

a. Serduno. Segedunum [237*a*].

b. Conderco. Condecor *Vat.* [237*c*].

c. Vindovala [237*d*].

d. Onno. Hunnum [237*e*].

e. Celunno. Celumno *Vat.* Cilurnum [237*f*].

f. Procoliti [237*g*].

266g. VOLURTION. VELURTION *Vat.* (" bol ritheadh "). Chesterwood by Rattenraw and Peelwell, 1 N.W. of Heydon Bridge.

h. AESICA. ESICA *Vat.* [237*j*].

i. BANNA (238*f*].

j. UXELUDIANO. Axelodunum [237*p*].

k. AVALARIA. AVALANA *Vat.* (" balladh uir "). Rochester [195*c*], on the Rede, under Balyardley Hill. Extensive vestiges. Inscription mentioning the Cohors Vardulorum, who either received their name from or bestowed it upon Balyardley Hill (" balladh Vardul ").

l. MAIA (" magh aoi "). Emblethorpe, under Oh Me (Maia) Edge, 6 S.W. of Rochester.

m. FANOCEDI. FANOCOCIDI *Vat.* (" fan siat "). Sidwood, on Tarset Burn, 3 N.E. of Falstone. Roman camp.

n. BROCARA (" bruach uir "). Brig, N. of Corsenside Church, near the confluence of the Brig Burn and the Rede.

o. CROUCINGO (" corr cnoc "). Risingham, on the Rede, under Corsenside Common. A stone found here mentions the neighbouring station of Habitancum [283*a*], and other stones mention the COH. I. VANG. and COH. IIII. GAL. EQ. [283*b*].

p. STODOION (" siat aith "). Stiddlethorpe, 6 E. of Bellingham. Roman camp on Aid Moss.

q. SINETRIADUM (" sunn eitre aith "). Great Swinburn, on Swin (or Dry) Burn. Camp where Chew Green Road crosses Dry Burn. Many posts in vicinity.

r. CLIDUM (" cladh "). Coldlaw, S. of the Wall, 4 miles from Great Swinburn.

267a. CARBANTIUM (" carr beannte "). Corbridge. The Roman station lay ⅓ mile W. between the Tyne and Cor Burn, and according to Horsley was called Corbow or Colcester. It has yielded many antiquities. Here Chew Green Road crossed the Tyne by a bridge, portions of which existed in the last century ; faint vestiges of another Roman bridge, which carried the same road across the Rede, may still be seen at Elishaw, near Otterburn. The antiquities of Corbow include Greek altars to Astarte and Hercules [48], and a silver plate called the Corbridge Lanx, which has bas-relief figures of Apollo, Vesta, Juno, Minerva, Diana. *Corbridge* is probably an attempted translation of Carbantium.

267b. TADORITON ("tod ritheadh"). Riding, 2 S.E. of Corbridge. Todburn Street, 2 S.W.

c. MAPORITON ("mob ritheadh"). Castlehill, Bradley in Ryton, Durham. Prudhoe, 2 W.

d. ALITACENON. ALITHACENON *Vat.* ("allt ceann"). Winlaton, 1 S. of Blaydon, Durh.

e. LOXA ("aill acha"). Ox Hill, by Kyo Laws, 3 E. of Leadgate, Durh. The Roman road from South Shields (near which it is called Wreken Dyke) to Wrekenton, 5 N. of Chester le Street, points to Kyo.

f. LOCHATRENE. LOCHATREVE *Vat.* ("aill-acha treabh"). Tribley, 4 E. of Kyo Laws, Durh.

g. CANIBROIANA. CAMBROIANNA *Vat.* ("ceann broin"). Chester le Street, on Long Burn, Durh.

h. SMETRI ("uisge-magh torr"). Mount Grace, Osmotherley, at the source of the Wiske, 6 N.E. of Northallerton. Numerous tumuli and vestiges of military works lie scattered upon the Cleveland Hills between this place and Pickering.

i. UXELA ("acha ail"). Uckerby, on Howl Beck, 1 W. of North Cowton, Yorks. The Roman road from Greta Bridge to Gatherley Moor points thence to this place.

j. LOCOTION ("aill cot"). Cote Hill, Yorks. 3 S.W. of Piercebridge. Vestiges of camp. Between Forcett and Aldbrough, 2 S.E., are traces of an entrenched post, about a mile square.

k. CORDA. Greta Bridge, Rokeby Park, Yorks. Roman camp, near the point where the road from Gatherley Moor crossed the Greta.

l. CAMULOSESSA ("cam Losess"). Howlsworth, 4½ N.W. of Barnard Castle, Durh., at the source of the Gaunless (the latter a form of the old name).

268a. PRÆSIDIUM [236b].

b. BRIGOMONO ("bruach moine). The Roman camp under Great Coum, at the confluence of the Lune and Borrow Beck, Westm. "Coum" is probably an abraded form of "Brigomono."

268c. ABISSON ("abh sunn"). Bousfield, Westm., 2½ N. of Tebay. Castlehowe in Wasdale, 1 W.; Castle Fold, near Sunbiggin, 3 N.E.

d. EBIO ("fè"). Byesteads, W. of the Lyvennet, by Reagill. Morland Bank, parallel to the river, with tumulus. Numerous British remains between this post and Bousfield.

e. CORIOTIOTAR ("carr toitear"). Roman camp at Setterah Park, on the Lowther, under Swarth Fell, Westm., 2 N. of Bampton.

f. CELERION. CELOVION *Vat.* ("aigeal rion"). Celleron, 1½ N.W. of Askham, Westm., on the Roman High Street [156].

269a. ITOCODON ("dic dun"). Hutton, between Penruddock and Dacre, Cumb. Roman camp at Bowerbank, Pooley Bridge, on Eamont Water, 3 S.E.

b. MAREMAGO. MAROMAGO *Vat.* ("iomaire magh"). Mockerkin, near Loweswater, E. of the Marrion, Cumb.

c. DUABLISIS. DUABSISSIS *Vat.* ("taip Liza"). Arlecdon, on Dub Beck, near the Ehen (Liza), Cumb.

d. VENUSIO ("beann ais"). Ponsonby, S. of the Calder, Cumb. Roman camp.

e. TRIMUNTIUM. TRIMINITIUM *Vat.* ("eitre monadh"). Hardknott Castle, Brotherilkeld, in Eskdale, Cumb. Roman camp near the Roman road from Muncaster to Ambleside.

f. EBUROCASSUM ("bruach caois"). Castlerigg, above Brockle Brook, Keswick, Cumb.

270a. BREMENIUM [195c].

b. COCUNEDA. COCENNEDA *Vat.* ("cuachan aite"). Cock Ridge, N. of Brig Burn, by Troughend Common, Northumb.

c. ALAUNA ("lon"). Elsdon, on Elsdon Burn, Northumb. Many military remains in vicinity.

d. OLEICLAVIS. OLEACLAVIS *Vat.* ("ol colbh"). Holystone, on the Coquet, Northumb. On the Roman road from High Rochester to the Devil's Causeway.

e. EJUDENSCA ("uchdan uisge"). Dancing Hall, by Yetlington and Callaley, 7 N.E. of Holystone. Camps at Callaley.

f. RUMABO ("airm fè"). Ingram ("ing airm") on the Breamish, 5 N.N.W. of Dancing Hall, and 3 W. of the Devil's

Causeway. Fawdon Hill ("fè dun"), 1 S.E. This district is thickly studded with camps, some of which (Crawley, Edlingham) are Roman, or have furnished Roman antiquities ; many are Gaelic, as at Greaves Ash, Lynhope Farne, 4 N.W. of Alnham, where there are the remains of a fortification containing 20 acres, with ramparts of unhewn stone.

271. Iterum sunt civitates in ipsa Britannia [recto tramite, una alteri connexa, ubi et ipsa Britannia] plus angustissima de oceano in oceano esse dignoscitur, id est :

a. VELUNIA ("baillean"). Blanefield, 1 E. of Kirkoswald, Ayrshire. Earthwork at Hollowshean, 1 S.W.

b. VOLITANIO. Tarbolton, on Water of Fail. Roman entrenchments.

c. PEXA ("uaigh"). Wexford, in Symington. Military remains in Dundonald, 1½ N.W.

d. BEGESSE ("beag ais"). Busbie, 2½ N.W. of Kilmarnock.

e. COLANICA ("guaillean acha"). Stancastle, between Annick Water and Eglinton, 1½ N.E. of Irvine.

f. MEDIO ("magh aite"). Amoton in Dalserf.

g. NEMETEM ("neimhead"). Nemphlar, 2 N.W. of Lanark.

[MEDIONEMETUM *Vat.*]

h. SUBDOBIADON ("stob don"). Stobilee, E. of Cleghorn, Lanark. Roman camp.

i. LITANA ("allt aon"). Castle Creg, Camilty Hill, co. Edin., 3 S.E. of West Calder. Roman camp.

j. CIBRA ("acha bra"). On Caw Burn, Pumpherston, 2 N. of Mid Calder, Edin. Roman remains.

k. CREDIGONE ("corr ducan"). Kair Eden [126]. Carriden, near the extremity of Graham's Dyke. Inscriptions of the LEG. XX. VAL. VICT., etc. [283*d*, *f*].

272. Iterum est civitas quæ dicitur :

a. JANO. LANO *Vat.* ("acha"). Achindavy, 1½ N.E. of Kirkintilloch. Inscription of the LEG. II. were found in the Castrum here in 1771 (*Roy's Mil. Ant., Plate* 30).

b. MAULION ("meallan"). Camelon ("acha maulion"). N.W. of Falkirk, near the most northern angle of Graham's Dyke. A Roman road connected this post with Stirling.

272c. DEMEROSESSA (" tom Rossie "). Rossie Law, 3 E. of Auchterarder. Roman fort.

d. CINDOCELLUM. Isle of Canty, 2½ N.E. of Toryburn, Fife. East Camps and West Camps, W. ; Easter Clune, N.E.

e. CERMO (" acha airm "). Crombie, by Torry Bay, on the Forth, 4 S.W. of Dunfermline.

f. VEROMO (" uir magh "). Dunfermline (" dun-verom "), once the Scottish capital.

g. MATOVION (" magh taip "). Downfield, Devon ; in Kettle, Fife. Forts.

h. UGRULENTUM. Lindores, by Newburgh, Fife. Fort.

i. RANATONIUM. RAVATONIUM *Vat.* (" roinn athan "). Rhynd, in the headland formed by the Tay and Earn. Forts on Moncreiffe Hill, towards Ronaldstone.

j. IBERRAN (" bru Earn "). Dunbarney, W. of Bridge of Earn, Perth.

273a. PRÆMATIS. PINNATIS *Vat.* (" bra miad "). Inchaffray (" innis præ "), in Madderty, 6 E. of Crieff. The *Vat.* Pinnatis seems a corruption of Præmatis ; yet it is answered by Findo Gask, an adjoining parish, and may therefore be an intentional variation by some copyist—præ paraphrased by pin (" beann ") *pin-matis.* A Roman road, trending from Drummond Castle to Perth, traverses Findo Gask, which also has vestiges of four Roman circular camps.

b. TUESSIS (" Tay eas "). Berry Hills, Thistlebridge, on Tay, 5 N. of Perth.

c. LEDONE. LODONE *Vat.* (" lodan "). Burrelton, 2 S.S.E. of Coupar Angus. Traces of Roman road ; Roman remains on Campmuir, N.E.

d. LITINMAGO (" Alyth magh "). Alyth, Perth. Fort at Bankhead, 1½ N.E.

274a. DEVONI (" taip "). Baldovie, in Kirkton of Kingoldrum, Forfar, 4½ N.E. of Bankhead.

b. MEMANTURUM (" mam torr"). Mems, with Castlehill and Mems Wood, N.E. of Kingoldrum.

c. DECHA (" dige "). Battle Dikes, in Oathlaw, Forfar ; 1 S.W. of Tannadice. Roman remains. Probably here, or at no great distance, was the camp of the Leg. IX., assailed by the Caledonii, A.D. 83 [95].

274d. BOGRANDIUM. Bogardo, 1½ E. of Oathlaw. Fort on Hill of Findhaven.

e. UGUESTE ("caios tigh"). Balgavies, 4 S.E. of Bogardo. Fort on Turin Hill, 2 N.W.

f. LEVIODANUM. LEVIODUNUM ("lab dun"). Dunlappe, in Stracathro, by Edzell, Forfar. The forts of White Caterthun and Brown Caterthun, 2½ W.S.W.

275a. PORREO. Forfar. Large Roman camp ½ N.E.

b. CLASSIS ("clais Eassie"). Denoon Law, near Egliston, and Eassie, 8 S.W. of Forfar. Fort.

c. LEVIOXANA. LEVIOXAVA *Vat.* ("lab ceann"). Delvine ("aith Levioxana"), Inchstuthill, between the Tay and Lethendy. Large Roman camp. Remains of Cleaven Dyke, 1 mile long, 1½ N.E. of Kinclaven, towards Lethendy.

276a. CERMIUM ("acha airm"). Ardoch, Strath Allan, near Corum Hill, 7 W. of Auchterarder. Extensive Roman camps, and remains of road pointing to Crieff. A stone from Ardoch mentions the Coh. I. Hispanorum.

b. VICTORIÆ [197g].

c. MARCOTAXON ("iomare cothachadh"). Catochill, near the Farg, 3 N.W. of Strathmiglo, Perth.

d. TAGEA. TAICHIA. Glenduckie Hill, near the Tay, co. Fife, 3 E. of Newburgh. Camp on Norman's Law, 1½ N.E.

e. VORAN ("broin"). Mount Hill, Kindifferon, Fife, 3 S.E. of Glenduckie.

277. Sunt autem in ipsâ Britanniâ diversa loca, ex quibus aliquanta nominari volumus, id est :

a. MAPONI ("mob"). Hamphall (Hampole), in Adwickle-Street, 6 N.W. of Doncaster. Site of mound called Castle Hill. A Roman road, connected with Ermine Street, points towards Mexborough.

b. MIXA ("magh acha"). Mexborough, Yorks. Vestiges of camp. Roman Ridge [151], a continuation of the road from Hamphall, passes S.W. towards Sheffield.

c. PANOVIUS. PANONIUS *Vat.* ("fè cnap"). Finningley, 6 S.E. of Doncaster. Site of Roman camp in Finningley Park, and fort N.E. at Pondoth Hill. Somewhere on the levels, within a few miles of this place, occurred in 633 the Battle of Hethfeld (*Sax. Chr.*) or Meicen (*Nenn.* 61), where

Edwin of Northumbria was slain by Penda and Cadwalla. This battle is usually placed at Hatfield village, but Meicen points rather to the boundary between Hatfield Chace and Misson Level, perhaps Pondoth.

277*d*. MINOX (" mein acha "). Munsborough, near Masborough, Rotherham. Circular camp at Wincobank, by Osgathorpe, on Roman Ridge.

e. TABA (" taip "). Castle Hill, Tupton, by Chesterfield, Derby. Site of station.

f. MANAVI (" magh cnap "). Mansfield, on the Maun, Notts. Roman camp at Whinney Hill, and Roman villa at Mansfield-Woodhouse. Leeming Lane (" aill man "), leading from Mansfield to Warsop, passes by the camp.

g. SEGLOES. Segelocum [218*j*].

h. DAUNONI*. DANNOM *Vat*. Cair Daun [289*c*.] (" aith," Aunoni, *Ank*). Thong Caster, in Caistor, Lincs., on the high ground E. of the Ankholme. Part of the Roman wall remained in Stukeley's time. Hengist and Rowena are said to have been married here.

278. Currunt autem per ipsam Britanniam plurima flumina, ex quibus aliquanta nominare volumus, id est :

a. FRAXULA (" fireach oil "). Hele Bay, Ilfracombe, Devon.

b. AXIUM. East Lynn River, Som., having its source in Haccombe Water, on Exmoor.

c. MAINA. Minehead Brook, Som.

d. SARVA. Severn [135*q*].

e. TAMARIS [136*b*].

f. NAURUM. Erme, Dev.

g. ABONA. Avon, Dev.

h. ISCA. Axe, Dev.

i. TAMION. TAIMON. Simene (now tributary of the Brid), Dorset.

j. AVENTIO. Avon, Hants and Wilts.

k. LEUCA. Beaulieu, Hants.

---

* This place, following Segelocum, may be thought to be Danum, which follows the same station in Ant. V., but the form of the name and the fact that Ravennas had already passed Danum without naming it, seems to favour Thong Caster.

278*l*. Juctius. Test, Hants. Military vestiges abound in the neighbourhood of this river.

m. Leugosena (" lua caois "). Itchen (*cf.* Megaslimen) [136*e*].

n. Coantia. Kent, Westm.

o. Dorvatium. Dorvantium. Derwent, Cumb.

p. Anava *Vat.* Wampool.

q. Bdora *Vat.* Petherill, tributary of the Ituna [135*e*].

r. Novitia *Vat.* Novius [135*d*].

s. Adron *Vat.* Adurnus [235*f*].

t. Certisnassa *Vat.* Char, Dors.

u. Antrum. Intraum *Vat.* Otter, Dev.

v. Tinoa. Tinea *Vat.* Teign.

w. Liar. Lynner, Corn.

x. Lenda. Looe, Corn.

y. Vividin. Fowey.

z. Durolani. Allen (now tributary of the Fal).

279*a*. Alauna. Helford River.

b. Conguvensuron. Coguveusuron *Vat.* Cober, Corn.

c. Durbis. Dubris [216].

d. Lemana [217, 302].

[Durbislemana *Vat.*]

e. Rovia. Novia *Vat.* Rother, Kent.

f. Ractomessa. Rartomessa *Vat.* Asten, by Hastings.

g. Senua. Ashbourne River, Pevensey.

h. Cimia. Cuckmere, Suss.

i. Velox. Ouse, Suss. (*cf.* Lewes).

[Cunia Velox *Vat.*]

Finitur autem ipsa Britannia, à facie Orientis, habens Insulam Thyle (Thile *Vat.*) [343] vel Insulam Dorcadas (Orcades *Vat.*) [327] ; à facie Occidentis, ex parte Provinciæ Galliam, et promontorium Pyrenæi ; à facie Septentrionalis, insulam Scotiam [301] ; à facie meridionali Germaniam antiquam.

MISCELLANEOUS TOWNS, ETC.

280*a*. The towns in this chapter are derived from three sources—(1) Classic authors ; (2) Roman grapholiths ; (3) the Notitia.

The long list of names preserved by Ravennas might be thought to afford the last materials available for the geography of Roman Britain, but discoveries of inscriptions containing words which have been regarded as geographical have tended to place additional names at the service of antiquaries. Habitancum [283*a*] and Alaterva [283*e*] belong to this class, and it cannot be doubted that both were names of posts garrisoned by Roman troops. This feature of the inscribed stones has not received the attention it deserves, and the deductions stated below, drawn from very limited sources, show that the inscriptions as a whole may be expected to afford a rich fund of geographical knowledge.

b. It is generally supposed that the Romans mainly garrisoned their Britannic possessions with " foreign " troops, and drafted the British levies away for continental service, but a study of the regimental names in the Notitia affords sufficient indication that, if this was their policy, they nevertheless frequently designated the cohorts and alæ here by native names. It appears, moreover, that such of the names as were unquestionably British were, perhaps without exception, territorial ; and the identification of the districts which supplied them not only adds many town names to the list, but throws interesting lights upon Roman strategy.

c. It is not to be expected that all the identifications proposed in this chapter will be found accurate. But while in some cases conjecture stands almost unsupported, in others the coincidences are convincing. Among the former occurs Dolichum, formed from an epithet of Jupiter, who was sometimes styled Dolichenus in Rome and Greece. On the whole, however, it is unlikely that this reflection of the god would receive acknowledgment in distant Britain ; hence the view that the deity intended was the Jupiter of Talgarth. Among the less doubtful class is Tanarum [282b], usually interpreted Thunderer, but probably simply a Gaelic name of a Gaelic village which possessed a Roman temple. Other names rest upon the appellative of a cohort. Of these Cartor receives recognition because it suggests relation to Durness and Durham, while Gugernum has an emphatic claim, for Gogar lies within a few miles of the spot which yielded the stone of the Coh. Gugernorum. This instance of a British place-name continuing virtually unchanged through seventeen centuries is by no means a solitary one.

280d. The greatest difficulty occurs with the Notitia, bringing into question the opinion that the vast majority of troops in Britain were extraneous. The N. Turnacensium and M. Tungricanorum seem clearly British in name ; and the Eq. Cataphractariorum, and such appellatives as Vigilium, Directorum, and Defensorum, which at first sight refute the argument, may be Gaelic relics in disguise. It must be conceded, however, that there was some admixture of non-British names. The Alæ Dacorum and the Mauri come within this class ; and the latter may have reached Britain with Peregrine when he came from Mauretania Cæsariensis [283w]. The fact, however, that these names answer those of distant Roman provinces is not of itself conclusive. It is a factor of the problem that the two troops last noticed are represented more or less accurately in the nomenclature of their districts [285i, j], and it is at least reasonable to suppose that they found the names already current there rather than that they introduced them. The liability of Gaelic to be confounded with Latin of similar orthography but different meaning seems exemplified by "Explorati" [284h.p], but another view is possible.

e. Occasionally a body of Notitian troops is distinguished by a double name. In these cases the second appellative may sometimes indicate the particular station from which the garrison noticed was detached. Thus N. MAURORUM AURELIANORUM may signify the Mauri from Aurelianum.

None of the restored names are inscribed in the map.

281a. GENONIA [46] ("gann"). Cononley, S.W. of Skipton, Yorks. Camp on Cononley Moor. *Temp.* Ant. Pius

[108] this town, then friendly to the Romans, was assailed by the Brigantes :

Ἀπετέμετο δέ καὶ τῶν ἐν Βριταννία Βριγάντων τὴν πολὴν, ὅτι ἐπεσβαίνειν
καὶ ὃυτοι σὺν τοῖς ὅπλοις ἦρξαν τὴν Γενουνίαν μοῖραν ὑπηκόους Ῥωμαίων.
—*Pausan in Arcad. è T. Gale*, 54.

281*b.* TRUTULENSIS PORTUS [103] (" traith aillean "). Helensburgh, E. of Gare Loch, co. Dumbarton. This allocation rests upon the inference that the fleet would be expected to join Agricola at his base (Grahams Dyke) ; and " Helensburgh," if ancient, supports this view.

c. BODOTRIA SINUS [93-94] (" badh eitre "). Torry Bay, in the Firth of Forth, co. Fife ; opposite Bowness, Linlithgow, where Grahams Dyke approaches the Forth. That the vicinity of this bay was fortified by Agricola may be assumed from the words of Tacitus : ATQUE *OMNIS PROPIOR SINUS* TENEBATUR. See [272*d, e, f.*]

282*a.* DOLICHUM (" tulach "). Talgarth, in Llanvaches, Mon. ; equidistant from Penhow and Castell Prin. Inscription from Isca Silurum : IOVI. O. M. DOLICHU . . . I.ONI°. AEMILIANUS. CALPURNIUS RUFILIANUS. EC. AUGUSTORUM. MONITU (*T. Gale*, 126).

b. TANARUM (" tuin uir "). Dinorwic, 4½ N.E. of Carnarvon. Extensive remains. Stone found at Chester in 1653 : I. O. M. TANARO. T. ELUPIUS. GALER. PRÆSENS. GUNTIA. PRI. LEG. XX. V.V. COMODO. ET. LATERANO. COSS. V. S. L. M. (*T. Gale*, 52). Præsens Guntia is probably a misreading of præses Seguntii [Segontium, 224*b*].

c. BRIG (" bruach "). Chester on Dee. This city still presents traces of its Roman occupation. Its numerous antiquities include a statue of the Phrygian Mithras, and inscriptions [282*b-e*]. North Watling Street connects it with Northwich, and the Roman road called Street Way runs from it towards Beeston. Though this was a station of the Leg. XX., the legion's headquarters were at Devnana [188*c*]. The name occurs on a stone found at Chester : DEAE NYMPHAE BRIG. (*T. Gale*, 53). The usual translation of this inscription, " to the nymph-goddess Brigantia," cannot be supported. In 1086 Bruge was a Manor in Cestre Hundred (D.B., 266).

282*d*. AVERNUM. The first part of an inscription from Chester has been read GENIO AVERNI. From the state of the stone it may be conjectured that the second word is incorrectly rendered, and perhaps it should be AVERVI, in which case it points to Werwin, 4 N.E. of Chester.

e. DOMUS SAMOSATA. Demage by Moston, 3 N. by W. of Chester. Inscription from Chester, dated in the reign of joint Emperors (unnamed) :

```
. . .  O SAL DOMIN
. . . . M. NN. INVI
. . .  SIMORUM
AUGG. GENIO . LOCI.
FLAVIUS . LONGUS.
TRIB. MIL. LEG. XX.
. . . LONGINUS FIL.
EIUS . DOMO.
SAMOSATA.
VS.
```
—*Coll. Ant.*, vi. 38.

Samosata is usually identified with Samosata on the Euphrates.

f. NAVIO (" cnap "). Brough, on the Noe, 10 N.E. of Buxton, Derb. Fragment of a milliare found in 1862 at Silverlands, Buxton, reads : A. NAVIONE M.P. X. (*Derb. Arch.*, 1904, p. 201). An inscription of the Coh. I. Aquitanorum, made in legation of Julius Verus in honour of Antonine Pius, found during excavations here in 1903 (*ibid.*, 197). Earthen rampart called Gray Ditch, 1 mile long, towards Bradwell (*broad wall*).

g. MASAVONÆ (" mais beann "). Magson, Winterburn Hill, 1 N.W. of Sowerby Bridge, Yorks. Military remains at Camp End. Mason Green and Ovenden 2 N.E. Inscription from Manchester : COHO. I. FRISIN. Ɔ. MASAVONIS. P. . . . XXIII (*T. Gale*, 49). Winterburn Hill is the required distance from Manchester, and midway between the two stations at the Roman camp by Friesland was probably the headquarters of the Coh. Frisinium.

FRISINUM (" fair sunn "). Friesland, between Saddleworth and Friar Mere. This name hangs entirely upon the Coh. Frisinium in the preceding article.

282h. NEHALENNIA ("innill innean"). St. Helens Ford, Newton Kyme, Yorks. Roman camp; and the Roman road forded the Wharfe here. Inscription from Domburg, Zealand: DEAE . NEHALENNIAE. OB. MERCES. RITE . CONSERVATAS. M. SECUND. SILVANUS. NEGOTTOR. CRETARIUS. BRITANNICIANUS . V.S.L.M. (*T. Gale*, 43, *è Reinesius*). Lime (" creta ") has been extensively produced in the vicinity.

i. VERBEIA ("Wharfe"). Wetherby, on the Wharfe. Inscription on altar : VERBEIAE. SACRUM. CLODIUS. FRONTO. PRAEF. COH. II. LINGON. (*T. Gale*, 44).

j. LINGONUM ("ailean ceann"). Ilkley. A stone found here mentions the Coh. Lingon. This cohort occurs in various places [135*f*, 265*c*, 282*i*] ; but it is questionable whether it had its name from Ilkley. There were Lingones in Gaul and Italy. Hollingley 2 N.E. of Ilkley.

k. BRIG ("bruach"). Bracken, W. of the strongly entrenched posts of Addingham, near Draughton. DUI. CI. BRIG. FL. NUM. MGG. ET. AURELIANUS. DD. PRO. SE. ET. SUIS. S. M. A. G. S. *In dextro latere :* ANTONINO. III. ET. GET. COS. (*Gruter.*, 130, *from stone in house of J. Savile at Bradley, Skipton*). The full town-name on this stone was probably DRUICOBRIGA.

l. VETTUM ("feith"). Pateley Bridge. Site of ancient fortress at Castlesteads. Stone from Bowes [214*i*].

m. BRACCHIO CÆMENTICIUM ("bruach"). Brough with Cams House in Bainbridge (Bainbrigg). Inscription found here :

> IMP. CÆS. L. SEPTIMIO . . .
> PIO. PERTINACI. AUGUSTO . . .
> IMP. CÆS. M. AURELIO . . .
> PIO. FELICI. AUGUSTO. ET. R.
> . . . . . .
> BRACCHIO. CÆMENTICIUM. . . .
> VI. NERVIORUM. SUB. CURA. L.A. . . .
> SENECION . . . (Etc.)
> —*Gruter.*, 266.

The antiquities of Brough include a statue of Commodus.

n. NEINBRICA [283*t*] ("Hening bruach"). Hening, 1½ S.W. of Brignall, Yorks. On altar found in 1702 at Rokeby : DEAI. NIMPHAI. NEINBRICA (*T. Gale*, 42).

282o. MAPONUM (" mob "). Woodplumpton, 4 N.W. of Preston, Lancs. This name depends upon a Ribchester inscription [263b] ; the modern name apparently a corruption of Apollo Mabon. The following also from the Ribchester inscriptions :

SARMATA. Sharoe Green, by Broughton, 2 N. of Preston.
ORDIANUM. Iddons with Burgh on the Yarrow, 2 S.W. of Chorley.
ASIATICUM. Stake House, on Grizedale, 4 N.E. of Garstang. Entrenchment called Calder Dike on Bleasdale Moor.

p. BELLONA (" baillean "). Blencogo (" cuach "), 4 W. of Old Carlisle. Inscription from Old Carlisle : DEAE. BELLONAE. RVFINUS. PRAE. EQ. ALÆ. AVG. ET. LAINIANVS. FIL.

q. BAETASIUM (" fè dus "). Fitz, Aspatria, at confluence of Bothel Beck and the Ellen, Cumb. Inscription from Ellenborough [283w], mentioning the Coh. I. Bætasiorum. The same troops are mentioned in the Malpas and Riveling Rescripts.

r. TRAMAI (" druim "). Thrimby, 2½ S.E. of Lowther, Westm. Inscription from Lowther : DEABUS. MATRIBUS. TRAMAI. VEX. CERMA. P. V. R. D. PRO. SALUTE. R. FUS. L.M. (*T. Gale,* 7).

CERMA. Crambe, Yorks.

s. SENINC (" sunn cnoc "). Knock, by Sink Beck, 3 N.E. of Kirkby Thore. Roman camp near Birks Head. Inscription from Old Penrith : D. M. FL. MARTIO. SENINC. CARVETIOR. QUESTORIO (*Gruter.* 411).

CARVETIUM (" carr feith "). Skirwith, Cumb., 6 N.E. of Penrith.

t. MAPONUM (" mob "). Plumpton, Cumb. Inscription found here: DEO. MAPONO. ET. N. AUG. See Ribchester inscription [263b]. T. Gale mentions the stones in this neighbourhood, 9 feet high, 14 thick, placed at distances of 1 mile.

u. CARTOR (" carr torr "). Durham, or perhaps near Stone Bridge, at confluence of the Durness and Wear, where there are entrenchments. The Coh. I. Cartor occurs on a stone from Binchester [265d].

282*v*. GYRUM. Jarrow, near South Shields. Inscription from Tynemouth : GYRUM. CUM. BAS. ET. TEMPLUM. FECIT. C. IU. MAXIMINUS. LEG. VI. VI. EX. VOTO. (*Hodg. Northumb*).

w. URINA ("roinn"). Carvoran, near Thirlwall ("tuirling balladh").

DEAE. SVRI
AE. SVB. GALP
VRNIO . AGR.
ICOLA . LEG. AVG.
PR. PR. A. LICINIVS.
CLEMENS. PRAEF.
COHI. HAMIORVM.
—*Arch. Journ*., xii. 225.

The name of this goddess, usually read Deæ Syriæ (*i.e.*, Ashtarte), is rather DEAE S(ACRAE) VRINAE.

x. BELUTUCADRUM ("balladh uachtar"). Foldsteads by Oughterby, 3 S. by W. from Burgh by Sands. Inscription from Burgh : DEO BELATUCA. Inscription from Great Chesters [285*g*] : DEO. MARTI. BELATVCADRO. (*T. Gale*, 34). This name is regarded as an epithet of Mars, but it merely signifies that the dedication was in the Martian temple at Belatucadrum, or rather that it was dedicated to Mars in the church there.

y. TURUM ("torr"). Thornbrough, 1 E. of Corbridge. Inscription from Corbridge : HPAKΛEI . TTPIΩ . ΔIOΔΩPA . APXIEPEIA—"Diodora arch-priestess of Hercules at Tyrios" (*Hodg. Northumb*. [48]).

z. HAMIUM. Humshaugh, N. of the Wall, near Chollerford. The Coh. I. Hamiorum occurs above [282 *w*] and at Miniabrugh, Stirling.

283*a*. HABITANCUM ("pait cnag"). Swine Hill, 1 N.E. of Buteland Fell, at the source of the Wansbeck. Large Roman camp with ramparts in good preservation. Inscription from Risingham [266*o*] : MOCONT. CAD. ET. N. D. N. AUG. M. G. SECUNDINUS. BF. COS. HABITANCI. PRIMA. STAT. PRO. SE. ET SUIS. POS. (*Arch. Jour*., xii. 217).

b. CADENUM ("ceide"). Roman camp at head of Cottonshope, 5 N. by W. of Rochester. Inscriptions from Risingham [266*o*] : DEO. MOUNO. CAD. (*Arch. Journ*., xii. 218). The district in charge of this garrison seems to have extended S. to Buteland.

Mocontum ("magh ganaid"). The Roman camps at Chew Green. Makendon 1 N.E.

283c. Grannum ("carn"). Cairnie, 2 S.W. of Inveresk, Edin. Inscription from Inveresk : APOLLINI. GRANNO. Q. VOLUSIUS. SABINIA. N. V. S. (*Gruter.*, 38). 1 S.W. are the Roman remains called the Kaim (*camp*).

d. Gugernum ("cuach roinn"). Gogar, 4 W. of Edinburgh. Inscription from Carriden : COH. I. GUGERNORVM. OPVS. TRIBUS. MILLIBUS. PASSUUM. FECIT. (*Hodg. Northumb.*).

e. Alaterva ("ail tairp"). Corstorphine ("cars terva "), co. Edinburgh. Inscription from Cramond adjoining : CAMPESTRIBUS ALATERVIS. *To the alatervan rural-gods.*

f. Statelesum. Near Kettlestoun, 2 S.W. of Linlithgow. Inscription from Carriden : COH. VIII. C. STATELES. (*Hodg. Northumb.*).

g. Silvanum ("Sloban"). Shilvington, 3 N. by E. of Benridge, Northumb. Translation of inscription from Burdoswald : " To the holy god Silvanus, the hunters of Banna consecrate this " [238*f*].

h. Vangio ("beann ach"). Bingfield, 3 E. of Chollerton, on the Chew Green Road. Inscription from Walwick Chesters [237*f*].

i. Aprilis. Bearl, 4 S.W. of Rudchester, Heddon-on-the Wall. Inscription from Rudchester : COH. VI. APRILIS.

j. Antenociticum. Anociticum (" ionad-cnoc teach "). E. of the Roman station at Benwell, towards Bentinck. Remains of temple with inscriptions to Antenociticus and the deities of the Emperors and to Anociticus, both by officials of the LEG. XX. VAL. ET. VICT.

k. Gordia. Cardew, 5 N.E. of Old Carlisle, by the Roman road to Carlisle. Earthworks and tumuli by Dalston Hall, near Cardewlees. ALA AUG. GORDIA [237*w*].

l. Caecilum ("cuach ail"). Cocklaw, ¾ S.E. of Chollerton, Northumb. Inscription at Oswalds Hill Head, on the Wall, 1 S. : CHO. VIII. CAECILI CLIIME (? CAECILIORUM).

m. Civitas Dumni. C. Dumnoni ("tom," "toman"). Spadeadam, 3 N. by W. of Burdoswald, on the Roman road to St. Cuthbert's. The first name was noticed by Brand on a stone at Glenwhelt, by Greenhead ; the second occurs on a stone from the Wall, E. of Thirlwall Castle. The corruption of " civitas " to " spade " is curious.

283n. HORTENSUM [237e] ("ard neass"). Rudchester, between Dunslaw and Heddon-on-the-Wall. In this neighbourhood occurred the Battle of Catscaul (Katty Shield, 1 N.) or Denisesburn in Heavenfield (Ovingham), where Oswald of Northumbria defeated and slew Cadwalla, King of the Britons, A° 635 (*Bed. Eccles. His.*, iii., 1 ; *Nenn.* 64).

o. CONDATE (" ceann dot "). Coniscliffe, Durh. ; the name perhaps from the tumulus by Carlbury.

MENE (" moine "). Hemingford, Hunts. Emmanuel Knowl in vicinity on Worsted Street. Inscription on an altar from Coniscliffe :

CONDATI
ATTONIVS
QVINTIANUS
MENE XCCI M.P.

—Gale, 50.

These numerals (191) are the distance from Coniscliffe to Hemingford, allowing 1 mile from Coniscliffe to Piercebridge, and proceeding by Iter. V. The altar was probably dedicated by Attonius after a safe journey from Mene.

p. VOCONTIUM. Wiggonby, 5 N.E. of Old Carlisle. Inscription from Grahams Dyke :

CAMPESTR.
SACRVMAEL
MARCVS . . .
DECALAEAUG
VOCONTIO.
V.S.L.L.M.

—Coll. Ant. vi. 24.

Inscription found in Holland :

DEAE VAGDAVER. CVSTI. SIM. . I.
CIVS SVPER. DEC. ALAE VOCONTIOR.
EXERCITVVS BRITANNICI.

—Ibid., 25.

This identification rests upon the AL. AUG., which was stationed at Old Carlisle (*cf.* AL. AUG. GORDIA [237w]).

283q. VICIBRIGUM. Fixby, 2 N. by W. of Huddersfield, on the hill (G. " bruach ") which extends to the Calder at Brighouse. Inscription from Greetland :

> DVIC BRIG.
> ET NVMM GG.
>
> —*Reyn.*, 194, *è Horsley.*

r. BRE(?). Inscribed bricks at Elland, 4 N.W. of Huddersfield : COH. IIII. BRE. (*Reyn.*, 193, *è Camd*).

s. TRIPUTIEN. Altar apud Amerbachium, in Otthonis Silva basis, Germany : NYMPHIS Ñ BRITTON TRIPVTIEN SVB CVRA M. VLPI MALCHI & LEG. XXII. PR. P. F. (*Gruter.*, 93). It has been conjectured that this refers to Tripontium [219*b*] ; it possibly refers to Bitton, Gloucs. (" eitre-Boyd "), but many allocations are possible.

t. LAUNA. Lonton, at the confluence of the Lune and Tees, Yorks.

NEINBRICA [282*n*].

IANUARIA. Gainford, Durh. ; Roman station.

> DEAE NYMPE LAVN
> NEINERICA ET
> IANVARIA . . .
>
> —*Horsley, Yorks. Inscr.*, 4.

u. (AUC). ARAB. (" Gwrfai "). Dinas, on the Gwrfai, 9 S.W. of Tŷ Coch, the latter 1½ S. of Bangor. Inscription found at Tŷ Coch, on the River Cegid, in 1806 : M. V. M. N. C. IMP. CAESAR M. AVREL. ANTONINUS PIVS P. IX AVC. ARAB. A comparison of this inscription with the one found at Lincoln [189*b*] suggests the following reading after the numeral : A VC. ARAB., *from Uc. to Arab.* If this is the correct rendering, Uc. is an abbreviation of the old name of Tŷ Coch ; and it is not impossible that the inscription itself gave name to the Hundred, Uwch-Gorfai (AVC. ARAB.), in which case the stone was the meeting-place of the Hundred Court.

v SAEGON (" aiseag "). Swag, D.B. Sugion, 3 N.W. of Gosport, Hants. SAEGON occurs upon a stone from Silchester, which appears to express a dedication to Hercules of Saegon (*Arch. Jour.*, 1851, pp.227-229). See Segontiaci (" aiseag ionad acha.") [172]). Caer Segon was destroyed by Ella, in his march from Sussex to Bath, A.D. 493 (*Hen. Hunt*). The

Roman road running from Winchester through Owslebury and Upham, and generally regarded as leading to Porchester, was rather the highroad to this station, to which it almost directly points. Saegon was perhaps the ferry from which Vespasian made his descent upon Wight.

283*w*. VOLANTIUM (" fe Ellen "). Maryport with Ellenborough, Cumb. Vestiges of Roman station. Numerous inscriptions :

> PRO SAL. ANTONINI AU. PII F.P. . . . PRAEF. COH.
> I. DELMATAR.—*Gruter.*, 114.
> GENIO. LOCI. FORTUNATAE. REDUCI. ROMAE. AETERNE.
> ET. FATO. BONO. C. CORNELIUS. PEREGRINUS. TRIB.
> COHORT. EX. PROVINCIA. MAUR. CAES. DOMOS. AEDES.
> DECOR. *In aversa :* VOLANTII. VIVAS.—*Ibid.*, 107.

The first part of the last inscription is probably corrupt, and must be translated: " To the Genius of the place for a fortunate return from Rome, Aternum and Patavinus."

x. LUTUDUM (" luaidh "). Perhaps Lea, D.B. Lede, near Dethick (" did ach "), E. of the Derwent, opposite Matlock and Wirksworth, Derb. Pigs of lead (which metal has been extensively worked there) mention LUT., LUTUD.

> IMP. CAES. HADRIANI. AUG. MET. LUT. Found on Cromford Moor, 1777.
> L. ARUCONI. VERECUND. METAL. LUTUD. Found near Matlock, 1783.
> TI. CL. TR. LUT. BR. EX. ARG. Found on Matlock Moor, 1787.

A comparison of these inscriptions with others found in many parts of Britain support the inference, however, that LUT. is not a place-name.

y. NODONS. (" ionad Nass "). Nass, Lydney, Gloucs. Two Roman camps in Lydney Park ; the largest, excavated in 1805, was found to contain a magnificent villa and temple, consisting together of sixty-four rooms and passages. The coins discovered ranged from Augustus to Arcadius, A.D. 14-408. The site of the temple has yielded three altars of the god Nodons (Nodens, Noduns), who was probably the genius loci of Nass.

z. IC. DURO. T. Quoted by T. Gale (p. 109) from coins found in the neighbourhood of Caistor, near Norwich, and supposed by him to refer to the River Tas. If this conjecture were correct, the town name would probably be " Durotas "; for Caistor is not Venta Icenorum, though commonly identified with it. The signification of IC. is still more uncertain ; it may stand for Iceni. Caistor has yielded many antiquities ; it has a Roman camp, and a Roman cemetery lies N.W. of the village towards Keswick.

283aa. PUNPEIUS CARANTORIUS. The usual reading of an inscription upon a stone standing on the roadside, Kenfig, Glamorgan. The possibility that Punpeius and Kenfig have the same meaning (pen, *ceann*) favour the view that the stone is a milliare :

PUNPEIUS CARANTORIUS

Suggested reading : PENPEIUS A BRANTONIO S̄ (SEPTEM).

If the present appearance of the stone warrants this reading, it records the true distance from Briton Ferry (Brantonium) to Kenfig—seven miles.

bb. SETLOCENIA. Settle, Yorks. Inscription from Ellenborough :

DEAE
SETLO
CENIAE
L. ABAR.

—Horsley.

cc. TRAMATRINÆ. Motherby in Greystoke, Cumb. Inscription from Lough, Plumpton Wall :

DEABUS MATRIBUS TRAMATRINIS
ET N. IMP. ALEXANDRI.

—Horsley.

dd. DOLOCHENUM. Talkin, 3 S.S.E. of Brampton, Cumb. Inscription from Risingham :

DOLOCHENO
C. IUL. PUBL.

—Horsley.

ee. COCIDI. Cock Law, 3½ S. of Burdoswald. Inscription at Scaleby Castle (supposed from Willowford or Burdoswald) :

DEO COCIDI
COH. I. AEL.

—Horsley.

283_ff_. CAESA Corionotota.   Hexham, with Hencotes ;
anciently Hagustad or Hagustald.   Inscription at Hexham :

> . . . PRAEF. EQ.
> CAESA . CORI
> ONOTATAR
> UM . . . . . .
> —_Horsley._

_gg_. DELIVIANA.   Tower Tay, W. of Walwick Chesters and
Lincoln Hill.   Inscription from Tower Tay :

> COH. VI.
> . . . DELIVIA
> NA.
> —_Horsley._

_hh_. VITIRI.   Fotherley, 5 S.E. of Corbridge.   Inscription
from Lanchester :

> DEO
> VITIRI.
> —_Horsley._

_ii_. MATUNO.   Manside Cross, 3 E. by S. of Elsdon.   Roman
station.   Inscription from Elsdon :

> DEO MATUNO
> PRO SALUTE.
> —_Horsley._

NOTITIA : SAXON SHORE [232].

284_a_. FORTIUM (" broth ").   Bradwell [235_a_].

_b_. TUNGRICANUM (" tuin cruachan ").   Dunkirk, with
Crockham, 5 W. of Canterbury, on Watling Street.

_c_. TURNACENA (" dronn ceann ").   Maginford, Berstead,
in Thornham, Kent.   Tumulus and Roman antiquities.   A
Roman road ran direct from Lymme to London via Berstead
(in Thornham), Farningham, and Eltham.

_d_. STABLESIANUM.   Lowestoft.   The modern name trans-
poses the ancient one (" les stab ").

_e_. VETASIUM (" feith ais ").   Whitstable (" vetas balla "),
Kent.   The sea has encroached here, and Roman remains
have been detected at a point called the Street Stones, now
washed by the tide.

284*f*. ABULCUM (" bolg "). Folkestone.

g. EXPLORATUM (" ach poll ard "). Cissbury at head of Lychpole Hill and Vineyard Hill, 3 N. of Worthing. See [157]. The mire referred to in this name is Broadwater.

DUCATUS BRITANNIARUM [234*a*].

h. CRISPIANUM (" greis beann "). Greasbrough, N. of Rotherham.

i. CATAPHRACTARIUM [230]. Castle Lidget (" alt acadh "), by Roche Abbey, 3 N.E. of Laughton-en-le-Morthen [236*c*]. Tumulus on Abbey Leys, Roche.

j. BRACIARIUM (" bruach uir "). Harborough, with Scray Wood and Chariot Nursery, Brassington (D.B. Branzinctune), Derb. This and neighbouring places have furnished many Roman antiquities ; it had a temple of Mars, as appears from an altar from Haddon, near Bakewell : DEO. MARTI. BRACIACAE. OSITIUS. CAECILIA. PRAEF. COH. I. AQUITANŌ. V.S. The term " Aquitani " points to the Haddon garrison as Gallic, but the neighbouring River Wye countenances another derivation (*cf.* Badecanwylla, *Sax. Chr.*, 924 ; Badequella, D.B. *Bakewell*). The district between Bakewell, Edensor, Chatsworth, Arbelows, and Brassington, contains many military and druidical antiquities, with tumuli.

k. TIGRISIUM (" aith greis "). Carsington (D.B. Ghersintune), by Brassington.

l. NERVIUM (" knar fè "). Knaresdale, on the Maiden Way, Northumb. The Coh. Nervionum [237*t*] are found at Alio, Dicte and Virosidum.

m. VIGILIS (" fè clais "). Temple Brough, by Ickles Hall, S. of the Don, Rotherham. Roman camp called Castle Garth.

n. EXPLORATUM (" ach poll ard "). Palliard on Yard Sike, Beldoo Hill, 7½ W. from Bowes, on the road to Brough on Stainsmoor. Roman fort. Large Roman camp 2 E. under Beldoo Hill.

o. DIRECTUM (" driuch aith "). Castlethwaite, Pendragon, 4 S. of Kirkby Stephen.

284*p*. DEFENSUM (" taip neas "). Tebay, at confluence of Tebay Gill and the Lune, Westm.

q. SOLENUM (" sal "). Haslingden, Lancs.

r. PACENUM (" beic "). Baxenden, 2 N.W. of Haslingden.

LINEA VALLI [234*b*].

285*a*. Coh. IV. Lergorum ("learg "). *Cf*. Laverock, in Horton, Northumb., 3 N. of Seghill ; Ellery Cleugh [2370].

b. CORNAVIO (" corr cnap "). Acorn Bank, 1 S. of Bedlington.

c. FRIXAGUM (" bruach ach "). Brixter, near Heugh, 1 S.E. of Stamfordham.

d. SABINIA (" spin "). High Spen, 3 S.W. of Winlaton, Durh.

e. TUNGRUM (" tighean carr "). House Steads (a paraphrase of the older name). Here are remains of a considerable town, vast military works, an amphitheatre, and a cave of Mithras. This cave, discovered in 1822, contained two altars, one dedicated by a centurion in the consulate of Gallus and Volusine, the other by a consular beneficiary. An altar, found in 1883, is dedicated to Mars Thingsus, and there are dedications to the goddesses Beda and Fimmilena, the former probably the *genio loci* of Peatrigg, 2 W. ; the latter of Hemmel Rigg, ½ N. of Sewing Shields.

f. ASTUM (" ast," *Haltwhistle Burn*). Great Chesters, by Burnhead and Cockmount Hill. Roman camp, hypocaust, and inscription :

IMP. CAES. M. AUR. SEVE
RUS. ALEXANDER. P.F. ET
AUG. HORREUM . VETU
STATE. CONLAPSUMM.
COH. II. ASTORUM. S . A.
A. SOLO. RESTITUERUNT.
PROVINCIA . REGNANTE
MAXIMO . LEG. AUG. P.R.P.
KAL. MARTI. MED. LEGA
TUS. CO. II. ET. DEXT.

—Hodg.

The Cohortes or Alæ Astorum are usually regarded as Astures from Hispania, but erroneously ; their name in nominative plural would be Asti.

285g. *The* Coh. I. Alæ Dacorum is generally assumed to have come from the Danubian province of Dacia; it may be supposed to have left its name in that of Desoglin ("Daci glinn," *Dacian Camp*), 2½ N.W. of Burdoswald. It is not impossible, however, that Desoglinn gave name to this cohort, which could consequently be regarded as a local corps (see Amboglanna [237*l*]). The following camps of the cohort are from inscriptions from Burdoswald :

CORDIA. Guardshill,* at confluence of King Water and Knorren Beck : I. O. M. CHO. I. AEL. DAC. CORDIANAE. (*Gruter*, 1063.)

TETRICIANUM. Tweedyhill, 1 S.E. of Desoglin : I. O. M. COH. I. AEL. DAC. TETRICIANORUM. (*Gruter.*, 1063).

ANIO. Naworth : I. O. M. COH. I. AEL. DAC. ANIO. (*Horsley*).

h. AURELIANUM (" uir Line "). Raw, on the White Line, 2 N.W. of St. Cuthberts.

MAURUM. Murrayholme, ½ S.W. of Raw.

i. HISPANUM. Spy Rigg, 6 N.E. of Gilsland.

j. THRACIS. Dargues, near Troughend, 2 N.W. of Otterburn. Large Roman camp on W. side of Chew Green Road.

k. CLASSICA (" gual uisge "). Belsay, between Ogle Burn (Gallowburn) and Coal Burn. Roman camp.

l. MORINUM. Ingoe with Moralees, 3 N.W. of Stamfordham.

m. **Armatura** (" Ar meidhe uir "). The fort in Ardale, Ousby, Cumb. The Cuneus Armaturarum has left its name in Cuns Fell, and perhaps in Smittergill, both in Ousby.

n. HERCULEA (" araiche ail "). Arkleby, 1½ S. of Aspatria.

NENNIUS'S THIRTY-THREE CITIES.

286. Nennius calls himself a Minister of the Church and a disciple of St. Elbod (a Welsh Bishop, who in 768 adopted the new cycle for regulating Easter). This circumstance combines with others to fix his period about A.D. 760-800. He enumerates thirty-three cities in Britain :

287a. (1) CAIR EBRAUC [191*j*].

b. (2) CAIR CEINT. Kendall, on the Kent [278*n*].

* Or Moorguards, between Desoglin and Tweedyhill.

287c. (3) CAIR GURCOC ("carr cuach"). Clawdd Gôch, Gro, near the confluence of the Vyrnwy and Tanat, Denbigh. Offas Dyke 1 E.

d. (4) CAIR GUORTHEGERN ("gard carn"). Cryniarth, Gartheryr, S. of the Tanat, 2 S.W. of Llangedwyn, Montg. Tomen, or fortified mound, at Maerdy. This is probably the place where Vortigern gave the western provinces of Britain to Ambrose (Embresguletic). See [291*l*].

e. (5) CAIR CUSTEINT. Stant, Llansilin, Montg., 3 N.E, of Llangedwyn.

f. (6) CAIR GUORANEGON ("acha Arenig"). Cair Gai. near the S.E. end of Bala Lake, Merioneth, in the neighbourhood of the hills Arenig and Arenig Fach. Antiquities : Coins of Domitian, an inscription which has been rendered HIC JACET SALVIANUS BURSOCAVI FILIUS CUPETIAN, and other Roman remains. Tomen y Bala, E. of Bala, was also a Roman fortress.

g. (7) CAIR SEGEINT. [224*b*].

h. (8) CAIR GUIN TRUIS ("ceann toirrse"). Trawsfynnydd, on Sarn Helen, Merioneth. Tumuli, among which one called Porus Grave, near Llech Idris, had a Roman inscription. The Roman camp of Tomen y Mur is 2 N., and that of Castle Prysor 3½ N.E.

288a. (9) CAIR MERDIN [225*b*].

b. (10). CAIR PERIS (" foras "). Cae Castell, Prescoed, St. Mellons, Mon. Military remains.

c. 11. CAIR LION [225*f*].

d. (12) CAIR MENCIPIT ("muine," *Monnow:* "ceap ait "). Grosmont, with Cupids Hill (D.B. Chipeete), S. of the Monnow, in Archenfield, Mon. Remains of entrenchments and raised roads.

e. (13) CAIR CARATAUC ("carr duc"). Caer Caradoc, near Knighton. Camden considered this place to be the scene of the overthrow of Caractacus [76].

f. (14) CAIR CERI. Kerry, 6 S.W. of Montgomery. Numerous remains. Kori, 1228 ; Keri, 1238, 1263 (*Brut y Tyw.*).

g. (15) CAIR GLOUI [226*d*].

289a (16) CAIR LUILID ("aill lod "). Burrow by Leesthorpe, 6 S.E. of Melton Mowbray, Leics. Roman camp,

16 acres ; parts of the vallum, 20 feet high. The name appears in Somerlidebie (now Somerby), under Burrow Hill, in 1086 a member of Burc Manor (D.B.).

289b. (17) CAIR GRANT (" gur ionad "). Grantham, Linc.

c. (18) CAIR DAUN [277h].

d. (19) CAIR BRITOC (" bru teach "). Tickhill, Yorks. A brass vase (" vas eneum ") (probably Roman) was discovered here in ploughing, *temp.* Edw. I. (*Rot. Hund.* i. 113).

e. (20) CAIR MEGUAID (" magh gead "). Fin Cop, 3 N.W. of Bakewell, Derb., situate above the Wye, in Monsall Dale (D.B., Muchedes). Remains of Roman camp. Fin Cop Low.

f. (21) CAIR MAUIGUID (" mob gead "). Catch Hills, Amberley, Derb. The castrum was at Castle Hill, E. of the Amber, 1 N. of Pentrich, and on Riknield Street.

g. (22) CAIR LIGION (" ail ach "). Carl Wark, by Burbage (" farb ach ", 1½ E. of Hathersage, Derb. Druidical remains on Higgaw Tor ; the last name contains the old one (" tor ail "). Carl Wark is an interesting fortress of uncemented, unhewn stones.

290a (23) CAIR GUENT [179b].

b. (24) CAIR COLLON [218c].

c. (25) CAIR LONDEIN [168b].

d. (26) CAIR GUORCON. Wroxeter [188d].

e. (27) CAIR LERION [219d].

f. (28) CAIR DRAITHOU (" dur Tove "). Towcester [214x].

291a. (29) CAIR PENSAVELCOIT (" beann siubhal-gead "). Benborough, by Buggilde Street, on the Cotswolds (" gead suibhal "), 1 S.E. of Temple Guiting, Gloucs. Cutsdean, 2½ N.W. This district probably supplied the name " Cotswold," which seems to refer either to an ancient road along the ridge of the hill or to the numerous roads converging in the vicinity.

b. (30) CAIR TEIM. Tenbury, on Teme.

c. (31) CAIR URNAHC (" Hafren," *Severn ;* " acha "). Worcester. Caer Wyrangon, *Triads.* Caer Wrangon, *Wel.*

d. (32) CAIR CELEMION (" acha luimean "). Culmington, near Callow Hill, Salop. Numerous camps in vicinity : Norton Camp 3 W. ; Corfham Castle, 3 N.E.

291*e*. (33) CAIR LOIT COIT (" allt gead "). The Burys, Lythwood, Lyth Hill, 2 S. of Shrewsbury. Camp. D.B. Ludecote.

Nennius mentions other names :

f. RUYM. The British name for the island which the Saxons called Thanet.

g. CEINT. The British name of Kent. Eng., *Centland*.

h. GUENET. North Wales.

i. MONTES HEREMI (" Heriri," " Eryri "). In the province of Guenet. Supposed to be the Snowdon Mountains. On the summit of one of these hills Vortigern commenced to build a castle (supposed to be Dinas Emrys, near Bethgelert), but being frustrated, bestowed the possession upon Ambrose (Embresguletic). But *cf*. Gartheryr [287*d*], which, however, also occurs elsewhere in Wales.

j. CAMPUS AELECTI, IN GLEVEŚING. Here the messengers of Vortigern found Ambrose. The place is perhaps Aber Cynllaith, with Bryn y gwalie, on the Tanat, near Pont Llanerch Emrys, 3 N.W. of Clawdd Goch.

k. GUENERI, a region in the Sinistral district of Britain. The Hundred of Geneur, near Aberystwith.

l. CAIR Guorthegirn. Built by Vortigern, in Gueneri, after the division of his kingdom with Ambrose, and named after himself. Borth near Llanfihangel-geneur-glynn.

m. GUORTHEGIRNAIM. Province, called after Vortigern, who fled hither when upbraided by Germanus. Vortigern's son Pascent succeeded him in the two provinces, Builth and Guorthegirnaim, by grant of Ambrose. In 1188 this province was called Warthrenion ; it contained the Church of St. Germanus (St. Harmans), and extended S. to near Cruker Castle. Rhaiadyr-Gwy was said to be near Warthrenion (*Girald. Camb.* i.). Warthrenion was later a comot of Arwystli, the name being then confined to a small district which Henry VIII. included in Radnorshire.

n. CAIR GUOTHERGIRN. Built by Vortigern in Dimetia, on the Towy, after his second flight from Germanus. Here he is said to have perished with his wives and all the inhabitants by fire from heaven. Pen-y-gnap, Llanegwad, near the confluence of the Towy and Cothi.

o. RENIS. River Aran, a tributary of the Ython, Radnor. Faustus, the incestuous son of Vortigern, built on its banks a large monastery, called after his name (*cf*. Llanbister on the Ython.

p. ELMETE. A district in Yorkshire, between Leeds and Tadcaster, still indicated by Barwick-in-Elmet. Edwin of Northumbria seized Elmete and expelled its King, Cerdic.

q. GUOLOPPUM, CATGWALOPH. Kidwelly, S. Wales. The text of Nennius is corrupt at the notice of this place, but he speaks of a quarrel between Guitolin and Ambrose, which occurred twelve years after Vortigern's reign, and probably the place was the scene of a battle between them.

ARTHUR'S TWELVE BATTLEFIELDS. (Nenn.).

292. This King is now regarded as mythical. Perhaps, however, he had a real existence, though the deeds accredited to him were the achievements of several heroes. Legend makes him ruler in Siluria, and it would seem that this was his kingdom, for the sites of his battles can be fixed within or at no great distance from it, and the names cannot be satisfactorily allocated to any other area. According to a work written A.D. 547, and erroneously attributed to Nennius, the King came into notice after the death of Hengist, and was twelve times chosen commander of the Kings and armies of the Britons, and was as often conqueror, the last of these exploits being the victory of Mons Badon (*Nenn*. 50). The death of Hengist probably occurred A.D. 488, when Æsc, his son, commenced to reign in Kent ; and this date is not inconsistent with Gildas, who states that the Battle of Mons Badon occurred forty-four years and one month after the landing of the Saxons—*i.e.*, in A.D. 491. From what can be gleaned out of the scanty records of those times, it appears that a Romano-Briton named Ambrose (who is possibly reflected in Arthur), and the victory of Mons Baden, seem to have temporarily freed the native British sovereignties from Saxon aggression (*Gild*., 26). The twelve battlefields were :

293a. (1) MOUTH OF THE RIVER GLENI. The confluence of the Cilieni with the Usk, Glam.

(2, 3, 4, 5) RIVER DUGLAS, in the district of LINUIS. The Dulas, Brec., which rises near the Elan, and falls into the Yrfon near Llanlleonfel. The Elan gave name to the Ellennith Mountains, (*Girald. Camb.*), now Plinlimon (" Ellennithluimean," Eng., *Moruge*).

(6) RIVER BASSAS. On the small stream which falls into the Ebwy at Bassalleg, Mon.

(7) THE WOOD CELIDON, Britannicè, *Cat Coit Celidon*. Golden Vale, Heref., within which, near Dorstone, is Arthur's Stone.

(8) Near GURNION CASTLE. Croes Carn Einion, near Bassalleg, Mon.

(9) CIVITAS LEGIONIS, CAIR LION [225*f*].

(10) RIVER TRAT TREUROIT (" traeth," Wel., *bank ;* Trothy). The Trothy, Mon.

(11) MONS BREGUOIN, Britannicè, *Cat Bregion*. Brecon.

(12) MONS BADON. Mynydd Baiden, 4 N.W. of Bridgend, Glam. Numerous remains, British and Roman. In this battle Arthur is said to have killed 940 men by his own hand. In the neighbourhood is the Roman camp of Y Bwlwarcan. This is the region of Gwlat Uorgan, Glam. (" Gual aith," *coalhill :* " obair," *work*), which was devastated by Maredudd and the Pagans in 991 (*Brut y Tyw.*). The abundance of coal in Glamorgan possibly explains " via Julia " as " Coal Road."

b. Whatever part Arthur played in the important events of his own age, it can hardly be doubted that the bardic poetry of later times associated him with the god Herakles, whose twelve tasks are perverted in the story of the twelve battles. Herakles' Phœnician original, Melqarth, may even have furnished the name of the British hero (" melq arth," *arth righ*). Arthur's Stone (Stone of Sketty, *Triads*), on Cefn-bryn, Gower, is a cromlech of eight perpendicular stones, terminating in small points, on which rests a ninth stone, weighing about 20 tons. Under it there is a spring called Lady's Well.

III
HIBERNIA

HIBERNIA

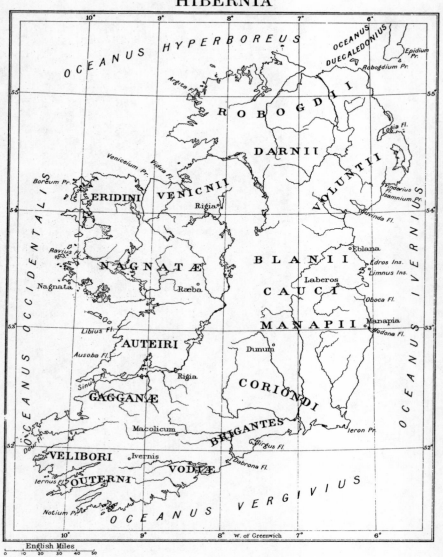

English Miles

III

HIBERNIA

Ἰερυίς, *Orph.*   Ἰέρυη, *De mundo, Strabo.*   Ἰρις, *Diod. Sic.*
Ἰουερυια, *Ptol. Marcian Stephanus.*   Ierne, *Lat. poets.*
Hibernia, *Cæs. Plin. Tac.*   Juverna, *Juvenal.*

294. Ireland, the most western of the Britannic group.
First mentioned in *Orpheus* [5], and again by Aristotle [9]
Avienus, writing of a period about five centuries B.C., calls it
Insula Sacra [7(109)] (Gr. ἱερος, *sacred*) ; and Ancæus the
Argonaut mentions its sacred heights [5].   Irish Religion
[18-21 ; Round Towers, 22 ; Clota, 331*b*].

295. Cæsar places Hibernia opposite Hispania and the W.
of Britain ; he considered it to be smaller than Britain by half,
and as far from Britain as the latter was from Gaul (*B. G.*,
v. 13).   Tacitus places it between Britain and Hispania, and
says it was smaller than Britain, but larger than the islands
in the Italian seas (*Agr.*, xxiv.).   According to Pliny, it was
300 miles broad and 600 long, and distant 30 miles from the
Silures by the shortest passage (*Hist. Nat.*, iv. 30).   Strabo's
knowledge of the island was less definite.   He says it was of
great extent, and lay beyond Britain, being parallel to it
towards the N., but at an unascertained distance from it, and
not more than 5,000 stadia from Keltica (*Gaul*).   It was said
that the farthest voyages then made N. of Keltica were to it,
and writers of the age mentioned nothing farther N.   In
Strabo's time (24 B.C. to A.D. 24) the Greeks thought Ierne
to be so extremely cold as to barely sustain life.   On this
account the inhabitants lived miserably and like savages,
being more savage than the Britons.   They fed on human
flesh, were enormous eaters, and deemed it commendable to
devour their deceased fathers, as well as opelny to have

301

commerce, not only with other women, but also with their own mothers and sisters. Strabo, however, thought this might be related without very competent authority, although to eat human flesh was said to be a Scythian custom ; and during the severities of a siege even the Kelts, Iberians, and many others were reported to have done the like (*Strab.* I. iv. 4 ; II. i. 13, 17 ; v. 8 ; IV. v. 4). Diodorus relates that the people who dwelt towards the north and on the confines of Scythia were said to be so savage as to eat men, and that the Britanni who inhabited Iris did the same (v. 32).

296. According to Mela, Iuverna was situated above Britain, and was almost the same size ; but each side had an equal extent of coast. The climate was unsuitable for maturing seed ; but the pasturage was so luxurious and excellent that the cattle were filled in a very short time, and if they were not driven away from the pastures they would burst. The inhabitants were barbarous, and, disregarding all useful arts, were exceedingly more despicable than other nations (*Mela*, iii.). But, according to the later information of Tacitus, the island did not differ much from Britain in soil or climate, or in the character and culture of its inhabitants ; while through commerce and traders its roadsteads and ports were better known. Tacitus considered that Ireland's convenient position with regard to Spain, Britain, and the Gaelic Sea, offered great opportunities to the strongest (*i.e.*, the western) portion of the Roman Empire, and he relates that in A.D. 82 Agricola meditated an invasion. With this object in view, Agricola received and kept in seeming friendship an Irish chieftain (*regulus*), who had been driven out by domestic war. He believed that a single legion with a few auxiliaries would be sufficient for the expedition, and that the conquest would facilitate the pacification of the Britons, because it would remove freedom from their sight (*Agric.*, xxiv.). Agricola's recall at the end of 84, prevented the design being carried into execution, and the Romans do not appear to have ever attacked the island. Juvenal, about A.D. 100, boasts that they had advanced beyond its shores [105], but he obviously means no more than that their conquests in Britain extended farther north ; thus showing better knowledge of the group than the Greeks had in Strabo's time, when Ierne was believed to overreach Albion in this direction.

297. Ptolemy amply describes the island [303-323], and evidence that coal was then known as a native mineral may be gathered from his pages [323*e*]. Solinus, the next geographer, says that in size it ranked next to Britain ; its inhabitants were inhuman and cruel ; but the pasturage was abundant, and it was necessary to drive off the cattle occasionally lest they should overfeed. No snake, and rarely a bird, was seen there. The people were inhospitable and warlike ; they drank the blood of slain enemies, having first smeared their faces with it ; and they would act dishonestly while professing justice. The mother placed the first food in the mouth of her male child on the point of her husband's sword, and with accustomed vows prayed that he would not die otherwise than in war and with weapons. Those who studied ornament adorned the hilts of their swords with the teeth of sea animals ; these had the whiteness of ivory. The chief delight of the men was in the brightness of their arms. They did not usually keep bees ; if even any dust or gravel was brought and scattered among the hives, the swarm would abandon the honeycomb (*Solinus*). Orosius placed the island between Britain and Spain, or, more broadly, in the course from Africa to the North. The nearest parts, particularly the promontory where the River Scena [304*e*] discharged and the Velabri [314] and Luceni [313] dwelt, lay along the Oceanus Cantabricus, looking towards, but at a great distance from, Brigantium, a city of Callecia (*Galicia, in Spain*) ; voyagers thither from Africa met the wind called Circium. The island was smaller than Britain, but its temperature was more advantageous ; it was inhabited by the Scots (*gentes Scotorum*) (*Oros.*, i. 2). According to Marcian, Ivernia was less than Britain, but lay near it, and more westerly. It was bounded N. by the Oceanus Hyperboreus, E. by the Oc. Hibernicus, W. by the Oc. Occidentalis, and S. by the Oc. Vergivius. The greatest length was from the Notium, or Australis, Promontory [304*h*] to the Rhobogdium Prom. [303*e*], estimated to be 170 (? 1850) stadia ; and the breadth, from the Sacrum Prom. [305*c*] to the Rhobogdium Prom.

was 1,834 stadia. The Arcticum Prom. [Boreum, 303*a*] was 14,250 stadia from the Arctic horizon. The circumference of the island was, in its greatest extent, 9,085 stadia ; in its smallest, 6,845. It contained sixteen tribes, and its noted features were eleven towns, fifteen rivers, five promontories, and six islands (*Marc. Herac.* ii. 41-43).

298. Avienus mentions the race of the Hiberni as inhabiting the Insula Sacra [7 (112)]. Diodorus calls them Britanni [295]. Ptolemy enumerates sixteen tribes—the Venicnii, Robogdii, Eridini, Nagnatæ, Autieri, Gagganæ, Velibori, Outerni, Vodiæ, Brigantes, Manapii, Cauci, Blanii, Voluntii, Darnii, and Coriondi [308-323]. Orosius mentions the Luceni [297] ; Richard the Scotti [310] and the Annales Ultoniensis the Cruithnei [Picts, 199*a*]. The Luceni, however, were part of the Gagganæ ; while Scotti and Cruithnei (connected in some way with the Eridini) were general terms designating several tribes. Richard must have suspected this identity, since he does not mention the Eridini, but introduces the Scotti.

b. The national legends start with Caesair, grand-daughter of Noah, who arrived in the island forty days before the flood, bringing with her fifty girls and three men. Her husband, Fionntan, alone survived the deluge. He existed through many ages at Dun-Tulcha, passing from notice about a century subsequent to St. Patrick's time. Partholan, the next immigrant, came from Migdonia, Greece, shortly before Abraham was born, and ten years later the Fomorians commenced a series of inroads. After three centuries of power Partholan's descendants were cut off by a plague, and the island remained uninhabited for thirty years, when Nemed, the twelth in descent from Noah, arrived with the Scythians, about B.C. 2,350. These newcomers held possession for 216 years, when they were destroyed by a plague and the Fomorians. Only thirty-three Nemedians survived ; some, escaping under the leadership of the son of Starn, son of Nemed, to Greece, became known as the Firbolgs (" fear," *man :* " bolg," *bag*), from the leather bags which they used in Greece for carrying soil to the rocks to form gardens ; others, under Britan Mael, grandson of Nemed, peopled Britain, and others, under

Beothach, another grandson, went into the N. and founded the race of the Tuatha de Danann. The Firbolgs, returning to Ireland in the eleventh generation, repossessed it ; but in thirty-six years they were themselves dispossessed by the Tuatha de Danann from Murias, who brought with them the Lia Fail, *Stone of Fate*, and also the famous caldron of the Dagda, from which no one ever went away unsatisfied. Two centuries later (*circa*, B.C. 1300) the Tuatha, then under three kings, were subdued by the Spanish Gaels, descended in the eighteenth degree from Gadelus, whose mother, Scota, Pharaoh's daughter, was the sixth in descent from Noah. The Gaels came in under Miled, whence they were called Milesians, and they gave to Ireland 171 kings, being still paramount at the introduction of Christianity.

298c. These legends, like the Kymric and Homeric poems, were apparently connected with the worship of Hea ; hence their explanation is to be sought in that part of the zodiac which constituted the region of Hea. Cæsair points to the sign Aquarius, which was presided over by the god Sar ; she is perhaps a reflection of Achiroë, grandmother of the fifty Danaids, all of whom but one murdered their husbands, and were in their punishment connected with the pitcher. The legend sprung from that notion which supplied the Welsh Lake of Floods ; and Partholan from Migdonia must be compared with Hu Gadarn from Defrobani ; their contemporaries, the Fomorians, and Kymry furnish a clue for the identity of Homer. The story, in this aspect, is that of Sagittarius the Archer [3c], whose Assyrian name, Yumu-nahri, may be compared with Ymir (or Örgelmir, *cf.* Herakles), who sprang from the union of cold and heat ; and the astronomical signification is that of the descending sun, who, when he entered this sign, stepped down into that part of his yearly course—the special province of Hea—which synchronized with the arrival of winter in the northern hemisphere. The invasion of the Scythians (G. " saighead," *arrow*) is another version of the same legend (*cf.* the arrow of Abaris the Hyperborean [17]). The Scythian scion Starn, who converted the rocks of Greece into flowery fields, is Saturn, the god of agriculture, answering the Scandinavian Asa-thor, the firstborn of Odin ; and the

similarly benign office of the kindred Tuatħa de Danann
(" race of the god Danann ") is symbolized by Dagda's caldron, the pitcher of Udgudûa [3c], which they brought with
them into the island. This vessel is obviously Aquarius, or
the water-pot. The Gadel were the worshippers of the wheel
—i.e., astronomers [21]. Their connection with Spain may
be compared with Tacitus's Iberian theory as applied to the
Silures [37]. Sagittarius is usually represented as a centaur
looking upon Scorpio, against which he draws his bow. It
is probable that this aspect of him as the slayer accounts for
his frequent occurrence in the W., where the passage of the sun
below the horizon led to the notion that there lay the entrance
to the caves of the dead. See 200c.

298d. The caldron of the Tuatha de Danann from Murias
is connected with the well of Hivergelmir, said to signify
" seething caldron " which the Scandinavian myth-makers
placed in the dark and wintry region of Niflheim. The icy
vapours of this tract joined with the heat of the southern
land of Muspelheim in forming the giant Ymir ; and the blood
from the wounds of Ymir when he was slain by the sons of
Bör formed the flood which drowned the giant race. Bergel-
mir and his wife, taking refuge in a boat, were the only mortals
who survived this flood. Bör was the father of the gods,
and thus the spring or source of life ; and his sons, Odin, Wili,
and We, who held between them the sovereignty of the universe, correspond to the three Kronids (Poseidon, Pluto, and
Zeus), as their respective kingdoms do to the Zodiacal
regions of Anu, Bel, and Hea. These stories indicate the
true significance of the Irish legends. Ymir is associated with
the Fomorians and with the caldron from Murias ; and the
Tuatha de Danann, the bearers of the caldron, are the followers of Odin, his name pointing to Denmark, the home of
the ancient Cimbri, whose name in turn suggests the caldron
of Hexampæus [38d]. The latter vessel was made of brass
from the arrow-heads collected when King Ariantas numbered
the Scythæ. Herodotus's explanation of Hexampæus, " sacred
ways " is not inconsistent with the ancient notion of Kimmeria.
Both referred, in one aspect, to the underworld ; and the
Bab. Ass. Kumaru, in its relation to Heb. " kemer " (*black-*

ness [*2e note*]), sufficiently describes that sign in which the sun, when killed by the arrows of the gloomy archer-sign or winter, embarks upon the river of death in the ship of Charon (Capricorn), only, however, to emerge gradually into new life through the revivifying flood, represented at one time by the seething caldron of Niflheim, and at another by the pitcher of Aquarius. The twelve streams which flowed from the Niflheim fountain are the signs of the solar zodiac ; and the zodiac itself is the great void of Ginnungagap, which lay between Niflheim and Muspelheim, and which may perhaps be interpreted Kiun-kakkab (" kiun," *Kronos ;* " kakkab," *star*), Kronos being the best known of the twelve Uranids.

298e. The region of Hea, being that of death, was naturally also the place of spirits (Ass. " sedu," *spirit*). The spirits crept into Irish religion as the Side (G. " sithich," *fairies*), reverenced as " deos terrenos," *Book of Armagh*, the word being connected mythologically with Uz, the goat or Capricorn, the sign which governed the sun's passage through Hades. " Uz " points to Asenheim, the Scandinavian Olympus, and to Asgard, the chief city of that region ; and to put the point beyond doubt, the Tuatha de Danann are sometimes called the Aes Side. So the Bab. " Enzu " (*Capricorn*) appears in the medieval Icelandic " Anse," applied to the worshipped dead ; and the phonetic Akkadian " alap," rendered in Assyrian as " sedu " (*spirit*), and connected in some aspects with the bull, still survives in Norse " Elf " (*fairy*)—a coincidence suggesting Elpenor, whose spirit, appearing to Ulysses in Hades, implored the honour of burial for his corpse. The tumulus raised over the remains of Elpenor, and the gruesome circumstances connected with his death and burial as related in the *Odyssey*, explain the purpose and significance of the Gaelic " sithain " or " sithdhun "—*i.e., fairy knolls* (Eng. *barrows*) ; they are the tombs of the worshipped or hallowed dead, and are met with in Ireland as well as in Britain.

299. Some assert that Hibernia was first colonized by Phœnicians. Whatever admixtures,however, may have taken place from the mainland of Europe and more distant countries,

it is unquestionable that it either received British elements or
sent emigrants into Britain. That its intercourse with the
latter was pronounced and permanent is shown by the circumstance that the Erse, or Irish vernacular is closely akin
to the Scotch, Gael, and Manx, and (in a less degree) to the
Welsh, all of which must have sprung from a common source.
Bede looked upon the Scots as the genuine inhabitants of
Ireland ; he says they occupied it before the Scythian Picts
settled in Britain, and that, afterwards emigrating to Britain,
they formed settlements among the Picts, either by agreement
or conquest (*Eccles. His.*, i.). These hypotheses were known to
and believed by writers of the fifth century and since, who
therefore called Ireland Scotia ; but we do not know whence
they derived their views, unless from the Latin poets, who
were generally reckless in matters of barbarian ethnology.
It is likely, however, that many Caledonians, calling themselves indifferently Picts or Scots, passed over to Ireland
under pressure from the Romans, both before and after the
time of Ptolemy, occasionally helping their kinsmen in Britain,
and even returning to their old homes when opportunity
offered. That such was the case towards the end of the
Roman period may be gathered from Claudian, according to
whom Ierne, after the victories of Theodosius, mourned
heaps of Scots [120]. Again, when Stilicho was driving back
the Caledonians, the same author says that the Scots moved
all Ierne, and the sea foamed with hostile oars [122]. The
latter statement, if not a poetic fiction, seems to indicate
that the Scots put Ierne into a ferment by their successful
solicitations for help.

300. The *De Situ* of Richard of Cirencester affirms that
Hybernia was the fatherland of the Scots, who passed hence
into Albion ; and that various Hybernian tribes, the *Damnii*,
Voluntii, Brigantes, Cangi, and others, were emigrants from
Albion at uncertain epochs ; also that the Menapii and Cauci
were certainly of Teutonic origin. These views, while suggested by the similarity of names, lack the concurrent testimony which satisfactorily explains the migrations of the
Gaidel. Moreover, Richard's Damnii of Hibernia is a mistake for Darnii, and the appellations of the other tribes men-

tioned by him do not need the theory of emigration, as they can be explained by local circumstances.

301. Scotia, a post-Roman name of Ireland, may have been poetical ; but if it was ever attached topographically to the soil, it was probably a form of G. " easgaidh "* (*quagmire*), in which acceptation it would describe very accurately the boglands of the central parts of the island, where, curiously, Richard placed the Scotti. Drepanius speaks of the Scot driven back to his marshes [120]. Here is perhaps the true signification of the mysterious term which early Albionic writers identified with " Scythæ." Yet Ierne, the appellation by which the island was known to the oldest classic authors, and which the Romans wrote Hibernia, always remained its name with the native historians. The Irish still call it Eire and Eirenn, the Highland Gaels Eirinn, the Manx Erin, the Welsh Iwerddon. From the fancied derivation of the name from " ur " (*green*, Wel. " gwyrdd "), it became known poetically as the " Emerald Isle." In the native mythical literature it is often called Fail, or Innisfail (" fail," *a ring*), in allusion to the basalts found upon its coasts [176a]— a name perhaps introduced by the Silures if the latter were really descendants of the Iberian Gael.

302. Early Welsh writers call the Irish Gwydyl—*i.e.*, Gadel, or Gael [38]. The *Brut y Tywysogion* mentions them several times : in A.D. 1084 died Terdelach brenhin Yscottieit nev y Gwydyl (*King of the Scots or Gwyddelians*) ; in 1087 an Irish fleet manned by Llygheswyr Yscotteit ar Gwydyl (*Scotch and Irish mariners*) assisted the Welsh prince Rhys ap Tewdwr ; in 1100 the Gwydyl sent armed ships to assist Robert Earl of Gloucester against the King of England ; in 1107 the Welsh Prince Madog ap Ridit, taking refuge in Ireland, soon left it again, being unable to endure the savage manners of the Gwydyl ; and in 1143 a fleet of the Gwydyl assisted Cadwallader.

* This word entered largely into British nomenclature. *Cf*. Scotter, Scotton, and Scotterthorpe in the marshes E. of the Isle of Axholme, Linc.

COAST-LINE : *PTOLEMY*.

303. Description of the N. side, above which lies the Oceanus Hyperboreus [351i] :

a. BOREUM PROM. [297]. Βόρειον ἄκρον. Lon. 11, Lat. 61. ("bior"). In the Peninsula of Mullet, perhaps the headland at Portafranka.

b. VENICEIUM PR. Οὐενίκηιον ἄκρ. Lon. 12.50, Lat. 61.20. ("beann cè"). Poolacheehy, Sligo. Venicnii [308].

c. VIDUA FLUV. Οὐιδούα ποταμοῦ ἐκβολαι. Lon. 13, Lat. 61. ("feith uaigh"). The stream which falls into the sea E. of Aughris Head ("uaigh ros"), Sligo.

d. ARGITA FL. Ἀργίτα ποτ. ἐκβ. Lon. 14.30, Lat. 61.30. ("ear gead"). Keadow Strand, N.E. of Burtonport Donegal.

e. ROBOGDIUM PR. [297]. Ῥοβόγδιον ἄκρ. Lon. 16.20, Lat. 61.30. ("ear uaghaidh"). Fair Head, Antrim. Columnar cliffs near, with Culfeightrin ("gual uaghaidh roinn"). ROBOGDII [309].

"Gual" (*coal*) [307d] is found here, and the following notice describes some ancient workings discovered about 1770 : "The miners, in pushing forward an adit or level toward the bed of the coal at an unexplored part of the Bally Castle Cliffs, unexpectedly discovered a passage cut through the rocks ; this passage was very narrow, owing to incrustations formed on its sides. On being sufficiently widened, some workmen went through it. In minutely examining this subterranean wonder, it was found to be a complete gallery, which had been driven forward many hundred yards into the bed of coal ; it branched out into thirty-six chambers, where coal miners had carried forward their works. The chambers were dressed quite square, and in a workmanlike manner ; pillars were left at proper intervals to support the roof ; and, in short, it was found to be an extensive mine, wrought by a set of people at least as expert as those of the present generation. Some remains of the tools, and even of the baskets used in the works, were discovered, but in such a decayed state that, on being touched, they fell in pieces. Some of the tools appear to have been of wood, thinly shod with iron. The great antiquity of the work is evident from the fact that there does not exist the most remote tradition of it in the country, but is more strongly demonstrable from the sides and pillars being covered with sparry incrustations, which the present workmen do not observe to be deposited in any definite portion of time " (*Rev. Dr. Hamilton, Letters on N. Coast of Antrim*).

304. Description of the W. side along the Oc. Occidentalis, after the Boreum Pr. :

a. RAVIUS FL. 'Ραουίου π. ἐ. Lon. 11.20, Lat. 60.40. (" earr abh "). The Errive, between counties Mayo and Galway.

b. NAGNATA. Νάγνατα πόλις ἐπίσημος. Lon. 11.15, Lat. 60.15. (" aonach," *hill :* " gnodh," *famous*). Illaunnameenoga, an island in Ballyconeely Bay, co. Galway. πολις επισημος, (*famous town*) was probably an interpretation of the native name. The place was, perhaps, like Iona, famous from a religious view ; that it was of local importance may be inferred from its giving name to the NAGNATÆ [311] and the province of Connaught.

c. LIBIUS FL. Λίβοιου π. ἐ. Lon. 10.30, Lat. 60. (" aill abh "). Aille River, S. of Doolin Point, Clare.

d. AUSOBA FL. Αὐσόβα π. ἐ. Lon. 10.30, Lat. 59.30 (" eas abh "). The stream flowing from Doo Lough and through Lough Donnell into the sea, co. Clare.

e. SINUS FL. [SCENA, 297]. Σίνου π. ἐ. Lon. 9.30, Lat. 59.30. (" sion "). The Sionan or Shannon.

The name probably refers to the many expansions
or lakes formed by the river, as if links in a
chain.

304f. DOUR FL. Δουρ π ἐ. Lon. 9.40, Lat. 58.40. The
stream near Kildurrihy, flowing into Ventry Harbour, Kerry.

g. IERNUS FL. Ἰέρνου π. ἐ. Lon. 8, Lat. 58. The
brook which rises in Knockoura and discharges
near Urhin, Coulagh Bay, S. of Kenmare River,
Kerry. Eyeries N.E. See Outerni [315].

h. NOTIUM PR. Νότιον ἄκρ. Lon. 7.40, Lat. 57.45.
(" aon aodann "). Brow Head, E. of Mizen Head
(" mais," *lump*), Cork. This name is usually
translated AUSTRALIS PR., *South Cape* [297].

305. Description of the S. side, lying near the Oc. Vergivius, after Notium Pr. :

a. DABRONA FL. Δαβρωνα π. ἐ. Lon. 11.4, Lat. 57.
(" dubh roinn "). The Blackwater, which falls
into the sea near Blackball Head.

b. BIRGUS FL. Βίργου π. ἐ. Lon. 12.30, Lat. 57.30.
(" bior acha "). The Brick, flowing into Dungarvan Harbour ; the name referring to the spit
bank which projects nearly to Dungarvan.
BRIGANTES [317], OC. VERGIVIUS [351c].

c. IERON PR. Ἱερὸν ἄκρ. Lon. 14, Lat. 57.30.
(? Iernian Cape). Carnsore Point, Wexford.
From confusion with Gr. Ἱερος, this name is
usually translated Sacrum Pr. [297]. *Cf.* Barna-
wheel and Ring, adjoining place-names.

306. Description of the E. side, lying near the Oc. Ivernius,
from Ieron Pr. :

a. MODONA FL. Μοδόνου π. ἐ. Lon. 13.40, Lat. 58.40.
"(magh tana.") Mouth of Broad Lough, Wicklow.

b. MANAPIA. Μαναπία πόλις. Lon. 13.30, Lat. 58.40.
" magh cnap "). Inchanappa, on the Vartry,
which flows into Broad Lough. MANAPII [322].

306c. Oboca Fl. 'Οβόκα π. ἐ. Lon. 13.10, Lat. 59. (" ob acha "). The stream flowing into the sea near Loughlinstown, S. of Killiney Bay, having one of its sources at Foxrock.

d. Eblana. Ἔβλανα πόλις. Lon. 14, Lat. 59.30. "(bla ain.") Julianstown on Nanny Water, Meath. Blanii [320].

e. Buvinda Fl. Βουουίνδα π. ἐ. Lon. 14.40, Lat. 59.40. (" beabh ionad "). Bavan Brook, flowing into Carlingford Lough.

f. Isamnium Pr. 'Ισάμνιον ἄκρ. Lon. 15, Lat. 60. (" sumain "). The coast at the mouth of the Shimna, near Mount St. Donard's, Down.

g. Vinderius Fl. Οὐινδέριος π. ἐ. Lon. 15, Lat. 60.15. (" beann doire "). Mount Panther, N. of Dundrum, Down.

h. Logia Fl. Λογία π. ἐ. Lon. 15.20, Lat. 60.40. (" log aoi "). The Lagan, on which Belfast (" beul ;" Vis, *cf.* Divis, *aite Vis*).

Then Robogdium Pr. [303*e*].

INLAND TOWNS: *PTOLEMY.*

307a. Rigia. 'Ριγία. Lon. 13, Lat. 60.20. (" araich "). Arigna, on Arigna River, W. of Lough Allen, Roscommon.

b. Raeba. 'Ραίβα. Lon. 12, Lat. 59.45. (" ar uaigh "). Ervallagh Oughter, 4 N.W. of Ballinasloe, Galway.

c. Laberos. Λάβηρος. Lon. 13, Lat. 59.15. (" lab," *cf.* Liffey ; " aros "). Leixlip, at the confluence of the Liffey and Rye Water, Kildare.

d. Macolicum. Μακόλικον. Lon. 11.30, Lat. 58.40. (" magh gualach "). Ballymagooly, on the Blackwater, 2 E. of Mallow, Cork. This name, if correctly interpreted, is interesting as indicating that coal was known, and probably worked, in this district eighteen centuries ago (see 303*e*).

e. Altera Rigia. Ἐτέραριγία. Lon. 11, Lat. 59.30. (ετερα, L. Altera, G. eile, *another:* Rigia). Limerick.

307.f. DUNUM. Δοῦνον. Lon. 12.30, Lat. 58.45. ("dun").
Doonane, E. of the Dinan, Queen's County.

g. IVERNIS. Ἰουερνίς. Lon. 11, Lat. 58.10. ("fè
raon"). Ballyvourny, at the confluence of the
Sullane and Bohill Rivers, Cork.

TRIBES: *PTOLEMY*.

VENICNII. Οὐενίκνιοι. ("? Veniceii" [303*b*]).

308. On the N. side of Hibernia towards the W., the
Robogdii being E. (*Ptolemy*). They extended from the Moy
(which may be regarded as their W. boundary) over the
countries of Sligo, Leitrim, and Fermanagh.

ROBOGDII. Ῥοβόγδιοι. [303*e*].

309. On the N. coast, E. of the Venicnii, the Darnii being
S. (*Ptolemy*) ; apparently occupying Donegal, Londonderry,
and N. Antrim. The columnar rocks or basalts abound on
this coast, especially W. of Bengore Head ("beann gearradh,"
hill of the carving), where a cluster of them forms the Giant's
Causeway. From the district called Mons Killaraus ("cala
ruis," *Portrush*), the Britons are fabled to have fetched the
monoliths of Stonehenge [173*d*]. In later times this territory
was called Reuta, or Routs, probably from Gael. "rod, rith,"
a path, in allusion to the step-like basaltic coast-line. The
inhabitants were the ancestors of the Irish Picts, the Cruithne
or Crutheni of the *Annales Ultonienses*; the English and Latin
versions of the annals, creating a distinction not found in
the original, confine the term Cruithne to the Irish Picts,
and give the name of Picti, Pictones, to the British Picts
(*cf. Ritson*). Some of the people of Reuta, under their
eponymous leader, Cruithne, or Reuda, passed, according to
native tradition, into N. Britain [200*d*].

ERIDINI. Ἐρίδινοι.

310. On the W. coast, between the Venicnii and the
Nagnatæ (*Ptolemy*), lying W. of the Moy in County Mayo.
Ric. does not mention the Eridini, but gives their territory

to the Venicnii ; it seems that through Reuda, King of the Scots, he identified them with the Scotti, placing the latter inland E. of the Shannon.

NAGNATÆ. Ναγνᾶται. [304b].

311. On the W. coast, below the Eridini and above the Auteiri (*Ptolemy*). They peopled the greater part of Galway, and their town was no doubt Nagnata.

AUTEIRI. Αὐτείροι. ("Uchda," *Aughty*: "ire").

312. Between the Nagnatæ and Gagganæ (*Ptolemy*), occupying Clare and the S. extreme of Galway, extending E. over Sleive Aughty to the Shannon, which also bounded them S.

GAGGANÆ. Γάγγαναι. ("Gagan").

313. Between the Auteiri and Velibori (*Ptolemy*), occupying the N. part of Kerry, and extending into Limerick. Their name refers to the clefts and caves on part of their Atlantic coast. They seem to be the LUCENI of Orosius, the last name, perhaps, from the village of Lixna, E. of the Brick, Kerry.

VELIBORI. Οὐελίβοροι, Οὐελλαβόριοι. ("Fail foir").

314. A western tribe, situated below the Gagganæ, towards the S.W. extremity of the island, and extending to the Outerni (*Ptolemy*). They occupied S. Kerry, and seem connected in name with Fogher Cliff in Valentia Island.

OUTERNI. Οὐτέρνοι. ("Aith Urhin" [304g]).

315. On the S. coast, between the Velibori and the Vodiae, and bordering on the Oc. Vergivius (*Ptolemy*). They occupied W. Cork.

VODIAE. Οὐοδίαι. ("Pait").

316. On the S. coast between the Outerni and the Brigantes, E. (*Ptolemy*), occupying E. Cork. The promontory suggested by their name is perhaps the Old Head of Kinsale, with Lispatrick.

BRIGANTES. Βρίγαντες. [305*b*].

317. On the S. coast, E. of the Vodiae (*Ptolemy*), seated in Waterford, about the Brick, whence their name.

DARNII. Δάρνιοι. (" Dur Oona," *Oona Water : cf.* Torrent River).

318. On the E. coast by the Oc. Ivernius, below and next to the Robogdii, the Voluntii lying S. (*Ptolemy*). They occupied Tyrone (which contains the name) and part of Antrim (" ncagh druim ").

VOLUNTII. Ουολούντιοι. (" Uileann aite ").

319. On the E. coast between the Darnii N. and the Blanii S. (*Ptolemy*), occupying Down and Armagh (*cf.* Castle Wellan).

BLANII. Βλάνιοι. (" Bla ain ").

320. On the E. coast, between the Voluntii N. and the Cauci S. (*Ptolemy*). They were seated at Julianstown (306*d*), and extended over Meath and Louth, and perhaps parts of Cavan and Monaghan (*cf.* Castle Blaney).

CAUCI. Καῦκοι. (" Cuach ").

321. On E. coast, between the Blanii N. and the Manapii S. They inhabited Dublin County, where their name survives in Cuckoo Stream (Mayne River) N. of Howth (" aoth "). The old name perhaps suggested by the peninsula of Howth.

MANAPII. Μανάπιοι. [306*b*].

322. Between the Cauci N. and the Coriondi (*Ptolemy*). They occupied Wicklow, their town being Manapia.

CORIONDI. Κοριόνδοι. (" Corr ionad ").

323. Between the Manapii and Brigantes (*Ptolemy*), occupying Wexford, and possibly Kilkenny and Carlow. Their name is traceable in Greenore Point, and in Kilscoran (a neighbouring village), and probably refers to the bill or long narrow bank which juts forwards from the same vicinity into Wexford Haven. See IERON PR. [305*c*].

IV
LESSER ISLANDS

IV

LESSER ISLANDS

SCANDINOVIA (*Mela.*).   SCANDIA (*Plin.*).
NERIGOS (*Plin.*).

324. The Norwegian Peninsula, or Scandinavia, anciently
believed to be an island, or island-group. Mentioned by
Mela, A.D. 50, in his chapter on the Islands of Hispania
Exterior and the Oc. Septentrionalis ; he says that it surpassed
the other islands of the Sinus Codanus [351*g*] both in fertility
and magnitude, and the Teutoni then held it.   Pliny mentions
Scandia as an island noticed by other writers ; and he also
mentions Nerigos as if unaware that it was identical with
Scandia [372]. Nerigos, *Norway, Norge,* is connected with
" njarga," a term still used in Finmark to denote a promontory—*e.g.,* Tsjorosj Njarga, Rago Nj., etc.

OCETIS INSULA.   MICTIS (*Plin.*).

325. Oκητις.   Lon. 32.40, Lat. 60.45., situated N.E. of the
Orcades (*Ptol. corr.*).   Mainland, the largest of the Shetland
Isles.   Timæus, the historian, related that at six days' sail
from Britain in the direction of the Continent lay the island
Mictis, in which tin was found; the Britanni sailed to it in
wicker vessels covered with skins (*Plin.* [372]).   The name
Mictis perhaps connected with Mio Ness in Mainland.   Chro-
mate of iron has been worked in Unst, the most Northern
of the Shetlands.   Ptolemy places the Shetlands S.E. of the
Orcades, instead of N.E., whence it may be inferred that his
calculations for these groups and Dumna were made from
Norway.

DUMNA (*Plin.*).   ["Tom"].

326. Δούμνα.   Lon. 30, Lat. 61. (*Ptolemy*).   Fair Island.
Ptolemy's particulars, when compared with those relating to
Pr. Orcas, seem to identify Dumna with Stroma, between
that cape and the Orcades ; but inasmuch as Dumna lies
under a line drawn from the Orcades to Ocetis, thus answering
to the position of Fair Island, the latter must be the island
intended.

ORCADES (*Mela, Plin., Orosius*).
ORCADÆ (*Tac.*).
ORCHADES (*Soline*).
[134*l*, 279*j*].

327. Beyond Dumna are the Orcades, Νῆσοι Ὀρκάδες, about
thirty in number, the middle of which has Lon. 30, Lat. 31.40.
(*Ptolemy*).   Orkney Islands.   Mela gives their number as
thirty, Pliny as forty, separated, according to both, by
narrow channels.   Soline says there were three (probably a
mistake for thirty) ; they were distant a voyage of seven days
and nights* from the Hebudes, were uninhabited, and without
woods, and were monotonous, with a rush-like herbage, or
consisted of bare sands (*Sol.*).   Orosius says there were
twenty islands desert and thirteen inhabited ; Jornandus
says there were thirty-five, Antonine three [374].

The islands were visited by the Roman fleet and subdued
temp. Claudius [72].   Tacitus, referring to the same event, says,
with unusual ignorance, that they were previously unknown :

Hanc oram novissimi maris tunc primum Romana classis circum-
vecta, insulam esse Britanniam adfirmavit ac simul incognitas ad id
tempus insulas, quas Orcadas vocant, invenit domuitque (*Agr.* x.).

---

* The distance from Britain to Thule, according to Pytheas, was
six days' sail [344], which allows about eighty miles per day [32, *note*],
reckoning from Cape Wrath ; and this rate agrees with Soline's two
days from Promontory Caledoniæ to the Hebudes [329].   But Soline
makes Thule five days' sail from the Orcades [347], representing
100 miles daily ; whereas the seven days from the Hebudes to the
Orcades, even if calculated from Promontory Caledoniæ, only represents about fifty miles daily.   Hence it must be inferred that the
voyages to the Hebudes, Orcades, and Thule, recorded by Soline, were
made under unequal conditions.

Euseby (died A.D. 340) says that Claudius annexed the islands, and Eutropius (C. 400), repeats the statement.

HÆBUDES (*Plin.*).
HEBUDES (*Soline*). ÆBUDES (*Marcian*).
(Epidii [199]).
NESIDES INSULÆ [13, 17, 22] (*Priscian*).

328a. The Hebrides, or Western Isles. These were known *temp.* Cæsar, who speaks of many islands less than Mona off this coast. Some writers had reported that there was continuous night in them for thirty days nearest the winter solstice ; but observations made by the Romans showed that nights were shorter in Britain than on the Continent (*B. G.*, *v.* 13). Pliny says there were thirty Hæbudes. Ptolemy describes them as lying above Hibernia, with which he groups them, and he says there were five :

EBUDA. Ἔβουδα. Lon. 15, Lat. 62. The most western, Long Island (Lewis and Harris).

EBUDA. Ὁμοίως Ἔβουδα. Lon. 15.40, Lat. 62. E. of the Western Ebuda. Skye.

RIKINA. Ῥικίνα. Lon. 17, Lat. 62. Next to East Ebuda. Canna [372].

MALEOS. Μαλεός. Lon. 17.30, Lat. 62.10. Next to Rikina. Mull. Mentioned in the *Argonautica* in terms implying that it was peculiarly sacred [5].

EPIDIUM. Ἐπίδιον. Lon. 18.30, Lat. 62. After Maleos. Bute, near the Epidium Pr., called Vectis by Pliny (who places it between Hibernia and Britain [372], and Vecta by Antonine [374].

Soline places the Hebudes at two days' sail from the Prom. Caledoniæ [134g], on the voyage to Thule ; their number was five. The inhabitants were unacquainted with corn and lived on fish and milk. One king was over the whole group, for, however many islands there were, they were divided only by a narrow strait. The king possessed no private property ; everything was enjoyed in common, equality being regulated by fixed laws, and unless he was drawn aside by avarice he learned justice from poverty. Since he had nothing of his own he was maintained at the public expense. No woman was specially given to him in marriage, but he enjoyed at any time whomsoever he pleased ; thus he had neither the promise or hope of children (*Sol.*). Marcian calls the group Britannic and says it contained five islands.

The thirty Hebudes of Pliny are perhaps the Hebrides Proper, as he separately mentions Rikina. The five of Soline must be identified with the Hebrides Proper, as they answer his two days' voyage from the Pr. Caledoniæ ; but the Hebudes from which he makes it a seven days' sail to the Orcades must be the Ebudæ of Ptolemy, which commenced near the Pr. Caledoniæ.

The Nesides, *pole islands*, were inhabited by the Amnites (Gael., " maon," *hero*). *Cf.* Isles of the Heroes [18]. Mona is still called poetically Ynys y Cedyrn (Wel. " cadarn," *mighty*).

ÆMODÆ (*Mela*). ACMODÆ (*Plin.*).

328b. Mela and Pliny give the number of these as seven ; Pliny mentions them after the Orcades and before the Hæbudes. They are the islands (including Eigg) lying off the coast of Moidart, Inverness.

MONA. CÆS.
MONAPIA (*Plin.*). Μονάοιδα, (*Ptol.*). MEVANIA (*Orosius*).
(" Muin, monadh ").

329. Isle of Man. Midway (*in medio cursu*) between Britain and Hibernia (*B.G. v.* 13), where Pliny also places it. Ptolemy places it E. of, and assigns it to, Hibernia, in Lon. 17.40, Lat. 61.30—too near Caledonia. Orosius says it was very near Hibernia, and not inconsiderable, possessing good soil and inhabited by the gentes Scotorum (*i.* 2). There is no evidence that it was attacked by the Romans.

MONA (*Plin.*, *Tac.*). Μόνα Νῆσος (*Ptol.*).

330. Anglesey, the old name surviving in Menai Straits. Pliny places it between Britain and Hibernia, and about 200 miles from Camaldunum [178b], which is nearly exact. (*H. N. ii.* 77, *iv.* 30). Ptolemy places it E. of, and assigns it to, Hibernia, in Lon. 15 Lat. 57.40, between Monaæda and

Edrum. It was conquered in 61 by Suetonius, who destroyed the Druidic groves and founded a station [80], but was called away by the Icenian revolt [83]. Being lost again, it was reconquered late in 79 by Agricola [90].

EDRUM DESERTUM. ANDROS (*Plin.*).

331*a*. Ἕδρου ἔρημος. Lon. 15, Lat. 59.30. (*Ptol.*). Drumnough, N.W. of Lambay Island, co. Dublin.

LIMNUM DESERTUM. LIMNUS (*Plin.*).

Λίμνου ἔρημος. Lon. 15, Lat. 59. (*Ptol.*). Lambay Island. The mention of the rocks Drumnough and Lambay by Ptolemy is inexplicable ; perhaps they were held in peculiar religious veneration. He assigns them to Hibernia, and Pliny places them between Hibernia and Britain.

CLOTA IN HIVERIONE [374].

331*b*. The holy island of Innis Caltra [22], in Loch Derg, co. Clare. It is situated towards the Bernagh Mountains, and probably Hiverio indicates the adjacent region and not Hibernia in general.

SILURA (*Soline*). SYLINA (*Sulp. Sev.*).

332. Lundy, off the coast of the Damnonii, in the strait between Britain and Hibernia. The inhabitants preserved their ancient manners, did not value money, traded by exchange or barter, and revered the gods ; both men and women equally pretended knowledge of the future (*Sol.*). The Emperor Maxim exiled some religious offenders to Sylina (*Sulp. Sev.*).

OESTRYMNIDES INSULÆ (*Avienus* [6]).
CASSITERIDES INS. (*Plin.* [372]). Νῆσοι Κασσιτερίδες (*Herod.* [4]).
CATTIDERIDES INS. (*Ptol.*).

333. The Scilly Islands. Avienus mentions the Oestrymnides as visited by Himilco. Herodotus had heard of the Cassiterides, or tin islands, but discredited their existence. Strabo definitely identifies them with the Scilly Isles, placing them in the open sea, N. of, and opposite to, Artabria in

Spain, but under nearly the same latitude as Britain, the latter lying more to the E. (II. v. 15) ; he enumerates them between the Island of Gadeira, *Cadiz*, and the Britannic Isles (*ibid*. 30), and states that tin was found in them and carried from the Britannic Isles to Marseilles (III. ii. 9). They were ten in number, and lay near each other, one being desert, the others inhabited by men who wore black cloaks, with tunics girt at the breast and reaching to the feet, and who walked with staves, like the Furies in tragedy. They subsisted by their cattle, and generally led a roving life, but worked tin and lead ; these, with skins, they bartered away to merchants for pottery, salt, and brass vessels. Formerly the Phœnicians, from Gades, alone held this trade, concealing the passage, and one shipmaster, when followed by some Romans, ran his vessel upon a shoal, escaping on wreckage, and the State reimbursed him for his cargo. The Romans at length won the secret, and Publius Crassus, finding, on a visit, that the metals were dug out at little depth, and that the inhabitants were peaceable, made known the discovery, though the passage was longer than to Britain (III. v. 11). Mela says that among the Celts there were some islands which, because they abounded in lead, were called by the one name Cassiterides (iii. 6).

334a. Pliny, who abridged what he found in other authors without reducing the materials to consistence, says that opposite Celtiberia there were many islands which the Greeks called Cassiterides, from their abounding in lead, and that lead was first brought from the Cassiteridan Isle by Midas· (Midacritas), King of Phrygia. He also says it was fabled that tin (plumbum candidum), which was more valuable than black lead (plumbum nigrum), was found in the islands of the Atlantic, whence it was conveyed in wicker boats covered with skins ; but he adds, apparently deriving his information from Isidore, that it was now known to be obtained from Lusitania and Galicia [372]. Ptolemy includes the islands in Hispania Tarraconensis, and says they lay in the Oc. Occidentalis, their number being ten, of which the middle had Lon. 4, Lat. 45.30. Soline says they were opposite the coast of Celtiberia and were rich in lead (xxiii.).

334b. The following islands seem to be members of this group :

BARSA.	*Ant.* [374].	Bryher.
LISIA.	,,	Illiswilgig.
ANDIUM.	,,	Annet.
SICDELIS.	,,	? Tresco, with the town Dolphin.
UXANTISINA.	,,	AXANTOS (*Plin.*). ? St. Mary's, with Hugh Town.
SIAMBIS.	*Plin.*	Sampson.
VINDILIS.	*Ant.* [374].	Toll's Island. This name seems to identify Richard's 40 VINDILIOS with the Scilly Islands.
SIATA.	,,	? St. Agnes.
ARICA.	,,	? Gorregan, or Ragged Island.

See [338].

The island adjacent to Britain, where Briareus watched over the sleeping Saturn [18a], is perhaps Bryher. The story seems to be that of the three Kyklopes reflected in the three Hekatoncheires (G. " ceud," *hundred :* " carr," *rock*), named Kottos, Gyges (*cf.* Gugha Island) and Briareus. The latter's mortal name of Ægæon suggests relation with the Genii, and Saturn is the Titan Kronos confined in Tartaros with the Hekatoncheires or Genii as his guards.

SENA [18a] (*Mela*).

335. Placed in the Mare Britannicum, opposite the shores of the Osismii, Armorica. Perhaps Ushant, or the Isle de Seins. Strictly, this island was not Britannic.

ICTIS (" acha dus ").

336. St. Michael's Mount, Cornwall ; an island at high water, but a peninsular at the ebb [45]. Part of the name possibly survives in Market Jew (Marazion).

VECTIS (*Suet.*). VECTA (*Eutrop.* vii). Νῆσος Ὀυίκτησις (*Ptol.*).

337. Isle of Wight ; ὑπὸ δὲ τὸν μέγαν λιμένα (*under the great haven. Cf* Megaslimen [136e]), having, in the centre, Lon. 19.20, Lat. 52.20. (*Ptol.*). Conquered by Vespasian, *circa* A.D. 43 [72], and said to have been peopled in post Roman times by the Jutes [131a]. Insula de Wit, D.B.

Riduna, Sarmia, Cæsarea (*Ant.* [374]).

338. Usually identified with Alderney, Guernsey, and Jersey, but probably to be sought amongst the Scilly Islands [334*b*]. Riduno, ? *Tean :* Sarmia, ? *St. Martins.*

Adtanatos (*Sol.*)

339. Isle of Thanet. According to Soline it adjoined the Fretum Gallicum [351*f*] and was separated from the mainland of Britain by the narrow estuary of the Wantsum ; it possessed good corn land and rich soil. No snake was found in it, and the soil, wherever carried, was fatal to those reptiles. Britannicè Ruym [291*f*].

Ruoichin, said to be an old British name of Thanet, probably designated the hill of Richborough, once undoubtedly an island, and usually, but incorrectly, identified with Portus Ritupiæ [168*d*].

Toliapis. Τολιάπις. ("Tul fe ").

340. Situated beside the Trinoantes [178], having Lon. 23, Lat. 54.15. (*Ptol.*). Canvey Island, Essex. The name perhaps connected with the Hope, stretching from Canvey towards Tilbury. The stated longitudes place this island and the next in the open sea towards Germany.

Counos. Γώουνος. (" Acha neas ").

341. Beside the Trinoantes ; Lon. 24, Lat. 54.30. (*Ptol.*). Foulness Island, Essex.

Glessariæ (" Glessum," *amber*).

342. Situated in the German Sea, E. of Britain, and called by the later Greeks Electrides, because amber, ηλεκτρον, was found in them (*Plin.*). Strictly they were not Britannic, being the Friesland Islands off the coasts of Holland and Germany.

Bergos. Burchana (*Plin.*).

Borkum, one of the Frisian Islands, E. of the Glessariæ.

V

THULE

V

THULE

Thule [12, 13, 66], *Tac.*, etc.   Thyle [259*j*], *Sol.*, etc.   ἡ Θούλη, *Ptol.*

("Toll," *a pit*).

343. Iceland ; the old name, either from the geysers, or
the observation that the island lay under the apex of the
celestial dome (θόλος).   About A.D. 70 it was said to be the
most distant (ultima) of the British Isles (*Plin.*).   Ptolemy
places it above the Orcades :

The most W. part	Lon. 29.	Lat. 63.
The most E. part	Lon. 31.40.	Lat. 63.
The most N. part	Lon. 30.20.	Lat. 63.15.
The most S. part	Lon. 30.20.	Lat. 62.40.
The middle ..	Lon. 30. 20.	Lat. 63.

344. Pytheas of Massilia affirmed that the farthest
country N. from the British Isles was Thule, which was six days'
sail from Britain, and near the Frozen Sea, where the Summer
Tropic and Arctic Circle were one.   He related that neither
earth, water, nor air existed separately there, but formed a
sort of mixture, resembling marine sponge, in which the earth,
sea, and all things were suspended, thus forming, as it were,
a link to unite the whole together ; it could neither be travelled
over nor sailed through.   He had seen this substance with
his own eyes ; the *rest he reported on the authority of others.*
He recorded no other particulars concerning the country—
whether it was an island or whether it continued habitable
up to the point where the Summer Tropic becomes one with
the Arctic Circle (*Strab.* I., iv. 1 ; II. v. 8 ; IV. v. 5.

345. Strabo states that, according to Eratosthenes, the
distance from the Borysthenes, *Dnieper*, to the parallel of
Thule was 11,500 stadia ; but he disputes this measure as a

mere guess. He further challenges the veracity of Pytheas, upon whom, he says, no reliance can be placed, and he remarks that other writers who had seen Britain and Ierne, although they noticed many islands around Britain, made no mention of Thule. His belief that it was scarcely possible to exist in Ierne owing to the cold [345] led him to conclude that the far region in which Eratosthenes placed Thule must be totally uninhabitable, and that the northern boundaries of the habitable earth lay considerably southward. He affirmed that the account of Thule was more uncertain than that of Ierne because of its secluded situation, being regarded the northernmost of all lands whose names were known (*Strab.* I. iv. 2, 3, 4 ; II. v. 8 ; IV. v. 5).

346. Pytheas, who visited Thule in 320 B.C., was not its discoverer, since some of his particulars respecting it were from other writers. Several geographers besides him and Strabo mention it. Isidorus computed it to be 1,200 miles from the mouth of the Tanais (*Plin., Hist. Nat.* ii. 112). Ptolemy placed it beyond the Orcades. Mela placed it opposite to (*i.e.*, in the same meridian as) the coast of the Belgæ (*Ric.* I., viii., § 20). Navigators sailed to it from Nerigos [324] (*Plin. Hist. Nat.* iv. 30).

347. The inhospitable, dark, and rigorous climate of Thule was proverbial in the earliest times. But, according to Pytheas, the days were continuous for six months in the Summer solstice when the sun passed the sign of Cancer, and nights were continuous in the Winter solstice (*Plin. Hist.Nat.* ii. 77 ; iv. 30) ; the zone in which this occurred extended from the Riphæan Mountains to Thule (*ib.* vi. 39). According to Tacitus, the extreme coast of Britain looked towards Thule, which, however, snow and winter were concealing ; it was said that the sea, which was sluggish, and heavy to the rowers, was not even raised by the winds* (*Agric.* x.). According to Solinus, Thule was the farthest of the Britannic Isles. In the Summer solstice, when the sun passed from the constellation of Cancer, there was scarcely any night ; in the

---

* Tacitus attributed this to the great distance of the island from land and mountains (*rariores terræ montesque*), which were productive of tempests, and also to the more unyielding stability of the open sea.

Winter solstice it so happened that the dawn seemed merged
in sunset. From the promontory of Caledonia voyagers
hither first passed the Hebudes, then the Orchades as the
second station, and from the latter it was distant a voyage
of five days and nights. The inhabitants, in the beginning of
Spring, lived with, and fed as, the cattle; then on milk; in
winter they used sparingly the fruit of trees. They had
wives in common, being unused to fixed marriage. Beyond
Thule the sea was sluggish and congealed (*Sol.*). Orosius
says the island was separated from the others by the bound-
less ocean ; lying towards the middle of this, it was only known
to a few.

348. The poets thus speak of Thule :

> Hyperboreo damnatum sidere Thulen.
> —CLAUD. *in Ruf.*
> [Thule condemned to Hyperborean star].

> Cæruleus . . . cum dimicat, incola Thules
> Agmina falcigero circumvenit arta covinno.
> —SILIUS ITALICUS, *Punic* xvii. 416.
> [When the dark-coloured inhabitant of Thule fights,
> He surrounds with scythed-chariot the thronged ranks].

Thule, in the last quotation, is figurative ; it is sometimes
used to express unbounded conquest. (120*a*, *c ;* 123*c*). A
passage in Claudian [120*b*] led Richard to imagine that part
of Caledonia was known by the name (*Ric.* I., vi. 50), unless,
indeed, the idea was suggested by Cairn Toul and Athole.
The Thule of Procopius, computed to be ten times larger
than Britannia [14], must be Greenland.

349. The phenomenon of continual day is noticed by
Avienus and Priscian :

> Longe dehinc [à Britanniâ] celeri si quis rate marmora currat
> Inque Lycaonias cymbam procul urgeat Arctos,
> Inveniet vasto surgentem vertice Thulen.
> Hic quum plaustra poli tangit Phoebeius ignis,
> Nocte sub illustri rota solis fomite flagrat.
> Continuo, clarumque diem nox æmula ducit.
> Nam sol obliquo torquetur cardine mundi,
> Directosque super radios vicinior axi
> Occiduo inclinat, donec juga rursus anhela

Devexo accipiat coelo Notus.   Inde fluenta
Tenduntur Scythici longe maris in facis ortum
Eoæ.

—AVIEN.: *Descript. Orb. Terr.*, 758-770.

Oceani tranans hinc [à Britanniâ] navibus æquor apertum
Ad Thulen venies ; quæ nocte dieque relucet
Titanis radiis, quum curru scandit ad axes
Signiferi, Boreas succendens lampade partes.
Ad navem pelago flectenti Aquilonis ab oris
Ad solem calido referentem lumen ab ortu,
Aurea spectetur tibi pinguibus insula glebis.

—PRISC.   *Periegesis*, 588-604

See [27-9].

VI
OCEANS

VI

OCEANS

350. The OCEANUS ATLANTICUS, ʼΩκεανὸς ʼΑτλαντικός, was generally regarded as being westward of the continents and islands of Europe and Africa. Particular portions had specific names : *e.g.*, (1) AETHIOPICUM MARE, N.W. of Africa ; from this sea Marcian (c. vi.) computed the distance to Thule. (2) OC. CANTABRICUS, or SINUS OESTRYMNICUS [7], extending from Artabria in Spain to the British Isles. (3) OC. GALLICUS, between the Pyrenees and the Sequana (Seine) (*Plin. Hist. Nat.* iv. 33). (4) OC. OCCIDENTALIS, ʼΩ. Δυτικός, washing the coast of Hibernia from Boreum Prom. to Notium Pr. [304], but sometimes as extensive as the term Atlantic itself.

351a. The arms of the Atlantic which washed the islands and peninsulas of N.W. Europe and the regions beyond were often designated under the general name of OC. SEPTENTRION-ALIS, *Northern Sea :* this extended from the Rhenus (Rhine) to the N. coast of Scythia (*Plin.* iv. 33), and was the N. boundary of Belgica and the two Germanies, the islands Britain and Hibernia being within it (*Marc.* II. i, 27) ; but numerous divisions were recognized :

b. (1) OCEANUS BRITANNICUS. ʼΩ. Βρεττανικός, BRITAN-NICUM MARE ; N. of Spain and Gaul ; extending from the Rhine to the Sequana (*Plin. ibid.*) ; washing Britain from Ocrinum Pr. to Cantium Pr. [136] : and lying N. of Gallia Lugdunensis (*Marc.*). Now the English Channel.

c. (2) OC. VERGIVIUS. ʼΩ. ʼΟνεργιούιος ; along the S. coast of Hibernia from Notium Pr. to Sacrum Pr. and washing Britain from about the Æst. Sabrina to Ocrinum Pr. [305, 135*q-u*]. The name probably from the Hibernian tribe Brigantes [317] ; it still survives as St. *George's* Channel.

d. (3) OC. IVERNIUS. ʼΩ. ʼΙουέρνιος, ʼΙουβέρνιος, HIBERNICUM MARE ; from Sacrum Pr. to Rhobogdium Pr. ; and from the

Novantum Pr. to Octapitarum Pr. [135, 306]. *St. George's Channel and Irish Sea.* Mare Gallwadiæ [127].

351e. (4) Oc. DUECALEDONIUS. 'Ω. Δουηκαληδόνιος; from Novantum Pr. to Orcas Pr. (*Ptol.*, *Marc.*) [134]. This name, signifying "Ocean of the Caledonian Promontory," must strictly have designated the sea between the Æst. Clotta and Hibernia ; and it points clearly to correct knowledge prior to Ptolemy, who confounds it with the Hyperborean.

f. (5) FRETUM GALLICUM. Straits of Dover [337].

g. (6) SINUS CODANUS. Kattegat ; the Gulf of Mentonomon [11]. The main extension of this arm inwards was called the Mare Suevicum, or Sarmaticum, *Baltic.* The immense island, Baltia, within it [11], in the neighbourhood of the Goths and Teutons, was apparently the mainland promontory between the Gulfs of Riga and Finland, now forming part of Russia's Baltic Provinces, and extending backwards to the Valdai Hills.

h. (7) Oc. GERMANICUS. 'Ω. Γερμανικός, Mare Cimbricum ; Mare Fresicum [199*f*] from Orcas Pr. to Cantium Pr. [137]. *German Ocean.* Mare Norwagiæ [127].

i. (8) Oc. HYPERBOREUS. 'Ω. 'Υπερβόρειος; a name for the Oc. Septentrionalis where it washes the N. coast of Scythia (*Plin. Hist. Nat.* iv. 27), and of Hibernia, from Boreum Pr. to Rhobogdium Pr. [303] ; called also the Oc. CRONIUS (Gael, " cron ") and MORTUUM MARE (*Dead Sea*) [5]. Hecatæus called it AMALCHIUM MARE,* from the River Paropamisus, where it washed Scythia, which name in the Scythian language signified " congealed " ; according to Philemon it was called MORIMARUSA MARE*—*i.e.*, MORTUUM MARE (Gael. " muir marbh "), from the Cimbri to Rubeas Pr. [5] ; beyond the latter point it was called CRONIUM (*Plin. ibid.*). At a day's voyage beyond Thule the sea was frozen (*concretum*), and was by some called Cronium (*ibid.* 30). The last name still appears in Greenland (cron-land).

---

* It is questionable whether these names had the actual meanings given to them by Hecatæus and Philemon. *Cf.* Amalchium with Gael. " meilg," *death*, " mulghart " [22] ; and Morimarusa with Russ. " moroz," *frost.* Morimarusa may still survive in Murman coast, part of the peninsula of Kola.

VII

APPENDIX

VII

APPENDIX

RELIGION OF THE GAULS.

352. The Gauls who were of any account were divided into two orders, the Druides and Equites. The Druids were engaged in the sacred offices, attended to public and private sacrifices, and interpreted matters of religion ; and a great number of young people came to them to be taught. They were held in great honour, decided nearly all controversies, public and private, and judged in cases of crime and murder, and in disputes as to heirships and boundaries. If any one, either of public or private rank, refused to abide by their decrees, they interdicted him from the sacrifices ; this was considered the greatest of punishments, and the excommunicated was reckoned in the number of impious and accursed. All the people shunned him for fear of disaster from contact with him, nor was any mitigation of punishment or any honour conceded to him notwithstanding penitence. The Druids were presided over by a chief, in whom the supreme power was vested. On his death the next in dignity succeeded ; if there were several with equal dignity the Druids had the right of election, and sometimes in such cases the competitors supported their claims by arms. At a certain time of the year they assembled in a consecrated place in the territory of Carnute (fines Carnutum), which was considered the middle of Gaul, and hither litigants flocked from all parts and submitted to their decrees and judgments (*De Bello Gall*. vi. 13).

353. The Druids enjoyed immunity from tribute, military service, and all obligations which attached to the other order.

Encouraged by these advantages many applied themselves to the discipline, either of their own will or at the instance of parents or relatives. These students were said to learn a large number of verses, so that sometimes their training lasted twenty years. It was held unlawful to commit those things to writing, though in matters outside religion writing was used. Cæsar considered that the reasons for this rule were, first, that the discipline should not be revealed to the uninitiated, secondly, that the use of letters would result in a looser training than would be imparted by the cultivation of memory. The Druids also taught the immortality of the soul, but considered that after death it passed from one body to another ; consequently death was not feared, and this gave great encouragement to valour. They also closely studied the stars and their motions, the size of the world and countries, natural science, and the power and majesty of the immortal gods, and handed down their beliefs to their disciples (*ibid.* 14).

354. The Gauls were exceedingly superstitious. On that account, those afflicted with grievous disease or about to engage in battle or other dangerous enterprises either immolated men as victims or vowed to immolate themselves, and such sacrifices were performed by the Druids. If the life of a man was taken, it was considered that nothing less than the life of another would appease the will of the immortal gods, and there were established public sacrifices of this kind. Others had wickerwork frames of enormous size which they filled with living men, and applying fire, consumed them in the flames. It was considered that on such occasions the sacrifice of those who were caught in thieving, robbing with violence, or other delinquencies, were more acceptable to the deities ; but when the number of these was not sufficient, they had recourse to innocent men (*ibid.* 16).

355. They chiefly worshipped the god Mercury, of whom there were many images. They held him to be the inventor of all arts, the guardian of roads, and journeyings, and the greatest patron of commerce. Next came Apollo, Mars, Jupiter, and Minerva, who had almost the same attributes as with other nations (*reliquæ gentes*). The first kept away disease ; Minerva imparted the rudiments of skill and handicraft ; Jupiter held the empire of the heavens ; Mars presided over war, and when about to engage in battle they commonly vowed the spoils to him.   The spoils with life (quæ super-averint animalia capta), were immolated ; the rest was heaped together in one place.   There were (*conspicari licet*), in con-secrated spots, in many States, tumuli piled up with these things, and if any person should dare to conceal any spoil, or remove it from the tumulus, he was given up to execution with torture (*ibid.* 17).   All the Gauls claimed descent from Dis Pater,* this belief being handed down by the Druids ; on this account they always measured time by the number of nights, instead of days, and they so observed birthdays, and the beginnings of months and years that day followed night (*ibid.* 18).   Their funerals, considering their social condition, were magnificent and costly ; everything which they imagined was pleasing to the deceased while living was cast in the fire, including even animals, and not much before Cæsar's time the slaves and dependents who were thought to have been esteemed by their master were burned together after the customary funeral ceremonies had been performed (*i.e.*, after the victims had been put to death† [*ibid.* 19]).

356. Among the Gauls there were generally three classes of men especially reverenced—the Bards, Βαρδοί μεν ‛υμνηταὶ καὶ ποιηταὶ ; Vates, ἱεροποιοί ; and Druids, φυσιολόγοι καὶ ἠθικοί. The Bards composed and chanted hymns ; the Vates occupied themselves with sacrifices and the study of nature ; while the Druids studied both nature and moral philosophy.   The belief in the justice of the Druids was so great that the de-cision of both public and private disputes was referred to them, and they had sometimes, by their decision, prevented armies from engaging when drawn up in battle array.   All cases of murder were particularly referred to them ; when there were plenty of these, they imagined there would be a plentiful

* Terrena vis omnis atque natura Diti patri dedicata est: qui *Dives*, ut apud Græcos πλούτων, quia et recidant omnia in terras, et orian-tur e terris.   Is rapuit Proserpinam, quod Græcorum nomen est; ea enim est, quæ Περσεφόνη Græce nominatur: quam frugum semen esse volunt, absconditamque quæri a matre fingunt.—*Cic. De Nat. Deor.*, ii. 26.

† Compare the funerals of Scythian kings (*Herod.* iv. 71, 72).

harvest. All three classes asserted that the soul was inde-
structible, and likewise the world, but that sometimes fire
and sometimes water had produced great changes (*Strab.
IV., iv. 4, Hamilton and Falconer's Translation,* 1854.)

357. To their simplicity and vehemence the Gauls joined
much folly, arrogance, and love of ornament. They wore
golden collars* round their necks, and bracelets on their
arms and wrists ; and those who were of any dignity had
garments dyed and worked with gold. This lightness of
character made them intolerable as conquerors, and threw
them into consternation in reverse. Besides their folly, they
had a barbarous and absurd custom, common to many
northern nations, of suspending the heads of enemies from
their horses' necks when returning from battle, and nailing
them as a spectacle to their gates. Posidonius said he witnessed this in many places, and was at first shocked, but
became familiar with it on account of its frequency. The
heads of many illustrious persons they embalmed with cedar,
exhibited them to strangers, and would not sell them for
their weight in gold. But the Romans put a stop to these
customs, and to their modes of sacrifice and divination, which
were quite opposite to Latin laws. They would strike a man,
devoted as an offering in his back with a sword, and divine
from his convulsions. They never sacrificed without the
Druids. They were said to have other modes of sacrificing
their human victims, piercing some with arrows, and crucify-
ing others in their temples ; and preparing a Colossus of hay
and wood, into which they put cattle, beasts of all kinds,
and men, and then set fire to it (*ibid.* 5).

358. It was a Gallic custom to make public atonement
with human offerings. Anyone compelled by very necessitous
circumstances might bind himself for this purpose on condition
that he should be provided with the best food at the public
expense for a full year ; he was then, on a fixed feast-day, led
through the whole town and outside the walls, where the people

---

* The golden collar, or torque, was in high favour with the Britons.
Aneurin says that 360 warriors went to the battle of Cattraeth [191 *e*]
wearing the golden torque ; and notices of it occur frequently in other
British bards.

killed him with stones (*Placid. Lactantius*).   It is also related
that persons condemned for crime were kept for five years,
that there might be a sufficient number available to make the
sacrifice respectable (*Diod.* v. 32).

359.   Et quibus immitis placatur sanguine diro
Teutates, horrensque feris altaribus Hesus ;
Et Taranis Scythicæ non mitior ara Dianæ.
Vos quoque qui fortes animas, belloque peremptas
Laudibus in longum vates dimittitis ævum,
Plurima securi fudistis carmina Bardi.
Et vos barbaricos ritus, moremque sinistrum
Sacrorum Druidæ positis repetistis ab armis.
Solis nosse deos, et cœli numina vobis,
Aut solis nescire datum : nemora alta remotis
Incolitis lucis.   Vobis auctoribus umbræ
Non tacitas Erebi sedes, Ditisque profundi
Pallida regna petunt ; regit idem spiritus artus
Orbe alio : longæ (canitis si cognita) vitæ
Mors media est. Certe populi, quos despicit Arctos,
Felices errore suo, quos ille timorum
Maximus, haud urget leti metus.   Inde ruendi
In ferrum mens prona viris, animæque capaces
Mortis, et ignavum redituræ parcere vitæ.
                    —Lucan, *Pharsal.*, i., 444.

360. The Druids held nothing more sacred than the
mistletoe, and the tree on which it grew, if an oak. They
chose groves of oaks, and performed no sacred ceremony
without its leaf, and it seemed possible (to Pliny) that they
thus had, by Greek interpretation, the name of Druids.   For
whatever grew on the oak was considered a gift from heaven,
and a sign that the tree had been selected by God Himself.
The mistletoe was rarely found upon it ; but on each occasion
it was cut with great ceremony. This occurred as the first
act on the sixth day of the moon, which was the beginning
of their months and years, and after the tree had passed its
thirtieth year, when it had already abundant strength, though
not half-grown.   In their language it was called " all heal."
Having prepared sacrifices and feasts under the tree, two
white bulls were brought forward, the horns of which were
then, for the first time, bound. The priest, clad in a white
robe, mounted the tree, and cut the mistletoe with a golden
sickle, and it was received on a white cloth.   The victims were

then killed, the people praying that God would add prosperity to the gift. The mistletoe was believed to cure animal barrenness and to be a remedy against all poisons (*Plin. Hist. Nat.* xvi. 95). The Gallic Druids also held the herb selago, *club moss*, in great veneration, gathering it with formal ceremonies, and holding it to be a charm against misfortune, and beneficial in all diseases of the eye (*ibid.* xxiv. 62) ; and another famous charm was the anguinum or serpent's egg (*ibid.* xxix. 12). The Magi (Druids) used the stone gagates in divination, affirming that it would not glow if the devotee was about to obtain what he wished (*ibid.* xxxvi. 34).

360*b*. Gentes (Galliæ) superbæ, superstitiosæ, aliquando etiam immanes adeo, ut hominem optimam et gratissimam diis victimam cæderent. Manent vestigia feritatis jam abolitæ, atque ut ab ultimis cædibus temperant, ita nihilominus ubi devotos altaribus admovere, delibant. Habent tamen et facundiam suam, magistrosque sapientiæ Druidas. Hi terræ mundique magnitudinem et formam, motus cœli ac syderum, ac quid Dii velint, scire profitentur. Docent multa nobilissimos gentis clam et diu vicenis annis in specu, aut in abditis saltibus. Unum ex iis quæ præcipiunt, in vulgus effluxit, videlicet ut forent ad bella meliores, æternas esse animas, vitamque alteram ad manes. Itaque cum mortius cremant ac defodiunt, apta viventibus olim. Negotiorum ratio etiam et exactio crediti deferebatur ad inferos ; erantque qui se in rogos suorum, velut unà victuri, libenter immitterent (*Mela* III. ii.).

RELIGION OF THE GERMANS.

361. The customs of the Germans differed much from those of the Gauls, for they neither had Druids over their divine affairs, nor were addicted to sacrifices. They only deified those things which they could see and which were of benefit to them, such as the sun, vulcan, and the moon. Report as to other gods was disregarded (*Cæs. B. G.* vi. 21). (But see [363]).

362. The Germans celebrated in ancient songs (which formed their poetry and records) the god Tuisco, sprung from the soil, and his son Mannus ; these were the origin

and founders of the race.   They assigned to Mannus three
sons, who gave names to the three great branches of the
race.   Some, relying on tradition, enumerated more nations
among the offspring of the god (*Tac. Germ* ii.).   They related
that Hercules visited them, and when they went to battle,
they sang in his praise as the strongest of all men.   They
had also a kind of song called barritum (barditum), by the
recital of which they inflamed their minds, and divined the
result of battle, for they caused terror or were terrified according to the sound ; in this they regarded harmony of voice
less than clamour.   Their effort was for discordant noise and
broken murmur, and they sought by striking their shields
on their mouths, to produce fuller and deeper sounds.   Some
thought that Ulysses, in his wanderings, visited Germany,
and also Asciburgium, which was situated on the Rhine and
was in Tacitus's time inhabited by people who were established
and named by him.   For example, an altar consecrated to
Ulysses, with the name of Lærtes his father, was formerly
found in the same place, and certain monuments and tumuli
inscribed with Greek letters still existed on the confines of
Germany and Rhetia.   Tacitus, however, could neither confirm or deny these antiquities, and left his readers to exercise
their own discretion (*ibid*. iii.).

363. The Germans especially worshipped Mercury, and
on certain days they considered it lawful to propitiate him
with human sacrifices.   Animals were sacrificed to Hercules
and Mars.   Part of the Suevi sacrificed to Isis, but the
presence of this foreign cult amongst them was not accounted
for, unless the symbol of the goddess, which was a Liburnian
galley   proved that it was imported.   They considered it
contrary to the greatness of the celestials to restrain them
within walls or to represent them in human shape.   They
consecrated groves and forest-clearings (*nemora*), which they
called by the names of deities and regarded with singular
veneration (*ibid*. ix.).

364. The priests had greater power than the kings or
military leaders (*duces*), who, without their permission, could
not order death, imprisonment, or flogging ; hence these
penalties were scarcely regarded as punishments, or as imposed

by, the leader, but rather as the will of the god, whom they believed to attend them in war, and whose effigies with certain standards the priests took from the groves and bore into battle. Omens and lots were highly esteemed. The casting of lots was simple ; a branch taken from a fruit-tree was cut in pieces, which were distinctively marked, and thrown broad-cast upon a white cloth. Then the State priest in public matters, or the family priest in private matters, having prayed to the gods, and looking heavenward, took up three pieces in succession, and interpreted according to the marks upon them. If inauspicious, nothing more was done in that matter the same day ; if auspicious, confirmation was sought by omens, which consisted of observing the noises or flights of birds or the neighing of horses. White horses were reared in the sacred places exclusively for this purpose ; they were harnessed in a sacred car, and the auspices were observed by the priest and the king or chief of the State. This kind of omen was in greatest favour, not only by the people but by the aristocracy and priests, for the horses being devoted to the service of the gods, were thought to be conscious of their will. In the event of a war of doubtful issue, the result was divined by means of a combat between one of their warriors and a captured enemy, each armed after the manner of his own nation (*ibid*. x.).

365. The princes decided small matters ; but the more important were determined by all, yet so that those matters which were in the decision of the people were deliberated by the princes. They met, except in exceptional and sudden circumstances, on fixed days, at the new or full moon, the new moon being considered most auspicious. They reckoned, not by days, as the Romans did, but by nights, so that night seemed to lead the day. Their liberty led to this looseness, that they did not assemble at once and as commanded, but the second and third day would be consumed by the delay of those summoned. At their assemblies the priests commanded silence, and had the right to enforce order (*ibid*. xi.). They did not despise the counsels of women, nor neglect their advice. Under Vespasian, Veleda was by many long revered as if a goddess ; and earlier, Aurinia and many others were venerated, though opinion did not deify them in their own time (*ibid.* viii.). The Germans did not make great funerals ; this only was observed—that the bodies of distinguished men were cremated with certain kinds of wood. They did not heap up the pyre with clothes or odours ; but the arms of the deceased were placed with him, and his horse was cast in the fire. The tombs were of sod. High and laborious monuments were spurned as heavy to the dead (*ibid.* xxvii.).

366. Special references occur in Tacitus to the religious customs of particular tribes. Among the Semnones, deputies from all peoples of the same blood met at stated times in a wood sanctified by ancestral auguries and ancient associations. There, after a man had been publicly killed, they performed ceremonies of a barbarous and dreadful kind. Another custom was observed in the grove : none entered unless bound with chains, thus acknowledging his inferiority to the god, and if any one fell he was not permitted to rise, but had to roll himself out. All superstition centred in this place, as if it was the cradle of the race and the house of the god, who governed all, everything else being subject and obedient (*ibid.* xxxix.). The Reudigni, Angli, Varini, etc., worshipped Herthum—*i.e.*, Terra Mater—in common and believed that she interfered in the affairs of men, and visited the people. There was in an island of the ocean an unpolluted grove having within it a consecrated carriage covered with tapestry, and only one priest was allowed to approach it. He perceived the goddess to appear in the interior, borne by female owls, and with great reverence he supplicated her. The day on which this occurred was one of joy, feasting, and hospitality ; on it they desisted from war and arms, put away all implements of toil, and so continued until the desire of the goddess for mortal conversation was satisfied, when the priest left her in the temple. Now the carriage and tapestry and, it was also said,the goddess herself, were washed in a secret lake, attended by slaves whom the lake immediately swallowed up (*ibid.* xl.). In the territory of the Naharvali the grove of the ancient religion was pointed out. Here the priest officiated in female attire, and acknowledged deities which, by Roman interpretation, were Castor

and Pollux; they had the same attributes, but were called
Alci.* Though there was no trace of foreign importation,
they were worshipped as faithful brothers (*ibid.* xliii.). The
nations of the Aestyi venerated the Mater Deum, whom they
represented under the figures of wild boars.† Her effigies was
borne into battle in front of the army, and it was even re-
spected by the enemy (*ibid.* xlv.).

SCANDINAVIAN RELIGION.‡

367. The Scandinavians had sacred groves. One of these,
attached to the temple of Upsal, in Sweden, and called
Odin's Grove, was full of the bodies of men and animals,
victims of sacrifice. In this grove every tree and leaf was
held in profound reverence. In or near the groves there
were altars; these consist generally of three upright pieces
of rock, supporting a large flat stone [249*h*] often with a
cavity underneath to receive the blood of the victims. They
are found in the middle of a plain or on a hill. Occasionally,
as seen in an example in Zealand, the altar, and the hill on
which it stands, are surrounded by a double circle of stones
which from their size have evidently been brought from a
distance, as masses of such magnitude are rarely found in the
island.

368. There were three great festivals in the year. The
first, named Jul (afterwards Yule, *Christmas*), was celebrated
in honour of the god Frey (*Sun*), at the Winter solstice, on
Mother-night (the night on which the Scandinavian year commenced). The second was kept at the first quarter of the
second moon of the year in honour of the Earth or the goddess
Goa. The third, which seems to have been anciently the
most considerable, was in honour of Odin. It was observed
at the beginning of Spring, to welcome that season, and to
obtain success in those freebooting expeditions which, commencing every year immediately after this festival, long
spread desolation along the coasts of Britain and N.W.
Europe. As with the Britons and Germans, human sacrifices

* The name suggests the Greek origin of the Alci (*cf.* Lakedæmon).
† The boar is frequently mentioned in Ossian.
‡ From Blackwell's edition of Mallet's *Northern Antiquities,* 1847

were amongst the offerings made on great occasions. At Upsal, a national festival was held every ninth year, at which nine victims were sacrificed. At another, held every year in January, at Lederan (now Lethra), in Denmark, ninety-nine were sacrificed, and the horrid practice also had a place in the religious rites of Iceland, where Norse elements were early implanted. The victims were generally selected from captives or the meaner orders of the people, but not always. A Norwegian king was burnt in honour of Odin to put an end to a dearth ; another offered his son to the same deity to obtain the victory in an intended expedition ; and Aun, King of Sweden, sacrificed his nine sons in order to obtain from Odin a prolongation of his life. The victims were usually strangled, or killed by a blow on the head ; some of their blood was sprinkled upon the bystanders, the sacred grove, the images of the gods, and the altars, and the bodies were either burnt or suspended in the grove.

369. With such a religion, extensive power must have been vested in the priests. In Scandinavia they consecrated the victims to the gods, pronouncing such words as " I devote thee to Odin ;" or " I devote thee for a good harvest, for the return of a fruitful season." Their oracles (for which Upsal and other places were famous) were held in as much reverence as the sacrifices. Poetry seems also to have been an instrument which, in the hands of the Skalds or poets, played as important a part in the national institutions as the bardic productions did in Britain and Germany.

WELSH TRADITIONS.

370. The following extracts from the Triads refer to the ancient inhabitants of Britain :

a. The Three Awful Events in the Isle of Britain.—The first was the bursting of the Lake of Floods and the rushing of an inundation over all the lands, until all persons were destroyed, except Dwyvan and Dwyvack, who escaped in an open vessel ; and from them the Isle was repeopled.

b. The Three Primary Works of the Isle.—The ship of Nwydd Nav Neivion, which brought in it a male and female

of all living things, when the Lake of Floods burst forth ;
the large horned oxen of Hu Gadarn (Hugh the Mighty),
that drew the crocodile from the lake of the land, so that
the lake did not burst forth any more ; and the stone of
Gwyddon Ganhebon, upon which all the arts and sciences
in the world are engraven.

370c. *The Three Pillars of the Nation of the Isle.*—The first
was Hu Gadarn, who brought the nation of the Kymry first
to the Isle ; and they came from the land of Haf, which is
called Defrobani,* and they came over the Môr Tawch
(Wel. "tawch," *hazy*) to the Isle and to Llydaw, *Armorica*,
where they settled. The second was Prydain, son of Aedd
the Great, who first organized a social state and sovereignty
in Britain ; for, before that time, there was no justice but
what was done by favour, nor any law except superior force.
The third was Dyvwall Moelmud, for he first made arrange-
ments respecting the laws, maxims, customs, and privileges
of the country and tribe. And for these reasons they were
called the three pillars of the nation of the Kymry.

d. The Three Social Tribes of the Isle.—The first was the
tribe of the Kymry, who came with Hu Gadarn because he
would not possess a country and land by fighting and pursuit, but by justice and tranquility. The second was the
tribe of the Lloegrwys from Gwasgwyn, *Gascony*. The third
were the Brython, from Llydaw. These were called the three
peaceful tribes, because they came by mutual consent and
tranquility ; and they were all descended from the primitive
tribe of the Kymry, and they had all the same language and
speech.

e. The Three Refuge-Seeking Tribes.—These came under
the peace and permission of the Kymry, without arms and
without opposition. The first was the tribe of the Celyddon
[201] in the north. The second was the Irish tribe, Gwyddyl,
from Alban [130]. The third were the people of Galedin,
who, when their country was drowned, came in vessels
without sails to the Isle of Wight, where they had land
granted them by the Kymry. They had no privilege or claim

---

* An interpolation, said to have been made in the twelfth century,
adds : " That is, where Constantinople now stands."

in the Isle of Britain, but they had land and protection assigned to them under certain conditions, and it was stipulated that they should not possess the rank of native Kymry until the ninth of their lineal descendants.

370 *f. The Three Usurping Tribes.*—The first were the Coraniaid from Pwyl, the second the Gwyddelian Fichti, who came over the sea of Llychlyn, the third the Saxons. These three tribes never went away again. The Coraniaid occupied the banks of the Humber, and the shores of the German Ocean ; they united with the Saxons on the arrival of the latter, and becoming incorporated with them, deprived the Lloegrwys of their government by wrong and oppression, and then also deprived the Kymry of the monarchial crown. All the Lloegrwys became one people with the Saxons, those only excepted who are found in Cornwall and in the comot of Carnoban in Deira and Bernicia. The Fichti dwelt in Alban on the shore of the Sea of Lochlyn. Though the Kymry lost the sovereignty of the Isle through the treachery of the protected tribes and the devastations of the three usurping tribes, yet they kept their country and language.

g. The Three Inventors of Song and Record of the Kymry Nation.—Gwyddon Ganhebon, the first in the world that composed vocal song ; Hu Gadarn, who first applied vocal song to strengthen memory and record ; and Tydain, the father of poetic genius, who first conferred art on poetic song, and made it the medium of record. From what was done by these, originated Bards and Bardism, and the privilege and institutes of these things were organized by the three primary bards, Plennydd, Alawn, and Gwron.

h. The Three chief Mechanics of the Isle.—The first, Corvinor, bard of Ceri Hir Llyngwyn, who first made a ship, sail, and helm for Kymry ; the second, Morddal Gwr Gweilgi, mason to Ceraint ap Greidiawl, who first taught the Britons to work stone and mortar about the time Alexander was subduing the world ; and the third, Coel, son of Cyllin, and grandson of Caradoc, son of Bran, who first made a mill turned by a wheel. These were three bards.

MELA.

371. *Hispaniæ exterioris et Septentrionalis oceani Insulæ.*—In Celticis aliquot sunt (insulæ), quas, quia plumbo abundant, uno omnes nomine Cassiterides appellant. Sena in Britannico Mari Osismicis adversa littoribus, Gallici nominis oraculo insignis est. Cujus antistites perpetua virginitate sanctæ, numero novem esse traduntur : Barrigenas vocant, putantque ingeniis singularibus præditas, maria ac ventos concitare carminibus, seque in quæ velint animalia vertere, sanare quæ apud alios insanabilia sunt, scire ventura et predicare : sed non nisi deditas navigantibus et in id tantum ut se consulerent profectis. Britannia qualis sit, qualesque progeneret, mox certiora et magis explorata dicentur. Quippe tamdiu clausam aperit ecce principum maximus, nec indomitarum modo ante se, verum ignotarum quoque gentium victor, qui propriarum rerum fidem ut bello affectavit, ita triumpho declaraturus portat. Cæterum ut adhuc habuimus, inter septentrionem occidentemque projecta, grandi angulo Rheni ostia prospicit, deinde obliqua retro latera abstrahit, altero Galliam, altero Germaniam spectans : tum rursus perpetuo margine directi littoris ab tergo abducta, iterum se in diversos angulos cuneat triquetra, et Siciliæ maximè similis, plana, ingens, fœcunda, verum iis quæ pecora quam homines benignius alant. Fert nemora, lacus ac prægrandia flumina, alternis motibus modò in pelagus, modò retro fluentia, et quædam gemmas margaritasque generantia. Fert populos regesque populorum : sed sunt inculti omnes, atque ut longius à continenti absunt, ita aliarum opum ignari magis, tantum pecore ac finibus dites, incertum ob decorem, an quid aluid, vitro corpora infecti. Causas autem et bella contrahunt, ac se frequenter invicem infestant, maximè imperitandi cupidine, studioque ea prolatandi quæ possident. Dimicant non equitatu modò aut pedite, verum et bigis et curribus, Gallicè armati : Covinos vocant, quorum falcatis axibus utuntur. Supra Britanniam Iuverna est, pene par spatio, sed utrinque æquali tractu littorum oblonga, cœli ad maturanda semina iniqui : verum adeo luxuriosa herbis non lætis modò sed etiam dulcibus, ut se exigua parte diei pecora

impleant, et nisi pabulo prohibeantur, diutius pasta dissi-
liant. Cultores ejus inconditi sunt, et omnium virtutum
ignari. Triginta sunt Orcades angustis inter se diductæ
spatiis. Septem Aemodæ. Contra Germaniam Vecta, in
illo sinu quem Codanum diximus. Ex iis Scandinovia, quam
adhuc Teutoni tenent, ut magnitudine alias, ita fœcunditate
antestat (iii. 6).

PLINY.

372. Ex adverso hujus situs [Rheni ostii] Britannia insula, clara Græcis nostrisque monumentis, inter septemtrionem et occidentem jacet : Germaniæ, Galliæ, Hispaniæ,
multo maximis Europæ partibus magno intervallo adversa.
Albion ipsi nomen fuit, cum Britanniæ vocarentur omnes :
de quibus mox paulo dicemus. Hæc abest a Gessoriaco
Morinorum gentis litore, proximo trajectu quinquagintu M.
circuitu vero patere tricies octies centena viginti quinque
M. Pytheas et Isodorus tradunt : triginta prope jam annis
notitiam ejus Romanis armis non ultra vicinitatem silvæ
Caledoniæ propagantibus. Agrippa longitudinem DCCC. M.
pass. esse : latitudinem CCC. M. credit. Eamdem Hiberniæ
latitudinem, sed longitudinem CC. mill. passuum minorem.
Super eam hæc sita abest brevissimo transitu a Silurum
gente XXX. M. pass. Reliquarum nulla CXXV. mill. circuitu amplior proditur. Sunt autem XL. Orcades, modicis
inter se discretæ spatiis. Septem Acmodæ, et XXX. Hæbudes :
et inter Hiberniam ac Britanniam, Mona, Monapia, Ricina,
Vectis, Limnus, Andros. Infra vero Siambis et Axantos.
Et ab adverso in Germanicum Mare sparsæ Glessariæ, quas
Electridas Græci recentiores appellavere, quod ibi electrum
nasceretur. Ultima omnium, quæ memorantur, Thule : in
qua solstitio nullas esse noctes indicavimus, Cancri signum
Sole transeunte, nullosque contra per brumam dies. Hoc
quidem senis mensibus continuis fieri arbitrantur. Timæus
historicus a Britannia introrsus sex dierum navigatione
abesse dicit insulam Mictim, in qua candidum plumbum
proveniat. Ad eam Britannos vitilibus navigiis corio circumsutis navigare. Sunt qui et alias prodant, Scandiam,
Dumnam, Bergos : maximamque omnium Nerigon, ex qua

in Thulen navigetur.   A Thule unius diei navigatione mare concretum, a nonnullis Cronium appellatur (*Nat. Hist.* iv. 30).

Ex adverso Celtiberiæ complures sunt insulæ, Cassiterides dictæ Græcis, a fertilitate plumbi : et e regione Arrotrebarum promontorii, Deorum sex, quas aliqui Fortunatas appellavere (*Ibid* 36).

Plumbum ex Cassiteride insula primus apportavit Midacritus (*Ibid.* vii. 57).

Sequitur natura plumbi. Cujus duc genera, nigrum, atque candidum. Pretiosissimum candidum, a Græcis appellatum cassiteron, fabuloseque narratum in insulas Atlantici Maris peti, vitilibusque navigiis circumsutis corio advehi. Nunc certum est, in Lusitania gigni, & in Gallæcia (*Ibid.* xxxiv. 47).

Solinus.

373. De Hyperboreis et Hyperboræ regionis situ.

Fabula erat de Hyperboreis et rumor irritus, si quæ illinc ad nos usque fluxerunt, temere forent credita. Sed cum probissimi auctores et satis vero idonei sententias pares faciant, nullus falsum reformidet.   De Hyperboreis rem loquimur. Incolunt pone Pterophoron, quam ultra aquilonem accipimus jacere. Gens beatissima. Eam Asiæ quidam magis quam Europæ dederunt. Alii statuunt mediam inter utrumque solem, antipodum occidentem, et nostrum renascentem ; quod aspernatur ratio, tam vasto mari duos orbeis interfluente.   Sunt igitur in Europa apud quos mundi cardines esse credunt, et extimos siderum ambitus, semestrem lucem, aversum uno tantum die solem : quamquam existant, qui putant non quotidie ibi solem ut nobis, sed vernali æquinoctio exoriri, autumnali occidere ; ita sex mensibus infinitum diem, sex aliis continuam esse noctem. De cœlo magna clementia : auræ spirant salubriter ; nihil noxii flatus habent. Domus sunt nemora vel luci. In diem victum arbores subministrant. Discordiam nesciunt. Ægritudine non inquietantur. Ad innocentiam omnibus æquale votum. Mortem accersunt, et voluntario interitu castigant obeundi tarditem : quos satietas tenet vitæ, epulati delibutique, de rupe nota præcipitem casum in maria destinant.

Hoc sepulturæ genus optimum arbitrantur. Ajunt etiam
solitos per virgines probatissimas primitiva frugum Apollini
Delio missitare. Verum hæ quoniam perfidia hospitium non
inlibatæ revenissent, devotionis quam peregre prosequebantur,
pontificium mox intra fines suos receperunt (xvi.).

374. Antonini Iter Britanniarum.

[Insulæ] in Mari (Oceano) quod Gallias et Britannias in-
terluit :

> Insulæ Orcades.   Num. III.
> Insula Clota in Hiverione
> Vecta.
> Riduna.
> Sarmia.
> Cæsarea.
> Barsa.
> Lisia.
> Andium.
> Sicdelis.
> Uxantisina.
> Vindilis.
> Siata.
> Arica.

GLOSSARY: GAELIC

ABBREVIATIONS: *f., feminine; nouns not so marked are generally masculine; a., adjective; dim., diminutive; pl., plural; W., Welsh; †, obsolete.*

A.

†ABH, water.
ABHAINN, *f.*, river.
ACH, ACHADH, field; plain.
ACHA (ACH), *f.*, mound; bank.
AIGEAL, an abyss; pool; *pl.*, aigealan.
†AIL, stone (see Aill).
AILBHE, AILBHEINN, *f.*, a flint; stone; rock.
AILEAN, a meadow; plain.
†AILL, *f.*, a rugged bank.
AILLEAN, a causeway.
†AIN, *f.*, water.
†AINN, a circle; ring.
†AIRM, a place.
†AIS, a hill; stronghold.
AISEAG, *f.*, a ferry.
AISRE, AISRIDH, an abode; hill; path.
AITE (AIT), a place.
AITEACH, a habitation.
†AITH, a hill.
AITREABH, an abode; dwelling.
†ALL, a rock; cliff.
ALLT, ALD, a mountain stream.
†ALT, a high place; hill.
AMHAINN, *f.*, a river.
AODANN, *f.*, brow.
†AOI, an island; hill.
†AON, a country; land.
AONACH, a hill; height.
ÀR, battle; field of battle.
†AR, land.
ARAICH, *f.*, a field of battle; a plain.
ARD, *a.*, high.
ARD, a height; eminence.
ARDAN, a knoll.
AROS, a house.
ART, a stone; a house.

†ART (*W.*, arth), a bear.
AT, a swelling.
ATHAN, a shallow.

B.

†BA, death.
BAD (*dim.*, badan), a tuft grove.
BADH, a harbour; bay.
†BAILLEAN, a boss; stud.
BALLA, BALLADH, a wall; rampart; the boss of a shield.
BAR, a top or summit; a height.
†BEABH, a tomb; grave.
BEAG, little.
BEANN, *f.*, a hill; mountain; *pl.*, beannta (beannte).
BEANNAN, a little hill.
BEIC, *f.*, a point; nib.
BEITHIR, *a.*, wild.
BEUL, an opening.
BEUM, a stream, ; torrent.
BINNEIN, a high conical hill.
BIOR, a spit.
†BIOR, water; a well.
†BLA, a town; village.
BOL, a bowl; cup.
BOLG, *f.*, a pimple; the boss of a shield.
†BOR, *a.*, high.
†BRÀ, a brow.
BRAID, *f.*, a mountain.
BREATH, *f.*, a row; rank.
†BRI, *f.*, a rising ground.
†BROIN, *f.*, a height.
†BROTH a mole; ditch.
†BRU (*W.*, bre), *f.*, a country; a bank.
BRUACH, *f.*, a bank; a steep.
BULG, a lump; knob.
BUS, a snout.

C.

CABRACH, a copse ; thicket.
CAISDEAL, a castle ; fort.
CALA, a harbour ; ferry.
†CALC, *f.*, lime.
CAM, *a.*, crooked ; bent.
CAMADH, a bending.
†CAOIS, *f.*, a furrow.
CARN, a cairn ; barrow ; *pl.*, cuirn.
CÀRR, a rock ; bog.
CASAIR, *f.*, a thorn ; slaughter.
CASAN, a footpath.
CATHAIR, *f.*, a town ; city ; bog.
CÉ, a pier.
CEANN, a head ; point.
CEAP, *f.*, the top (as of a hill) ; a head.
†CEIDE, *f.*, a green ; hillock.
CEUM, a path.
CIADAN, a moor ; height.
CIAN, *a.*, long ; distant.
CLADH (*W.*, clawdd), a bank ; mound ; dike.
CLAIS, *f.*, a furrow ; trench.
CLUAIN, *f.*, a pasture.
CNAG, a knob.
CNAP, a knob ; lump ; a little hill.
CNOC, a hillock.
COILLE, *f.*, a wood ; *pl.*, coiltean, coillte.
COIT, *f.*, a small boat; quoit.
COLBH, a pillar.
COMAR, a way.
COR, a turn.
CORR, a snout ; corner.
†COT, a cottage.
COTHACHADH, a battle.
CRATH, to shake ; hence cràthrach, *f.*, criathrach, a bog.
CROM, a circle.
CRUACH, *f.* (*dim.*, cruachan), hill.
CUACH, *f.* (*dim.*, cuachan), a bowl.
CUAILLE, *f.*, a pole ; stake.
CUAN, a large lake.
CURACH, *f.*, a marsh.

D.

†DID, *f.*, a pap.
DIDEAN, a fort.
DIG, DIC, *f.*, a dike ; ditch.
DION, a shelter ; fence.
†DOBHAR, water.
DOIRE, *f.*, a grove.
DOIREACH, woody

DORR, rough.
DOT (see Did).
DRIUCH, a beak.
DRONN, *m.*, druim, *f.*, a ridge.
DUBH, black.
DÙC (*dim.*, ducan), a heap ; hillock.
DÙN, a fort ; hill.
†DUR, water.
†DUS, a fort.

E.

†EAR, a head.
EARR, an end ; limit.
EAS, a cataract.
EASGAIDH, *f.*, a quagmire.
†EITRE, *f.*, a trench.
EUBH, a cry.

F.

FAD, long ; distant.
†FÀIL, *f.*, a ring.
FAILL (FÀIL), *f.*, a precipice.
FÀIR, *f.*, a ridge.
FAN, FANADH, a declivity.
FAOB, a lump.
FASAIL, desolate.
FÈ, FÉITH, a bog.
†FEARB, *f.*, a pimple.
FEORAN, a green.
†FICH, a castle.
FINID, *f.*, an end, close.
FIREACH, a hill ; moor.
FORAS, a river-ford.
FOIR, *f.*, a brink.
†FORAOS, a forest.
†FOS (FOSS), a ditch ; wall.

G.

GABAIR, a tattler.
GÀG, a cleft ; *pl.*, gagan.
GAIN, *f.*, sand.
GALL, a rock ; stone.
GALLAN, a rock.
GANAID, *f.*, a fence.
†GANN, a fort.
†GARD, a fenced place.
GEAD, a ridge.
GEADACH, ridgy.
†GIL, *f.*, water.
GLAIB, *f.*, a bog.
GLEANN, a valley ; *pl.*, gleanntaidh.
GLINN, a fortress.
GNUIS, *f.*, a notch.

GREIS, *f.*, battle.
†GRIOM, battle.
GUAL, coal ; guaillean, a cinder.
GUALACH, coaly.
†GUR, a pimple.

I.

I, an island.
IADHADH, a winding ; circuit.
IARUÑN, iron.
INÑEAN, a navel ; middle of a pool.
†INNILL, *f.*, a fort.
INNIS, *f.*, island.
IOMAIRE, *f.*, a ridge ; furrow.
IONAD, a place ; stead.
IRE, *f.*, earth ; land.
IÙL, a guide ; way.
IUMAIDH, *f.*, level ground.

L.

LÀB, LAIB, dirt ; a bog.
LÀBACH, LÀPACH, boggy.
LANN, *f.*, an enclosure ; house.
LÀRAOH, a battle-field.
LEAC, *f.*, a flag ; declivity.
LEÀNAG, a small plain ; meadow.
LEARG, *f.*, a green slope ; little eminence.
LEÒG, a marsh.
LIA, a stream ; stone.
LINNE, *f.*, a pool ; pond ; *pl.*, linnte, linntean, etc.
LIOS, *f.*, a palace ; fortified place.
LOD, LODAN, a puddle ; marsh.
†LOG, a pit ; water-dike.
†LOICH, LOIC, *f.*, a place.
LOM, bare ; smooth ; a field.
LÒN, a meadow.
LÒNACH, marshy.
LONAIG, lane.
†LUA, water.
LUAIDH, *f.*, lead.
LUIMEAN, a bare barren hillock.

M.

MAB (see Mob).
MAGH (*W.*, mai), a field.
MAIS, *f.*, a lump ; heap.
MÀM, a large round hill.
†MATA (MAT), great.
MEALL, a lump ; knob ; hill (*dim.*, mealian).
†MEAS, a point or edge.
MEIDHE, *f.*, a stump.

MEIN, *f.*, a mine ; ore.
MIAD, a meadow (*dim.*, miadan).
MOB, *f.*, a mob ; tuft.
MÒINE (MOINE), *f.*, peat ; a bog.
MONADH, a hill ; mountain.
†MORC, great, huge.
MUIN, *f.*, a mountain.
MÙR, a wall ; hill.
MURACH, walled.

N.

†NEAR, water ; river.
NEAS, *f.*, a fortified hill.
NEIMHEAD, consecrated ground.
†NITH, *f.*, battle.
NIÙC, a corner.

O.

OB, a bay ; harbour.
OIL, *f.*, a rock.
OIR, *f.*, a boundary.
OITIR, *f.*, a seabank ; shoal.
†OLL, high ; great.
ORD, a mountain.

P.

PAIT, *f.*, a lump ; protuberance.
PÉAC, any sharp-pointed thing (see Beic).
POLL, mire ; a pool.

R.

†RAIS, RUIS, *f.*, a path.
RÀMH, a wood.
RAON, a plain ; field.
RIASG, *f.*, a moor ; marsh.
†RION, a way ; road.
†RITHEADH, a grove.
ROD, RITH, a road.
ROINN, *f.*, a point.
RÒS, a promontory.
RÙCAN, RUCHD, a conical rick (of hay) ; ? a barrow.
RUGHA, a cape.

S.

SAL, dirt ; mire.
SALANN, salt.
SCORR, a rock ; cliff.
†SEAD, a way ; road.
†SEIDEAN, a quicksand.
SGARBH, a ford.
SGEALB, a cliff (*cf.* Scalpcliff).

SIAT, a swelling.
†SION, *f.*, a chain.
SIUBHAL, a course (road).
SLINN, *f.*, a flat stone ; tile.
SLOB, SLOBAN, a puddle.
SLOC, a pit ; ditch ; marsh.
SLUG, a gulping.
SLUGAITE, a quicksand.
SOC, a beak ; point.
†SOPAR, a well.
†SPIN, a thorn.
STÀDH, a working.
STOB, a thorn.
STÒITE, prominent.
STUADH, a pillar ; street.
SUMAIN, *f.*, a wave.
SUMAIR, a gulf ; whirlpool.
SUNN, a wall.

T.

TACAID, *f.*, a knob.
TAIN, *f.*, water.
TAIP, *f.*, a lump ; rock.
TAIRP, a clod.
TANA, thin ; ? narrow.
TEACH, TIGH, a house ; *pl.*. tighean.
TIOBAIR, *f.*, a well.
TIR, *f.*, country ; land.
TOCHAIL, *f.*, a mine ; quarry.
†TOCHAR, a causeway.
TOD, a clod.
TOIRRSE, *f.*, a lump.

TOITEAR, lumpy.
TOLL, a pit ; cave.
TOM, a hillock ; conical knoll (*dim.*, toman).
TORR, a tower ; mound.
TORRACH, having mounds.
†TOT, a sod.
TRAIGH, TRÀITH, *f.*, a shore.
TREABH, *f.*, a farmed village (*W.*, tref, town).
TUATH, the north.
TUIN, *f.*, a dwelling-place.
†TUIR, a pillar.
TUL, a hillock.
TULACH, a mound ; knoll.

U.

UACHDAR, the top ; surface (a height).
UADH, UADHAIDH, *f.*, cave.
UAGH, UAGHAIDH, *f.*, cave.
UAIGH, *f.*, a grave (*pl.*, uaighean).
UAIMH, UAMH, *f.*, a grave ; cave.
†UATH, earth.
UBH, a point.
UCHDACH, UCHDAN, a steep ascent.
UIG, *f.*, a pebble.
UILEANN, *f.*, a corner.
UIR, *f.*, a mound.
UISGE, water.
†UR, heath.
UR, a brink.

INDEX

I.—ANCIENT AND ANTIQUARIAN NAMES

ABBREVIATIONS:

| Æ., Æstuarium. | I., Insula (–ae). | P., Promontorium. |
| F., Fluvius. | O., Oceanus. | S., Sinus. |

Antiquarian names, etc., are printed in Italics.   *Numbers refer to paragraphs.*

II.—MODERN NAMES

ENGLAND

THE END